FOREWORD

This publication is based on papers prepared for a conference, "Beyond 2000: The New Social Policy Agenda", convened by the OECD in November 1996. The conference, which was chaired by Mr. A.P.W. Melkert, the Netherlands Minister for Social Affairs and Employment, provided social policy ministers, their senior policy advisors and invited academics with the opportunity to review the socio-economic changes that have affected social protection systems, and to discuss new policy instruments better able to meet policy objectives.

Systems of social protection in OECD countries are facing pressures from many directions: changing labour markets are leaving many who wish to work unable to do so, or are requiring them to work for low wages; families are more unstable and many parents are finding it difficult to combine work and family responsibilities; and the ageing of the population is increasing pension payments and is leading to increased demands for long-term care services. At the same time, there are strong pressures to reduce public spending, not least because the high costs of financing social expenditure may adversely affect employment.

Social protection systems are sometimes using the wrong policy instruments to insure the wrong people against the wrong risks. Thus, social policy must be reoriented to give a higher priority to some social problems which are not being properly addressed. It is equally clear that new resources are unlikely to be forthcoming from public budgets to meet such needs.

Policy development must proceed from clear redefinition of the goals of social protection. Perhaps surprisingly, the conference discussion revealed relatively little disagreement about the objectives of social policies. However, there is dispute about the appropriate policies to meet these goals. Such differences of opinion arise from two sources: disagreement about the effectiveness of policy instruments; and disagreement about the priorities to be given to different policy objectives. Hence, policy development requires both the evaluation of new policy instruments in the light of policy objectives, and the development of a framework that will assist in the setting of social policy priorities and in achieving public acceptance for a reorientation of social policy.

The conference stressed the need for trust in the social protection institutions and warned that trust has been eroded by the belief that talk of social policy "reform" is simply a code for reducing existing protection. If new social needs are to be addressed without additional resources being made available, a framework for deciding policy priorities is necessary. Ad hoc decisions are unlikely to make best use of resources, nor to imbue confidence and trust in systems of social protection.

The policy challenge for the coming decades is to ensure that the returns to social expenditure are maximised in the form of social cohesion and active participation in society and the labour market. This approach stresses interventions that take place early in the life-cycle or that improve integration into the labour market and society. Particular attention needs to be directed to supporting those who have low earnings but are working or in training, and to those who are caring for others. A social investment approach also requires a realistic assessment of whether provision of welfare services through public-sector institutions is always appropriate. The roles played by government, the market, the community and the family in providing necessary social support may need to be reconsidered.

Sometimes social policy is claimed to harm economic performance. As this conference has shown, the opposite is the case. Good social policy is likely to improve economic performance as well as achieve legitimate social goals.

The contributed papers were edited by Patrick Hennessy and Mark Pearson of the OECD Secretariat. The report is published on the responsibility of the Secretary-General.

TABLE OF CONTENTS

Introduction *by* Donald J. Johnston 9

Chapter 1
Socio-economic change and social policy
by Peter Scherer

Introduction 13
Achievements and failures of welfare systems 14
The challenges to social protection 28
Social policy and the life cycle 43
Balancing sustainability and security in social policy 52
Notes 57
Bibliography 60

Chapter 2
Welfare states at the end of the century:
the impact of labour market, family and demographic change
by Gosta Esping-Andersen

Introduction: the perennial crisis of the welfare state 63
Welfare state responses to the employment problem 66
The new demographics: ageing and family change 69
Social spending, servicing and redistributive efficacy 70
The risks of entrapment and welfare state policy 73
The politics of welfare state reform 75
Notes 77
Bibliography 79

Chapter 3
Family change, family policies and the restructuring of welfare
by Chiara Saraceno

Introduction 81
Changes in family organisation and behaviour 81
Ageing of the population 86
Family obligations and social policies 87
A new approach to family policies 93
Notes 96
Bibliography 98

Chapter 4
Employment and social protection: are they compatible?
by Robert Haveman

Income protection systems among OECD countries 101
The pros and cons of a generous and accessible social protection system 102
Trends in employment, inequality and social protection within the OECD countries 103
Is there no alternative approach? 107
Obstacles to an employment-centered social policy reform 110
Notes 112
Bibliography 114

Chapter 5
The challenge of poverty and exclusion
by Bea Cantillon

Introduction 115
Financial poverty: levels and trends 115
The impact of social expenditure 121
Socio-demographic change and poverty 123
Employment and poverty 125
Financial poverty and social exclusion: "new poverty" 130
New policy avenues 131
Notes 138
Appendix 1: Methods of poverty measurement 141
Appendix 2: Comparability of the Luxembourg Income Study (LIS) datasets 144
Bibliography 161

Chapter 6
Can we afford to grow old? Adjusting pension policies to a more aged society
by Lans Bovenberg and Anja van der Linden

Introduction 167
Strengths and weaknesses of various pension systems 167
Scenarios 172
Policies to insure against ageing 174
Conclusions 182
Notes 186
Bibliography 187

Chapter 7
Developing health and long-term care for a more aged society
by Riyoji Kobayashi

Introduction 189
Development of health-care services and long-term care 192
Residential care 195
Community care 198
Family care 201
Local health and welfare planning for the aged 202
Bibliography 204
Appendix: Commentary on Mr. Kobayashi's paper *by Claes Örtendahl* 207

Chapter 8
Balancing sustainability and security in social policy
by Fritz W. Scharpf

Introduction 211
Sustainability under different problem loads 213
Sustainability under different modes of financing 215
Most vulnerable: payroll taxes and generous rates of income replacement 216
Perspectives 218
Bibliography 221

Chapter 9
Social protection and the low-skilled
The debate 223

Conclusion *by* A.P.W. Melkert 229

List of Tables

Table 1.1.   Net income replacement ratios (net retirement pension/net earnings)
              for pensioners without a dependent spouse, 1990 25
Table 1.2.   Population aged 65 and over as a percentage of the population aged 15-64,
              1960-2030 26
Table 1.3.   Employment, unemployment and population, 1972 to 1995 30
Table 1.4.   Number of people in full- and part-time employment in 15 OECD countries,
              in 1975 and 1995 34
Table 1.5.   Proportion of young people in education and in employment, by sex, for 15-19
              and 20-24 year-olds 35
Table 1.6.   Proportion of the population in four age groups that had attained at least upper
              secondary education, 1992 44
Table 1.7.   Proportion of population aged 25-35, attending school or in training, by sex
              and labour force status, in 1984 (or 1989) and 1994 45
Table 1.8.   Age at first childbirth 46
Table 1.9.   Completed fertility by year of birth of the mother, 1930-60 47
Table 1.10a. Percentage of births attributable to young women, 1960-94 48
Table 1.10b. Age specific birth rates per 1 000 (within and outside marriage), 1960-94 49
Table 1.11.   Proportion of adults in prison, by sex, in 1990 51
Table 1.12.   Average tax rates for persons of working age and at pensionable age, 1995 51
Table 1.13.   Annual non-profit sector operating expenditure by ICNPO group, and annual
              revenue by source and by country, as a percentage of GDP, 1990 54
Table 1.14.   Gross to net expenditure adjustment as a percentage of GDP, 1993 56
Table 2.1.   Welfare states in crisis, then and now 63
Table 2.2.   Social expenditure and their age distribution 65
Table 2.3.   Indices of "equality" and employment performance 68
Table 2.4.   Households with disposable income below half median income 69
Table 2.5.   Public and private spending on social protection 71
Table 3.1.   Percentage employed full-time and part-time (less than 30 hours per week),
              for married/cohabiting mothers, and lone mothers 83
Table 3.2.   Average ranking of selected OECD countries on the basis of family supports 92
Table 5.1.   Extent of financial poverty in OECD countries, using two different measures
              of poverty 116

Tables of Appendix 2 of Chapter 5

Table A.1.   Comparability of LIS surveys across years within countries   146
Table A.2a.   Extent of poverty in a number of OECD countries, using relative poverty lines . . .   148
Table A.2b.   Poverty rates in a number of OECD countries, using "absolute" poverty lines   150
Table A.3.   Poverty rates and poverty gaps for persons, by age   152
Table A.4.   Impact of social security transfers on poverty rates and poverty gaps
              by age of persons   154
Table A.5.   Poverty rates and composition of the poor by sex of the head of household   156
Table A.6.   Poverty rates by age of head of household, using 50 per cent relative poverty
              line   158
Table A.7.   Poverty rates for households whose head is at active age, by household-type . . .   160

Table 6.1.   Pension schemes in selected OECD countries   168
Table 6.2.   Real wage growth contrasted with real returns on capital, selected OECD
              countries, 1971-90   171
Table 6.3.   Input scenarios   173
Table 6.4.   Market scenario   173
Table 6.5.   Intergenerational solidarity scenario   174
Table 6.6.   Participation rates and effective retirement age in the EC, Japan
              and the United States, 1990   176
Table 6.7.   Participation rate, effective retirement age and life expectancy, 1950-80   177
Table 6.8.   Ratio of number in employment to the number of retired in OECD countries
              under alternative assumptions   180
Table 6.9.   Contribution rate with comprehensive package   181
Table 7.1.   Percentage of elderly people aged over 80 in the whole population   190
Table 7.2.   Percentage of elderly people over 65 living alone or with the family
              in the whole population   191
Table 7.3.   Percentage of women aged 45-60 in the labour market   191
Table 7.4.   Percentage of elderly people over 65 in residential care and receiving elderly
              home help services   192
Table 7.5.   Models of care for the elderly   193

List of Charts

Chart 1.1.   GDP per capita, at price levels and exchange rates of 1990   15
Chart 1.2a.   Health expenditure (public and private) and extent of ageing, 1994   16
Chart 1.2b.   Health expenditure (public and private) per capita, and GDP per capita,
              in dollars using purchasing power parities (PPPs), 1994   16
Chart 1.3.   Cash transfers and expenditure on services, by type, 1980-85 and 1992-93   18
Chart 1.4.   Changes in Gini coefficients   27
Chart 1.5.   Labour market and schooling status, in selected OECD countries,
              persons aged 15-19   39
Chart 5.1.   Unemployment and poverty   127
Chart 5.2.   Long-term unemployment and poverty   128
Chart 5.3.   Employment and poverty   128
Chart 5.4.   Low pay and poverty   129
Chart 8.1.   Income supplement for low-wage jobs   219

INTRODUCTION

Opening address by Mr. Donald J. Johnston,
Secretary-General of the OECD, Paris,
Tuesday, 12 November 1996

Minister Melkert, may I warmly welcome you and your fellow Ministers, other delegates and invited experts to the OECD.

I am delighted to open this conference. I believe that your discussions on the new social policy agenda over the next two days will touch upon topics which are central to the concerns of policy makers and citizens in all OECD countries. I would like to take a few minutes to describe briefly how the OECD is contributing to this debate.

Let me begin by reminding you of the mission statement of the OECD: the preamble to the founding Convention in 1960 talked of the need for Member countries to consult and co-operate "(...) to promote the highest sustainable growth of their economies and improve the economic and social well-being of their peoples".

From its beginning, therefore, the OECD has been concerned with keeping in harmony the twin goals of economic growth and social well-being. At the same time, the OECD has always been mindful that there are close interactions between economic and social objectives. Social policies have a profound impact on the workings of the economy. How could it be otherwise?

In 1960, the OECD Member countries devoted, on average, around 10 per cent of GDP to public expenditure on social protection: on health, pensions and other social programmes. By 1980, this had risen to almost 20 per cent on average, and OECD felt sufficiently concerned about the situation to hold a conference, which some of you may have attended, on the subject of the "crisis" in the welfare state.

It is interesting to see, with the benefit of hindsight, how far the prediction of crisis has been upheld, and to what extent it has not. For a decade after the 1980 conference, predictions of imminent fiscal crisis would have been dismissed as far-fetched. For example, by 1990 – not, it has to be said, without some effort at cost-containment – the portion of OECD GDP devoted to public expenditure on social protection had risen on average by only 1 to 2 per cent: hardly a crisis.

However, as we found all too soon, this encouraging performance had been sustained by several years of above-average growth. With the onset of the economic down-turn of the early 1990s, too many countries that had already allowed large public deficits to accumulate were ill-prepared to weather the storm.

Today, we find that public expenditure on social programmes and the control of public spending are at the heart of daily political debate in parliaments and among the public. It is not a comfortable time to be a politician.

But it is encouraging that, despite the political difficulties, there is a broad consensus among Member countries around an economic strategy of prudent macroeconomic policy, including fiscal consolidation, structural reform and market liberalisation. However, I am concerned that we risk a backlash against this strategy because of the impression that it places too little emphasis on social objectives. Indeed we have already been witnessing in some OECD countries signs of social unrest and protest movements as well as low popularity ratings for many governments and a "feel bad" factor which may reflect a lack of confidence in these policies.

The language of sacrifice is not designed to win hearts and minds. The message we would like to promote from the OECD is that bringing public-sector deficits and debt under control through fiscal consolidation is not an alternative to policies to promote social protection and social well-being: on the contrary, it is a necessary condition for maintaining such policies in future years.

At the same time, if OECD societies are to retain the capacity to maintain social cohesion in the future, they must review priorities and the ways in which social programmes are implemented. It is essential for the cohesion of our societies to maintain a sound basis for social protection, but this has to be made more sustainable, both in terms of public finances and, in some countries, in terms of public opinion.

One approach that has been advocated by OECD Social and Labour Ministers for a number of years is to move away from passive income maintenance towards more active policies: putting the stress on participation in the labour market in return for support. Through the OECD *Jobs Study* we have sought to show how labour market policies may be moved in this direction, and we have initiated a process of review of social assistance policies to identify how minimum income support policies can also be made active rather than passive.

In the longer term, our societies are ageing and the economy will have to support more older people in future decades. This makes it all the more important to find ways to raise the level of employment in our economies and to reduce long-term unemployment to a minimum. It also calls for a new approach to employment, learning and saving for retirement in which a number of current barriers to a more flexible life-course must be addressed.

We have begun to outline this new approach in a recent report entitled *Ageing in OECD Countries – A Critical Policy Challenge*, and will report to the OECD Ministerial Council in 1998 with a range of options that could be pursued to deal with the challenges posed by ageing populations.

When OECD Social and Health Ministers last met here in 1992, at the trough of the economic down-turn, they affirmed that " (...) the role of social policy (...) is to provide a framework which enables the fullest participation possible in all aspects of society for all its citizens – supporting them in their efforts to balance work, learning, care for dependents, and leisure throughout the stages of the life cycle (...)".

This statement makes clear that the concerns of social, employment and education policies are now very closely interwoven. No set of policies in one of these areas of responsibility will achieve its goals without a corresponding and supporting contribution from the other policy sectors. I believe that this has been clearly recognised in the Japanese "Initiative for a Caring World" which Prime Minister Hashimoto proposed at the Lyon Summit in June 1996, with strong support from President Clinton and President Chirac. The work of the OECD has also been guided by this perspective.

It is also clear from this statement that the concern of social policy is nothing less than the effective functioning of our societies, not merely the effective supervision of public social programmes. By this I mean supporting the efforts of individuals, families, voluntary groups and enterprises to improve the well-being of the population in general.

That is why the papers prepared for this conference do not focus narrowly on the performance of specific social and health programmes. Instead, they deal more broadly with the ways that markets, families and social programmes together are impacting on human welfare, and on how the wider policy framework may have to change if it is to support, rather than hinder, the contributions that market and family can make to welfare.

We have already emphasised through the OECD *Jobs Study* that policy makers across the board have always to ask the question, "how does this proposal affect the prospects for employment?". From perusal of the documents to this meeting I would propose that we should now add the question, "how will this proposal affect the prospects for families?".

A particular concern is with those groups and individuals who, for whatever reason, are unable to benefit from economic growth to the same extent as the majority of the population. Whatever concept one uses to describe this phenomenon in your countries – the socially excluded, the underclass, the truly disadvantaged – there is a shared concern that the benefits of the macroeconomic and social policies we are pursuing are failing to reach some groups who, as a result, are losing the capacity for full social and economic participation.

This is contrary to social equity, and, if this trend persists and worsens, it could threaten social stability and undermine the other gains from economic growth. If this conference can propose more effective means of lifting these groups into the social mainstream, it will have more than fulfilled its purpose.

As my opening quotation from the preamble to our Charter indicates, the OECD has always been in the vanguard of policy thinking intended to promote social well-being as well as economic growth. I see this conference as a very important step in reaffirming that dual commitment and updating our views on the social policies relevant for the 21st century.

SOCIO-ECONOMIC CHANGE AND SOCIAL POLICY

by

Peter Scherer
OECD, Paris

INTRODUCTION

The slowdown in the growth of OECD economies over the past twenty-five years has been accompanied by fears about the sustainability of current systems of social protection. These concerns are increasingly focused on the growth in cash transfers: transfers to the elderly have increased, as have those to people not in employment, including not only unemployment benefits, but also (and increasingly) social assistance, invalidity and early retirement benefits. The relative gap between households at the top and bottom of the income distribution has widened in many countries. Maintaining lone parents and the long-term unemployed on benefits is seen as a problem rather than a solution.

Policies have been influenced by a feeling that the strains on the social protection system are the result of economic disequilibria. The evidence does not support this view. Per capita economic growth has continued steadily over the last quarter century and, although the structure of employment has changed, the proportion of the population in employment has not altered dramatically. Working time has been re-arranged amongst the population and labour markets show every sign of having successfully capitalised on the talents of the most educated and highly skilled parts of the population. However, a number of factors – education, employment, race, housing, family structure and benefit rule – are acting together to marginalise some groups. The policy objective is to break the cycle of dependency by "making work pay". The strategy must be to move from passive income support to active support of those in, or attempting to enter, work.

Social policy systems are based on securing families against interruptions to regular earnings. The social basis of these systems is eroding: employment is shifting from one-earner to two-earner families and the latter are paying two premiums with a reduced risk of being without any earnings; low-skilled job opportunities are restricted by the cost of social insurance charges payable by the employer; and low wage rates can make the income received in work lower than income support payments. The result is that the system is providing insurance which they do not really need to those who fund it, but is failing to provide employment to those who desperately need it.

Policies which will be successful "beyond 2000" must take account of new realities. Families are adjusting to changes in society and the labour market. Policies should ensure that those responsible for children are able to combine family and career responsibilities. Parents need access to child care and educational facilities which are consistent with their employment patterns.

Old age no longer implies low income. Current pension arrangements and asset accumulation have significantly reduced old-age poverty in most countries, but the burden on the working population of supporting the elderly is becoming painfully high. A majority of the elderly will continue to depend on public pensions, but reform is required in countries where even those with high earnings are provided with pensions in excess of their contributions.

The need to provide long-term care for dependent elderly people has increased public expenditure on the elderly. Even adequate pensions are not sufficient to finance intensive care costs, and countries are turning to social insurance arrangements to spread the burden away from social security.

Financing social transfers from a broad tax base is an option which should be considered – provided the tax system does not itself exempt the incomes of particular age groups.

Further policy initiatives taking social, demographic and labour market trends into account could include: moving toward income support arrangements which encourage beneficiaries to be flexible and to take risks, including experimenting with case management, training and unpaid trial employment for those who would otherwise be reliant on benefit income, the repayment of income-support benefit when income rises above a certain floor, the support of those who care for elderly and infirm relatives and policy interventions which are earlier in life, and which are preventive, not remedial.

ACHIEVEMENTS AND FAILURES OF WELFARE SYSTEMS

The past twenty-five years

In 1980, the OECD held a conference the proceedings of which were published the following year under the title *The Welfare State in Crisis* (OECD, 1981). As Esping-Anderson observes, that conference identified a number of challenges facing the welfare state largely associated with the consequences of the slowdown in economic growth and the rise in unemployment at the time. Many of these concerns were generated by the slowdown in growth which had been experienced over the previous decade. The initial response to the slowdown had been for nominal growth to continue at the same or even an accelerating rate, leading to "stagflation": slow growth and high inflation rates. Slower growth has meant that it has not been possible to increase transfers and public provision of services at the same real rate as in the past without committing increasingly larger proportions of national income. In some OECD countries, public expenditure did in fact continue to increase as a proportion of GDP throughout the decade which followed, and the recession of the early 1990s caused a further cyclical increase.

Nonetheless, over the past twenty-five years, continued, if occasionally halting growth, has been experienced in the OECD area.[1] By 1994, per capita GDP was 55 per cent higher in the OECD area than in 1970: 104 per cent in Japan, 62 per cent in the countries comprising the European Union until 1994, and 47 per cent in the United States[2] (Chart 1.1). On the whole the OECD economies have grown enough to allow aggregate household incomes to grow.[3] However, it is true that the rate of growth has been slower than that which characterised the first quarter century after the second World War – the period during which the main building blocks of the social policy frameworks in OECD countries were laid down.

In spite of its economic growth, the OECD area has witnessed mounting problems in sustaining its welfare systems. In most countries these systems have become unstable for reasons ranging from purely demographic changes to changes in the composition of employment. The economic interests of the households which finance transfers are diverging more from those of the beneficiaries, leading to a loss of social cohesion and even, in some countries, of consensus on the desirability of the systems themselves. Growing tensions of unsustainability are most apparent in disputes about how to fund social expenditure – and even about whether they should be funded publicly. At the time of the 1980 conference, it was feared that the lower growth which was already evident would doom the welfare state by eliminating the growth in resources on which it relied. These fears have proved to be exaggerated. Thinking on these issues was at the time explicitly or implicitly influenced by the "Baumol paradox" (Baumol, 1967): market economies were composed of capital-intensive primary and secondary sectors characterised by high rates of productivity growth, and a labour-intensive service sector, characterised by stagnant productivity. Relative demand for the output of the two sectors was believed to be price inelastic, so that a future exponential increase in the aggregate labour intensity of the economy could be projected – with the health care sector the classic illustration of these pressures. In fact, it has proved possible to control the rate of increase of such expenditure (although they have risen as a proportion of GDP), both by increasing productivity[4] in the provision of health care and by controlling usage (OECD, 1996c).

Current concerns about future health care costs are often concentrated on the implications of ageing populations for such expenditure. Health care expenditure are higher for elderly people than for younger age groups, and so a simple extrapolation of this ratio into the future suggests that health care

◆ Chart 1.1. **GDP per capita, at price levels and exchange rates of 1990**

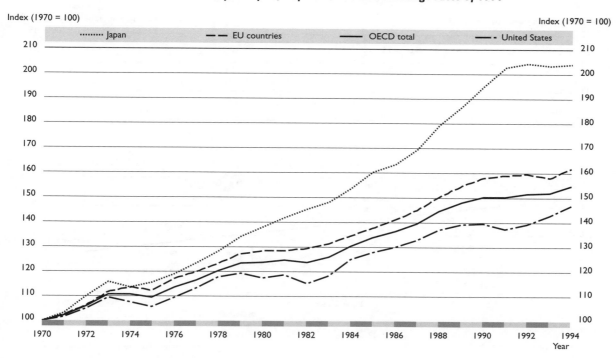

Source: OECD National Accounts database (1996).

expenditure will rise in *per capita* terms for this reason alone. However, if countries can control health care expenditure so that, as populations age, the ratio between expenditure on the elderly and the young is reduced,[5] it may be possible to avoid this. Also, to the extent that health care expenditure are concentrated in the final years of life, ageing of the existing population may not result in higher expenditure in the future, but of course this will not compensate for a rise in the ratio of old people due to a previous fall in the birth rate.

Comparisons across OECD countries are encouraging in this regard. If health care expenditure were necessarily higher when populations are older, one would expect that countries which have more elderly populations would show a systematic tendency to have higher per capita health care expenditure than those with younger populations. This does not appear to be the case: across OECD countries there does not appear to be any relationship between the extent of ageing and aggregate health care expenditure. It is real per capita GDP, and not the proportion of the population who are elderly, which is closely correlated with the proportion of national income devoted to health care (Scherer, 1996) (Charts 1.2a and 1.2b).

This said, it is clearly important to understand more thoroughly the likely implications of future demographic trends on health care burdens: is healthy life expectancy increasing at least in line with the increase in life expectancy itself, with expensive care concentrated in a smaller part of the population, or can demand for health care in the future be estimated by extrapolating from current age-specific expenditure? (For a preliminary discussion of this issue, see OECD, 1996e.)

Current policy preoccupations

Fears about the viability of social commitments have now shifted to cash transfers. Publicly funded provision of various forms of care ("in-kind" benefits) – of which health care is the major item –

◆ Chart 1.2a. **Health expenditure (public and private) and extent of ageing, 1994**

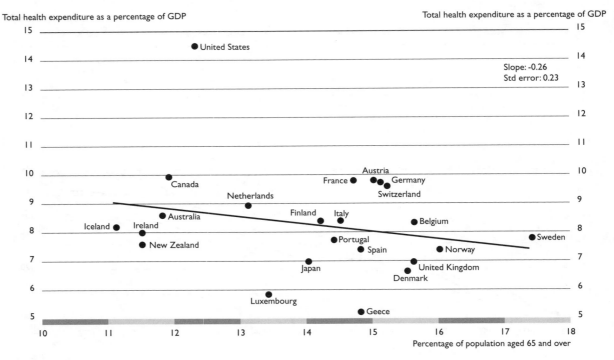

Source: OECD health database (1996).

◆ Chart 1.2b. **Health expenditure (public and private) per capita, and GDP per capita, in dollars using purchasing power parities (PPPs), 1994**

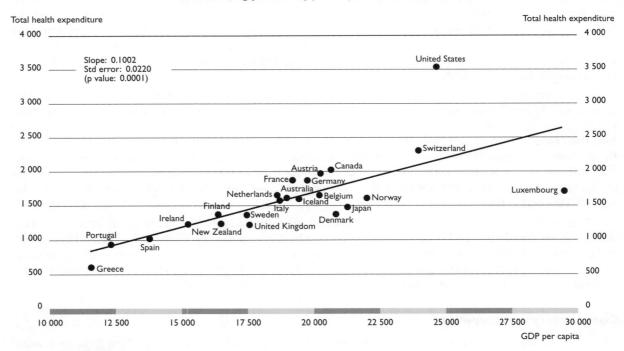

Source: OECD health database (1996).

represents a direct use of resources which would otherwise be available to households to spend (although they would often have to meet the same costs themselves, so that the effect on net household incomes is indeterminate, and varies with the economic situation of individual households and their use of such services). In contrast, cash transfers re-assign incomes between households, and do not change national expenditure in a national accounting sense. They may affect aggregate incomes (apart from the administrative costs of the transfers) due to distortions in the price mechanisms of the economy, because of the taxes used to finance the transfers and the dissuasive effects which transfers can have on their recipients (OECD, 1996b) (Chart 1.3).

Some of these increases were planned, or at least largely foreseeable. Expenditure on public transfers to the elderly in the form of old age pensions have increased as pension systems based on social insurance principles have matured (OECD, 1988b), and as the life expectancy of retired people has increased. The high levels of expenditure now being experienced were implicit in many European countries in the benefit entitlement formulae in their pension systems (Table 1.1).

In all OECD countries, public pension systems involve, either explicitly or implicitly, a flat rate component (often with adjustments for household size) and an earnings-related component. The increase in life expectancy and future demographic changes in the proportion of elderly people in the population is putting pressure on the financing of even the flat-rate component, and in many countries this is now subject to reduction if other income (either earnings-related pension entitlements or aggregate income) is high.[6]

But it is the earnings-related component of public systems which is under the greatest strain. Currently, the formulae for determining pension entitlements often imply that all contributors will receive a yield on the contributions which are made on their behalf which is greater than the sum of the growth rates of employment and of individual earnings. While it is always possible to achieve this for some contributors (and most public pension systems are biased towards higher replacement rates for those with low lifetime earnings – this is in fact the way the flat rate component is instituted in many instances), this cannot be the case for the pension system as a whole – unless it receives a subsidy from the general tax system.[7]

As a result, earnings-related pension systems have been reformed or are under reform in the United Kingdom, France, Italy, Sweden, Japan and other countries. In many cases, this reform has been initially oriented to changing the formulae for pension accrual so that, in the future, pension rights will be based on lifetime contributions rather than on final salaries. In some cases, the reforms have introduced an element of capitalised funding of future provision, in order to ensure that, at least for the proportion of the pension which is funded in this way, pension entitlements will be based on accumulated capital and the revenue from investing it.[8] Unfortunately, these reforms, while bringing the growth of pension expenditure under control, seem likely to leave the systems with severe strains (OECD, 1996e, Chapter 2). This is because the ageing of OECD populations and the changing patterns of lifetime labour force participation will both lead, for the foreseeable future, to a shrinkage of the base of pension contributors relative to beneficiaries (Table 1.2).

For those countries which continue to rely on currently financed pension systems, the nature of the pension promise needs to be recalled. These pension systems were designed to ensure that those who had retired would be able to share in economic growth and prosperity – and in their initial years they frequently were implemented to allow those who had recently retired to do so, although their own contributions had been for a short duration.[9] It is necessary now to ensure that this basic design principle is not forgotten. Most public pension systems have an element of redistribution to those with low earnings, or to those with dependents. However, it is impossible for a pension system to redistribute towards all contributors and still remain viable once it is mature without a general budgetary subsidy. Hence, where the design of pension systems is such that those with high earnings receive a yield on the contributions which are made on their behalf greater than the sum of the growth rates of employment and of individual earnings, immediate reform is called for. Clearly, the overall relation between pension recipients and other citizens involves much wider issues than pensions alone. This involves the consideration of life-cycle issues, to which this paper will return below.

◆ Chart 1.3. **Cash transfers and expenditure on services, by type**
(1980-85 and 1992-93)

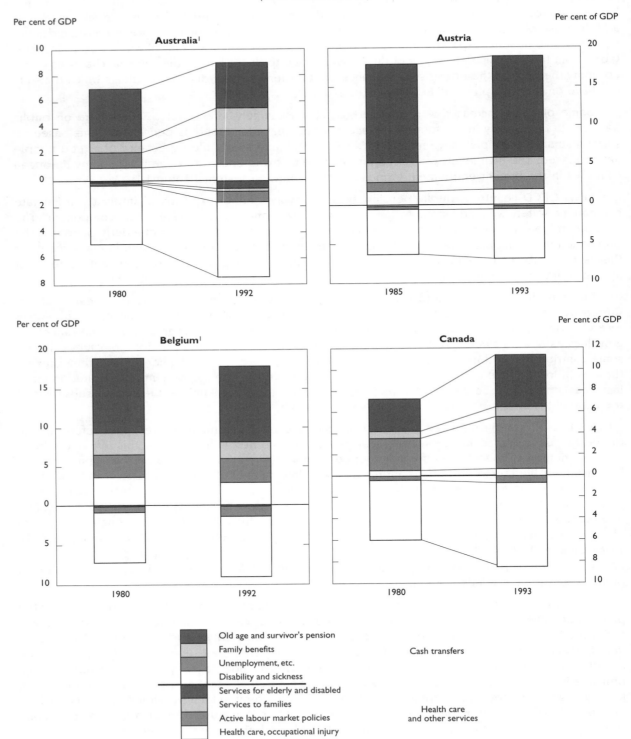

Note: In order to show the evolution, values for health care and other services, found under the zero line, are positive.
1. For the 1980 expenditure on active labour market policies (ALMP) an estimate was calculated by taking the ratio between ALMP and unemployment for the most recent year available, and applying this ratio to the unemployment figure for 1980.

◆ Chart 1.3. *(cont.)* **Cash transfers and expenditure on services, by type**
(1980-85 and 1992-93)

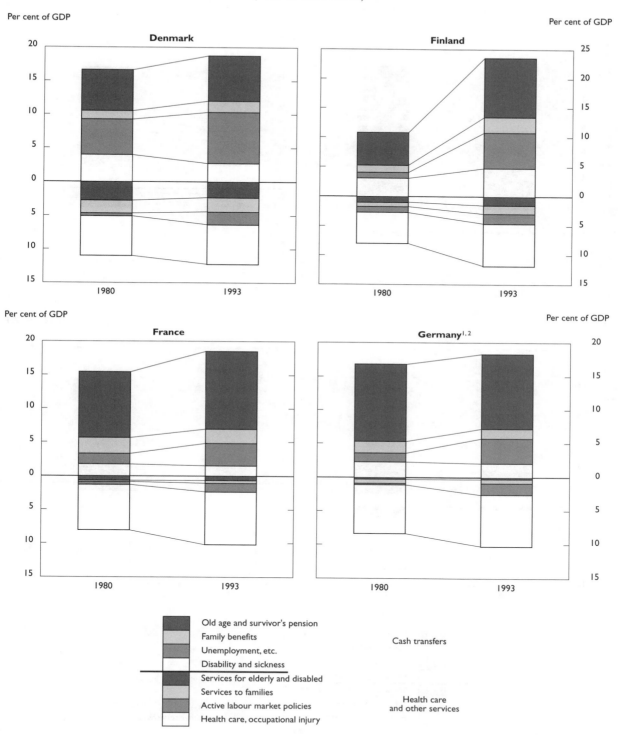

Per cent of GDP

Per cent of GDP

Per cent of GDP

Per cent of GDP

Old age and survivor's pension
Family benefits
Unemployment, etc.
Disability and sickness

Services for elderly and disabled
Services to families
Active labour market policies
Health care, occupational injury

Cash transfers

Health care
and other services

Note: In order to show the evolution, values for health care and other services, found under the zero line, are positive.
1. For the 1980 expenditure on active labour market policies (ALMP) an estimate was calculated by taking the ratio between ALMP and unemployment for the most recent year available, and applying this ratio to the unemployment figure for 1980.
2. The 1980 figures are for western Germany, 1993 figures are for unified Germany.

◆ Chart 1.3. (cont.) **Cash transfers and expenditure on services, by type**
(1980-85 and 1992-93)

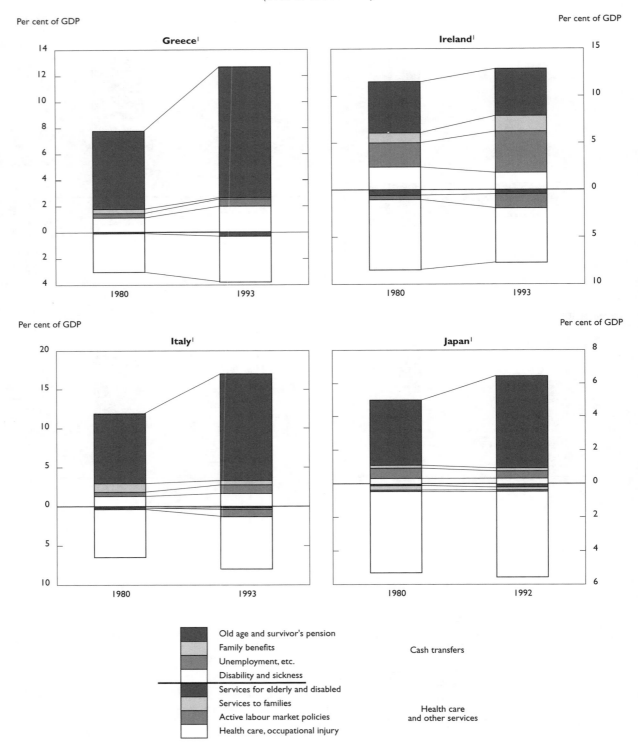

Old age and survivor's pension
Family benefits
Unemployment, etc.
Disability and sickness

Cash transfers

Services for elderly and disabled
Services to families
Active labour market policies
Health care, occupational injury

Health care
and other services

Note: In order to show the evolution, values for health care and other services, found under the zero line, are positive.
1. For the 1980 expenditure on active labour market policies (ALMP) an estimate was calculated by taking the ratio between ALMP and unemployment for the most recent year available, and applying this ratio to the unemployment figure for 1980.

◆ Chart 1.3. *(cont.)* **Cash transfers and expenditure on services, by type**
(1980-85 and 1992-93)

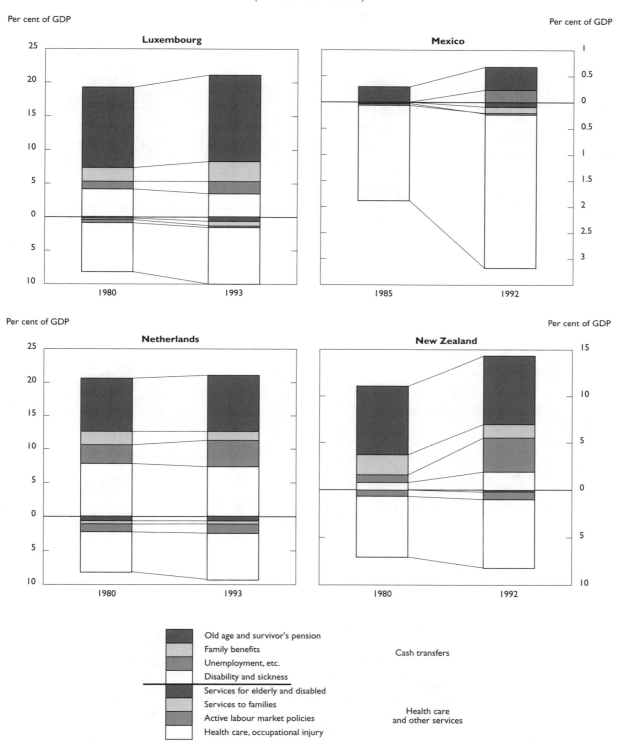

Per cent of GDP

Per cent of GDP

Per cent of GDP

Per cent of GDP

Old age and survivor's pension
Family benefits
Unemployment, etc.
Disability and sickness

Cash transfers

Services for elderly and disabled
Services to families
Active labour market policies
Health care, occupational injury

Health care
and other services

Note: In order to show the evolution, values for health care and other services, found under the zero line, are positive.

◆   Chart 1.3. *(cont.)* **Cash transfers and expenditure on services, by type**
(1980-85 and 1992-93)

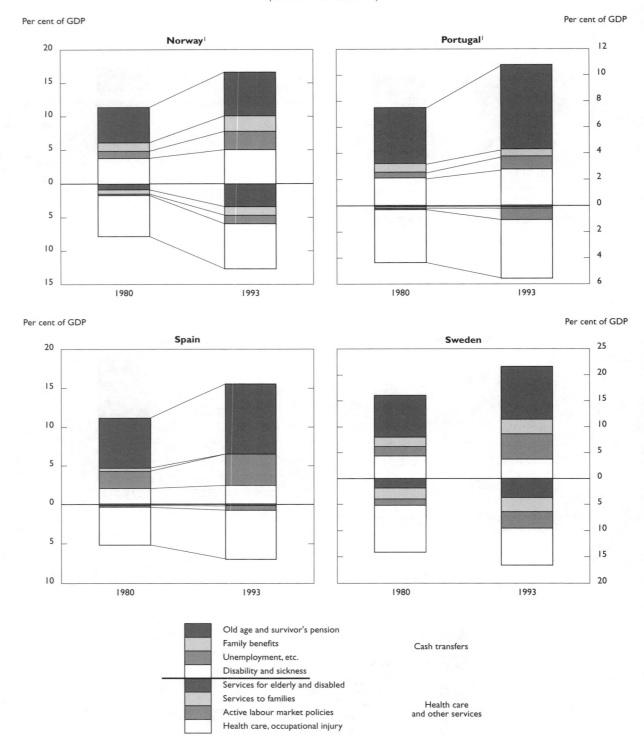

Note: In order to show the evolution, values for health care and other services, found under the zero line, are positive.
1.   For the 1980 expenditure on active labour market policies (ALMP) an estimate was calculated by taking the ratio between ALMP and unemployment for
     the most recent year available, and applying this ratio to the unemployment figure for 1980.

◆   Chart 1.3. *(cont.)* **Cash transfers and expenditure on services, by type**
(1980-85 and 1992-93)

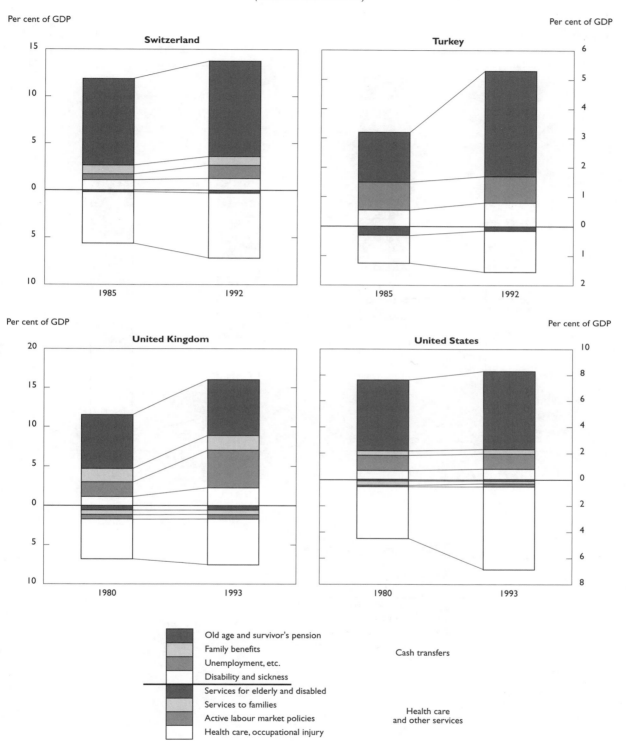

Per cent of GDP

Per cent of GDP

Per cent of GDP

Per cent of GDP

	Old age and survivor's pension	
	Family benefits	
	Unemployment, etc.	Cash transfers
	Disability and sickness	
	Services for elderly and disabled	
	Services to families	
	Active labour market policies	Health care
	Health care, occupational injury	and other services

Note: In order to show the evolution, values for health care and other services, found under the zero line, are positive.

◆ Chart 1.3. *(cont.)* ***Cash transfers and expenditure on services, by type***
(1980-85 and 1992-93)

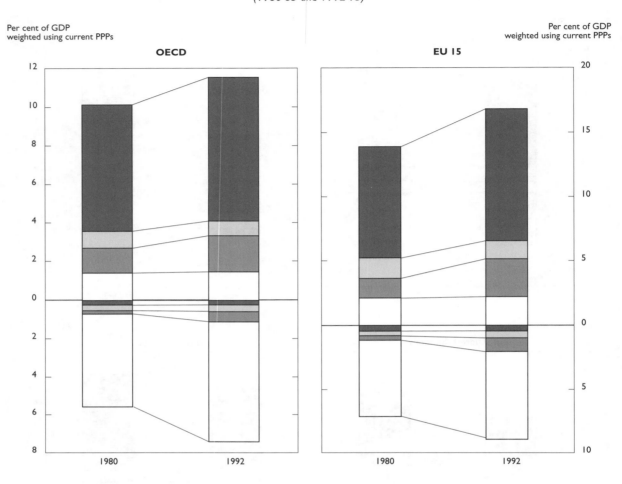

Per cent of GDP
weighted using current PPPs

Per cent of GDP
weighted using current PPPs

OECD

EU 15

Old age and survivor's pension
Family benefits
Unemployment, etc.
Disability and sickness

Cash transfers

Services for elderly and disabled
Services to families
Active labour market policies
Health care, occupational injury

Health care
and other services

Note: In order to show the evolution, values for health care and other services, found under the zero line, are positive.
Sources: OECD social expenditure database as at June 1996; for GDP, OECD analytical database as at June 1996.

Table 1.1. **Net income replacement ratios (net retirement pension/net earnings)
for pensioners without a dependent spouse, 1990[1]**

	Qualifying years	Average income level		
		²/₃	1	2
Australia[2]	n/a	45	33	19
Belgium	45	81	73	53
	20	34	39	34
Czech Republic	40	84	75	53
	25	66	59	41
Denmark	40	83	60	37
	20	82	59	36
France	37.5	96	88	75
	20	52	50	49
Germany	45	72	77	63
	20	32	34	28
Greece	35	125	107	97
	20	118	81	68
Ireland	40	57	42	26
	20	57	42	26
Italy	35	91	89	94
	20	56	56	56
Luxembourg	40	86	78	69
	20	48	48	44
Netherlands	40	66	49	27
	20	66	49	27
Portugal	37	89	94	102
	20	56	53	58
Spain	35	98	97	97
	20	70	73	71
United Kingdom	45	53	44	30
	20	31	28	23

1. The replacement rates presented here are based on the design features of the pension systems and do not show actual average replacement rates for the population. In particular for Italy, they reflect the inclusion of an estimation of the pension value of severance allowances.
2. Data refers to July 1990. Qualifying years are not applicable.
Source: Australia: Department of Social Security.
　　　　Czech Republic: Ministry of Labour and Social Affairs.
　　　　EU members: EUROSTAT (1993), *Old Age Replacement Ratios,* Vol. 1.

The other source of increase in the transfer burden has been the growth in the expenditure devoted to unemployment compensation. The specific issue of unemployment will be discussed below, but in addition to unemployment benefits the change in the structure of employment has resulted in a spillover of income maintenance payments into other categories. Invalidity benefits and early retirement benefits (in many countries these are interchangeable terms) have added to the pensions burden. Since such benefits are often funded in the same way as the old-age pension system, they represent a "premature ageing" of the population which has the same implications for expenditure as demographic ageing itself. Growth in the proportion of the population in receipt of invalidity benefits has been experienced in a number of OECD countries, and is one of the main factors contributing to increases in total outlays. The use of such benefits as a substitute for unemployment benefits may be a far more important source of "welfare dependence" than social assistance to the most disadvantaged.[10]

Table 1.2. **Population aged 65 and over as a percentage
of the population aged 15-64, 1960-2030**

	1960	1990	2000	2010	2020	2030
United States	15.4	19.1	19.0	20.4	27.6	36.8
Japan	9.5	17.1	24.3	33.0	43.0	44.5
Germany	16.0	21.7	23.8	30.3	35.4	49.2
France	18.8	20.8	23.6	24.6	32.3	39.1
Italy	13.3	21.6	26.5	31.2	37.5	48.3
United Kingdom	17.9	24.0	24.4	25.8	31.2	38.7
Canada	13.0	16.7	18.2	20.4	28.4	39.1
Australia	13.9	16.0	16.7	18.6	25.1	33.0
Austria	18.6	22.4	23.3	27.7	32.6	44.0
Belgium	18.5	22.4	25.1	25.6	31.9	41.1
Czech Republic	11.9	19.1	19.9	22.1	31.6	..
Denmark	16.5	22.7	21.6	24.9	31.7	37.7
Finland	11.7	19.7	21.5	24.3	34.7	41.1
Greece	12.3	21.2	25.5	28.8	33.3	40.9
Iceland	14.1	16.6	17.3	18.1	24.1	32.1
Ireland	18.6	18.4	16.7	18.0	21.7	25.3
Luxembourg	15.9	19.9	21.9	25.9	33.2	44.2
Mexico	..	6.4	7.0	8.0	10.4	14.8
Netherlands	14.7	19.1	20.8	24.2	33.9	45.1
New Zealand	..	16.7	17.1	18.9	24.6	30.5
Norway	17.3	25.2	23.9	24.0	31.2	38.7
Portugal	12.7	19.5	20.9	22.0	25.3	33.5
Spain	12.7	19.8	23.5	25.9	30.7	41.0
Sweden	17.8	27.6	26.9	29.1	35.6	39.4
Switzerland	15.5	22.0	23.6	29.4	37.8	48.6
Turkey	6.7	7.1	8.9	9.4	11.7	16.2
OECD Total (except Czech Republic)	14.9	19.3	20.9	23.5	29.8	37.7
OECD Europe	15.3	20.6	22.1	24.7	30.8	39.2

Source: Bos, E., Vu, M.T., Massiah, E. and Bulatao, R. (1994), *World Population Projections, 1994-95,* The International Bank for Reconstruction and Development/The World Bank.
Czech Republic: Ministry of Labour and Social Affairs.

The welfare state and family incomes

There has been a strong growth since 1980 in the dispersion of household incomes in a number of OECD countries, although by no means in all. This change has been greatest in absolute terms in Anglo-Saxon countries, and has on the whole been less pronounced in continental Europe and in the Nordic countries (Chart 1.4).[11]

The causes of this change are not fully understood. Two important factors have been the broadening of the distribution of hourly earnings amongst individuals (OECD, 1996a; Gottschalk and Danziger, 1993; Picot and Myles, 1995) and changes in household composition – though the latter have, overall, reduced the extent of the change. In the United States, where the rate of growth of per capita GDP has been slower than in most other OECD countries and the initial differentials between households were wider than elsewhere, the growth in dispersion between households has been greatest (United States Government, 1995; and United States Department of Labour, 1996).

This change in income distribution and the growth of concern about its implications is new. Around the time of the 1980 OECD conference, there was a consensus that one of the empirical economic constants for the United States was the inter-household distribution of income (Danziger and Gottschalk, 1993). Perhaps as a result, concern about the distributional consequences of changes in tax and transfer systems was not high on the agenda, and is not raised in the discussion in *The Welfare State*

◆ Chart 1.4. **Changes in Gini coefficients (1980-81 = 100)**

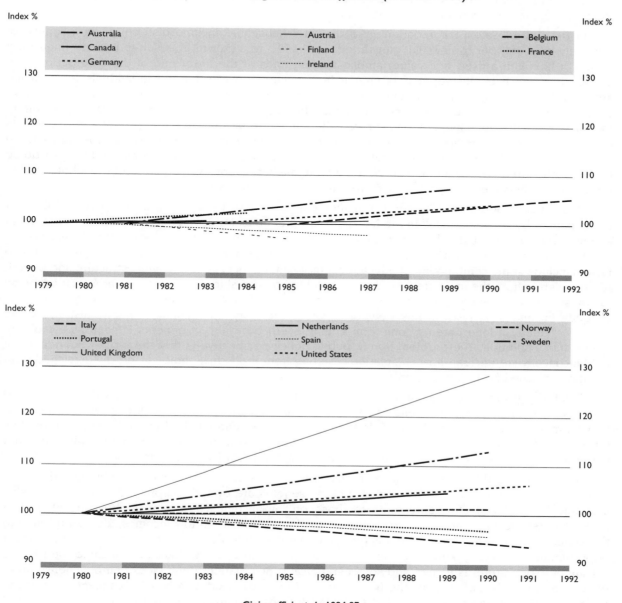

Gini coefficients in 1984-87		
	Year	Gini coefficient
Finland	1987	20.7
Sweden	1987	22.0
Norway	1986	23.4
Belgium	1988	23.5
Germany	1984	25.0
Netherlands	1987	26.8
Canada	1987	28.9
Australia	1985	29.5
France	1984	29.6
United Kingdom	1986	30.4
Italy	1986	31.0
Ireland	1987	33.0
United States	1986	34.1

Source: OECD (1995), *Income Distribution in OECD Countries*, Social Policy Studies No. 18, Paris.

in Crisis (OECD, 1981), other than in the context of suggesting that the egalitarian goals of the welfare state were inhibiting economic adjustment and growth.

In the United Sates, the broadening of the inter-household income distribution in a context of relatively slow real per capita GDP growth led, until 1994, to a growth in absolute poverty (measured against a line with a fixed real value) amongst households at the lower end of the distribution. It is unclear how much of this represents growth in persistent poverty for the individuals in particular households, and how much of it represents transient low incomes in the course of life cycles, with greater variation in incomes over time.[12] In most other OECD countries, real incomes at the bottom of the income distribution have not, on average, fallen in real terms, and in particular not after the effects of the tax transfer system are taken into account. However, the relative gap between households at the top and bottom of the income distribution has widened in many countries – and is likely to do so further in the future, as labour markets become more market responsive and as access to labour market opportunities becomes less uniformly distributed amongst households.

It is a matter of debate whether a broadening in income distribution in itself – provided it is not accompanied by an absolute fall in the incomes of poorer households – is a matter of policy concern. In a sense, concern about this has been superseded in Europe by a debate about "social exclusion" – broadly the notion that a number of factors are acting together to marginalise some groups. These factors include some combination of education, employment, race, housing, family structure and benefit rules. Isolation from the mainstream of society can lead to a total loss of economic and social adhesion for those affected, made worse by cultural isolation. Whether or not the benefits system prevents absolute income poverty is, in this view, only part of the story. Maintaining someone just above the poverty "line" (*e.g.* lone parents, long-term unemployed) but only on benefits is seen as a problem rather than a solution. The problem from a public policy perspective is that the proper boundaries of public concern are unclear: how is isolation resulting from individual choice to be distinguished from isolation imposed by lack of opportunity?

Related concerns underlie the desire to end "welfare dependency" in countries with means-tested systems.[13] In a major reform intended to achieve this aim, the United States has just legislated to transfer most authority for provision of aid to families with dependent children to the States, providing for a limit of two years in the duration of income support for a non-exempt[14] parent who does not undertake paid work. No adult may receive more than a total of five years' assistance.

Accompanying this growth in income disparities has been a growth in geographical disparity. Particularly in countries in which a majority of households are owner occupiers, the stock of housing available for rental at affordable rents to those on low incomes has come to be concentrated in particular areas. Social housing, when access is confined to those on low incomes, also contributes to this concentration, particularly when it is provided in geographically concentrated estates. Employment opportunities are more likely to be found in areas in which average household income (and hence consumer expenditure) is higher, and so geographical concentration of the lack of employment opportunities compounds and worsens the income disparities associated with housing concentration. It has become clear that any policy intended to lessen income disparities needs to address geographical disparities as well.[15]

THE CHALLENGES TO SOCIAL PROTECTION

Social protection has come under severe stress due to changes in the composition and nature of employment. While initially devised as an economic stabiliser, its function has gradually changed. But this is not due to any fall in overall employment levels. Over the past 25 years, the proportion of the population in employment has been more or less stable in the OECD area: for the twelve countries for which data are available continuously since 1972, 63 per cent of the working age population was engaged in paid employment in 1972, versus 66 per cent in 1995. In the eight European countries included in this total, there was a slight fall: from 61 to 58 per cent. Hence, in terms of a simplistic count of numbers employed, if the OECD area can be considered to have been fully employed in 1972, it still

is today.

The overall stability in the employment rate masks massive changes in the composition of employment. One is age related. The 25-54 year age group accounted for 75 per cent of employment in 1995, versus 65 per cent in 1972: the proportion of that age group in employment grew from 70 to 76 per cent. This represented a shift in employment away from young people,[16] and also away from older men. The growth in the employment share of adults[17] was itself the product of two contradictory trends. There has been a fall in the proportion of adult men in employment (though this has been on average balanced by the increase in this age group as a proportion of the population), and a strong increase in the employment rate of adult women (Table 1.3).

There has also been a growth in the proportion of employment which is classified as part-time (Table 1.4).[18] Although part-time workers are actively involved in the world of work, they earn less than full-time workers, so the distributional effects of the growth in the share of part-time employment are significant. As women also generally earn less than men (even when working full-time) the shift in employment share from men to women has also had a distributional effect – as has the growth (in some countries) in the share of full-time employment (amongst both sexes) with low earnings (OECD, 1996c).

Unemployment[19] grew in the OECD area in spite of the stability in employment rates. Nor was it linked in a simple manner to the falls in employment which did occur. Amongst young people, the rise of unemployment was not nearly as great as the fall in employment, which in the majority of European countries (where it was most pronounced), was accompanied by a growth in full-time participation in education (Table 1.5). Because the unemployment rate is influenced by employment rates (which are low where simultaneous schooling and employment are rare, as in France, and high in "dual" education systems such as those of Germany and Austria), and because it is possible (and in some countries common) to combine educational participation with jobseeking, the unemployment rate is a particularly misleading indicator of social distress amongst young people. It is the large proportion of young people who are neither at school nor at work which is the clearest sign of social distress: in many countries it is as high or higher for young men as for young women. Those engaged full-time in child raising will also be found in this category, but the proportion of young people neither in school nor in work has not fallen as the birth-rate has fallen.

Countries have responded to this problem in different ways. Some have emphasised increasing flexibility in the youth labour market and the removal of entitlements to income support which seemed to encourage young people to quit school and look for work.[20] Others have concentrated on increasing school participation, and have experienced both a fall in the proportion of young people in employment and a fall in the proportion neither in school nor in work (Chart 1.5).[21]

Amongst older men, most of the fall in employment rates was accompanied by withdrawal from the labour force (encouraged by reductions in the standard retirement age, and by subsidised early retirement which lowered the effective retirement age) (OECD, 1995b and 1995c). Amongst adult men, participation in the labour force did not decline appreciably despite falling employment, so that the rise in unemployment roughly matched the fall in employment. However, amongst adult women unemployment rose sharply throughout the period, in spite of the strong growth in employment, and now accounts for over a quarter of all unemployment in the OECD area.

Unemployment is not randomly distributed. As detailed reviews of social insurance systems have shown (Government of Canada, 1994; Swedish Department of Finance, 1993), even systems which are, in principle, based on social insurance principles do not have any of the features of an insurance market. Those who are repeated claimants are easily identifiable, and would not be insurable in any insurance market, even if insurance were compulsory. Social insurance against unemployment always represents the transfer of resources to bad risks. As the Swedish authorities observe, the distinction between social insurance and targeted assistance can be, for this reason, formal rather than substantive in countries in which most persons losing a job and willing to work receive some form of income support.

The change in female employment has not been uniform in its impact. In all OECD countries for which data are available, employment growth has been concentrated in married couple households, so that the two-earner households have grown as a proportion of all households: female employment growth has not reduced the proportion of households in which no one is receiving an earned income,

Table 1.3. **Employment, unemployment and population, 1972 to 1995**
12 OECD countries[1]

	Employment				Unemployment				Population			
	1972	1979	1989	1995	1972	1979	1989	1995	1972	1979	1989	1995
(Millions)												
Men 15-24	27.6	27.5	25.1	22.3	2.2	3.2	3.5	3.8	45.9	48.8	48.1	46.4
Men 25-54	99.4	109.9	122.2	130.4	2.0	3.2	5.5	7.8	105.5	118.5	135.2	148.9
Men 55-64	20.4	20.1	21.4	21.0	0.5	0.7	1.1	1.3	26.4	28.1	33.9	34.6
Women 15-24	21.9	23.0	22.0	19.5	1.7	3.2	3.5	3.5	46.3	48.5	47.2	45.0
Women 25-54	50.8	65.3	86.5	97.7	1.5	3.1	5.8	7.5	109.7	121.0	136.7	150.1
Women 55-64	10.2	11.4	12.7	13.6	0.2	0.4	0.5	0.7	30.5	32.9	36.9	37.0
All 15-24	49.4	50.5	47.2	41.9	3.9	6.5	7.0	7.2	92.2	97.3	95.4	91.4
All 25-54	150.2	175.2	208.7	228.1	3.5	6.3	11.4	15.3	215.2	239.5	272.0	299.0
All 55-64	30.5	31.5	34.1	34.6	0.7	1.1	1.6	2.0	57.0	61.0	70.7	71.6
All 15-65	230.2	257.2	289.9	304.6	8.1	13.8	20.0	24.5	364.4	397.7	438.1	462.0
(Per cent distribution)												
Men 15-24	12.0	10.7	8.7	7.3	27.2	23.3	17.4	15.4				
Men 25-54	43.2	42.7	42.1	42.8	24.5	23.4	27.7	31.9				
Men 55-64	8.9	7.8	7.4	6.9	6.4	5.0	5.3	5.2				
Women 15-24	9.5	8.9	7.6	6.4	20.8	23.5	17.7	14.1				
Women 25-54	22.1	25.4	29.8	32.1	18.4	22.1	29.2	30.6				
Women 55-64	4.4	4.4	4.4	4.5	2.7	2.8	2.7	2.8				
All 15-24	21.5	19.6	16.3	13.7	48.1	46.7	35.1	29.5				
All 25-54	65.3	68.1	72.0	74.9	42.8	45.5	56.9	62.5				
All 55-64	13.3	12.3	11.7	11.4	9.1	7.8	8.0	8.0				
All 15-65	100.0	100.0	100.0	100.0	100.0	100.0	100.0	100.0				
Ratio to population (per cent)									**Unemployment rate (per cent)**			
Men 15-24	60.0	56.3	52.3	48.2	4.8	6.6	7.2	8.1	7.4	10.5	12.1	14.4
Men 25-54	94.2	92.8	90.4	87.5	1.9	2.7	4.1	5.2	2.0	2.9	4.3	5.7
Men 55-64	77.2	71.7	63.2	60.6	2.0	2.5	3.1	3.6	2.5	3.3	4.7	5.7
Women 15-24	47.3	47.4	46.6	43.4	3.7	6.7	7.5	7.7	7.2	12.4	13.8	15.1
Women 25-54	46.3	54.0	63.2	65.1	1.4	2.5	4.3	5.0	2.9	4.5	6.3	7.1
Women 55-64	33.2	34.6	34.3	36.8	0.7	1.2	1.5	1.9	2.1	3.2	4.1	4.8
All 15-24	53.6	51.9	49.5	45.8	4.2	6.6	7.3	7.9	7.3	11.4	12.9	14.8
All 25-54	69.8	73.2	76.7	76.3	1.6	2.6	4.2	5.1	2.3	3.5	5.2	6.3
All 55-64	53.6	51.7	48.1	48.3	1.3	1.8	2.3	2.7	2.4	3.3	4.5	5.4
All 15-65	63.2	64.7	66.2	65.9	2.2	3.5	4.6	5.3	3.4	5.1	6.4	7.5

1. Australia, Canada, Finland, France, Italy, Japan, Netherlands, Norway, Spain, Sweden, United States, Western Germany.

Table 1.3. **Employment, unemployment and population, 1972 to 1995** *(cont.)*
8 European OECD countries[1]

(Millions)

	Employment 1972	1979	1989	1995	Unemployment 1972	1979	1989	1995	Population 1972	1979	1989	1995
Men 15-24	10.3	9.6	8.8	6.2	0.5	1.2	1.7	1.7	17.3	18.8	19.2	17.3
Men 25-54	40.0	41.5	43.1	47.1	0.5	1.2	2.7	4.2	42.2	44.7	48.7	55.7
Men 55-64	9.0	8.5	8.3	7.6	0.2	0.3	0.5	0.6	12.2	12.3	15.1	15.3
Women 15-24	7.8	7.4	6.7	4.8	0.4	1.4	2.0	1.7	16.8	18.2	18.4	16.5
Women 25-54	17.8	21.8	26.8	32.0	0.3	1.1	3.3	4.4	42.8	44.7	48.2	55.1
Women 55-64	3.6	3.9	3.9	4.1	0.1	0.2	0.3	0.4	14.4	14.4	16.3	16.2
All 15-24	18.1	17.0	15.5	11.0	0.9	2.6	3.7	3.5	34.1	37.0	37.6	33.8
All 25-54	57.8	63.3	69.8	79.1	0.8	2.4	6.1	8.7	85.0	89.4	96.9	110.8
All 55-64	12.7	12.4	12.2	11.7	0.2	0.5	0.8	1.0	26.6	26.7	31.4	31.6
All 15-65	88.5	92.6	97.5	101.8	2.0	5.4	10.6	13.1	145.7	153.1	166.0	176.2

Employment — Ratio to population (per cent); Unemployment and Population — (Distribution en pourcentage)

	Employment 1972	1979	1989	1995	Unemployment 1972	1979	1989	1995	Population 1972	1979	1989	1995
Men 15-24	59.2	51.0	45.6	35.8	26.5	22.1	15.8	13.0	11.6	10.4	9.0	6.1
Men 25-54	94.9	92.8	88.4	84.5	26.2	22.7	25.8	32.3	45.2	44.8	44.2	46.3
Men 55-64	73.9	69.1	55.1	49.8	9.0	5.3	5.0	4.7	10.2	9.2	8.5	7.5
Women 15-24	46.5	40.5	36.5	29.1	19.0	25.9	19.2	13.3	8.8	8.0	6.9	4.7
Women 25-54	41.4	48.7	55.5	58.0	16.4	20.6	31.2	33.7	20.1	23.5	27.4	31.4
Women 55-64	25.3	27.0	23.6	25.2	2.8	3.3	2.9	2.9	4.1	4.2	4.0	4.0
All 15-24	53.0	45.9	41.2	32.6	45.5	48.0	35.0	26.4	20.4	18.3	15.9	10.8
All 25-54	68.0	70.8	72.1	71.3	42.6	43.3	57.1	66.0	65.3	68.3	71.6	77.7
All 55-64	47.6	46.4	38.7	37.1	11.9	8.7	7.9	7.6	14.3	13.4	12.5	11.5
All 15-65	60.7	60.5	58.7	57.8	100.0	100.0	100.0	100.0	100.0	100.0	100.0	100.0

Unemployment rate (per cent)

	1972	1979	1989	1995
Men 15-24	4.9	11.2	16.0	21.7
Men 25-54	1.3	2.9	6.0	8.3
Men 55-64	1.9	3.3	6.1	7.5
Women 15-24	4.6	16.1	23.3	26.6
Women 25-54	1.8	4.9	11.0	12.2
Women 55-64	1.5	4.5	7.3	8.4
All 15-24	4.8	13.4	19.3	23.9
All 25-54	1.4	3.6	8.0	9.9
All 55-64	1.8	3.7	6.5	7.8
All 15-65	2.2	5.5	9.8	11.4

1. Finland, France, Italy, Netherlands, Norway, Spain, Sweden, Western Germany.

Table 1.3. **Employment, unemployment and population, 1972 to 1995** *(cont.)*
United States, Canada and Australia

	Employment				Unemployment				Population			
	1972	1979	1989	1995	1972	1979	1989	1995	1972	1979	1989	1995
(Millions)												
Men 15-24	11.8	14.4	12.5	11.9	1.5	1.9	1.6	1.8	18.9	21.8	19.3	19.6
Men 25-54	38.0	43.4	53.9	57.9	1.2	1.6	2.4	3.0	41.2	47.7	60.1	66.5
Men 55-64	8.1	8.2	7.7	7.3	0.3	0.2	0.3	0.3	10.3	11.5	12.0	11.8
Women 15-24	9.4	12.3	11.5	10.7	1.2	1.7	1.3	1.5	20.0	22.4	19.7	19.4
Women 25-54	20.9	29.1	43.5	49.1	1.0	1.7	2.2	2.6	43.9	50.1	62.3	68.6
Women 55-64	4.5	5.0	5.5	5.8	0.2	0.2	0.2	0.2	11.6	13.0	13.3	12.9
All 15-24	21.2	26.7	24.0	22.5	2.8	3.6	2.9	3.2	38.9	44.3	39.0	39.0
All 25-54	58.9	72.5	97.3	107.0	2.3	3.2	4.6	5.6	85.1	97.7	122.4	135.1
All 55-64	12.6	13.2	13.2	13.1	0.4	0.4	0.5	0.6	21.9	24.6	25.2	24.7
All 15-65	92.6	112.4	134.5	142.6	5.5	7.3	8.0	9.4	145.9	166.6	186.6	198.8
(Per cent distribution)												
Men 15-24	12.8	12.8	9.3	8.3	28.2	25.9	20.1	19.0	13.0	13.1	10.3	9.8
Men 25-54	41.0	38.6	40.0	40.6	22.7	21.9	30.1	32.0	28.2	28.6	32.2	33.5
Men 55-64	8.7	7.3	5.7	5.1	5.0	3.3	3.9	3.7	7.1	6.9	6.4	6.0
Women 15-24	10.1	10.9	8.5	7.5	22.3	23.7	16.6	15.6	13.7	13.5	10.5	9.8
Women 25-54	22.5	25.8	32.3	34.4	19.0	22.8	27.1	27.3	30.1	30.0	33.4	34.5
Women 55-64	4.9	4.5	4.1	4.1	2.8	2.3	2.2	2.5	7.9	7.8	7.1	6.5
All 15-24	22.9	23.7	17.8	15.8	50.5	49.7	36.7	34.5	26.7	26.6	20.9	19.6
All 25-54	63.6	64.5	72.4	75.0	41.7	44.7	57.2	59.3	58.3	58.7	65.6	67.9
All 55-64	13.6	11.8	9.8	9.2	7.8	5.7	6.1	6.2	15.0	14.8	13.5	12.4
All 15-65	100.0	100.0	100.0	100.0	100.0	100.0	100.0	100.0	100.0	100.0	100.0	100.0
Ratio to population (per cent)												
Men 15-24	62.6	66.1	64.8	60.6	8.2	8.6	8.3	9.1				
Men 25-54	92.3	91.1	89.6	87.0	3.0	3.3	4.0	4.5				
Men 55-64	78.2	70.8	64.2	62.0	2.6	2.1	2.6	2.9				
Women 15-24	46.8	54.7	58.2	55.0	6.1	7.7	6.7	7.5				
Women 25-54	47.6	58.0	69.8	71.5	2.4	3.3	3.5	3.7				
Women 55-64	39.0	38.7	41.5	44.9	1.3	1.3	1.3	1.8				
All 15-24	54.4	60.3	61.5	57.8	7.1	8.2	7.5	8.3				
All 25-54	69.2	74.2	79.5	79.2	2.7	3.3	3.7	4.1				
All 55-64	57.4	53.8	52.3	53.1	1.9	1.7	1.9	2.4				
All 15-65	63.5	67.5	72.1	71.7	3.7	4.4	4.3	4.7				
Unemployment rate (per cent)												
Men 15-24									11.5	11.6	11.4	13.1
Men 25-54									3.2	3.5	4.3	4.9
Men 55-64									3.3	2.9	3.9	4.5
Women 15-24									11.5	12.4	10.4	12.0
Women 25-54									4.7	5.4	4.7	5.0
Women 55-64									3.3	3.3	3.1	4.0
All 15-24									11.5	11.9	10.9	12.6
All 25-54									3.7	4.3	4.5	5.0
All 55-64									3.3	3.0	3.5	4.2
All 15-65									5.6	6.1	5.6	6.2

Table 1.3. **Employment, unemployment and population, 1972 to 1995** (cont.)
Japan

	Employment				Unemployment				Population			
	1972	1979	1989	1995	1972	1979	1989	1995	1972	1979	1989	1995
(Millions)												
Men 15-24	5.5	3.5	3.9	4.3	0.2	0.1	0.2	0.3	9.7	8.2	9.6	9.5
Men 25-54	21.4	25.0	25.3	25.4	0.2	0.4	0.4	0.6	22.2	26.1	26.4	26.7
Men 55-64	3.3	3.5	5.4	6.0	0.1	0.2	0.2	0.3	3.9	4.3	6.8	7.5
Women 15-24	4.7	3.4	3.9	4.0	0.1	0.1	0.2	0.3	9.5	7.9	9.1	9.1
Women 25-54	12.2	14.5	16.3	16.7	0.1	0.3	0.4	0.5	23.0	26.2	26.3	26.4
Women 55-64	2.0	2.4	3.3	3.7	0.0	0.0	0.1	0.1	4.6	5.4	7.3	7.9
All 15-24	10.2	6.8	7.7	8.3	0.3	0.2	0.4	0.5	19.3	16.0	18.7	18.6
All 25-54	33.6	39.4	41.5	42.1	0.4	0.7	0.7	1.1	45.2	52.3	52.7	53.1
All 55-64	5.3	5.9	8.7	9.8	0.1	0.2	0.3	0.4	8.5	9.7	14.1	15.3
All 15-65	49.1	52.2	57.9	60.2	0.7	1.1	1.4	2.0	72.9	78.0	85.5	87.0
(Per cent distribution)												
Men 15-24	11.2	6.6	6.7	7.1	21.7	11.6	13.8	13.8	13.3	10.5	11.2	11.0
Men 25-54	43.5	47.9	43.6	42.2	33.3	36.6	27.5	28.6	30.4	33.5	30.9	30.6
Men 55-64	6.7	6.7	9.3	10.0	10.1	14.3	15.9	14.8	5.3	5.5	8.0	8.6
Women 15-24	9.7	6.5	6.6	6.7	14.5	9.8	12.3	12.8	13.1	10.1	10.7	10.4
Women 25-54	24.9	27.7	28.1	27.8	18.8	25.0	26.1	26.1	31.6	33.6	30.7	30.4
Women 55-64	4.1	4.7	5.7	6.2	1.4	2.7	4.3	3.9	6.3	6.9	8.5	9.0
All 15-24	20.8	13.1	13.3	13.8	36.2	21.4	26.1	26.6	26.4	20.6	21.9	21.4
All 25-54	68.4	75.6	71.7	70.0	52.2	61.6	53.6	54.7	61.9	67.0	61.6	61.0
All 55-64	10.8	11.3	15.0	16.2	11.6	17.0	20.3	18.7	11.6	12.4	16.5	17.6
All 15-65	100.0	100.0	100.0	100.0	100.0	100.0	100.0	100.0	100.0	100.0	100.0	100.0

Ratio to population (per cent)

	Employment				Unemployment			
	1972	1979	1989	1995	1972	1979	1989	1995
Men 15-24	56.2	42.3	40.3	45.1	1.5	1.6	2.0	2.9
Men 25-54	96.4	95.7	95.5	95.3	1.0	1.6	1.4	2.2
Men 55-64	84.8	81.5	79.2	80.8	1.8	3.8	3.2	4.0
Women 15-24	49.7	42.9	42.1	44.4	1.0	1.4	1.9	2.9
Women 25-54	53.0	55.2	61.9	63.2	0.6	1.1	1.4	2.0
Women 55-64	43.6	44.8	45.3	47.5	0.2	0.6	0.8	1.0
All 15-24	53.0	42.6	41.2	44.7	1.3	1.5	1.9	2.9
All 25-54	74.3	75.4	78.7	79.3	0.8	1.3	1.4	2.1
All 55-64	62.5	61.0	61.7	63.7	0.9	2.0	2.0	2.5
All 15-65	67.3	66.8	67.7	69.2	0.9	1.4	1.6	2.3

Unemployment rate (per cent)

	1972	1979	1989	1995
Men 15-24	2.7	3.6	4.7	6.1
Men 25-54	1.1	1.6	1.5	2.2
Men 55-64	2.1	4.4	3.9	4.7
Women 15-24	2.1	3.2	4.2	6.1
Women 25-54	1.1	1.9	2.2	3.1
Women 55-64	0.5	1.2	1.8	2.1
All 15-24	2.4	3.4	4.5	6.1
All 25-54	1.1	1.7	1.4	2.6
All 55-64	1.5	3.1	1.8	3.7
All 15-65	1.4	2.1	1.6	3.3

Source: OECD *Labour Force Statistics database* (1996).

Table 1.4. **Number of people in full- and part-time employment in 15 OECD countries,**[1]
in 1975 and 1995

(millions)

	Full-time			Part-time[2]			Proportion part-time/full-time	
	1975	1995	Change	1975	1995	Change	1975	1955
Males	162.6	186.3	23.7	9.9	16.4	6.5	6.1%	8.8%
Females	96.2	142.6	46.4	25.7	45.2	19.5	26.7%	31.7%
All	258.8	328.9	70.1	35.6	61.6	26.0	13.8%	18.7%

1. Australia, Austria, Belgium, Canada, Denmark, France, Italy, Japan, Luxembourg, Netherlands, New Zealand, Norway, United Kingdom, United States, Western Germany.
2. Definitions of part-time work differ accross countries.
Source: OECD full-time/part-time database.

but there is no clear evidence either of that proportion's increasing over the decade (Gregg and Wadsworth, 1996*a* and 1996*b*). In the United States, analysis of census year data over four decades shows that, at least since 1970, it has been households in which the male earner has high wages that male participation and earnings have increased, and it is also in such households that female participation and earnings had increased most (Juhn and Murphy, 1996). Although the increase in female participation has had the overall effect of increasing equality of incomes amongst households as a whole, due to the shift from one-earner households to two-earner households, inequalities of income amongst households with two earners have increased.

Social policy systems in OECD countries are generally based on protecting families against fluctuations in their income, which consists basically of regular earnings from a "regular" job. Interruptions of regular earnings – due to unemployment, illness, family responsibilities or invalidity – are regarded as "risks" against which insurance is necessary. This is the idea behind the international conventions on social security (including those sponsored by the ILO and the Council of Europe).

To the extent that the industrialised societies are adjusting to the changing patterns of labour demand in the ways described above, the social basis of this system is being eroded. If most households have a single earner, then the risk to that household of the loss of income from interruption of employment is considerable, and the conjunctural nature of such an occurrence makes private insurance impractical. Social insurance meets a need which is difficult to satisfy in other ways.

However, once employment shifts from the young to two-earner families, the system is eroded at both ends. Two-earner families are better able to accumulate cash reserves and other resources which provide a cushion against income fluctuations. Hence, to the extent that social insurance (and in particular insurance for non-employment related services such as health care) is funded by specific levies (rather than from the general tax system), they may (if they each receive an adequate income in work) find themselves paying two premiums for a cover neither of them really needs.[22] At the same time, those trying to enter the labour market with low qualifications or few marketable skills can find that the cost of social insurance charges payable by the employer makes job opportunities hard to find. Furthermore, low rates of pay may result in lower income when in work than when on income support, particularly in the case of part-time work. Hence the system as a whole provides some of those who fund it with an insurance which they do not really need, while failing to provide employment opportunities to those who desperately need them. In addition to the labour market distortions caused by financing and paying cash transfers to those without employment, there is a growing divergence of economic interests between those who fund them and those who receive them.

This is not the result of any "failure" in the labour market. The labour market is changing its nature in response to technological change – and in response to the feedback into the derived demand for labour from these processes themselves: the patterns in demand in twin-income households are different from those in single-earner households.[23] Nor is there any evidence of "moral" failure on the

Table 1.5. **Proportion of young people in education and in employment, by sex, for 15-19 and 20-24 year-olds**

Men 15-19

| | | At work only | | At school and at work | At school | | Jobseeking while at school | Total jobseeking | Neither at school nor at work | | Total | Per cent | Total in age cohort | | | |
		Total at work	At work only		Total at school	At school only			Looking for work	Not looking for work			Thousands	Labour force participation rate	Unemployment rate	School attendance rate
Australia	1984	49.3	28.5	20.8	59.9	35.4	3.7	13.4	9.7	1.9	11.6	100.0	643.6	62.7	21.3	59.9
	1994	42.3	18.2	24.1	71.5	42.6	4.8	13.1	8.3	2.0	10.3	100.0	650.0	55.4	23.7	71.5
Canada	1985	36.7	14.4	22.2	73.8	46.3	5.3	12.8	7.5	4.2	11.7	100.0	1 028.8	49.5	25.9	73.8
	1995	35.3	10.7	24.6	80.3	51.0	4.8	9.2	4.4	4.6	9.0	100.0	992.4	44.4	20.6	80.3
Japan	1982	18.1	15.3	2.9	81.6	78.7	–	–	–	3.2	3.2	100.0	4 277	–	–	81.6
	1992	18.2	13.8	4.4	81.1	76.6	–	–	1.2	4.0	5.2	100.0	4 990	–	–	81.1
Switzerland	1980	56.3	15.8	40.6	83.3	42.7	0.0	0.4	0.4	0.5	1.0	100.0	262.0	56.7	0.7	83.3
	1990	55.4	10.6	44.8	88.3	43.4	0.1	0.6	0.5	0.6	1.1	100.0	218.1	56.0	1.0	88.3
United States	1983	36.9	20.0	16.9	68.4	44.9	6.6	13.6	7.1	4.6	11.6	100.0	7 731.9	50.5	26.9	68.4
	1993	38.4	20.0	18.5	70.6	46.1	6.1	10.7	4.7	4.7	9.4	100.0	6 640.5	49.2	21.8	70.6
Belgium	1984	13.2	10.0	3.2	82.2	78.3	0.7	4.7	4.1	3.8	7.8	100.0	383.6	17.9	26.5	82.2
	1994	6.3	4.2	2.1	84.5	82.1	0.3	3.0	2.8	8.6	11.3	100.0	311.5	9.4	32.5	84.5
Denmark	1984	60.9	17.7	43.1	77.2	30.3	3.8	7.2	3.4	1.7	5.1	100.0	199.0	68.0	10.6	77.2
	1994	63.6	9.5	54.1	88.5	29.6	4.9	5.9	1.0	0.9	1.9	100.0	166.5	69.5	8.5	88.5
Germany	1984	39.7	11.1	28.6	85.9	55.4	2.0	4.3	2.3	0.7	3.0	100.0	2 532.6	44.0	9.7	85.9
	1994	33.5	4.8	28.7	92.8	63.3	0.9	2.2	1.3	1.1	2.4	100.0	2 157.2	35.7	6.2	92.8
Greece	1984	25.3	23.2	2.1	68.7	65.4	1.2	5.1	3.8	4.2	8.1	100.0	346.0	30.4	16.7	68.7
	1994	14.2	13.3	0.9	80.1	78.7	0.5	3.7	3.2	3.5	6.7	100.0	350.5	17.8	20.5	80.1
France	1984	20.2	12.7	7.5	71.5	63.8	0.2	8.7	8.5	7.3	15.8	100.0	1 792.8	28.9	30.0	71.5
	1994	8.3	2.3	6.0	92.5	85.8	0.6	4.1	3.5	1.7	5.2	100.0	1 762.9	12.5	33.1	92.5
Ireland	1984	27.9	18.7	9.2	68.0	56.9	2.0	14.0	12.0	1.3	13.2	100.0	166.1	41.8	33.4	68.0
	1994	17.0	11.0	6.0	80.0	72.8	1.2	7.7	6.4	2.5	8.9	100.0	160.2	24.7	31.1	80.0
Italy	1984	23.5	22.2	1.4	63.2	60.7	1.1	11.2	10.1	4.6	14.6	100.0	2 197.4	34.7	32.2	63.2
	1994	15.6	14.7	0.8	71.4	69.9	0.7	8.1	7.4	6.4	13.9	100.0	1 932.5	23.7	34.3	71.4
Luxembourg	1984	37.2	21.2	16.1	73.0	56.2	0.7	4.4	3.6	2.2	5.8	100.0	13.7	41.6	10.5	73.0
	1994	15.7	10.2	5.6	81.5	75.9	0.0	1.9	1.9	6.5	8.3	100.0	10.8	17.6	10.5	81.5
Netherlands	1989	33.1	7.8	25.3	89.5	59.8	4.3	5.8	1.5	1.3	2.8	100.0	562.1	38.9	15.0	89.5
	1994	37.3	7.0	30.2	89.0	53.8	5.0	7.1	2.1	1.9	4.0	100.0	462.3	44.4	16.0	89.0
Portugal	1989	48.9	44.6	4.3	49.0	43.9	0.8	4.3	3.5	2.9	6.4	100.0	457.9	53.2	8.0	49.0
	1994	26.5	22.7	3.8	70.6	65.7	1.0	3.5	2.5	4.2	6.7	100.0	440.1	30.1	11.7	70.6
Spain	1989	20.3	18.6	1.7	69.7	66.6	1.5	9.2	7.7	3.9	11.7	100.0	1 652.4	29.5	31.1	69.7
	1994	13.2	11.6	1.6	75.0	70.8	2.6	12.1	9.4	4.0	13.4	100.0	1 624.1	25.3	47.7	75.0
United Kingdom	1984	41.9	21.9	19.9	63.8	42.0	1.8	13.0	11.2	3.1	14.3	100.0	2 328.7	54.9	23.7	63.8
	1994	39.8	17.5	22.3	67.1	42.9	1.9	10.5	8.6	6.8	15.4	100.0	1 686.7	50.3	20.9	67.1

Table 1.5. **Proportion of young people in education and in employment, by sex, for 15-19 and 20-24 year-olds** (cont.)

Women 15-19

		At work only	Total at work	At school and at work	At school — Total at school	At school only	Jobseeking while at school	Total jobseeking	Neither at school nor at work — Looking for work	Not looking for work	Total	Per cent	Thousands	Labour force participation rate	Unemployment rate	School attendance rate
Australia	1984	30.9	47.6	16.8	55.6	35.4	3.3	11.6	8.3	5.3	13.6	100.0	626.2	59.3	19.6	55.6
	1994	15.4	42.7	27.3	74.3	40.6	6.4	12.5	6.2	4.1	10.3	100.0	621.2	55.3	22.7	74.3
Canada	1985	14.9	39.4	24.5	73.5	45.2	3.8	9.1	5.3	6.3	11.6	100.0	977.5	48.5	18.8	73.5
	1995	8.7	36.3	27.6	81.2	49.5	4.1	7.7	3.6	6.5	10.1	100.0	946.1	44.0	17.5	81.2
Japan	1982	15.5	18.1	2.7	81.4	78.7	–	–	–	3.2	3.2	100.0	4 102	–	–	81.4
	1992	12.0	17.2	5.3	84.7	79.4	–	–	1.3	2.1	3.3	100.0	4 702	–	–	84.7
Switzerland	1980	24.7	50.5	25.8	73.0	47.3	0.0	0.6	0.6	1.6	2.2	100.0	249.7	51.1	1.3	73.0
	1990	14.8	48.4	33.5	83.3	49.6	0.1	0.9	0.7	1.2	1.9	100.0	205.0	49.2	1.7	83.3
United States	1983	19.1	36.0	16.8	65.9	44.0	5.1	10.1	5.0	10.0	15.0	100.0	7 696.8	46.1	21.9	65.9
	1993	17.8	36.4	18.6	68.6	45.6	4.4	8.3	3.9	9.7	13.6	100.0	6 510.6	44.7	18.6	68.6
Belgium	1984	7.0	8.7	1.7	84.0	81.4	0.9	5.8	4.9	4.1	9.0	100.0	376.5	14.5	40.0	84.0
	1994	3.2	3.9	0.7	83.6	82.4	0.4	2.4	2.0	11.3	13.3	100.0	299.6	6.3	37.8	83.6
Denmark	1984	16.5	53.1	36.6	77.3	36.9	3.7	7.8	4.1	2.2	6.2	100.0	198.7	60.9	12.8	77.3
	1994	10.7	58.2	47.6	85.4	35.4	2.4	3.2	0.7	3.2	3.9	100.0	147.4	61.4	5.2	85.4
Germany	1984	11.5	33.9	22.4	83.8	58.9	2.5	5.4	2.9	1.9	4.7	100.0	2 465	39.2	13.7	83.8
	1994	4.5	27.6	23.1	92.8	69.1	0.6	1.6	1.0	1.7	2.7	100.0	1 942.1	29.2	5.5	92.8
Greece	1984	13.6	14.4	0.8	61.5	59.1	1.6	8.2	6.6	18.3	24.9	100.0	376.8	22.6	36.4	61.5
	1994	7.3	7.9	0.6	78.5	76.8	1.1	7.1	6.1	8.2	14.2	100.0	377.9	15.0	47.6	78.5
France	1984	9.9	12.6	2.7	71.1	68.1	0.2	11.2	11.0	8.0	19.1	100.0	1 851.6	23.8	47.2	71.1
	1994	2.2	5.0	2.8	92.6	89.4	0.4	3.6	3.2	2.0	5.2	100.0	1 754.6	8.6	41.7	92.6
Ireland	1984	18.6	23.9	5.3	70.7	62.5	3.0	11.6	8.6	2.1	10.7	100.0	158.8	35.5	32.7	70.7
	1994	7.4	12.1	4.7	85.1	79.1	1.3	6.0	4.7	2.8	7.5	100.0	153.1	18.1	33.2	85.1
Italy	1984	14.4	15.0	0.6	61.3	59.5	1.2	13.5	12.3	12.0	24.3	100.0	2 286.8	28.5	47.4	61.3
	1994	9.0	9.9	0.9	72.5	70.9	0.6	6.6	6.0	12.5	18.5	100.0	1 947.9	16.6	40.0	72.5
Luxembourg	1984	26.7	34.1	7.4	66.7	59.3	0.0	3.7	3.7	3.0	6.7	100.0	13.5	37.8	9.8	66.7
	1994	11.4	16.2	4.8	79.0	74.3	0.0	3.8	3.8	5.7	9.5	100.0	10.5	20.0	19.0	79.0
Netherlands	1989	10.4	30.4	20.0	84.9	59.1	5.8	7.9	2.0	2.7	4.7	100.0	554.7	38.2	20.6	84.9
	1994	7.7	34.4	26.7	88.3	58.6	3.0	4.7	1.7	2.3	4.0	100.0	450.0	39.0	12.0	88.3
Portugal	1989	31.0	33.2	2.2	54.5	51.1	1.3	6.4	5.2	9.3	14.5	100.0	436.0	39.6	16.2	54.5
	1994	18.6	21.5	2.9	71.8	67.7	1.2	5.3	4.1	5.5	9.6	100.0	441.7	26.8	19.6	71.8
Spain	1989	12.7	14.0	1.3	70.5	67.2	2.0	11.7	9.7	7.1	16.8	100.0	1 624.8	25.7	45.5	70.5
	1994	7.0	8.3	1.3	79.9	75.7	2.9	11.4	8.5	4.6	13.1	100.0	1 626.9	19.7	58.1	79.9
United Kingdom	1984	25.4	40.0	14.6	58.3	41.8	1.9	10.4	8.5	7.7	16.3	100.0	2 227.9	50.4	20.6	58.3
	1994	20.1	39.6	19.5	64.0	42.4	2.0	7.6	5.6	10.3	15.9	100.0	1 591.8	47.3	16.1	64.0

Table 1.5. **Proportion of young people in education and in employment, by sex, for 15-19 and 20-24 year-olds** *(cont.)*

Men 20-24

		Percentage of age cohort											Total in age cohort			
					At school				Neither at school nor at work							
		At work only	Total at work	At school and at work	Total at school	At school only	Jobseeking while at school	Total jobseeking	Looking for work	Not looking for work	Total	Per cent	Thousands	Labour force participation rate	Unemployment rate	School attendance rate
Australia	1984	63.8	77.6	13.8	22.4	7.1	1.5	13.0	11.5	2.4	13.8	100.0	656.9	90.6	14.3	22.4
	1994	57.8	72.8	15.0	27.3	10.2	2.1	14.0	11.9	3.1	15.0	100.0	718.7	86.7	16.1	27.3
Canada	1985	54.0	63.7	9.6	24.3	13.6	1.1	17.8	16.8	4.9	21.7	100.0	1 258.1	81.5	21.9	24.3
	1995	47.1	62.6	15.5	36.5	19.1	1.9	12.9	11.0	5.4	16.4	100.0	1 012.1	75.5	17.0	36.5
Japan	1982	67.1	71.7	4.7	29.0	24.3	–	–	–	4.0	4.0	100.0	3 934	–	–	29.0
	1992	65.5	73.4	8.0	29.6	21.6	–	–	2.4	2.5	4.9	100.0	4 858	–	–	29.6
Switzerland	1980	77.0	83.3	6.3	20.5	14.2	0.0	1.6	1.6	0.8	2.5	100.0	245.8	84.9	1.9	20.5
	1990	71.1	80.2	9.0	23.9	14.7	0.2	3.6	3.4	1.5	4.9	100.0	277.0	83.8	4.3	23.9
United States	1983	63.0	68.5	5.4	18.1	11.1	1.6	15.3	13.7	5.2	18.9	100.0	12 209.5	83.7	18.2	18.1
	1993	66.1	72.9	6.8	19.1	11.4	0.9	10.2	9.3	5.5	14.8	100.0	10 472.5	83.1	12.3	19.1
Belgium	1984	51.0	55.7	4.8	34.3	28.7	0.8	13.0	12.3	2.5	14.7	100.0	393.4	68.8	19.0	34.3
	1994	48.4	50.2	1.8	33.8	31.5	0.5	11.7	11.3	6.6	17.8	100.0	354.2	61.9	19.0	33.8
Denmark	1984	57.3	74.8	17.5	28.6	9.3	1.9	12.1	10.3	3.8	14.1	100.0	194.1	86.9	13.9	28.6
	1994	43.0	69.5	26.5	47.3	18.7	2.0	9.0	7.0	2.7	9.7	100.0	186.5	78.6	11.5	47.3
Germany	1984	61.7	69.9	8.2	29.0	20.4	0.4	7.4	6.9	2.4	9.3	100.0	2 348.9	77.2	9.5	29.0
	1994	52.0	66.5	14.5	38.1	23.3	0.3	7.4	7.2	2.7	9.9	100.0	2 134.4	73.9	10.1	38.1
Greece	1984	60.4	62.9	2.5	24.0	19.5	1.9	13.6	11.7	3.9	15.6	100.0	248.6	76.5	17.8	24.0
	1994	53.1	55.0	2.0	29.9	26.9	1.0	13.4	12.4	4.7	17.0	100.0	315.5	68.4	19.6	29.9
France	1984	66.8	68.6	1.8	13.9	11.9	0.2	14.7	14.5	4.8	19.3	100.0	1 836.6	83.3	17.6	13.9
	1994	41.7	47.0	5.3	39.4	33.1	1.0	16.6	15.6	3.3	18.9	100.0	1 860.7	63.7	26.1	39.4
Ireland	1984	60.7	68.9	8.2	19.1	9.9	1.0	19.5	18.5	1.7	20.2	100.0	142.9	88.4	22.1	19.1
	1994	50.4	59.0	8.6	29.2	19.3	1.2	17.5	16.2	4.2	20.4	100.0	145.3	76.5	22.9	29.2
Italy	1984	57.3	58.8	1.4	23.5	20.3	1.7	17.6	15.9	3.3	19.2	100.0	1 938.8	76.3	23.0	23.5
	1994	44.5	45.9	1.3	29.7	27.1	1.3	16.7	15.4	10.3	25.8	100.0	2 127.1	62.6	26.7	29.7
Luxembourg	1984	73.8	78.0	4.3	22.0	17.7	0.0	2.1	2.1	2.1	4.3	100.0	14.1	80.1	2.7	22.0
	1994	60.4	66.4	6.0	31.3	25.4	0.0	5.2	5.2	3.0	8.2	100.0	13.4	71.6	7.3	31.3
Netherlands	1989	43.7	67.0	23.3	48.4	22.4	2.6	8.5	5.8	2.1	7.9	100.0	602.2	75.5	11.2	48.4
	1994	42.4	65.8	23.4	46.5	20.5	2.6	9.3	6.7	4.4	11.1	100.0	585.7	75.1	12.4	46.5
Portugal	1989	69.9	75.9	6.0	20.9	13.5	1.4	7.0	5.5	3.6	9.2	100.0	337.4	82.9	8.4	20.9
	1994	56.0	62.6	6.6	32.2	24.0	1.5	9.4	7.8	4.0	11.8	100.0	376.5	72.0	13.0	32.2
Spain	1989	53.1	55.7	2.6	26.1	20.9	2.6	19.6	17.0	3.8	20.8	100.0	1 577.3	75.3	26.0	26.1
	1994	39.2	42.2	3.0	34.2	26.8	4.5	27.0	22.6	4.0	26.6	100.0	1 612.3	69.2	39.1	34.2
United Kingdom	1984	61.8	72.6	10.8	17.8	6.4	0.6	17.1	16.4	3.9	20.3	100.0	2 280.8	89.7	19.0	17.8
	1994	57.9	70.0	12.1	19.8	6.6	1.1	15.7	14.6	7.7	22.2	100.0	2 040.5	85.7	18.3	19.8

Table 1.5. **Proportion of young people in education and in employment, by sex, for 15-19 and 20-24 year-olds** (cont.)

Women 20-24

| | | Percentage of age cohort | | | | | | | | | | | Total in age cohort | | | |
| | | At work only | | At school | | | | Neither at school nor at work | | | | | | | | |
Country	Year	Total at work	At work only	At school and at work	Total at school	At school only	Jobseeking while at school	Total jobseeking	Looking for work	Not looking for work	Total	Per cent	Thousands	Labour force participation rate	Unemployment rate	School attendance rate
Australia	1984	65.2	56.0	9.2	15.6	5.1	1.3	8.9	7.6	20.9	28.4	100.0	662.9	74.1	12.0	15.6
	1994	68.6	52.7	15.8	25.8	8.3	1.7	8.9	7.2	14.2	21.4	100.0	708.7	77.4	11.4	25.8
Canada	1985	63.5	53.6	9.8	22.7	12.1	0.8	9.9	9.1	14.5	23.7	100.0	1 224.2	73.4	13.5	22.7
	1995	60.8	43.2	17.6	37.3	18.6	1.2	9.0	7.8	11.6	19.4	100.0	995.5	69.8	12.9	37.3
Japan	1982	69.6	67.7	1.9	12.6	10.7	–	–	–	19.8	19.8	100.0	3 883	–	–	12.6
	1992	73.4	69.2	4.2	17.0	12.9	–	–	4.9	8.8	13.7	100.0	4 695	–	–	17.0
Switzerland	1980	74.8	69.9	4.9	13.6	8.7	0.0	1.4	1.4	15.1	16.5	100.0	237.7	76.2	1.9	13.6
	1990	77.1	70.1	7.0	18.3	11.1	0.2	3.3	3.1	8.5	11.6	100.0	258.9	80.4	4.0	18.3
United States	1983	59.9	55.4	4.6	14.0	8.5	1.0	9.2	8.2	22.4	30.6	100.0	12 708.3	69.1	13.2	14.0
	1993	64.2	57.5	6.7	17.8	10.4	0.8	5.9	5.2	19.4	24.6	100.0	10 855.8	70.2	8.5	17.8
Belgium	1984	47.5	43.8	3.7	29.0	23.9	1.3	18.7	17.4	9.9	27.3	100.0	390.1	66.2	28.3	29.0
	1994	43.8	42.5	1.4	33.4	31.5	0.5	12.4	11.8	12.3	24.2	100.0	344.5	56.2	22.0	33.4
Denmark	1984	69.1	49.3	19.8	29.8	8.9	1.2	14.9	13.8	7.1	20.9	100.0	185.3	84.0	17.8	29.8
	1994	64.6	36.1	28.5	49.3	17.0	3.8	10.1	6.3	8.3	14.6	100.0	172.1	74.7	13.5	49.3
Germany	1984	63.3	55.7	7.6	23.8	15.8	0.4	6.7	6.4	14.2	20.5	100.0	2 374.8	70.0	9.6	23.8
	1994	64.4	50.5	13.9	33.9	19.8	0.3	6.4	6.2	9.4	15.6	100.0	2 164.3	70.8	9.1	33.9
Greece	1984	34.2	32.8	1.4	14.5	11.5	1.6	14.3	12.6	40.1	52.7	100.0	328.8	48.4	29.4	14.5
	1994	33.9	32.7	1.3	30.1	27.3	1.6	17.2	15.6	21.5	37.2	100.0	357.9	51.2	33.6	30.1
France	1984	55.4	53.1	2.3	13.7	11.0	0.4	16.6	16.3	17.0	33.2	100.0	2 029	72.0	23.1	13.7
	1994	40.5	34.3	6.2	42.4	34.4	1.8	16.6	14.8	8.6	23.3	100.0	2 034.4	57.1	29.0	42.4
Ireland	1984	66.1	60.0	6.1	14.8	7.8	0.9	10.2	9.3	15.9	25.1	100.0	139.4	76.3	13.3	14.8
	1994	58.9	50.6	8.3	27.5	17.8	1.4	12.2	10.8	11.2	22.0	100.0	140.6	71.1	17.1	27.5
Italy	1984	39.6	38.4	1.2	20.5	17.2	2.1	19.3	17.2	23.9	41.0	100.0	2 047	58.9	32.8	20.5
	1994	33.1	31.5	1.6	32.9	29.3	1.9	17.1	15.1	20.5	35.6	100.0	2 169.8	50.1	34.0	32.9
Luxembourg	1984	70.3	67.6	2.8	14.5	11.7	0.0	2.1	2.1	15.9	17.9	100.0	14.5	72.4	2.9	14.5
	1994	61.8	57.3	4.6	24.4	19.8	0.0	3.1	3.1	15.3	18.3	100.0	13.1	64.9	4.7	24.4
Netherlands	1989	66.7	48.6	18.1	35.4	15.1	2.2	8.0	5.8	10.2	16.0	100.0	610.2	74.6	10.7	35.4
	1994	69.5	49.5	19.9	36.8	15.5	1.3	5.9	4.6	9.1	13.7	100.0	588.7	75.4	7.8	36.8
Portugal	1989	58.2	52.3	5.9	24.8	17.1	1.7	10.8	9.1	13.9	22.9	100.0	380.7	69.0	15.6	24.8
	1994	50.2	43.2	7.0	40.6	31.6	2.0	9.0	6.9	9.2	16.1	100.0	380.2	59.2	15.1	40.6
Spain	1989	36.2	33.4	2.8	30.6	23.1	4.7	25.5	20.9	15.2	36.1	100.0	1 554.6	61.7	41.3	30.6
	1994	31.1	27.3	3.8	42.3	31.7	6.7	27.3	20.6	9.9	30.5	100.0	1 562.6	58.4	46.8	42.3
United Kingdom	1984	59.8	53.6	6.2	11.4	4.8	0.5	10.0	9.5	25.4	35.0	100.0	2 235.9	69.8	14.3	11.4
	1994	63.5	53.4	10.0	16.9	6.2	0.7	7.8	7.2	22.5	29.7	100.0	1 953.3	71.3	11.0	16.9

Source: Australia: Australian Bureau of Statistics. Canada: Statistics Canada. Japan: Statistics Bureau. Employment Status Survey, 1982 and 1992. United States: US Bureau of Labor Statistics. European Union members: Unpublished data supplied by EUROSTAT.

◆ Chart 1.5. *Labour market and schooling status, in selected OECD countries, persons aged 15-19*

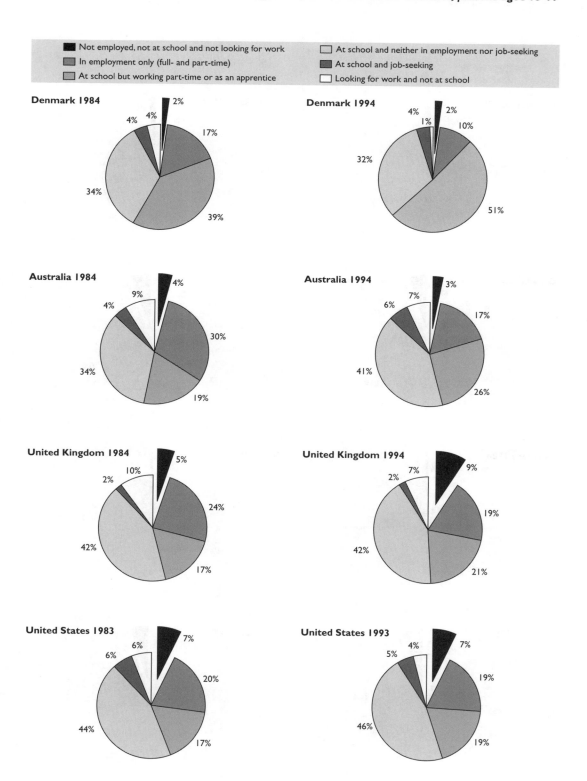

■ Not employed, not at school and not looking for work □ At school and neither in employment nor job-seeking
■ In employment only (full- and part-time) ■ At school and job-seeking
□ At school but working part-time or as an apprentice □ Looking for work and not at school

Denmark 1984
2% • 4% • 4% • 17% • 34% • 39%

Denmark 1994
4% • 2% • 1% • 10% • 32% • 51%

Australia 1984
4% • 9% • 4% • 30% • 34% • 19%

Australia 1994
3% • 7% • 6% • 17% • 41% • 26%

United Kingdom 1984
5% • 10% • 2% • 24% • 42% • 17%

United Kingdom 1994
9% • 7% • 2% • 19% • 42% • 21%

United States 1983
7% • 6% • 6% • 20% • 44% • 17%

United States 1993
7% • 4% • 5% • 19% • 46% • 19%

Source: OECD Labour Force Statistics.

◆　Chart 1.5. *(cont.)* ***Labour market and schooling status, in selected OECD countries, persons aged 15-19***

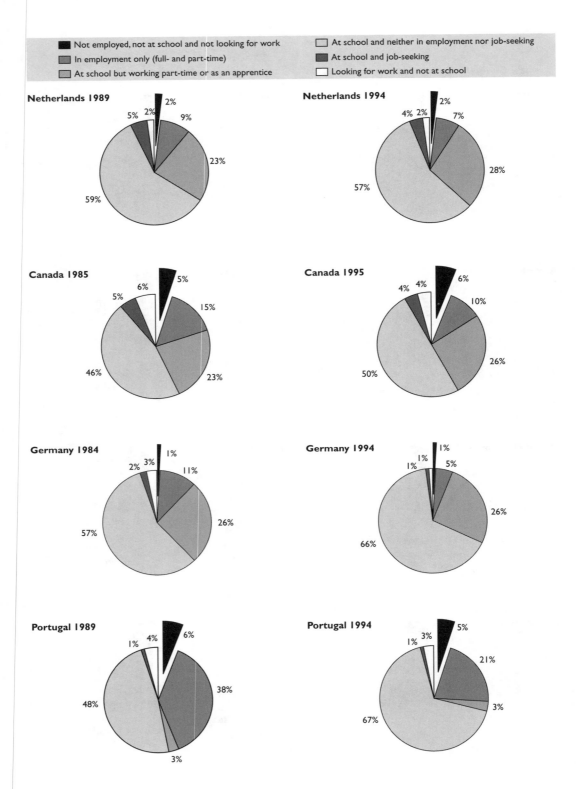

■ Not employed, not at school and not looking for work
▨ In employment only (full- and part-time)
▤ At school but working part-time or as an apprentice
□ At school and neither in employment nor job-seeking
▨ At school and job-seeking
□ Looking for work and not at school

Netherlands 1989
2% · 9% · 23% · 59% · 5% · 2%

Netherlands 1994
2% · 7% · 28% · 57% · 4% · 2%

Canada 1985
5% · 15% · 23% · 46% · 5% · 6%

Canada 1995
6% · 10% · 26% · 50% · 4% · 4%

Germany 1984
1% · 11% · 26% · 57% · 2% · 3%

Germany 1994
1% · 5% · 26% · 66% · 1% · 1%

Portugal 1989
6% · 38% · 3% · 48% · 1% · 4%

Portugal 1994
5% · 21% · 3% · 67% · 1% · 3%

　Source:　OECD Labour Force Statistics.

◆   Chart 1.5. *(cont.)*   **Labour market and schooling status, in selected OECD countries, persons aged 15-19**

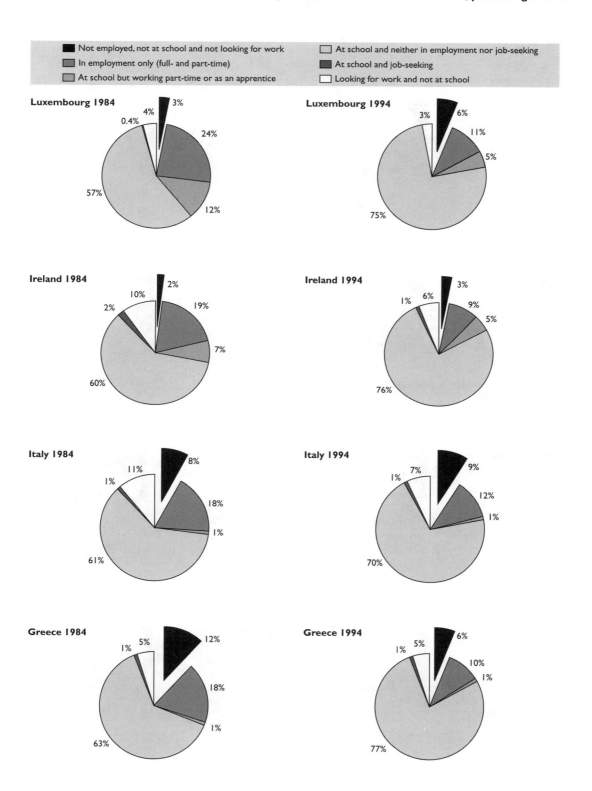

■ Not employed, not at school and not looking for work   ☐ At school and neither in employment nor job-seeking
▨ In employment only (full- and part-time)   ▨ At school and job-seeking
▨ At school but working part-time or as an apprentice   ☐ Looking for work and not at school

Luxembourg 1984
4% 3%
0.4%
24%
57%
12%

Luxembourg 1994
3% 6%
11%
5%
75%

Ireland 1984
10% 2%
2% 19%
7%
60%

Ireland 1994
1% 6% 3%
9%
5%
76%

Italy 1984
11% 8%
1% 18%
1%
61%

Italy 1994
1% 7% 9%
12%
1%
70%

Greece 1984
1% 5% 12%
18%
1%
63%

Greece 1994
1% 5% 6%
10%
1%
77%

Source: OECD Labour Force Statistics.

◆   Chart 1.5. *(cont.)*   **Labour market and schooling status, in selected OECD countries, persons aged 15-19**

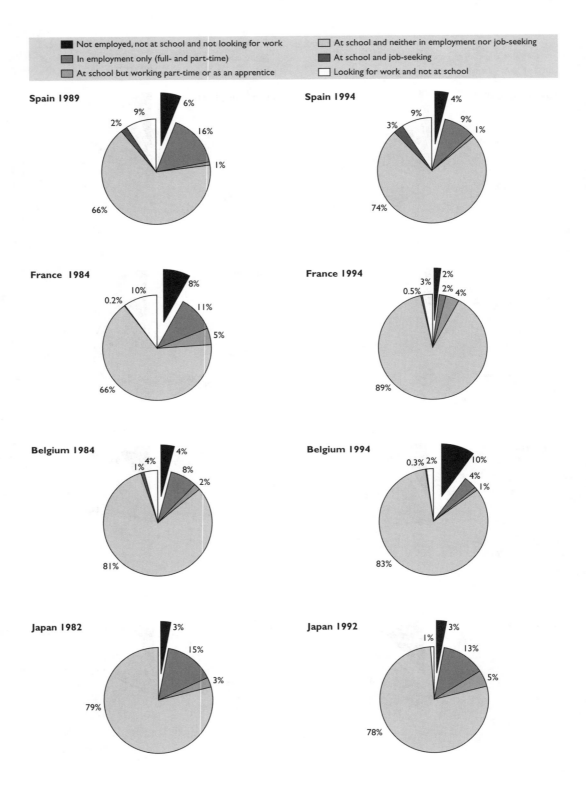

Not employed, not at school and not looking for work

In employment only (full- and part-time)

At school but working part-time or as an apprentice

At school and neither in employment nor job-seeking

At school and job-seeking

Looking for work and not at school

Spain 1989
6%, 16%, 1%, 66%, 2%, 9%

Spain 1994
4%, 9%, 1%, 74%, 3%, 9%

France 1984
8%, 11%, 5%, 66%, 0.2%, 10%

France 1994
2%, 2%, 4%, 89%, 0.5%, 3%

Belgium 1984
4%, 8%, 2%, 81%, 1%, 4%

Belgium 1994
10%, 4%, 1%, 83%, 0.3%, 2%

Japan 1982
3%, 15%, 3%, 79%

Japan 1992
3%, 13%, 5%, 78%, 1%

Source: OECD Labour Force Statistics.

◆   Chart 1.5. *(cont.)*   **Labour market and schooling status, in selected OECD countries, persons aged 15-19**

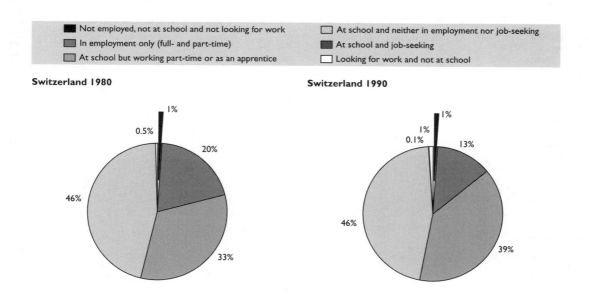

■ Not employed, not at school and not looking for work   ☐ At school and neither in employment nor job-seeking
■ In employment only (full- and part-time)   ■ At school and job-seeking
☐ At school but working part-time or as an apprentice   ☐ Looking for work and not at school

Switzerland 1980   **Switzerland 1990**

Source: OECD Labour Force Statistics.

part of those who have been excluded from employment and still seek it: the growth in the number of job seekers is a sign of the desire for economic participation.

Hence the social policy makers must face a twofold challenge. Firstly, there are a number of people who are unable to support themselves and their families through work. Secondly, an increasing number of families may perceive that they will get less out of the State than they contribute to it. The divergence of interests between gainers and losers has always been there, but in the past it was blurred by the attempt to ensure that all citizens shared in the benefits conferred by the system.[24] The middle classes supported welfare to get health, education, better pensions and family support; the working classes supported it mainly for greater economic security in times of sickness, unemployment and old age. Now there is a greater divide between those in regular employment (of any "class") and those in casual or no employment.

SOCIAL POLICY AND THE LIFE CYCLE

Family formation and family policy

Family formation patterns have adjusted in the light of these pressures. First, educational attainment has been growing in almost all OECD countries over the past fifty years, so that successive cohorts have higher rates of educational attainment (Table 1.6). However, with current institutional arrangements this can be a slow process: if educational attainment is determined for life at an early age, increased skill requirements will not be attainable by the current labour force. Early retirement from the labour force is no solution to this lack of adaptability as OECD populations age. This has led to a shift to lifelong learning (OECD, 1996*f*): adult participation in continuing education is expanding (Table 1.7).

Age at first marriage and age at first childbirth are increasing: family formation is being deferred until education and integration into the labour market have been completed (Table 1.8). The deferment

Table 1.6. **Proportion of the population in four age groups that had attained at least upper secondary education, 1992**

	25 to 34	35 to 44	45 to 54	55 to 64
North America				
Canada	81	78	65	49
United States	86	88	83	73
Pacific Area				
Australia[1]	57	56	51	42
New Zealand	60	58	55	49
European Community				
Belgium	60	51	38	24
Denmark[2]	67	61	58	44
France	67	57	47	29
Germany	89	87	81	69
Ireland	56	44	35	25
Italy	42	34	21	12
Netherlands	68	61	52	42
Portugal[3]	21	17	10	7
Spain	41	24	14	8
United Kingdom	81	71	62	51
Other Europe – OECD				
Austria	79	71	65	50
Czech Republic[3]	43	36	34	26[4]
Finland	82	69	52	31
Norway	88	83	75	61
Sweden	85	78	63	46
Switzerland	87	84	77	70
Turkey	21	14	9	5
Weighted mean OECD (except Czech Republic)	*72*	*69*	*60*	*48*

1. 1993.
2. A relatively large number of the 25- to 34-year-olds are still enrolled in education. Data may therefore underestimate the true values.
3. 1991.
4. Refers to 55-59.
Source: OECD (1996f), *Lifelong Learning for All*, Paris.
Czech Republic: Ministry of Labour and Social Affairs.

of marriage and childbirth means that when families are formed the parents are better educated and more likely to be established in their careers – which increasingly are dual careers. This reduces poverty rates amongst families with children,[25] to some extent through a "stretching out" of the passage from one generation to the next: the proportion of young people in their 20s living with their parents has ceased to fall and is rising in many OECD countries.

Even after marriage or first childbirth, completion of family formation is further deferred in the light of employment and child care opportunities. It can even be deferred indefinitely, so that completed family size falls. However, it is not yet clear how general this is: fertility has fallen amongst younger women in all OECD countries, but is rising amongst older women: completed fertility has not yet fallen in most OECD countries (Table 1.9). In countries with parental leave entitlements and comprehensive child care facilities for young children, such as Sweden and France, or in which child care is available in a deregulated private market, such as the United Kingdom, completed fertility seems not to have fallen below about two, but it has clearly done so in some other countries, including Germany. Nonetheless, even deferment of family formation, when generalised across a community, will have wide social and economic consequences: it means that there will be a small cohort moving through the education system and a further fall in the future ratio of working age to retirement age adults.

In some countries, very early family formation has also been evident, suggesting fading confidence in career opportunities: some young women despair of finding a place in the labour market or finding a

Table 1.7. **Proportion of population aged 25-35, attending school or in training, by sex and labour force status, in 1984 (or 1989) and 1994**

		Men and women	Men				Women			
		Total	Total	of which:			Total	of which:		
				Employed	Unemployed	Not in the labour force		Employed	Unemployed	Not in the labour force
Australia	1984	9.0	10.2	8.8	0.5	0.9	7.9	4.7	0.4	2.8
	1994	8.9	9.1	6.9	0.6	1.6	8.7	5.7	0.5	2.6
Canada	1984	5.2	5.4	3.1	0.3	2.0	5.1	3.0	0.3	1.8
	1994	7.4	6.9	3.5	0.4	3.0	7.8	3.6	0.4	3.9
Sweden (25-34)	1989	12.4	11.7	7.4	0.2	4.0	13.2	9.7	0.1	3.5
	1994	13.6	13.7	6.3	2.5	4.9	13.5	6.4	2.4	4.7
United States	1984	2.9	3.2	0.8	0.3	2.0	2.6	0.6	0.1	1.9
	1993	3.1	2.9	0.9	0.2	1.7	3.3	0.8	0.2	2.3
Germany	1984	6.7	9.0	2.0	0.3	6.7	4.4	1.1	0.1	3.2
	1994	9.9	12.4	5.0	0.4	7.0	7.2	3.0	0.2	3.9
France	1984	1.7	2.0	1.1	0.1	0.9	1.4	0.8	0.0	0.5
	1994	6.3	6.3	3.8	0.7	1.8	6.4	3.4	0.8	2.2
Italy	1984	4.1	4.8	1.6	0.4	2.8	3.4	1.0	0.5	1.8
	1994	7.6	8.2	1.9	0.4	5.9	7.0	1.6	0.6	4.8
Luxembourg	1984	2.4	3.4	0.9	0.0	2.2	1.3	0.7	0.0	0.7
	1994	6.1	7.8	4.1	0.3	3.6	4.3	2.1	0.3	1.9
United Kingdom	1984	5.5	6.5	5.1	0.2	1.2	4.5	3.3	0.2	1.0
	1994	10.6	11.2	9.4	0.6	1.3	10.1	8.0	0.4	1.6
Ireland	1984	3.2	4.0	3.2	0.2	0.7	2.3	1.6	0.1	0.6
	1994	6.4	6.6	5.0	0.4	1.2	6.3	4.8	0.3	1.2
Denmark	1984	11.4	11.8	8.3	0.9	2.5	10.9	7.7	0.8	2.5
	1994	22.2	20.4	14.8	1.3	4.3	24.1	15.3	1.6	7.2
Greece	1984	1.7	2.1	1.0	0.1	0.9	1.4	0.5	0.3	0.6
	1994	2.6	3.1	0.9	0.3	1.9	2.2	0.6	0.3	1.3
Spain	1989	5.4	5.3	2.0	0.9	2.4	5.5	1.8	1.5	2.1
	1994	7.8	7.1	2.6	1.6	3.0	8.5	2.4	2.7	3.3
Portugal	1989	4.7	4.9	3.2	0.3	1.4	4.4	2.5	0.4	1.5
	1994	8.5	8.4	5.7	0.5	2.2	8.7	4.9	0.8	3.0

Source: European Union members (except Sweden): unpublished data supplied by EUROSTAT.
Australia: ABS, Surveys of Transition from Education to Work, May 1984 and 1994.
Canada and Sweden: Labour Force Surveys.
United States: Monthly Current Population Survey, March.

Table 1.8. **Age at first childbirth**

	1970	1975	1980	1985	1990	1993
Australia[1]	23.2	24.2	25.3	26.3	27.6	28.3
Austria					25.0	25.5
Belgium	24.0	24.1	24.6	24.9	26.5	
Canada	23.1	23.8	24.6	25.5	26.4	26.8
Czech Republic	22.5	22.5	22.4	22.4	22.4	22.3
Denmark	23.7	24.0	24.6	25.5	26.4	27.2
Finland					26.8	27.2
France	23.8	24.2	24.9	25.9	27.0	27.6
Germany[2]	24.3	24.8	25.2	26.2	26.9	27.5
Greece	24.0	23.6	23.3	23.7	24.7	25.9
Iceland		21.8	21.9	23.1	24.0	24.8
Ireland	25.3	24.8	24.9	25.6	26.3	26.6
Italy	25.1	24.7	25.1	25.9	26.9	27.5
Japan	25.6	25.7	26.4	26.7	27.0	27.2
Luxembourg					26.5	
Netherlands	24.3	25.0	25.6	26.5	27.6	28.3
New Zealand[3]		23.9	24.9	26.3	27.6	28.7
Norway	23.6	24.2	25.2	26.1	25.5	26.0
Portugal	24.4	24.0	23.6	23.8	24.7	25.2
Spain		24.5	24.6	25.4	26.5	27.1
Sweden	24.8	24.5	25.5	26.1	26.3	27.0
Switzerland[4]	25.1	25.7	26.4	27.0	27.6	28.1
United Kingdom	23.9	24.6	25.1	25.9	27.3	27.4
United States[5]	25.4	25.3	25.7	26.1	26.3	26.4

1. Median age of mothers at nuptial first confinement. Data are for 1971, 1976 and 1981.
2. Data for 1970 to 1990: former West Germany.
3. Figures relate to live nuptial first births of the current union only.
    Data are for 1976, 1981, 1986, 1991 and 1995.
4. Data for Switzerland are for married women only.
5. Median age of mothers at first child birth.
Source: European Union members: EUROSTAT (1996), NEWCRONOS.
    Australia: Australian Bureau of Statistics (1995), *Social Trends*.
    Canada: Statistics Canada.
    Czech Republic: Ministry of Labour and Social Affairs.
    Japan: Ministry of Health and Welfare (1994), *Vital Statistics of Japan*.
    Netherlands: Statistics Netherlands (1994), *Statistical Yearbook*.
    Portugal: Ministerio para a Qualificaçao e o Emprego.
    New Zealand: Statistics New Zealand, Population and Demography Division.
    United States: National Center for Health Statistics (1995), *Annual Report on Vital Statistics*.

steady partner, and bear children without either, often without completing their secondary education. These young women are the counterpart of the young men who "drop out" and leave school with no qualifications: by 25 they have 10 years non-employment, no skills and perhaps a "prison record" (Freeman, 1996) (Tables 1.10a, 1.10b and 1.11).

Even in the United States, where this tendency has been most pronounced, it does not outweigh the general tendency to defer family formation in its impact on the overall growth of poverty (so that, overall, demographic change has had a positive effect on the poverty rate). Nonetheless, it remains a tragic path to family formation in a modern economy, and the current United States reform of welfare support for the children born in these circumstances has been inspired by a public perception that the support system has contributed to this tendency (although whether this perception is correct is a hotly disputed issue).

Support for families, through family allowances and child care provision, is modest compared to other items of social expenditure in all OECD countries: Sweden, with the highest effort, devotes 5.3 per cent of GDP (this largely accounts for the higher overall level of Swedish social expenditure, once the double counting through the taxation of benefits is taken into account) (Chart 1.3) (Bradshaw, 1993). Such subsidies cannot be sufficient to compensate families fully for the cost of child raising (Davies and Joshi, 1994) – and would be perceived as inequitable if they did, as children are of greatest

Table 1.9. **Completed fertility by year of birth of the mother, 1930-60**[1]

	1930	1935	1940	1945	1950	1955	1956	1957	1958	1959	1960
Australia	3.07	3.09	2.87	2.49	2.36	2.26	2.23	2.23	2.22	2.18	2.16
Austria	2.32	2.45	2.17	1.77	1.89	1.70	1.73	1.71	1.68	1.69	1.66
Belgium	2.30	2.27	2.17	1.94	1.84	1.83	1.83	1.84	1.84	1.83	1.85
Czech Republic	2.15	1.68	..	2.67	2.83	2.58	2.56	2.48	2.28	2.09	2.09
Denmark	2.36	2.38	2.24	2.06	1.90	1.84	1.84	1.85	1.85	1.86	1.87
Finland	2.51	2.30	2.03	1.87	1.85	1.88	1.90	1.92	1.93	1.93	1.93
France	2.64	2.58	2.41	2.22	2.11	2.13	2.13	2.12	2.11	2.09	2.07
Germany	2.17	2.16	1.98	1.79	1.72	1.67	1.67	1.65	1.65	1.64	1.63
Greece	2.21	2.02	2.01	2.00	2.07	2.03	1.99	1.92	1.90	1.93	1.93
Iceland	3.50				2.7	2.5	2.43	2.49	2.48	2.46	2.49
Ireland	3.50	3.44	3.27	3.27	3.00	2.67	2.57	2.53	2.47	2.42	2.37
Italy	2.29	2.29	2.14	2.07	1.90	1.79	1.76	1.73	1.69	1.67	1.63
Luxembourg	1.97	2.00	..	1.82	1.72	1.68	1.69	1.68	1.66	1.70	1.71
Netherlands	2.65	2.50	2.21	1.99	1.90	1.87	1.87	1.86	1.86	1.83	1.84
Norway	2.49	2.57	2.45	2.21	2.09	2.05	2.05	2.06	2.06	2.06	2.06
Portugal	2.95	2.85	2.61	2.31	2.12	1.97	1.95	1.93	1.94	1.90	1.86
Spain	2.59	2.67	2.59	2.43	2.19	1.90	1.87	1.85	1.80	1.75	1.69
Sweden	2.11	2.14	2.05	1.96	2.00	2.03	2.04	2.05	2.06	2.05	2.06
Switzerland	2.17	2.17	2.08	1.86	1.80	1.75	1.75	1.73	1.74	1.76	1.75
United Kingdom	2.35	2.41	2.36	2.17	2.03	2.02	2.02	2.00	1.98	1.96	1.94

1. For EUROSTAT countries, estimates for generations which have not yet completed their reproductive career are based upon the *ceteris paribus* assumption that future rates will be the same as the most recent observations available.
Source: European Union members: EUROSTAT (1996), Demographic statistics 1996.
Australia: Australian Bureau of Statistics.
Czech Republic: Ministry of Labour and Social Affairs.
Switzerland: Office fédéral des assurances sociales.

value to their own parents. A more fruitful path for policy – one which experience in a number of OECD countries suggests is effective – is to ensure that public policy ensures that those responsible for children are able to combine their careers with their responsibilities for their children. This in particular means that parents need access to child care and educational facilities which are consistent with a full working life. It also involves availability of full-time care for pre-school children, and also schooling hours and arrangements which do not suppose the continuous availability of one parent.

In Japan and in many European countries, support for family formation has been structured on different lines. The emphasis of support has been on enabling the one-earner family to prosper, through insurance arrangements designed to assure the income security of the principal earner, both during working life and after retirement. Where unemployment has grown, this has been interpreted as resulting from an overall shortage of jobs, and early retirement and late entry into the work force have both been encouraged in order to ration out the jobs amongst those who "really" need them. While the right of women to pursue careers has been recognised, it has not been seen as a major goal of public policy to facilitate this, and schooling systems have continued to rely on the active availability of a parent. Early childhood education services are often offered widely, but these do not necessarily meet the needs of working mothers.[26] In these countries, family formation has declined, and completed family sizes continue to fall.

Support for the elderly

The maturation of pension systems in OECD countries has significantly reduced, and in some countries eliminated, old-age poverty (except for groups left out of this system, such as women left without adequate pension cover through divorce or other breakdown in family-related income security provision). However, this was not the primary goal of earnings-related pension systems, in which entitlements are positively related to past earnings. Such pension systems are designed to prevent sharp changes in standards of living at retirement, and they therefore perpetuate into retirement the earnings differentials of working life. Frequently, public systems are supplemented by tax-encouraged

Table 1.10a.   **Percentage of births attributable to young women, 1960-94**

	Age of women	1960	1970	1980	1990	1994
Australia[1]	15-19	–	11.0	7.6	5.7	4.9
	20-24	–	35.6	29.2	20.1	18.9
Austria	15-19	7.6	9.8	9.5	4.5	3.4
	20-24	29.6	35.1	37.3	28.0	23.3
Belgium	15-19	3.0	5.7	4.7	2.2	–
	20-24	25.7	35.6	32.7	19.9	–
Canada	15-19	8.4	11.8	8.7	5.9	6.1
	20-24	28.8	35.4	31.2	20.5	18.9
Czech Republic	15-19	12.2	11.6	11.5	14.1	13.5
	20-24	40.0	48.3	44.6	44.8	44.4
Denmark	15-19	7.8	6.3	3.9	2.6	1.6
	20-24	32.6	34.9	29.7	22.2	14.6
Finland	15-19	4.6	7.7	4.2	1.9	1.7
	20-24	29.0	38.7	25.2	16.7	14.4
France	15-19	3.9	6.5	4.7	2.5	1.9
	20-24	27.9	39.3	31.8	20.7	17.2
Germany	15-19	5.6	9.3	7.5	3.4	2.7
	20-24	33.0	31.0	35.0	24.0	17.4
Greece	15-19	–	–	9.9	5.4	3.8
	20-24	–	–	35.5	30.0	23.1
Ireland	15-19	–	–	3.7	3.9	3.9
	20-24	–	–	20.7	14.6	14.0
Iceland	15-19	–	–	11.3	6.6	4.2
	20-24	–	–	32.7	25.5	21.2
Italy	15-19	2.8	4.4	5.0	2.4	–
	20-24	21.8	27.7	28.9	19.4	–
Japan	15-19	–	1.0	0.9	1.4	1.4
	20-24	–	26.5	18.8	15.7	16.5
Luxembourg	15-19	–	5.4	4.0	3.0	1.7
	20-24	–	32.7	27.4	19.4	15.3
Netherlands	15-19	2.3	3.9	2.3	1.6	1.2
	20-24	17.8	30.7	22.8	13.1	10.5
New Zealand[2]	15-19	–	–	10.9	7.9	7.4
	20-24	–	–	32.5	23.1	20.7
Norway	15-19	5.4	7.7	5.8	3.1	2.3
	20-24	27.0	37.8	30.2	23.0	18.7
Portugal	15-19	4.2	6.4	11.4	8.6	7.8
	20-24	26.0	27.5	34.8	29.4	25.4
Spain	15-19	–	–	5.6	3.7	–
	20-24	–	–	27.3	18.0	–
Sweden	15-19	7.6	6.4	3.2	2.1	1.5
	20-24	27.5	32.9	24.4	20.9	16.5
Switzerland	15-19	2.4	3.6	2.4	1.2	0.9
	20-24	23.2	29.5	22.7	15.3	12.0
United Kingdom	15-19	–	–	7.0	6.2	5.0
	20-24	–	–	29.2	24.2	19.8
United States	15-19	13.8	17.3	15.3	12.6	12.8
	20-24	33.5	38.0	33.9	26.3	25.3

occupational pensions which have similar goals, and which are frequently "integrated" with public systems in a way which counteracts any redistributive elements in the public pension formula. Finally, those who have had a successful lifetime career are likely to have accumulated wealth in the form of owner occupied dwellings and other property. The extent to which these systems have over-provided for the consumption needs of the elderly can be observed in the high savings rates which typify the elderly in many OECD countries.

Public pension transfers are thus increasingly flowing to a sector of the population which, on average, has considerable other incomes and assets. There can be no question of reneging on the pension promise: incomes and asset holdings are skewed, and a majority whose life situation is

Table 1.10b. **Age specific birth rates per 1 000 (within and outside marriage), 1960-94**

| | | Age of females | | | | | | | | | |
| | | 15-19 | | | | | 20-24 | | | | |
		1960	1970	1980	1990	1994	1960	1970	1980	1990	1994
Australia[1]	In marriage				4.3	2.4				50.0	36.8
	Out of marriage				17.7	18.3				29.6	32.4
	Total	47.4	55.5	28.2	22.0	20.7	225.8	181.9	107.5	79.6	69.2
Austria	In marriage		27.4	13.3	6.1	4.9		137.1	90.3	51.1	44.2
	Out of marriage		17.4	13.4	9.6	9.1		25.8	26.6	28.0	28.1
	Total	33.7	44.9	26.7	15.7	14.0	168.5	162.9	116.9	79.1	72.3
Canada	In marriage			11.7	4.6	2.9			80.9	49.9	35.9
	Out of marriage			15.3	20.9	22.1			14.3	31.2	36.3
	Total			29.0	25.5	25.1			95.2	79.2	72.2
Czech Republic	In marriage										
	Out of marriage										
	Total	44.0	49.0	53.1	44.7	32.6	184.6	174.4	196.2	174.3	121.8
Belgium	In marriage				4.9						56.6
	Out of marriage				3.4						11.0
	Total	17.6	23.0	15.0	8.3			138.1	145.3	105.3	67.6
Denmark	In marriage				2.6	1.3				25.9	18.6
	Out of marriage				6.6	5.2				46.1	36.8
	Total	32.6	24.6	11.6	9.2	6.6	167.6	121.0	94.1	72.0	55.4
Finland	In marriage					1.3					30.2
	Out of marriage					5.7					32.6
	Total	22.8	23.8	14.0	8.7	7.0	154.7	114.6	84.1	63.2	62.8
France	In marriage										
	Out of marriage										
	Total	23.6	26.7	17.8	8.9	7.0	160.0	168.1	121.6	74.5	56.8
Germany	In marriage					4.6					37.5
	Out of marriage					5.5					13.4
	Total	25.8	37.4	20.4	13.7	10.1	139.8	143.5	106.1	68.5	51.0
Greece	In marriage					9.1					60.0
	Out of marriage					1.4					2.2
	Total				14.8	10.5				80.0	62.2
Ireland	In marriage										
	Out of marriage										
	Total				12.8	12.0				59.1	46.8
Iceland	In marriage					0.1					11.4
	Out of marriage					18.5					82.7
	Total			51.3	31.5	18.6			148.1	121.4	94.1
Italy	In marriage				3.9					45.2	
	Out of marriage				2.4					3.3	
	Total	13.6	20.7	14.5	6.4		100.1	126.1	93.4	48.5	
Japan	In marriage										
	Out of marriage										
	Total	4.3	4.5	3.6	3.6	4.0	107.2	96.5	77.1	44.8	42.4
Luxembourg	In marriage				8.2	5.3				51.7	47.1
	Out of marriage				5.4	3.7				12.1	12.6
	Total		24.0	11.0	13.5	9.0		144.2	76.1	63.8	59.7
Netherlands	In marriage				3.6	2.6				33.0	25.1
	Out of marriage				2.4	2.4				9.0	9.5
	Total	12.2	17.1	6.9	5.9	5.0	107.8	129.4	70.8	42.0	34.6

Table 1.10*b*. **Age specific birth rates per 1 000 (within and outside marriage), 1960-94** *(cont.)*

		Age of females									
		15-19					20-24				
		1960	1970	1980	1990	1994	1960	1970	1980	1990	1994
New Zealand[2]	In marriage										
	Out of marriage										
	Total		130.5	95.6	73.3			333.4	177.9	141.2	
Norway	In marriage				1.2	0.6				32.0	19.5
	Out of marriage				10.7	9.4				52.8	49.8
	Total	27.2	34.2	19.4	11.9	10.1	166.8	160.4	102.0	84.9	69.3
Portugal	In marriage	10.1	12.8		7.5	5.5	69.1	73.2		37.7	27.3
	Out of marriage	3.3	3.2		4.4	5.0	9.4	6.3		6.7	6.6
	Total	13.4	16.0		11.9	10.5	78.5	79.5		44.4	33.9
Spain	In marriage				5.8					38.1	
	Out of marriage				3.6					6.8	
	Total			20.7	9.4				106.7	44.9	
Sweden	In marriage		6.2	1.8	1.3	1.1		81.4	34.1	28.1	19.3
	Out of marriage		19.7	9.7	8.3	5.5		29.9	52.6	58.6	46.0
	Total	28.4	25.9	11.5	9.6	6.5	125.0	111.2	86.7	86.7	65.3
Switzerland	In marriage					2.8					37.9
	Out of marriage					1.3					4.4
	Total	11.0	16.0	7.2	4.6	4.0	111.9	114.0		50.4	42.3
United Kingdom	In marriage										
	Out of marriage										
	Total			23.1	25.6	22.6			109.0	85.2	72.5
United States	In marriage		48.5	28.2	20.6			152.8	92.8	73.5	
	Out of marriage		19.8	24.8	39.3			15.0	22.3	43.0	
	Total	89.1	68.3	53.0	59.9	58.9	258.1	167.8	115.1	116.5	111.1

1. Data for Australia are for 1971, 1981, 1991. Births 15-19 represent under 20.
2. Data for New Zealand are for 1971, 1981, 1991 and 1995.
Source: European Union members: NEWCRONOS (1996).
   Non European Union members: UNITED NATIONS (1994), World population prospects.
   Australia: Australian Bureau of Statistics.
   Canada: Statistics Canada.
   Czech Republic: Ministry of Labour and Social Affairs.
   Japan: Ministry of Health and Welfare (1994), *Vital Statistics of Japan.*
   New Zealand: New Zealand Statistics.
   Portugal: Ministerio para a Qualificaçao e o Emprego.
   United States: Statistical Abstract of the United States (1995).

structured around their pension income is situated below that average. However, it may now be time to reconsider the favoured fiscal treatment which the elderly often receive: they are often exempt from social charges (which are levied on earned income in many countries) and also often receive favoured treatment in the general tax system. Those with extensive capital assets in the form of housing stock are often unable to access this to fund income needs, or are encouraged not to do so by exemption of such assets from tax assessment and (at least in Australia) from the criteria which determine entitlement to means-tested support. Similarly, general publicly subsidised concessions to the elderly represent further "in-kind" benefits (which are not generally captured in the data) – benefits which are often not available to younger low-income families. Old age is no longer a useful "proxy" for income distress, although many tax systems do still reflect that assumption (Table 1.12).[27]

   This issue has come to a head in many countries as a result of the need to provide for long-term care for dependent elderly people (OECD, 1996*d*). Even adequate pensions are not sufficient to finance

Table 1.11. **Proportion of adults in prison, by sex, in 1990**

(per million of the total population)

	Men	Women	Men and women
Australia	1 058	61	1 119
Austria	541	20	562
Belgium	603	32	635
Canada	–	–	1 051
Czech Republic	775	22	792
Finland	534	18	552
France	743	35	778
Greece	705	33	739
Italy	180	10	190
Japan	308	13	322
Netherlands	283	13	295
New Zealand	1 017	51	1 068
Portugal	588	30	618
Spain	417	27	444
Sweden	414	20	434
Switzerland	542	29	570
Turkey	480	10	490
United Kingdom	566	21	587
United States[1]	5 236	n.a.	n.a.

n.a.: Not available.
1. 1993 data.
Source: UN Fourth Crime Survey, 1990.
Australia: Australian Bureau of Statistics.
Canada: Statistics Canada, Canadian Centre for Justice Statistics.
Czech Republic: Ministry of Labour and Social Affairs.
United States: US Bureau of Justice Statistics, *Bulletin Prisoners* of 1993, *Bulletin Jail Inmates* of 1991.

Table 1.12. **Average tax rates for persons of working age
and at pensionable age, 1995**

Panel A. Average production worker income level

Age	Income source	Canada	France	Germany	Italy	Japan	United Kingdom	United States
40	Earnings	26.9%	26.7%	38.3%	26.7%	15.5%	26.5%	25.9%
70	Earnings	24.0%	26.7%	38.3%	26.7%	11.0%	26.4%	16.2%
70	Pensions	0.0%	5.1%	0.0%	19.7%	0.0%	18.0%	7.2%

Panel B. ⅔ of average production worker income level

Age	Income source	Canada	France	Germany	Italy	Japan	United Kingdom	United States
40	Earnings	22.9%	23.1%	33.8%	22.9%	13.7%	22.2%	23.9%
70	Earnings	18.6%	17.3%	33.8%	22.9%	9.6%	20.7%	14.2%
70	Pensions	0.0%	0.0%	0.0%	15.7%	0.0%	13.1%	6.6%

Notes: The following assumptions have been made for each panel (at average production worker level, and at ⅔ average production worker level):
– the first row displays average tax rates on earned income for a 40-year-old single worker without children;
– the second row gives average tax rates on earned income for a 70-year-old single worker without children;
– the third row represents average tax rates on state age pensions at a level equal to earned income for a 70-year-old single pensioner without children.
A state pension at the gross level equal to earned income may not be attainable, these hypothetical cases are used nevertheless to facilitate comparison.
Private pensions or investment/savings income to older people are not considered.
Source: OECD Secretariat calculations.

intensive-care costs, and so countries are turning to social insurance arrangements to spread the burden away from the estates of those who are stricken with senile dementia and other afflictions requiring intensive care (Hennessy and Wiener, 1996). To avoid institutionalisation, the families of frail elderly people frequently provide care themselves, and often do so for cost reasons, even where institutional care has become appropriate. Social insurance can spread this burden by providing income support to those who provide this care, and by financing the costs of institutionalisation when this is essential. However, if this new branch of social insurance is financed in the traditional way (through levies paid by, or on behalf of, those in paid employment)[28] a fresh burden is placed on working age people as a whole. Even if social charges are extended to public pension receipts, the rate of charge has to be kept low, since many pensioners are totally reliant on their pension incomes. France, with a system of generalised social contributions, has taken the first step towards spreading the financing of social benefits over a wider tax base. Another way to acheive this is to finance social transfers by the general tax system (which is policy in Australia, New Zealand and Denmark – countries with very divergent benefit systems) provided the tax system does not itself exempt the incomes of particular age groups.

The issue of pension burdens is often formalised in analyses of the net tax burden on succeeding generations. Perhaps a more immediate issue is the question of the extent to which the financing of current pension systems (including disability and early retirement benefits – many of which have come to finance "premature ageing") is in a sense "crowding out" arrangements which enable parents to combine child raising and careers. These arrangements might be in the form of direct public service provision, or through modification of relative wage levels and relief from taxation and charges so that households can be confident of being able to afford their own arrangements.

BALANCING SUSTAINABILITY AND SECURITY IN SOCIAL POLICY

As it has developed to date, the welfare state has been successful in providing income security for those already established in the labour force,[29] both during their working life and after retirement. However, the main risk that families face today is that their children will not be able to establish themselves in careers. As a result, they are deferring childbirth and, if they can, pouring resources into their children's education in a bid to ensure that their children do have the educational attainment necessary for entry into working life.

Traditional social insurance arrangements are powerless against these risks. They are predicated on the assumption that each generation will make its own way into working life, and individuals will both establish their own career and, through income transfers, support those who have retired or who are temporarily unemployed.

Substituting targeted income support for those out of work while avoiding the problem of leaving those not integrated into the labour force without cover, raises its own problems: for those with low earnings potential in the current labour market, the differential between earnings in an (often unappealing) low wage job and basic income support payments can be low, and the gains from working are small as a result of the abatement of income support as earned income increases (the poverty trap).

A growth in the proportion of the population in receipt of income support also saps public confidence. Where recipients of such support are regionally concentrated, severe political pressures can result: some of the recent strains concerning regional policy in Belgium, Canada and Italy have reflected this. Geographic or social concentration of receipt of benefits, particularly when it is associated with a feeling on the part of recipients that they have to manipulate the system in order to make ends meet, can also jeopardise their legitimacy: the fact that the very word "welfare" has become "politically incorrect" in the United States illustrates this sharply. It is therefore very important that social protection systems are administered fairly but firmly; lax administration can jeopardise the very existence of the protection itself.

Policy in the face of these trends had often been influenced by a feeling that the apparent shortage of jobs, as evidenced by the high levels of unemployment, is the result of economic disequilibria: either a lack of aggregate demand (the Keynesian view) or distortions in the economic system due to wage rigidities and the benefits system. Thus the only possible role for social policy is to paper over the cracks in the social fabric and wait for *la crise* to come to an end.

The evidence does not support this view. Per capita economic growth has continued steadily over the last quarter century, and has been, if anything, faster in the European region than in North America, where unemployment has remained lower. Although the structure of employment has changed extensively, the proportion of the population in employment has not altered dramatically, in spite of social developments (early retirement, increases in initial schooling) which might have been predicted to reduce it. There has of course been a shift to part-time employment: working time as well as employment itself has been re-arranged amongst the population. Labour markets in OECD countries show every sign of having successfully capitalising on the talents of the most educated and highly skilled sections of their populations.

The success of these economies in generating opportunities is illustrated by the immigration pressures which OECD countries are experiencing. The willingness of immigrants to work at low wages – and in some countries without social protection cover – requires a new approach to the labour market difficulties facing existing residents if xenophobic responses are to be countered. This is particularly the case for existing disadvantaged ethnic minorities, who can find themselves squeezed between their own educational and geographic marginalisation from current opportunities, and the ability of immigrants to draw on social capital from their home communities to establish themselves in a new home.

Perhaps it is time to see current labour market trends as the basis on which social policy should be constructed, rather than as the scapegoat for its failures. As the above description has suggested, the labour market and other economic processes have certainly generated social strains and distress, and there is no room for complacency. The challenge is to find ways to reform social policy and protection against distress in ways which will enhance growth without increasing disparities of access to its fruits: if economic growth is accompanied by stagnation of the incomes of the majority of the population or absolute falls for the most disadvantaged, its very desirability can be called into question. This almost certainly will involve moving away from income transfers as the main means of providing for distress, and towards measures which positively enhance the social and labour market circumstances of those in need. The short-term budgetary costs of such measures are unlikely to be less than those of the transfer payments they are intended to supersede:[30] which is why it is essential that pilot trials of new approaches should be carried out before they are implemented and that they should be evaluated afterwards.

It is also necessary to move away from the idea that social policy is implemented solely by formal governmental institutions. As Table 1.13 shows, the non-profit sector is a significant part of OECD market economies. While non-profit institutions receive government funding, which is in turn included in government expenditure totals, in many countries such institutions are largely funded from outside the government sector (though tax concessions undoubtedly help also). These non-governmental bodies carrying governmental functions are particularly important in countries (such as the United States and the United Kingdom) where direct governmental expenditure is a lower proportion of GDP.

Such an approach might have features such as the following:

– Employment opportunities are likely increasingly to favour those with the ability to be flexible, whether through belonging to a household including other earners (so that weekly fluctuations in income are supportable) or because of their own adaptability. Hence income support arrangements should be structured to encourage those in receipt of support to be flexible and to take risks in seeking new opportunities. This implies a greater degree of medium-term stability of income support, particularly for those with family commitments.[31]

– For the foreseeable future, there is likely to be an excess potential supply of labour, and it makes no sense to require those receiving income support to confine their main activity to looking for work. However, other activities attracting income support should be based on improving employment prospects, although that might include various forms of training, community work, and unpaid trial employment.

Table 1.13. **Annual non-profit sector operating expenditure by ICNPO[1] group, and annual revenue by source and by country, as a percentage of GDP, 1990**

	France	Germany	Hungary	Italy (1991)	Japan	Sweden (1992)	United Kingdom	United States
Expenditure								
Total operating expenditure								
– in millions of national currency	FF 216 649	DM 86 808	HUF 25 922	L 26 606 932	¥ 13 716 653	SKr 56 800	£26 352	$346 355
– as a percentage of GDP	3.34	3.58	1.25	1.99	3.22	3.95	4.80	6.42
Major ICNPO group (as a percentage of GDP)								
Culture, recreation	0.59	0.26	0.70	0.23	0.04	1.09	0.98	0.20
Education, research	0.83	0.42	0.05	0.43	1.27	0.57	2.04	1.46
Health	0.48	1.24	0.01	0.33	0.89	0.11	0.17	3.38
Social services	0.97	0.83	0.31	0.45	0.44	0.39	0.55	0.64
Environment	0.02	0.01	0.02	0.00	0.01	0.06	0.10	0.04
Development and housing	0.21	0.53	0.02	0.03	0.01	0.36	0.37	0.20
Civic and advocacy	0.10	0.04	0.01	0.05	0.03	0.15	0.03	0.02
Philanthropy	0.00	0.01	0.01	0.02	0.00	0.08	0.03	0.02
Internal activities	0.04	0.05	0.00	0.03	0.02	0.17	0.18	0.08
Business associations	0.10	0.19	0.12	0.46	0.37	0.90	0.34	0.33
Other	0.00	0.00	0.01	0.00	0.15	0.08	0.00	0.06
Revenue								
Total revenue								
– in millions of national currency	FF 218 001	DM 93 412	HUF 30 865	L 28 180 382	¥ 19 508 519	SKr 63 538	£29 993	$423 519
– as a percentage of GDP	3.36	3.85	1.48	2.16	4.58	4.42	5.46	7.85
Source of revenue (as a proportion of total revenue):								
Public sector payments	59.45	68.19	23.31	40.73	38.31	26.57	39.80	29.59
Private donations	7.07	3.88	19.72	4.94	1.30	9.38	12.05	18.65
Private fees and payments	33.48	27.92	56.97	55.67	60.39	64.07	48.15	51.78

1. International Classification of Non-Profit Organisations.
Source: Salamon, L.M., Helmut, K.A., Wojciech, S. *et al.* (1996). *The Emerging Sector: A Statistical Supplement*. The Johns Hopkins Institute for Policy Studies, Baltimore.

- The principle of capitalisation of income security, which has been advocated (World Bank, 1994) as a very long-term solution to financing old age income security, might be more immediately applied to income support during working life. Those in receipt of income support (apart from the supplements payable for children and other dependents) should be expected to repay a certain part of their receipts when and if their income is above a certain floor.[32] On average, the disadvantaged would still be net recipients and the advantaged net contributors, but by giving all individuals an interest in improving their circumstances, and providing a basis for support of those who currently have no insurance-based record, the split between "insurance" and "assistance" clients could be narrowed.

- "Case management" procedures need to be developed in an active rather than a passive way: rather than carefully controlling income support entitlements on the basis of past entitlements, the emphasis for working-age people should be on ensuring that income support (whether or not on a "capitalised" basis) is used to support activities which are likely to lead to re-entry into employment.

- Caring for others, including children and elderly or infirm relatives, should be recognised as "active" participation and supported in its own right (Bradbury, 1996).

Such measures could be components of a new approach which would look at inter-relationship of policy interventions (whether education, health or social security) at different stages of the life-course. This would put greater emphasis on policies that impact on the transition points in life, with more interventions earlier in life and more preventive (and less remedial) measures. The goal would be to re-define equity and security in terms of barriers towards life-course flexibility, and to avoid definitions which suggest that the goal of social policy is to provide protection against flexibility. If it is not developed deliberately, a new approach may well be imposed by the reduction in the abilities of governments to act autonomously as a result of the process of globalisation of economic and social life. An approach imposed solely by these constraints could fail to provide either protection or flexibility.

Reform of systems of social protection is often represented as being synonymous with reductions in public expenditure. But, as noted, the short-run budgetary costs of the measures to increase opportunities for the disadvantaged are unlikely to be less than those of the transfer payments they are intended to supersede. Indeed, unless accompanied by basic reforms in methods of provision (such as those currently under way in the Netherlands and Australia), they could easily be more. In view of the primacy given to fiscal retrenchment as a policy objective in most OECD countries, can countries afford reforms of the sort suggested?

Three observations are pertinent in answering this question. First, the degree of social protection available in a given country cannot be measured only by the amount which its government spends on social policy. In truth, spending is a poor indicator. Differences in the volume of social-protection expenditure across countries appear much larger than they actually are. Countries with apparently low social spending often do not tax income transfers, mandate employers to provide social benefits (pensions and sick payments, for example) or encourage private provision through tax subsidies. Table 1.14 illustrates how important these factors can be. Social-protection expenditure in Denmark, Germany and the Netherlands are not twice as high as those in the United States: fully half of the apparent difference can be ascribed to alternative institutional arrangements. If private spending on health is included, the remaining difference is almost eliminated.

Furthermore, cutting government expenditure will increase the pressure on individual households to provide for themselves. In Sweden, for example, taxes paid by households are 36.8 per cent of private household expenditure, compared with just 10.4 per cent in the United States. But expenditure on private health, education, day care and pensions are equivalent to 29.2 per cent of consumer expenditure in the United States, compared with an equivalent figure of 4.4 per cent in Sweden (see Esping-Andersen, Chapter 2 in this volume). Cutting public social expenditure will not necessarily lead to a reduction in the total resources which an economy devotes to "social" ends – though it will alter the distribution of those resources across the population.

Table 1.14. **Gross to net expenditure adjustment as a percentage of GDP,[1] 1993**

	Denmark	Germany	Netherlands[2]	Sweden	United Kingdom	United States
Gross direct public social expenditure	30.51	28.66	30.64	38.25	23.41	15.04
Direct taxes and social contributions paid on transfers	3.91	2.57	5.86	5.31	0.19	0.08
Net cash direct public social expenditure	26.60	26.09	24.78	32.94	23.22	14.96
Indirect taxes	3.87	2.90	2.47	3.70	2.30	0.47
Net direct public social expenditure	22.73	23.19	22.31	29.24	20.92	14.49
Social/fiscal measures on public and private social expenditure	0.08	0.78	0.08	–	0.36	1.15
Net current public social expenditure	22.81	23.97	22.39	29.24	21.28	15.64
Gross direct mandatory private social expenditure	0.43	1.60	–	0.62	0.23	0.48
Direct taxes and social contributions paid on transfers	0.12	0.51	–	0.19	0.01	0.003
Indirect taxes	0.08	0.18	–	0.08	0.03	0.03
Net current mandatory private social expenditure	0.23	0.91	–	0.35	0.19	0.46
Net current publicly mandated direct social expenditure	23.05	24.88	22.39	29.58	21.47	16.10
Memorandum items:						
Pensions under administrative extension	–	–	0.60	–	–	–
For information: non-public health expenditure[3]	1.18	2.51	1.97	1.28	1.06	7.65

1. All data presented in percentage of GDP at market prices.
2. Values of social-fiscal measures for the Netherlands concern 1994.
3. OECD (1996), *Health Data 1996* (diskette), Paris. Non-public health expenditure is defined as the difference between total health expenditure and public health expenditure.
Source: Adema *et al.* (1997).

Second, most social expenditure is on pensions and health care, the two areas where political resistance to scaling back the role of the state is most intense and where changes inevitably have to be phased in over time. Perhaps the biggest achievement of the welfare state has been to almost eliminate poverty amongst the elderly in many countries. But whereas a large proportion of the elderly rely on public provision for most or all of their income, there are increasing signs of over-provision of public support for others. There is a strong case for reviewing the balance of provision of income support to the elderly and refocusing expenditure on younger generations where social problems are growing in importance.

The third reason for seriously considering pre-emptive, preventative policies, despite their cost, is that the alternative is so unattractive. Failure to prevent long-term exclusion from the labour market leaves OECD societies with the options either of continued high costs of paying income support to a significant proportion of the population throughout their life, or of sharply reducing these payments, with the possibility of bitter consequences for social cohesion and transmission of disadvantage across generations.

NOTES

1. In this account, "the OECD area" omits, unless otherwise stated, the countries which became members in 1995-96 (Czech Republic, Hungary, Poland and the Republic of Korea), as data for them have not yet been incorporated in the database, or else are not available retrospectively.

2. As a result, GDP per capita has converged: in 1970, American GDP per capita, when compared using purchasing power parities for that year, was 45 per cent greater than the rest of the OECD; in 1994, this had fallen to 35 per cent. Japan, which had been at 85 per cent of the OECD average, had risen to 11 per cent above the average by 1994.

3. In those countries in which the dispersion of incomes between households has grown, this aggregate growth has nonetheless left many households worse off. Also, some of this growth represents the use of resources to alleviate damage (pollution control, health care). However, even supposing that the increases in environmental and health spending were all damage limitation (implying that none of the observed reductions in morbidity or mortality were due to health care provision) they only involve a very small proportion of overall GDP per capita growth – total health expenditure has only risen by 2.5 percentage points of GDP since 1970.

4. The slowdown in productivity growth elsewhere in the economy has itself contributed to slowing the relative productivity deficiency of the health care sector.

5. For example, by avoiding the unnecessary use of acute care hospitals to provide long-term care. Health insurance arrangements tend to encourage inappropriate use of acute care facilities in a number of OECD countries, in particular Japan.

6. Flat-rate benefits are sometimes only paid as last resort assistance benefits.

7. It is possible also for each generation to receive a pension higher in value than the contributions paid in a pay-as-you-go system if the number of contributors and the earnings on which they pay contributions are growing. This is the famous "Aaron condition" for a high rate of return to contributors from pay-as-you-go schemes.

8. All OECD countries which have introduced such provisions (the United Kingdom, Sweden and Australia, so far) as part of compulsory public provision have a flat-rate basic pension as a basis of their system, to which the capitalised funds will be added – though in the case of the latter two, the flat-rate pension is reduced when either total pension entitlements (Sweden) or total income and assets are high (Australia). In addition, most OECD countries (New Zealand is an exception) offer tax advantages for capitalised pension funds which supplement public provision: these are generally used most by those with high incomes for whom the public pension systems offer a low pension in relation to their income.

9. For an extensive discussion of the extent to which initial generations were favoured as the United States Old Age and Disability Insurance (OASI) was implemented, see Steuerle and Bakija (1994).

10. In 14 out of 23 OECD countries in 1992, the number in receipt of invalidity or early retirement benefits equalled or exceeded the total number of unemployed (Blondal and Pearson, 1996, Table 1). In 11 out of 23 countries in 1993 expenditure on disability benefits alone exceeded expenditure on unemployment and early retirement benefits combined (OECD, 1996f, Table 3).

11. The rise in Sweden is from a low initial degree of inequality, and that country still has one of the most compressed income distributions in the OECD.

12. In Mexico, where inter-household income distribution is wide compared to the rest of the OECD, the economic crisis of 1995 increased considerably the number of households in poverty.

13. The New Zealand Department of Social Welfare held a major international conference on 16 to 19 March 1997 on this issue, under the title "Beyond dependency: a watershed for welfare".

14. Exempt parents include single parents with children under the age of 6 years.

15. The Territorial Development Service of the OECD has been developing programmes on social distress in urban areas and in isolated rural communities.

16. Even if employment rates have remained unchanged, demographic changes would have led to a fall in the employment share of young people in any case. But this has been compounded by a dramatic fall in the proportion of this age group in employment from one cohort to the next.

17. To avoid verbosity, this account uses "adults" as a shorthand for persons aged 25-54, "young people" for those 15-24, and "older workers" for those aged 55-64.

18. From 1975 to 1995, the proportion of total employment classified as part-time in 15 OECD countries rose from 26.7 to 31.7 per cent (Table 1.4). This has largely been due to the increase in the proportion of both men and of women who are working part-time: if this had not increased between 1975 and 1995, the increase in the proportion of employment held by women would have only resulted in a quarter of the increase in the part-time proportion which did in fact occur. Although the proportion of men working part-time increased less than that of women, they still have a greater overall employment share, and this means that this increase (2.7 percentage points for men) has the same effect on the overall average as the 5 percentage point increase for women. In many countries, a growing proportion of the labour force consists of involuntary part-time workers (OECD, 1995d).

19. By unemployment is meant, of course, those counted as satisfying the ILO criteria (not in paid employment, taking active steps to find employment, available to take up employment). The "non-employed" include those not in employment who do not satisfy these criteria, who are classified as outside the labour force.

20. The United Kingdom has abolished entitlement to unemployment benefits for teenagers under 18, and have made income support conditional on participation in youth training schemes, while in Australia the Youth Training Allowance has replaced the Jobsearch allowance for this age group, to emphasise the priority attached to participation in education and training.

21. France instituted a strong drive to increase the proportion of young people completing the *baccalaureate* in the 1980s, and succeeded in reducing the proportion of teenagers neither in school nor in work from 17 per cent in 1985 to 5 per cent in 1995. The proportion of teenagers looking for work fell, but as the proportion in employment fell even faster, the unemployment rate rose. In Germany, where the proportion neither in work nor at school, and the proportion looking for work, is now similar to France, the unemployment rate is lower because those enrolled in the dual system are counted as employed, and the denominator of the unemployment rate is larger. In Sweden, responsibility for integrating young people was transferred from national labour market authorities to local authorities responsible for schools and children's services, while in Japan for fifty years schools have had the responsibility for integrating their pupils into either the world of work or higher education.

22. As a result, in Spain and other countries with relaxed administrative controls, families try to arrange things so that only one member is registered in the formal economy and liable to social insurance contributions (de la Rica and Lemieux, 1994).

23. For example, the sports and leisure industry is changing: low-priced sports events and gymnasiums with Spartan facilities are being displaced by more highly capitalised facilities which do not cater for those with time to spare but little income to spend.

24. For example, in Sweden, sickness insurance became a means for financing extra days off for a large proportion of the work force.

25. Although, to the extent that young people have left their parental home, poverty rates amongst single people and childless couples would be correspondingly higher.

26. For example, in Austria, only 54 per cent of existing kindergartens for children aged between three and six, are open throughout the day: of the remainder, half require children to return home for lunch, and the other half only open half a day. If the wishes of parents were fulfilled, 85 per cent of Austrian children would attend kindergarten: to achieve this it would be necessary to increase the number of places by 40 per cent (Austrian Federal Ministry for Women, 1995).

27. One indicator of the extent to which pension flows are "overcompensating" is the volume of transfers between generations within families: INSEE has estimated (de Barry et al., 1996) that in France these approximate half of bequests each year. Such flows have been studied extensively in the United States as well, although the longitudinal data sets on which these studies are based do not appear to readily yield estimates of the total volume of such flows. These transfers are between generations but within families. To a large extent they replace bequests, and to the extent this is true they have no redistributional effect in life-cycle terms. However, if included in survey data they may reduce the measured "income poverty" amongst young people starting out in their careers.

28. The "fourth arm" of the German social insurance system, instituted in 1995, is financed in this way. The current debate in Japan on how to finance long-term care insurance raises this issue. France has suspended the institution of long-term care benefits announced in 1995 due to financing issues.

29. Although where insurance cover is dependent on a settled earnings record, some of those in precarious employment may not benefit. Optional employer-provided benefits – even if they are encouraged by tax concessions – are often not available to low income employees: this is a particular issue in the United States, where many low-income employees do not receive health insurance cover from their employers.

30. The United States administration recognises that providing job opportunities is essential to reforming welfare and has proposed a three pronged $3.4 billion initiative to create job opportunities for the hardest to employ welfare recipients. This proposal includes a targeted jobs tax credit to create new job opportunities for long-term welfare recipients and tax incentives to increase investment in distressed areas.

31. The twelve-month period used when determining family payment in Australia and the six-month period for family credit in the United Kingdom are examples of such provisions.

32. The Australian arrangements for income support for tertiary students have some of these features. In order to avoid disincentive effects, the extra marginal tax on earned income in any one year is low, and this would be necessary in any capitalised benefit system.

BIBLIOGRAPHY

ADEMA, W., EINERHAND, M., EKLIND, B., LOTZ, J. and PEARSON, M. (1997), "Net public social expenditure", Labour Market and Social Policy Occasional Papers No. 19, OECD, Paris.

AUSTRIAN FEDERAL MINISTRY FOR WOMEN (1995), *Women in Austria 1985-1995.*

BAUMOL, W. (1967), "The macro-economics of unbalanced growth", *American Economic Review,* Vol. 57, pp. 415-426.

BLONDAL, S. and PEARSON, M. (1996), "Unemployment and other non-employment benefits", *Oxford Review of Economic Policy,* Vol.11, No.1, pp.136-169.

BRADBURY, B. (1996), *Income Support for Parents and Other Carers*, SPRC Reports and Proceedings No. 127, University of New South Wales, Australia.

BRADSHAW, J. (1993), *Support for Children: A Comparison of Arrangements in 15 countries*, DSS Research Report No. 21, HMSO, London.

DANZIGER, S. and GOTTSCHALK, P. (1993), "Introduction", *Uneven Tides*, The Russell Sage Foundation, New York.

DAVIES, H.B. and JOSHI, H.(1994), "The foregone earnings of Europe's mothers", in O. Ekert-Jaffe (ed.), *Standards of Living and Families: Observation and Analysis,* John Libbey, Montrouge, London and Rome.

DE BARRY, C., ENEAU, D. and HOURRIEZ, J-M. (1996), "Les aides financières entre ménages", *INSEE Première,* No. 441, April.

DE LA RICA, S. and LEMIEUX, T. (1994), "Does public health insurance reduce labour market flexibility or encourage the underground economy?", in M. Blank (ed.), *Social Protect vs. Economic Flexibility: Is There a Trade-off?*, University of Chicago Press, Chicago.

FREEMAN, R.B. (1996), *Why Do So Many Young American Men Commit Crimes and What Might We Do About It?*, NBER Working Paper Series No 5451, Cambridge, MA.

GOTTSCHALK, P. and DANZIGER, S. (1993), "Family structure, family size, and family income: accounting for changes in the economic well-being of children, 1968-1986", *Uneven Tides,* The Russell Sage Foundation, New York.

GOVERNMENT OF CANADA (1994), *From Unemployment Insurance to Employment Insurance,* A supplementary paper to "Improving social security in Canada", Ministry of Human Resources Development, Canada.

GREGG, P. and WADSWORTH, J. (1996a), "The rise of the no-job household", *Centre Piece*, Centre for Economic Performance, London School of Economics and Political Science, Economic and Social Research Council, London, United Kingdom.

GREGG, P. and WADSWORTH, J. (1996b), *It Takes Two: Employment Polarisation in the OECD,* Centre for Economic Performance Discussion Paper No. 304, CEPR, London School of Economics, London.

HENNESSY, P. and WIENER, J. (1996), "Paying for care for the elderly", *The OECD Observer*, No. 201, Aug./Sept., Paris.

JUHN, C. and MURPHY, K.M. (1996), *Wage Inequality and Family Labor Supply*, NBER Working Paper No. 5459, Cambridge, MA.

OECD (1981), *The Welfare State in Crisis – An Account of the Conference on Social Policies in the 1980s*, Paris.

OECD (1988a), *Ageing Populations: The Social Policy Implications*, Paris.

OECD (1988b), *Reforming Public Pensions*, Social Policy Studies No. 5, Paris.

OECD (1995a), *New Directions in Health Care Policy*, Health Policy Studies No. 7, Paris.

OECD (1995b), *The Transition from Work to Retirement*, Social Policy Studies No. 16, Paris.

OECD (1995c), *The Labour Market and Older Workers*, Social Policy Studies No. 17, Paris.

OECD (1995d), "Supplementary measures of labour market slack: an analysis of discouraged and involuntary part-time workers", *Employment Outlook*, Paris, Chapter 2.

OECD (1996a), "Earnings inequality, low-paid employment and earnings mobility", *Employment Outlook*, Paris, Chapter 3.

OECD (1996b), "Making work pay", *Employment Outlook*, Paris, Chapter 2.

OECD (1996c), *Health Care Reform: The Will to Change*, Health Policy Studies No. 8, Paris.

OECD (1996d), *Caring for Frail Elderly People: Policies in Evolution*, Social Policy Studies No. 19, Paris.

OECD (1996e), *Ageing in OECD Countries – A Critical Policy Challenge*, Social Policy Studies No. 20, Paris.

OECD (1996f), *Lifelong Learning for All*, Paris.

OECD (1996g), "Social expenditure statistics of OECD Member countries: provisional version", Labour Market and Social Policy Occasional Papers No. 17, Paris.

PICOT, G. and MYLES, J. (1995), *Social Transfers, Changing Family Structure, and Low Income Among Children*, Research Paper Series No. 82, Analytical Studies Branch, Canada.

SCHERER, P. (1996), "The myth of the demographic imperative", in C.E. Steuerle and M. Kawai (eds.), *The New World Fiscal Order: Implications for Industrialized Nations*, The Urban Institute Press, Washington, D.C.

STEUERLE, C.E. and BAKIJA, J.M. (1994), *Retooling Social Security for the 21st Century*, Urban Institute Press, Washington, D.C.

SWEDISH DEPARTMENT OF FINANCE (1993), *Social Security in Sweden and Other European Countries – Three Essays*, Report of the Expert Group for Studying Open Economies, Stockholm, Sweden.

UNITED STATES DEPARTMENT OF LABOUR (1996), *Report on the American Workforce*, Government Printing Office, Washington, D.C.

UNITED STATES GOVERNMENT (1995), *Economic Report of the President*, US Government Printing Office, Washington, D.C.

WORLD BANK (1994), *Averting the Old Age Crisis*, Oxford University Press, Oxford, United Kingdom.

WELFARE STATES AT THE END OF THE CENTURY
The Impact of Labour Market, Family and Demographic Change

by

Gosta Esping-Andersen
University of Trento, Italy

INTRODUCTION: THE PERENNIAL CRISIS OF THE WELFARE STATE[1]

As Heclo (1981) once noted, the welfare state has been crisis-ridden since its inception. In the 1950s, conservatives criticised it for its inflationary effects. Ten years later, the left attacked it for its inadequate equalitarian achievements. The pendulum swung once again to the right in the 1970s with tax and welfare backlash movements, and diagnoses of government "overload". Today, as Table 2.1 suggests, the crisis is associated with population ageing, family decline, and mass unemployment. Not only is the pendulum in constant motion, the malaise always seems to be different.

It is widely claimed that the current crisis is deeper and more damaging than earlier. Whether this is true or not depends on what we mean by "the welfare state". Pension systems may very well be unviable but this may reveal little about welfare states which, as a postwar construct, meant something very different than the mere sum of social programmes on offer. The ideal, when launched in the 1940s, was in juxtaposition to the authoritarian welfare state. Social citizenship and universal solidarities spoke to the pressing wartime needs for nation-building and social integration in the face of the fascist and bolshevik menace. Full employment and redistribution and, more generally, the dismantling of class, ethnic or regional cleavages, were seen as fundamental prerequisites for stable liberal democracy.

If we judge by these objectives, the postwar welfare state was a crowning success; in part because social security became more comprehensive and people found jobs; in part because it harnessed the capacity of the labour market and the family to assure social welfare. The architects of the modern welfare state, such as Lord Beveridge in Britain or Gustav Moeller in Sweden, were adamant that work and family, and not the state, should constitute the principal foundation of social welfare.

Now, at the close of the 20th century, the challenge of communism is fading and new social divisions are emerging. Once viewed as a prospective haven of prosperity, post-industrial society appears instead to produce a "two-thirds" society of winners and losers. Many believe that a new class of the excluded, a modern day *lumpen proletariat*, is emerging. Where jobs are not on the increase, this is likely to be a class of marginals and outsiders; where they are, it will be a class of working poor.

Table 2.1. **Welfare states in crisis, then and now**

1950s	1960s	1970s	1990s
Too much state Inflation	Too little equality	Government overload Stagflation Unemployment	Family values decay Ageing Globalisation Unemployment

Note: The symptoms of crisis for the 1970s are taken from OECD (1981).

The novelty of the current welfare state crisis is that it springs from simultaneous "failure" of the family and labour market to provide the basic level of security that Beveridge and his contemporaries relied upon. Rather than offering well-paid, stable jobs for the "standard production worker", the contemporary labour market puts at risk youth, the low-skilled, and workers in declining industries. Similarly, family change gives rise to divorce, lower fertility, and atypical households which, in turn, raises the risk of poverty, especially among women and children. The dysfunction of labour markets and families threatens the equilibrium of welfare states whose social programmes were constructed in an era with a wholly different risk profile. Populations are ageing and needs intensifying, whereas the financial means to address both are diminishing. Trapped in this kind of double whammy, few remain optimistic about finding a "win-win" policy formula. Whatever the political colour of governments, the single overriding issue is simply how to reduce social obligations with minimum pain.

The catch, however, is that an erosion of social protection will threaten not only the losers but, even more importantly, also the winners. The more universalistic the welfare state, the more it has built formidable loyalties. Where social entitlements have become an integral part of the life-course calculations of the entire population, both interest groups and the average voter will logically resist entitlement reductions across-the-board.

The challenges to the welfare state come mainly from outside: the turbulence of labour markets, due to new technologies and the globalisation of trade and capital; the decline of the homogeneous mass worker, due to much greater social differentiation; the ageing of populations; and family change. All undercut the basic assumptions that underpinned postwar social policy. If there is a crisis in the welfare state, it is because it is institutionally frozen in a social order that no longer prevails. The crisis may in fact be more political than institutional, to the extent that vested interests block change and reform.

Popular discourse has already recognised the arrival of a new class of losers. Witness labels such as the "A-team" and "B-team", or the new underclass. Behind such labels lurks the idea that there is a class of marginals trapped in lifelong underprivilege. But whether this is empirically true remains an open question. It is undeniable that bad jobs, low pay, unemployment, and poverty afflict more and more people. Yet if peoples' experience of marginality and want is only temporary, life chances will probably not be seriously impaired. Indeed, if systematic entrapment can be avoided, low-end "lousy" jobs may even be socially beneficial, because they provide easy labour market entry for young people, immigrants and women. We face a real crisis of social polarisation only if the losers of today are losers for life, and if they pass their underprivilege on to the next generation.

The contemporary challenge lies in the need to rethink and update earlier assumptions about work, family and social risk. Since the architects of postwar welfare state could assume stable families and well-functioning, full employment labour markets, they concentrated their social policies on those unable to work, and particularly the elderly. Income support for the able-bodied young was designed to cushion temporary income loss; not, as has happened, to park populations on long-term maintenance. Apart from education and health, the postwar welfare state was also very lean in terms of services provided; it was implied that families would internalise social care.

For these reasons, the postwar welfare state became extraordinarily biased towards transfer benefits to the aged. In some countries, notably Scandinavia, this bias weakened as the accent of policy came to privilege services, active labour market programmes, and income security for women and young families. Other nations, including Japan, the United States and, *par excellence*, Southern Europe, have actually strengthened the bias towards the elderly; in part because pensions constitute the principal welfare state programme and in part, because of early retirement. The prevalence of "familism" in Southern European and Japanese social policy is also a chief reason. Some countries, Austria and Italy especially, are really "pensioner states" rather than "welfare states" (see Table 2.2). Passive income maintenance, once intended to provide a guarantee for people in their inactive years, tends to be also the major response to the risks and needs of families in their active years. This may safeguard against poverty, but does little to promote life chances. The life cycle distribution of economic risk has changed radically in recent decades (Myles, 1996).

Table 2.2. **Social expenditure and their age distribution**

	Social expenditure (% GDP)		Spending on services as a percentage of transfer spending	Transfers to elderly/transfers to non-elderly	
	1980	1993	1993	1980	1993
Australia[1]	11.7	16.5	15	1.3	0.7
Canada	13.3	20.1	34	1.2	1.2
New Zealand[1]	18.2	23.3	2	1.8	0.8
United Kingdom	18.3	23.4	19	1.6	1.0
United States	12.7	15.3	10	2.3	2.5
Denmark	27.6	30.9	31	0.6	0.6
Finland	18.9	35.3	16	1.1	0.8
Norway	18.9	29.3	37	0.9	0.7
Sweden	30.4	38.3	34	1.0	0.9
Austria	22.3	25.7	2	2.5	2.2
Belgium[1]	25.6	27.0	3	1.0	1.2
France	23.5	28.7	7	1.5	1.6
Western Germany	25.0	24.7	8	1.9	1.7
Italy	18.2	25.0	2	2.7	3.5
Netherlands	28.8	36.4	10	0.7	0.7
Spain	16.5	22.5	2	1.3	1.3
Japan[1]	10.2	12.0	8	3.4	5.5

1. 1992 instead of 1993.
Source: OECD social expenditure database.

In this paper I argue the following. Firstly, welfare states are being compelled to redefine their egalitarian promise. The static equality-of-result approach that came to dominate redistributive policy is no longer practical and may even be counterproductive. The principles of egalitarianism, universalism, and solidarity that postwar welfare states endorsed spoke to a society dominated by a homogeneous industrial worker mass (captured in OECD's "standard worker"). A hallmark of post-industrial society is rising occupational, familial and life-course differentials and destandardisation – all of which give rise to new needs and also to new inequalities "here and now". The question is how to redefine egalitarianism and rebuild social integration.

The neo-liberal answer is to scale back the welfare state, thus allowing greater individual choice and markets to "clear". The accent is on individual equity: you get only what you have earned. The "welfare society" strategy, as a second answer, advocates a shift in responsibilities back to families and community voluntary provisions. A third response, widely popular in Europe, promotes work sharing and a guaranteed citizens' income, the assumption being that the total volume of work is limited. A fourth and, as yet, vaguer vision is a recast welfare state that emphasises supply-side measures: proactive income maintenance and active social investment policies. Behind contemporary policy concepts, such as lifelong learning or active labour market policy, lurks the idea of moving from static egalitarianism to a dynamic obligation to guarantee life chances.

My second argument addresses the changing status of women. Traditional "familism", built around the male breadwinner logic, is negative both for employment and for family formation. Hence the pressing need for a radical rethinking of family policy: one that helps reduce dependence on a single income earner, and one that makes it possible to combine high fertility rates with female careers. My third argument is that the pensioner bias in contemporary welfare states is doubly problematic. It crowds out spending on the young, and will in any case become unsustainable given population ageing.

WELFARE STATE RESPONSES TO THE EMPLOYMENT PROBLEM

It is generally agreed that the postwar harmony of welfare state growth, equality and full employment has been lost. The erstwhile capacity of OECD countries to sustain full employment was based on a combination of circumstances that no longer exist – and are certain not to return. Firstly, it was anchored to an economy driven by industrial mass production and consumption. Secondly, income redistribution, high wages and a high social wage helped consolidate and even out demand. Thirdly, the full employment commitment was basically limited to males, the wage setting norm was a "family wage", and social protection standards addressed one-earner families.

De-industrialisation since the 1970s has created mass unemployment, particularly eroding the position of younger and less-skilled workers. Jobs in the service economy are potentially abundant, but are subject to two constraints that did not exist in industrial mass production. Firstly, a large proportion of services tend to be high skilled, especially in business and health services. Labour intensive demand comes mainly from personal or social services (such as restaurants, laundries, day care or home helpers), but these often require social and cultural skills.[2] Secondly, following Baumol (1967), the gap in productivity growth between services and manufacturing implies that service jobs will grow only if labour costs are lower or, alternatively, if subsidised (i.e. through government employment). Welfare state services, as we have seen in Scandinavia since the late 1960s, can compensate for stagnant market services and can also boost aggregate participation levels through their promotion of women's employment. But in an egalitarian wage regime, such as that in the Nordic countries, the long-term effect is mounting fiscal crisis or a drain on the tradable sector.

It is therefore often argued that a return to full employment will require more wage inequality and flexibility, lower taxes and social benefits. The alternative is chronically high unemployment that will adversely affect young people and the less skilled.[3] Here a historical parallel is warranted. In the postwar process of "de-ruralisation", large numbers of unqualified workers easily found well-paid and stable factory jobs. Their "reserve wage" was very low, and they probably experienced a sense of upward mobility in terms of pay, consumption and security; their "family wage" could permit mothers the luxury of housewife status. The low-skilled today cannot count on well-paid jobs, let alone upward mobility; in Europe, their reserve wage can be high.

Welfare states respond to the new employment problem very differently. The typical contrast is between a rigid, "sclerotic Europe" and a dynamic, deregulated North America. European labour markets are characterised by their high labour costs, earnings compression, and strong job protection. In the EU countries, average legislated labour costs are three times higher than in the United States, and the ratio of unskilled to skilled worker earnings hover around 80 per cent, compared to about 50 per cent in the United States (OECD, 1994b).[4] The guaranteed social minimum income – whether measured in terms of wages or in terms of social benefit standards – is substantially higher in Europe (excluding the United Kingdom). In the United States, real wages stagnated and the minimum declined during the 1980s; this did not happen in Europe (Blank, 1994; McFate et al., 1995; OECD, 1994b). Job protection (employee dismissal rules, for example) is clearly much stronger and more rigidly enforced in Europe. Thus, on the OECD index of labour market rigidity, the Anglo-Saxon nations score an average of 1.6 compared to 8 in Scandinavia, and 10.8 in continental Europe (OECD, 1994b). High wage costs and job protection are held to be major causes of youth unemployment.

The prevailing view that Europe prioritises worker protection at the expense of jobs obscures the widely differing national profiles of employment and non-employment. A combination of strong protection and joblessness is a peculiar trait of many, if not most, continental European countries, and is arguably the outcome of two strategic considerations. The first is the perceived necessity of safeguarding family welfare. In a male breadwinner-dominated society, the entire family and not just individuals would be threatened by wage erosion and job insecurity in two ways: day-to-day living standards rely on the "family wage" principle, and unbroken, lifelong careers are necessary for pensions and other social entitlements.[5] It is therefore no wonder that political majorities (and trade unions) consistently uphold the existing welfare state edifice. The second consideration relates to strategies of industrial adaptation and competition. Deregulation and low wages may, as in America, clear labour markets but at the possible cost of what Soskice calls a "low-skill equilibrium". European nations, in contrast, have generally opted for a high-wage, quality-production strategy that privileges the skilled core workers at the expense of the "outsiders" (Soskice, 1994). In the latter model, the downsizing of the workforce has been politically brokered with the help of income guarantees and early retirement. It was hoped that the budgetary burden of mass retirement could be covered by the associated productivity dividend.[6]

The Nordic approach to "equality" and worker protection has been distinctly different. With the partial exception of Denmark, Scandinavia avoided mass unemployment (until recently) through a mix of government service growth and active labour market policies, backed up by nationwide consensual wage bargaining. This has resulted in a massive rise in women's employment, largely in the public sector, and a comparatively much smaller decline in (older) male participation. Hence, aggregate employment-to-population ratios are 15-20 percentage points higher than in the EU, and female participation rates now hover around 80 per cent. The policy intention was primarily to equalise women's economic status; the pre-condition was strong taxation powers. As a natural consequence, the two-earner, dual career family has become the norm. There is little doubt that the costs of harmonising women's family and work responsibilities with generous paid leave and child care provisions are very high. The gain, however, is stable and even rising fertility combined with minimal risks of poverty entrapment and welfare dependence among vulnerable groups such as single mothers.[7] Also France, with its rather extensive network of child care (the *maternelles* infant schools and crèches), demonstrates that fertility can be compatible with female employment.

Scandinavian policy has always pursued equality by work promotion rather than by income maintenance or job protection. Two incomes is a good hedge against family poverty. And the main reason why single mother poverty rates in Denmark and Sweden are no higher than average is that they have earned incomes (because of free child care), which are topped up by transfers.[8] Continental Europe, in contrast, has favoured income maintenance and early retirement as a means to uphold wages and job security for the core workforce.[9] The concomitant discouragement of female labour supply in many countries, both via the tax regime and via "familistic" social policy (*e.g.* a reluctance to provide public care services), means that total activity rates remain low and are even declining.[10] With rising educational attainment, women decide nonetheless to pursue careers. In fact, participation (but not employment) levels of young female cohorts today are no lower than in Scandinavia or North America. But since this occurs in a hostile environment in terms of youth unemployment, and from the point of view of harmonising careers and family responsibilities, the result is delayed family formation and declining and even record-low fertility. The paradox of pro-family social policy in countries like Italy and Spain (and also Japan) is that it maintains family responsibilities, but at the expense of family formation.

Prioritising a largely male, core workforce in the context of increasing unemployment, results in a fortification of an "insider-outsider" divide: the high wages and job security enjoyed by male breadwinner "insiders" accounts for the unemployment and exclusion of their sons, daughters, and wives. Hence, in most EU countries (Germany is the notable exception) unemployment is highly concentrated among the young, and is normally of very long duration.[11] This, in turn, fosters increased family dependence on the male breadwinner's earnings and social entitlements. In Southern Europe today, about 50 per cent of young adults (aged 20-30) still live with their parents. Among unemployed young people, the figure rises to 90 per cent (Esping-Andersen, 1996).

The notion that "equality" and "jobs" are at loggerheads seems compelling – especially in view of the rising unemployment in Scandinavia. North America, Australia and New Zealand exhibit rising inequality and have enjoyed stronger job growth. There is less poverty and less inequality in Europe, but also much less employment growth.[12] Yet, it is clear from Table 2.3, that when we probe behind the general concepts of "equality" and "jobs", the trade-off appears less crystal clear. On the one hand, deregulation and rising inequalities do not automatically translate into improved job performance. In terms of unemployment, the United States seems to be the exception, not the rule, that labour markets "clear" if wages are unequal and social protection is minimal. If we judge by unemployment rather than job expansion, the famous "equality or jobs" trade-off appears to be based on this one single case. Also, the British experience of the last decades does not suggest that deregulation brings immediate employment benefits. Here, as in the United States, a sharp increase in earnings differentials coincided

Table 2.3. **Indices of "equality" and employment performance**

	Earnings spread			Job security	Employment rate	Unemployment rate	Long-term unemployment
	Year	Ratio	Change since 1990	1985-93	1995	1995	1995
Canada	94	4.2	(−)	3	68	9.5	13.8
Australia	95	2.9	(+)	4	69	8.5	30.8
United Kingdom	95	3.4	(+)	7	68	8.7	43.5
United States	95	4.4	(+)	1	74	5.5	9.7
Denmark	90	2.2	n.a.	5	73	n.a.	27.9
Finland	94	2.4	(−)	10	61	17.1	32.3
Norway	91	2.0	n.a.	11	74	4.9	26.5
Sweden	93	2.1	(+)	13	71	9.2	15.7
Austria	94	3.7	(+)	16	69	n.a.	17.4
Belgium	93	2.2	(−)	17	56	9.4	62.4
France	94	3.3	(0)	14	60	11.6	45.6
Germany	93	2.3	(−)	15	65	8.2	48.3
Italy	93	2.8	(+)	21	52	12.2	62.9
Netherlands	94	2.6	(0)	9	64	6.5	43.2

Notes: Earnings spread is measured as the ratio of earnings at the 90th percentile to that at the 10th percentile.
A (+), (−) or (0) indicates trend towards more, less, or no change in inequality since 1990 (OECD, 1996).
Job security is a national ranking of degree of worker protection with lowest=1 (OECD, 1994b, Table 6.7).
Employment, unemployment and long-term unemployment (12 months-plus as a percentage of total) data are from OECD (1996), Tables A, L and Q.

with a lowering of social benefit levels as a proportion of average earnings[13] and a fall-off in trade union strength (Pierson, 1995). The incidence of post-tax and transfer poverty has, on one definition of poverty, jumped from 8.5 per cent to 12.5 per cent over the 1980s (McFate *et al.*, 1995, Table 1.10), and for some groups, such as young families and single mothers, poverty rates are exceptionally high (see Table 2.4). Yet, British unemployment rates (8.7 per cent in 1995) remain high (although lower than the European average); the incidence of long-term unemployment is worrying (43.5 per cent of the unemployed had been so for a year or more in 1995), and the employment/population ratio has actually fallen since 1979 (although at 67.8 per cent it remains significantly higher than the EU average of 60.2 per cent). (See Table 2.3 in this chapter, and OECD, 1996, Tables A, L and Q.)

On the other hand, there are marked differences in the "equality-jobs" profile across Europe. Although aggregate unemployment rates are now converging, in the Nordic countries this occurs against a background of much higher employment levels (even when adjusting for part-time work), lower youth unemployment (except Finland), and below-average long-term unemployment. And, as is well-known, Scandinavia is distinctive in terms of equality, with a very high degree of earnings compression and very low poverty rates across all social groups (Table 2.4).[14] In turn, most continental European countries combine low employment levels with high unemployment and exceptionally high long-term and youth unemployment. Wage inequality is quite high in some countries (such as Austria and France), but low in others (Germany). Trends in earnings distribution and poverty are stable, but overall modest poverty levels often mask high levels in groups with a loose attachment to the labour market, such as single mothers or widows. The social insurance-based continental European welfare states perpetuate their existing labour market structures: good, even luxurious, entitlements for the core (male) worker; residual assistance for others.

The lack of any straightforward connection between equality and job protection, on the one hand, and employment performance, on the other hand, is what one would expect. Clearly, this simple nexus is governed by other factors: one of these is the family, the provision of the welfare states is another. And, as I shall discuss in the concluding part, politics is a third factor.

Table 2.4. **Households with disposable income below half median income**

	Year	Couples with children		Single mothers	Aged households	
		Young	All		Single	Couples
Australia	85	13.0	9.1	71.1	58.3	11.1
	89	14.2	9.4	62.7	56.8	13.1
Canada	87	19.8	10.9	66.1	26.1	5.5
	91	14.4	9.2	61.4	12.2	3.2
United Kingdom	86	18.9	11.6	20.7	13.6	3.8
	91	24.9	13.0		42.3	17.9
United States	86	23.5	14.5	67.5	45.6	12.4
	91	26.7	14.1	63.3	41.1	12.7
Denmark	87	5.5	4.1	6.7	37.1	2.2
	92	5.4	3.5	13.9	19.8	2.9
Finland	87	4.3	2.8	6.6	28.1	3.2
	91	1.8	2.2	8.6	28.1	3.2
Sweden	87	3.4	3.1	5.7	13.5	0.8
Belgium	85	4.6	3.1	23.0	11.1	11.8
	92	2.1	3.7	14.7	11.8	12.4
Germany	84	14.6	5.1	39.4	15.5	8.4
	89	6.8	6.9	29.5	14.4	5.1
Netherlands	87	11.6	4.2	17.0	–	0.3
	91	9.8	5.9	34.8	2.8	4.7

Notes: Poverty rates refer to households with disposable income below 50 per cent of the national median, using an equivalence scale of 0.5 per additional person.
Young couples = head of household under 30 years of age; elderly = 65+. The data exclude units with co-habitating "other adults". Children = all under age 18.
Source: Luxembourg Income Study (see OECD, 1995*b*). Calculations kindly provided by Koen Vleminckx.

THE NEW DEMOGRAPHICS: AGEING AND FAMILY CHANGE

Postwar social policy could rely on stable and fertile families, largely capable of providing for their own caring needs. It also assumed a very standardised life-course, with female withdrawal from work at childbirth and with unbroken male careers from, say, age 16 to 65. These assumptions are now anachronistic. Families are much less stable, divorce rates and out-of-wedlock births are now "typical", and single-parent households account for a large and growing share of all child families.[15]

Family instability is a major catalyst of poverty, and the risks of social entrapment and welfare dependence are considerable, particularly for women and children. Here, however, welfare state design makes a difference. The key issue is how the mix of income support and care services facilitate work. Divorced women and single mothers are much less likely to be (and remain) in poverty in Scandinavia (and possibly France), in part because they have benefit entitlements due to being already integrated in the labour force and, in part, because widely available and affordable day care allows them to work. Elsewhere, single mothers easily find themselves in a welfare trap, with an unfavorable relationship between the cost of child care and expected earnings. Welfare entrapment is especially likely where, as in the United States, easy-entry jobs pay very low wages.[16]

Rising family instability is, of course, related to women's educational attainment, entry into paid employment, and enhanced economic independence. This complex of factors goes a long way in explaining declining fertility. Yet, it is important to recognise that the effect is far from linear. Scandinavia has both record high female participation rates and comparatively high fertility rates; Japan and continental (especially southern) Europe score low on both counts. The difference lies in welfare state policy, especially extensive day-care and paid-leave provisions and, for Europe, also in youth unemployment. Delayed job-entry and difficulties of harmonising work and family obligations lead to postponed family formation and fewer births (Bettio and Villa, 1995; Goldin, 1995; Gustavsson and Stafford, 1994). The lack of births and low activity levels combine to worsen the impact of population ageing. The issue of how to stimulate employment and fertility is therefore especially acute.

As is well known, ageing populations pose a severe threat to welfare state finances. OECD (1988) projections indicate that if current benefit standards are maintained, ageing alone will cause expenditure on pensions and health to double or even triple by 2040.[17] The problem is especially intense in countries, like Japan, where the demographic shift is unusually rapid. But as an indication of the overall trend, the European Union age/dependence ratio will increase by 50 per cent within the next two decades or so (European Commission, 1993). Many countries, especially Belgium, the Netherlands, and Italy, already face severe deficits in their pension systems as contributions fall far short of benefit payments. In Italy, an admittedly extreme example, about one-third of total annual public deficits are caused by pension contribution shortfalls.

The ageing crisis should, however, not be considered in isolation from employment and family policies. The burden of ageing depends, in the first instance, on birth rates, on employment structure, and on retirement practice. Welfare state policies and human longevity have provoked dramatic changes in the normal life-course. Since the 1950s longevity has increased on average by 8-10 years while the number of economically active years has shrunk by about the same number of years. The shift is even more pronounced where early retirement is prevalent. Arithmetically speaking, we have doubled pension benefit years while cutting contributing years by around 25 per cent. To a degree, this can be offset by higher productivity but, still, the inter-generational redistribution burden is mounting. In the extreme Italian case, there is now only one active contributor for each pensioner. Even with a larger share of elderly, Sweden, with very high activity rates, has about 2.5 actives for each pensioner. In other words, the intensity of the ageing crisis depends not only on pure demographics, but also on employment policies.

Population ageing may also threaten the welfare of the young. For one thing, with increased longevity the share of highly care-intensive "ultra-aged" grows.[18] Even in "familistic" societies, such as Japan and southern Europe, it is unrealistic to assume that this burden can be managed within the family. The absence of caring services for the aged frequently implies unnecessary and very costly hospitalisation.

Secondly, pensions and health care together usually account for the lion's share of social expenditure. And the political power of the aged, combined with early retirement, conspire to push up spending – frequently at the expense of programmes for the young. The problem is that this crowding-out effect is occuring at the same time as the life cycle distribution of economic risk increasingly disfavours young families.

Once again, differences in approach make a huge difference. As shown in Table 2.2, one group of countries, predominantly the already transfer-biased Japanese and continental European welfare states, but also the United States, is increasingly pensioner biased. On average, the continental European nations spend 2.3 times as much on the old as on the young, and the Anglo-Saxon nations, 1.1 times as much. A few welfare states, particularly the Scandinavian countries, but also Canada, Australia and New Zealand, are more youth-oriented.

SOCIAL SPENDING, SERVICING AND REDISTRIBUTIVE EFFICACY

The capacity of OECD welfare states to manage emerging social problems may be less related to size than to structure. Existing welfare state differences make it possible, to some extent, to assess the comparative efficacy of families, the market, or welfare states to meet the "postindustrial" challenge.

As we have seen from Table 2.2, welfare states vary in terms of size and commitment. In essence, Richard Titmuss' old distinction between residual and institutional welfare states still holds. Although there is a slight convergence in overall social expenditure levels, differences are widening for other attributes. In 1960, the most generous welfare spender, Germany, exceeded the average by a ratio of

1.8, while the leanest, the United States, spent 0.7 times the average. By 1990, Sweden had become the most generous spender at 1.4 times the average, and Australia the leanest at 0.6 times the average (based on OECD, 1994a). Generally speaking, the Anglo-Saxon welfare states have been stagnant at comparatively modest spending levels, whereas continental European and especially Scandinavian welfare states – now similar in terms of spending levels – have continued to grow, albeit at a vastly reduced pace, since the late 1970s.

Such similarities and differences are nonetheless deceptive. For one thing, where public welfare is lean, private social spending may fill the gap; for another, aggregate expenditure tell us little about what precisely welfare states provide. The welfare state may be lean or generous, residual or comprehensive, yet the underlying quest for social protection barely differs. Modest public welfare commitments imply that responsibilities are reallocated from the State to either employers or families. And *vice versa*. Hence, it is unlikely that any effort at cost-shifting between state, market, and families will affect aggregate national social protection costs. But it will affect societies' ability to adapt to family and labour market changes. Therefore, the public-private mix has profound distributive implications.

Market alternatives are often presented as the most attractive solution to fiscally beleaguered welfare states. The Chilean pension reform has in fact become a model to emulate. The advantages of privatisation are three-fold. Firstly, it should augment savings and thus lower interest rates; secondly, it allows individuals more choice in tailoring their welfare package according to need; and thirdly, although less egalitarian, it is more equitable: you get what you earned.

Privatisation generally implies less complete coverage and more benefit inequality, but not necessarily any macroeconomic savings. The logic can be seen from a comparison of two welfare state extremes: the "residual", highly-marketised American and the unusually comprehensive Swedish systems (see Table 2.5). Swedish public spending is more than double the American figure, but the two begin to converge when we add private outlays. In Sweden, the state dominates. In the United States, both employers and families carry a significant welfare burden.[19]

American welfare philosophy has always stressed employer-provided occupational plans. Indeed, by 1979 these covered the "primary" workforce reasonable well (around 50 per cent of all wage earners for pensions; 70 per cent for health). In the primary economy, therefore, combined legislated and

Table 2.5. **Public and private spending on social protection**

	Sweden	United States
	As a percentage of GDP	
Public social expenditure, 1990	33.1	14.6
Private education	0.1	2.5
Private health[1]	1.1	8.2
Private pensions[1]	1.8	3.0
Total	35.5	28.3
	As a percentage of private household expenditure, 1990	
Private health, education and pensions	2.7	18.8
Day care (child families)	1.7	10.4
Total	4.4	29.2
Taxes	36.8	10.4
Total + taxes	41.2	39.6

1. Private health data for Sweden are for 1992. American data include "other social welfare". Private pensions for Sweden are estimated from employer-provided pension benefits in the OECD *National Accounts*. Swedish tax data are from *Statistisk Aarsbook*, 1994, Table T 226. American private pensions and health expenditure data are from *Social Security Bulletin, Annual Statistical Supplement*, 1992, Table 3A4.
Sources: OECD, *National Accounts*, detailed tables (1994); US Bureau of Labour Statistics, *Consumer Expenditures in 1990*; Mishel and Bernstein (1993), Table 8.37.

negotiated employer labour costs are quite similar to prevailing European levels (on average, 23 per cent of wages in the United States and 29 per cent in the European Union) (Blank, 1994, p. 167). Substituting employers for the state poses, however, the problem that a substantial gap remains because employer coverage is partial. A menacing aspect of the "American model" is that this gap is now widening; partly because those firms that traditionally furnished occupational welfare – basically traditional large industries – are in decline; and partly because new employment concentrates in sectors and firms where unions and occupational benefit plans are scarce. Thus, in America employer-provided pension coverage has declined, notably in the 1980s, and there has been a simultaneous shift from defined-benefits to individual savings or defined-contribution plans. Also employer-provided health coverage has declined. There are now an estimated 30 or 40 million Americans without health insurance (Myles, 1996).

Where public and corporate welfare guarantees decline in tandem, as is the case in the United States, welfare gaps will widen and the cost will shift to families themselves. As Table 2.5 shows (bottom half), the enviably low taxes that Americans pay are matched by very heavy household social spending obligations, the net result being that disposable income for alternative consumption or savings is crowded out. The net result is also that the distribution of welfare suffers. Thus, health expenditure absorb 8-10 per cent of income of households in the two lowest quintiles compared to 5 per cent for households with average incomes. And, as is well known, private pensions create much greater inequality amongst the elderly than do public pensions (Pestieau, 1992; West Pedersen, 1994). The rich can save, the poor cannot.

Since government social security in Europe is comprehensive and generous, employer plans and household welfare purchasing remain marginal.[20] In European welfare states, the main difference in the public-private mix has to do with service provision and family social care. The Nordic countries' comprehensive approach to social care is internationally unique. In Japan and most continental European countries, relatively high labour costs imply that the market-option is prohibitive. The result is that caring is mainly internalised in the family and that women therefore delay and reduce fertility, or interrupt work at child birth (Bettio and Villa, 1996). In the United States, neither public nor employer provision is extensive, but higher wage differentials should make day care affordable for large sections of the population.[21] As shown in Table 2.5, family outlays on day care is negligible in Sweden, but quite substantial in the United States and, for low income families, the cost is often prohibitive.

More generally, care services reduce the burden of unpaid domestic work and thus help to induce greater female labour supply. Their absence saddles families with the double care burden for the young and the elderly. This shows up in the average time women spend on unpaid domestic work, which ranges from less than 25 hours a week in Denmark, 31 hours in the United States, to a full 45-50 hours in Italy and Spain (Bonke, 1995).

If the issue is how to relieve welfare state finances, there appears to be no ready made win-win solution. Shifting costs to the market might reduce public deficits and encourage greater savings, but if we prioritise social protection this is clearly not optimal.[22] For one thing, the public savings may be less than impressive since private plans – be they of the individual, group, or employer type – usually require public subsidies in the form of tax expenditure.[23]

More importantly, it is difficult to imagine that marketised welfare is compatible with current trends in employment and family structure. Where job growth is associated with low-wages and a high proportion of part-time or casual employment, there will remain huge gaps in private coverage because employers are unlikely to extend benefits to their contingent workforce. Indeed, low-income earners may require social transfers just to live above poverty. Alternatively, in a European "insider-outsider" scenario – as in the Japanese system – the core workforce would probably do equally well with private schemes but, virtually by definition, the "outsiders" would be as excluded as are American low-wage workers. Since marketised welfare assumes decent earnings and a stable attachment to the labour market, it is also unlikely to cover the exigencies of family instability, particularly in countries where women and mothers cannot count on public care provision.

The high levels of public social expenditure that prevail across Europe today probably rule out any significant increases in the future; given current budget imbalances, cumulated public debt, and taxation limits, the contrary is more likely. If this is the case, the existing structure of spending becomes exceedingly important if, that is, new inequalities and poverty risks are emerging.

At similar expenditure levels, the typical continental European welfare state is mainly targeted towards "passive" and pensioner-related transfers, whereas the Nordic systems favour services and young families. Both types of welfare states perform well in terms of minimising poverty amongst the elderly, the Nordic system arguably better. This is however not the case with respect to the risk menu of working age families.

The capacity of the more "residual" Anglo-Saxon welfare states to combat poverty is much weaker, as can be seen in Table 2.4. Certainly, poverty among the aged has diminished considerably[24] in Canada, Australia, the United Kingdom, and the United States, but, except for Britain, aged poverty rates are much higher (in the range of two or three times higher) than in European welfare states. Also, the more residual welfare states are clearly less capable of stemming the tide of market inequalities. During the 1980s, the post tax-transfer poverty rate among young (aged 20-29) households has risen by 45 per cent in the United States, and 53 per cent in the United Kingdom (McFate et al., 1995).

In contrast to most European countries, income maintenance to working-age families in the Anglo-Saxon welfare states is dominated by targeted, means-tested programmes. Targeting benefits to the demonstrably needy is widely believed to be a more efficient approach to social protection, and it is in fact becoming a favoured policy alternative to costly universal or even insurance-based systems. In terms of poverty reduction, targeted programmes are, in fact, generally less efficient than universal schemes. This is especially the case where means tests target the really "deserving" poor. The efficiency of targeting does, however, seem to increase markedly where it is less stigmatising and more comprehensive. This is illustrated by the recent experience in Australia and Canada where targeting, in a sense, has taken the form of a negative income tax: need is ascertained via the more innocuous, and less stigmatising, tax return; and the philosophy of selectivity is to screen out the middle class rather than narrowly address absolute poverty (Castles, 1996; Myles, 1996). There is an argument to be made that the negative income tax approach can combine the advantages of universalism and selectivity. Still, more or less the same combination can be derived from an effective tax-clawback of universal benefits.

If the goal is to combat child poverty, it is evident that the Australian and Canadian approach is more effective than narrow targeting. Still, universal benefit systems clearly perform much better. The percentage of child families lifted out of poverty by taxes and transfers is essentially zero in the United States, around 18 per cent in Canada, 28 per cent in Germany and a full 50 per cent in France and the Netherlands (McFate et al., 1995, Table 1.6). Child poverty in general, and single-parent child poverty in particular, remains alarmingly high in basically all the Anglo-Saxon countries.[25]

THE RISKS OF ENTRAPMENT AND WELFARE STATE POLICY

If the crisis of the welfare state has its origins in poorly functioning families and labour markets, it is difficult to see how a strategy of resurrecting familial welfare or of privatisation will enhance our societies' ability to maximise welfare. The question, then, turns to the possibilities of recasting the existing welfare state. This involves both a technical problem: what should it look like? and a political problem: how to build it?

This is of course not the place to propose a blueprint for an optimal future welfare state. We can, however, identify what are the basic parameters required to equilibrate the three principal institutional actors: for households welfare maximisation is primarily a function of jobs and income adequacy; in contrast, for labour markets, job growth is said to require less job security (i.e. deregulation) and more wage inequality; and for welfare states, long-term financial solidity means greater fertility and less unemployment. Is it possible to envisage a win-win combination of these apparently contradictory requirements?

If we begin with the dilemma of fertility and family well-being, our analyses do suggest a positive-sum strategy. Since it is unrealistic to assume a return to the stable, traditional one-earner family, a return to high fertility rates assumes lower youth unemployment but, above all, adequate and affordable family care services, so that women's work and family obligations can be harmonised. Encouraging the double-earner family has an additional positive effect, because it helps offset possibly low earnings of one spouse by reducing the household's narrow dependence on one "family wage" and on the breadwinner's job security, and because two-income families constitute the best hedge against child poverty. In most countries, the poverty rate amongst two-income child families is one-half or even one-third that amongst single-earner child families. The need for care services is especially acute for the growing proportion of single-parent households, although their reduced availability as a source of labour supply (and thus of earnings) implies the need for additional social transfers to ward off poverty. Furnishing family services by the public sector may be constrained for budgetary reasons, implying the likelihood of reliance on (possibly regulated and at least partially subsidised) private care in order to ensure broad access. In brief, a new philosophy of socialising the costs of children is needed.

Turning to the "jobs/equality" trade-off, if it is true that job growth requires deregulation and wage flexibility, a positive-sum solution will only be possible if welfare states radically redefine their commitment to equality in general, and their aged-transfer bias in particular. In the first instance, the pressures for high wages and job security are especially intense where families depend on one income. Maximising female employment clearly decreases the trade-off. Yet, if as most believe, it is difficult to avert skill redundancies, mass job-losses, and a large low-wage labour market (in the labour intensive services especially), the core question is how to assure against lifelong entrapment, against the emergence of a "B-team" locked into chronic underprivilege. The risks of entrapment are, in fact, multiplied when we consider family instability. The issue can be likened to Joseph Schumpeter's famous omnibus analogy: social classes do not consolidate if, like the omnibus, they are always full, but always of different people.

Secure, well-paid jobs for the less skilled will probably not return. Hence, one burning issue is how to ensure that the proportion of poorly qualified workers in each new entering youth cohort remains at a minimum, and how to assure that those at risk of entrapment (whether for family or labour market reasons) do not find themselves in an omnibus with locked doors. Data on long-term, let alone life-time entrapment are difficult to come by. Nonetheless, it is clear that there is a real risk that people may find themselves locked into the "B-team". Recent American research shows that for a person in poverty in any given year, there is a 50 per cent chance for blacks and 30 per cent chance for whites that family income will fall below poverty in at least 5 out of the next 10 years (Stevens, 1995). The risks of extended poverty and welfare dependence among single mothers in America is also well-documented, and appears principally related to lack of cheap day care combined with the poverty trap problem built into Aid to Families with Dependent Children (AFDC). Worse still, this stratum tends to pass on underprivilege to succeeding generations. By and large, the (relatively scarce) comparative data available, indicate that poverty, low-income and single parent entrapment is much less common in Europe (Duncan et al., 1995; Duncan and Voges, 1993; Burkhauser et al., 1993; Burkhauser and Poupore, 1993). The Duncan et al. study indicates that the percentage of families with children living in poverty for three consecutive years is about 12 per cent in Canada and 14 per cent in the United States, versus only 1.5 per cent in Germany and France (Alsace-Lorraine), and 0.4 per cent in the Netherlands. On the other hand, Europe (except Scandinavia) is much more likely than North America to generate long-term entrapment for the unemployed. Mean unemployment duration in Germany is 14 months and in Italy 39 months, compared to 3 in the United States (and 4 in Sweden) (OECD, 1994b). For Denmark, an unusually thorough and detailed study comes to the conclusion that, overall, movement out of underprivilege and marginalisation is very high, but that there remains a rather small chronic loser class, typically condemned to rotate between marginal jobs, assistance and unemployment (Velfaerdskommissionen, 1995).

As this, and most other research shows, escape from unemployment and marginality is vastly enhanced with skills and education. Thus, the probability of escape rises by 30 per cent with vocational training, and doubles with more theoretical education (Bjorn, 1995). The impact of educational deficiencies on B-team entrapment will almost certainly intensify in the future. A win-win policy therefore requires, firstly, a social investment strategy that emphasises lifelong learning, training and re-education in general, and a concerted policy to minimise the proportion of individuals with low qualifications amongst successively entering youth cohorts. Secondly, it requires a greater emphasis by the welfare state on securing adequate resources for young families in order to facilitate their capacity to cope with, and adjust to, a world that breeds risk rather than security.[26] At the very least, welfare state guarantees against permanent exclusion must be positive overall.

The welfare state's emphasis on the elderly reflects the postwar view that most risks are concentrated in peoples' non-working years. Over the past five decades, welfare states have indeed scored a huge success in diminishing poverty amongst the elderly. It may even be that the effort has overshot the target. Household expenditure data for two such different countries as Finland and Italy show that pensioner households on average save 25-30 per cent of income. In Italy, even pensioners in the lowest income quintiles save.[27]

If social transfers to the aged exceed needs, the result is in a double sense distributionally perverse. In the case of Italy – which may be extreme but hardly unique – pension financial shortfalls account for roughly one third of annual budget deficits, yet pensioners on average receive one-third more in income than they need. Their savings allow, of course, for intra-family redistribution from the old to the young but in such a manner that broader social inequalities are perpetuated. It is, then, obvious that contemporary welfare states will need to re-orient their policies in favour of youth and working-age adults. Not only does aged-spending crowd out programmes for the young, but it also misallocates purchasing power from a job-creation point of view. The aged are intensive consumers of mainly public social services, but are the least prone to consume market services.

THE POLITICS OF WELFARE STATE REFORM

The welfare state may be in crisis, yet it remains hugely popular in public opinion. The more comprehensive (and thus costly) the welfare state, the more will peoples' lives be organised around its programmes. And, as we know, universal "rights" programmes enjoy the greatest support: pensions and health in particular. The average voter, to whom governments must respond, is growing older and this certainly accounts for the bias towards the elderly. The clout of the elderly is also bolstered by life-course-specific social security needs. Since everybody eventually ages, there is a ready-made coalition in favour of generous pensions. The problem is that those already old lose personal interest in programmes for the young, be it child allowances, maternity benefits, day-care services, or worker training.[28]

Nonetheless, contemporary retrenchment policies tend to focus primarily on cost containment in health care and, above all, on pension reform.[29] Everywhere, governments are reversing two decades of falling retirement ages; where social insurance pensions prevail, there is a shift back to the "defined contribution" formula; where the flat-rate universal model prevails, there is a drift towards income-tested benefits. In both cases, there is a retreat from the promise of an adequate "retirement wage". The trend, currently spearheaded by Australia and Canada, towards "negative income tax" targeting implies similarly a shift from income security guarantees to an implicit subsidy for low-wage or under-employed workers (Myles, 1996).

A comparison of governments' policies over the past years reveals, however, a very important pre-condition for reform. The average voter's "veto" is more easily overcome where governments can negotiate a broad consensus with strong, nationally encompassing, interest organisations, such as occurred in Germany in 1989, in Sweden over the past years, and in Italy in 1995. A policy of imposition, as pursued by the Berlusconi cabinet in Italy in 1994, and the Juppé government in France in 1995, is more likely to trigger massive social unrest.

In brief, as political scientists and economists have repeatedly shown, the ability of countries to achieve positive sum solutions under conditions of acute conflict of interest is closely related to their institutional structure of political mediation. Strong interest groups can, on the one hand, insist that a bargained consensus is preferable to sabotage or instability. On the other hand, comprehensive social pacts will more easily overcome the entrenched opposition of narrower special interest groups, and are more likely to arrive at binding agreements based on trust.

The problem is that countries are unequally endowed with a strong social partnership infrastructure capable of delivering sustained, across-the-board wage or social benefit moderation in return for, say, job expansion or deficit reductions. Two types of policies are especially ill-equipped to produce such positive sum formulae: those in which strong interest representation (especially trade unions) is limited to the core workforce, and those with a weak and fragmented interest organisational system. In the former case, the likely result is that existing privileges of the "insiders" are safeguarded at the expense of the "outsiders"; in the latter case, governments are more easily captive to the short-term dictates of the median voter or to the most powerful and resourceful organised lobbies.

NOTES

1. The author would like to thank Francis Castles, John Myles, Vicente Navarro and Peter Scherer for their helpful comments, and especially Koen Vleminckx for his generous help in computing poverty data from the Luxembourg Income Study (see OECD, 1995b). The author assumes full responsibility for any errors that remain.

2. Distributive services, once a major source of employment growth, are now stagnant. They account for roughly 15 per cent of total employment in advanced economies.

3. Exaggerated equality, it is said, may also adversely affect the development of human capital if there are not adequate returns for more education (Lindbeck, 1993).

4. The difference is much smaller (and disappears almost entirely) when the comparison is with the American "primary" economy where employer-provided occupational benefits average 12 per cent of wages. However, a high proportion of growth, not only of low-skilled jobs, but more generally, of all job growth in the United States occurs in firms and sectors which are not covered by occupational benefit plans (Burtless, 1990; Blank, 1994; Mishel and Bernstein, 1993).

5. The urgency of job protection is obviously enhanced where, as in most of Europe, delayed job entry and early retirement reduce possible active years. The number of potentially active years for males has, on average, declined by 8-10 years in recent decades.

6. If compensated labour exclusion were to be targeted on older and primarily less-skilled workers, such a productivity dividend would be more likely. However, almost everywhere early retirement rates are similar for both high- and low-skilled workers.

7. In Denmark and Sweden, the participation rate of mothers with small children (under 6 years of age) exceeds 80 per cent, and Scandinavian fertility rates are now among Europe's highest. The costs of permitting mothers, especially single mothers, to work may easily exceed their marginal productivity (especially considering their high absenteeism rates). However, any reasonable cost calculus should also take into account the long-term, dynamic effects in terms of minimising entrapment and chronic welfare dependence.

8. In Sweden, earned income accounts for 65 per cent, and transfers for 35 per cent, of the total income of single mothers. The employment rate of single mothers in Germany, the United Kingdom and the United States is much lower (respectively, 50, 30, and 45 per cent), and their poverty rates much higher.

9. Some countries, such as Italy and the Netherlands, have made heavy use of disability insurance; most have lowered the de facto retirement age.

10. Public or semi-public child care for small children caters for 30-50 per cent of children in Scandinavia, but less than 5 per cent in EU countries, except in France and Belgium where coverage is 15-20 per cent (Esping-Andersen, 1996). The proportion of elderly people living with their children is less than 10 and even 5 per cent in Northern Europe, but around 40 per cent in Italy and Spain and 65 per cent in Japan.

11. The average duration of unemployment (OECD estimates) is around 40 months in Italy and Spain, around 20 months in Germany, France, the Netherlands and Belgium. This compares to less than 10 months in both the Nordic and Anglo-Saxon countries (OECD, 1994c, Table 13).

12. Only Norway, with its abundant oil revenues and pervasive industrial subsidisation, has managed to contain unemployment.

13. For most groups, benefit levels have been increased in line with prices. For some groups, such as families with children, benefits have been increased above the level of inflation.

14. There has been some increase in earnings differentials in Sweden during the 1980s, but this must be viewed against an extremely high degree of equality to begin with.

15. The divorce rate is now 50 per cent of the marriage rate in the United States, and on average 23 per cent in Europe; the share of children born out-of-wedlock is, at 25-30 per cent, similar in North America and Europe. In

both instances, however, southern European rates are much lower – albeit climbing. Single-mother families constitute about 5 per cent of the total in Southern Europe, about 10-15 per cent in Canada, the Netherlands, Sweden, and the United Kingdom, and a full 20 per cent in the United States (Bettio and Villa, 1995; United States Department of Health and Human Services, 1995; and the author's calculations from Luxembourg Income Study data: see OECD, 1995*b*).

16. Research shows that a much larger proportion of American than European welfare mothers are locked into long-term poverty and dependence. Also, there is strong evidence that this has substantial adverse effects on the life chances of their children – such as higher drop-out rates in school (Gottschalk *et al.*, 1994). For a comparative study of poverty entrapment, see Duncan *et al.* (1995).

17. Still, as the OECD (1988) report suggests, the rising financial burden can be covered by productivity (and thus real income) growth. An estimated real annual productivity growth of 0.5 to 1.2 per cent (depending on country) will suffice to finance the forecast expenditure increase. This ignores, of course, the fact that many countries are counting on growth just to bring down their heavy public debt.

18. The population aged 80+, at 3-5 per cent today, has doubled since 1960 and will double again by year 2040.

19. Note that the American data exclude the additional tax-expenditure effect that comes from generous tax deductions on employer and individual welfare plans.

20. There are indications that individual retirement-savings accounts are growing quite rapidly across all European countries, the main reasons being attractive tax-savings and decaying confidence in governments' future pension commitments. Also, household purchase of private health care has risen slightly in such widely different countries as Italy and Sweden, although mainly among high-income households.

21. Data for the mid-1980s indicate that only 2 per cent of American firms provide child care arrangements. About half of children of employed mothers are cared for by paid carers, half by family and relatives (Statistical Abstract of the United States, 1987, Tables 613 and 673).

22. It is dubious whether low public welfare expenditure and modest social entitlements encourage private savings. Certainly, the privatisation of pensions in Chile has raised national savings, but the case of Chile is not comparable to the OECD countries. Doubts arise when we consider net national private savings rates. The residual welfare state countries score systematically below the OECD average. As a per cent of GDP (1990-1994), the United States savings rate is 6.2 per cent; the Canadian, 7.1; the United Kingdom's, 5.3; and the Australian, 3.4. The weighted OECD average is 7.7 per cent, and the weighted European average 8.2 per cent (Leibfritz *et al.*, 1995).

23. The Thatcher government's privatisation of sickness allowances, which was meant to produce savings of 400 million pounds to the public budget, required tax concessions that resulted in a final savings of only 40 million pounds (Saunders, 1994; O'Higgins, 1986).

24. Japan is often considered a "residual" welfare state (in part because its pension system has not yet fully matured; in part because of the prominence of private welfare), and yet does not display high poverty rates (unfortunately, comparable data are lacking). Sustained full employment and rapid economic growth are doubtlessly a major factor.

25. Note that these figures on poverty reduction do not take into account indirect taxes. Substantially higher consumption tax rates in Europe than in North America imply that European government's *de facto* poverty reduction performance may be, comparatively, less impressive. Yet, against this one must also weigh the heavier social protection spending burden that falls on North American households (as discussed earlier in this paper).

26. It is often claimed that more training and education is futile when there are no jobs or, at best, if available jobs tend to demand few skills anyhow. This is a deeply falacious argument, mainly because it is static. The real issue is how to maximise the chances of individuals to move on from poor jobs to good jobs along their life-course.

27. Author's own analyses on the 1993 Italian household expenditure survey, and personal communication from professor Kangas at the University of Turku in Finland.

28. Recent voter studies in both Denmark and Finland show the basic same age/social programme support pattern. Support for pensions and health is equally high and strong across all age groups while support for "youth-related" welfare benefits falls dramatically among older voters (Forma, 1996; Goul Andersen, 1995).

29. Although it should be noted that many countries, including the Netherlands and Sweden, have undertaken substantial reductions in other benefit programmes such as sickness and unemployment pay (for an overview, see Ploug and Kvist, 1994).

BIBLIOGRAPHY

BAUMOL, W. (1967), "The macro-economics of unbalanced growth", *The American Economic Review*, No. 57, pp. 415-426.

BETTIO, F. and VILLA, C. (1995), "A Mediterranean perspective on the break-down of the relationship between participation and fertility", Unpublished paper, University of Sienna, Department of Economics, December.

BJORKLUND, A. and FREEMAN, R. (1994), "Generating equality and eliminating poverty, the Swedish way", NBER Working Paper, No. 4945.

BJORN, N.H. (1995), "Causes and consequences of persistent unemployment", Ph.D. dissertation, Department of Economics, University of Copenhagen.

BLANK, R. (1994), *Social Protection versus Economic Flexibility*, University of Chicago Press, Chicago.

BONKE, J. (1995), *Arbejde, Tid og Kon i Udvalgte Lande*, Socialforsknings Instituttet, Copenhagen.

BURKHAUSER, R. and POUPORE, J.G. (1993), "A cross-national comparison of permanent inequality in the United States and Germany", *Cross-National Studies in Aging*, Programme Project Paper, No. 10, Syracuse University.

BURKHAUSER, R., HOLTZ-EAKIN, D. and RHODY, S. (1993), "Labor earnings mobility and inequality in the United States and Germany during the 1980s", *Cross-National Studies in Aging*, Programme Project Paper, No. 12, Syracuse University.

BURTLESS, G. (1990), *A Future of Lousy Jobs?*, Brookings Institute, Washington, DC.

CASTLES, F. (1996), "Australia and New Zealand: needs-based social guarantees and working class life cycles", in G. Esping-Andersen (ed.), *Welfare States in Transition*, Sage, London.

DUNCAN, G. and VOGES, W. (1993), "Do generous social assistance programmes lead to dependence?", ZeS-Arbeitspapier, No. 11, Center for Social Policy Research, University of Bremen.

DUNCAN, G. *et al.* (1995), "Poverty and social assistance dynamics in the United States, Canada, and Europe", in K. McFate, R. Lawson and W.J. Wilson (eds.), *Poverty, Inequality and the Future of Social Policy*, Russell Sage, New York, pp. 67-108.

ESPING-ANDERSEN, G. (1996), *Welfare States in Transition*, Sage, London.

EUROPEAN COMMISSION (1993), *Social Protection in Europe*, Brussels.

FORMA, P. (1996), "Rational legitimacy of the welfare state: popular support for ten income transfer schemes in Finland", Unpublished paper, Department of Social Policy, University of Turku, Finland.

FREEMAN, R. (1988), "Labor market institutions and economic performance", *Economic Policy*, No. 6, pp. 63-80.

GOLDIN, C. (1995), "Career and family", NBER Working Paper, No. 5188.

GOTTSCHALK, P., MCLANAHAN, S. and SANDEFUR, G. (1994), "The dynamics of intergenerational transmission of poverty and welfare participation", in S. Danziger, G. Sandefur and D. Weinberg (eds.), *Confronting Poverty: Prescriptions for Change*, Harvard University Press, Cambridge, MA, pp. 85-108.

GOUL ANDERSEN, J. (1995), "Velfaerdsstatens folkelige opbakning", *Social Forskning*, August, pp. 34-45.

GUSTAVSSON, S. and STAFFORD, F. (1994), "Three regimes of child care: the United States, the Netherlands, and Sweden", in R. Blank (ed.), *Social Protection versus Economic Flexibility*, University of Chicago Press, Chicago.

HECLO, H. (1981), "Toward a new welfare state?", in P. Flora and A. Heidenheimer (eds.), *The Development of Welfare States in Europe and America*, Transaction Books, New Brunswick, pp. 383-406.

LEIBFRITZ, W., ROSEVEARE, D., FORE, D. and WURZEL, E. (1995), "Ageing populations, pension systems and government budgets: how do they affect savings?", OECD Economics Department Working Papers, No. 156, Paris.

LINDBECK, A. (1993), "The welfare state and the employment problem", *The American Economic Review*, May, pp. 71-75.

MARSHALL, T.H. (1950), *Citizenship and Social Class*, Oxford University Press, Oxford.

MCFATE, K., SMEEDING, T. and RAINWATER, L. (1995), "Markets and states: poverty trends and transfer system effectiveness in the 1980s", in K. McFate *et al.* (eds.), *Poverty, Inequality and the Future of Social Policy*, Russell Sage Foundation, New York, pp. 29-66.

MISHEL, L. and BERNSTEIN, J. (1993), *The State of Working America*, M.E. Sharpe, New York.

MYLES, J. (1996), "When markets fail", in G. Esping-Andersen (ed.), *Welfare States in Transition*, Sage, London.

OECD (1981), *The Welfare State in Crisis*, Paris.

OECD (1988), *Ageing Populations – The Social Policy Implications*, Paris.

OECD (1994*a*), *New Orientations for Social Policy*, Social Policy Studies No. 12, Paris.

OECD (1994*b*), *The OECD Jobs Study: Evidence and Explanations*, Part II, Paris.

OECD (1994*c*), *Economic Outlook*, December, Paris.

OECD (1995*a*), *Employment Outlook*, Paris.

OECD (1995*b*), *Income Distribution in OECD Countries*, Social Policy Studies No.18, Paris.

OECD (1996), *Employment Outlook*, Paris.

O'HIGGINS, M. (1986), "Privatisation and social welfare: concepts, analysis and the British experience", in S. Kamerman and A. Kahn (eds.), *Privatisation and Social Welfare*, Princeton University Press, Princeton pp. 55-177

PESTIEAU, P. (1992), "The distribution of private pension benefits: how fair is it?", in E. Duskin (ed.), *Private Pensions and Public Policy*, Social Policy Studies No. 9, OECD, Paris.

PIERSON, P. (1995), *Dismantling the Welfare State?*, Cambridge University Press, Cambridge.

PLOUG, N. and KVIST, J. (1994), *Recent Trends in Cash Benefits in Europe*, Socialforskningsinstituttet, Copenhagen.

SAUNDERS, P. (1994), *Welfare and Equality*, Cambridge University Press, Cambridge.

SOSKICE, D. (1994), "Reconciling markets and institutions: the German apprenticeship system", in L. Lynch (ed.), *Training and the Private Sector*, University of Chicago Press, Chicago.

STEVENS, A.H. (1995), "Climbing out of poverty, falling back in", NBER Working paper, No. 5390.

UNITED STATES DEPARTMENT OF HEALTH AND HUMAN SERVICES (1995), "Report to Congress on Out-of-Wedlock Childbearing", Government Printing Office, Washington, DC.

VELFAERDSKOMMISSIONEN (1995), *Velstand og Velfaerd – en Analysesammenfatning*, Ministries of Commerce, Finances, Interior and Economy, Copenhagen.

WEST PEDERSEN, A. (1994), "What makes the difference? Cross-national variation in pension systems and their distributional outcomes", in P. Kosonen and P.K. Madsen (eds.), *Convergence or Divergence? Welfare States Facing European Integration*, European Commission, Brussels, pp. 125-156.

FAMILY CHANGE, FAMILY POLICIES AND THE RESTRUCTURING OF WELFARE

by

Chiara Saraceno
University of Turin, Italy

INTRODUCTION

In the industrialised countries the family is the subject of social policy debates from two perspectives. First, changes in family and individual behaviour are modifying the way these societies reproduce themselves; this involves not only changes in the age-structure profile of the population, but also shifts in the gender division of labour, inter-generational redistribution and solidarity, and the balance between caring needs and caring resources. Secondly, welfare restructuring increasingly involves a re-drawing of the lines between governmental and family responsibilities, redefining individual expectations and family obligations.

These processes are not homogeneous across the industrialised countries. However, in all of them the "family question" (Martin, 1996), in this dual sense, as a possible source of social problems and as a resource for addressing these same problems, is at the centre of policy debates around the restructuring of the welfare state. In addition, the way that other, indirect "family questions", such as the ageing of the population or the greater fragility of labour market attachment, are defined in policy debates is greatly influenced by the way this central "family question" is interpreted in each society.

CHANGES IN FAMILY ORGANISATION AND BEHAVIOUR

Among the behavioural changes which are found to some degree in all the industrialised countries, and which have a profound impact on social policies, are three in particular:

- growing labour force participation by women with family responsibilities, particularly by mothers of young children;
- growing marital instability, and greater fragility of the father-child relationship. There is also a rising proportion of births out-of-wedlock, although there are considerable cross-national differences in the size and meaning of this trend (Kamerman, 1995);
- declining fertility, or at least stabilisation of fertility at under-replacement rates.

Growing participation of women in the labour force

Women's lives have changed quite dramatically in the industrialised countries over one or two generations. In all OECD countries, women's activity rate increased substantially from the 1970s, and women's share of total employment has grown (Commission of the European Communities, 1993; OECD, 1995). At the same time, women in the younger cohorts now tend to remain in the labour force throughout their adult life, even if and when they have children (see Saraceno, 1993).[1] In 1991, half of all mothers with children under 10 in Europe were employed outside the home (Millar and Warman, 1996).

Of course, both the activity rate and the relative presence of women in the different activity sectors vary between countries and within each country. Thus, in the Scandinavian countries, Canada and the United States, women's activity rate is consistently above 60 per cent (touching 70-80 per cent in the

Scandinavian countries). In Australia, Belgium, France, Germany, the Netherlands, Switzerland and the United Kingdom it is above or around 50 per cent. In other countries, such as Ireland, Italy and Spain it remains below 50 per cent. However, even in these latter countries, the activity rates of the youngest cohorts are similar to those in the first group of countries, particularly among better educated young women; for example, in Italy, in the 25-50 age bracket the activity rate of women holding a high school or university degree is 77 per cent, compared to 46 per cent for women with minimum compulsory schooling (Carmignani and Pruna, 1991). Women's share in the overall increase of the labour force since the 1980s has been larger in the European Free Trade Association (EFTA) countries than in the United States and Japan, where men and women contributed more evenly to the total increase (Commission of the European Communities, 1994).

These differences are partly due to the size of the service sector, which, with the exception of Germany, is larger in the more prosperous countries. In particular, the larger the extent of welfare provisions in each country, the greater the participation of women as workers in welfare services and administration. For example, in Denmark and the Netherlands service sector employment is around 70 per cent, compared to 48 per cent in Greece and 44 per cent in Portugal. In countries with a larger service sector, women's participation in the labour market is made easier not only by the greater availability of jobs in this sector, but also by this sector's providing personal and social services, some of which would otherwise be shouldered by families, and by women within them. In these countries a greater portion of what traditionally has been women's family work has been transformed into women's paid work.[2]

The comparative picture is complicated by two additional factors. First, some countries with a low overall women's activity rate, such as Italy, not only have a higher percentage of women working full-time, but also have a lower gender gap in earnings than countries, such as Denmark, where women's activity rate is almost double. Secondly, in countries with a lower activity rate of women and high rates of unemployment, such as Spain and Italy, a substantial number of women work in the informal sector. In these countries, women in employment may have greater difficulty in balancing the demands of family and work, because of a lack of social services and because of a longer working day. In addition, a higher proportion of working women are vulnerable to labour market and life-course risks because they do not benefit from the social protection granted to formal workers. Their economic security, particularly, but not only, in old age, remains highly dependent on their attachment to a husband.

Irrespective of these important differences, in all the industrialised countries it is mothers with young children who have most increased their labour force participation, and the number of families in which both parents hold a regular part-time or full-time job is growing (Jallinoia, 1989; Saraceno, 1992). In Japan, "working wives" outnumbered full-time housewives for the first time in 1983 (Carney and O'Kelly, 1990). Table 3.1 shows the level of employment participation of mothers, both married and alone. This phenomenon, which reverses the trend of the 1950s and 1960s, when young mothers were the largest group of women outside the labour force, has a number of causes:

- First, young women are on average better educated than older women, aspire to better jobs, and have grown up in the expectation of gender equality.

- Secondly, the experience of growing male unemployment, and the resultant weakening of the "male breadwinner" role, is rendering the dual worker family a normal strategy for maintaining economic security, not only for women but for households.

- Finally, young mothers are motivated to enter and remain in the labour force by the greater instability of marriage, and therefore of lifelong attachment to a male breadwinner. Holding a job is an insurance for oneself and one's children against the uncertainty of marriage.

The growing labour force participation of women is not only changing women's lives, but also family and wider kinship ties; in particular, it affects the availability of women to provide care. This has hitherto been the assumption underlying both the division of labour within the family and the division of responsibilities between government and the family which has shaped modern welfare states.

Table 3.1. **Percentage employed full-time and part-time (less than 30 hours per week), for married/cohabiting mothers, and lone mothers, most recent available data**

		Married/cohabiting mothers				Lone mothers			
		Full-time	Part-time	All employed	% of employed who work full-time	Full-time	Part-time	All employed	% of employed who work full-time
Australia	1994	24	32	56	43	23	20	43	53
Austria	1993	28	18	46[1]	61	43	15	58[1]	74
Belgium	1992	36	22	61	59	52	16	68	76
Denmark	–	64	20	84	76	59	10	69	86
Finland	1993	62	8	70	89	61	4	65	94
France	1992	49	20	68	72	67	15	82	82
Germany (reunited)[2]	1992	21	20	41	51	28	12	40	70
Greece[3]	–	–	–	32	–	–	–	23	–
Ireland	1993	29	12	41	71	58	11	69	84
Italy	1993	17[4]	20[4]	54[4]	31[4]	53[5]	34[6]	87[7]	61
Japan	1993	32	13	45	71	61	13	73	82
Luxembourg	1992	13	39	52	25	16	24	40	40
Netherlands	1994	31	27	58	53	17	10	27	63
New Zealand	1991	40	37	77	52	44	17	61	72
Norway	1991	48	7	55	87	43	7	50	86
Portugal[8]	1991	–	–	38	–	–	–	68	–
Spain (Madrid region)	1991	–	–	–	–	41	29	70	59
Sweden	1994	42	38	80	53	17	24	41	41
United Kingdom	1990-92	21	41	62	34	47	24	70	59
United States	1992	45	19	64	70	47	13	60	78

1. Excludes 13 per cent of married/cohabiting mothers and 20 per cent of lone mothers who are on parental leave.
2. 36+ hours.
3. Information not available in this form, but 51 per cent of women in likely age group were economically active and 5 per cent of working women worked part-time.
4. For married/cohabiting women with or without dependent children (1992).
5. Including self-employed.
6. Including working for family.
7. Includes self-employed who may work full-time or part-time.
8. If the definition of lone mothers was restricted to single, separated and divorced women (to counter the bias resulting from the disproportionate number of widowed women in the Portuguese definition of lone mothers), Portugal would have a much higher level of lone mothers in paid work.

Source: Bradshaw et al. (1996).

Growing instability of marriage and the father-child relationship

Marital instability, with its resultant one-parent families, is not a new phenomenon. Only during the 20th century has the sudden death of a parent-spouse at a young age ceased to be a common event, even in the most affluent regions of the world (Anderson, 1985). In most of the industrialised nations, with the possible exception of the Scandinavian countries and the United States, the rate of family break-up today, due to separation and divorce, is far lower than that a century ago arising from the death of the husband or wife. However, while divorce and separation were permitted in many countries in the past, they did not occur as frequently as they do today.[3]

The growing instability of marriage due to desertion, separation and divorce today must be read against this background. While separation and divorce affect only a minority of all children even in countries with high divorce rates (Duncan and Rodgers 1990; Kiernan and Wicks, 1990), they are leading to a growing proportion of children living with only one parent, and to a growing number of women acting as the only, or main, responsible parent both for care and for maintenance. National levels of lone parenthood vary: children in Canada, Great Britain, Sweden and the United States are more likely to be affected than those in France or Germany, and far more likely than in Italy, Portugal or Spain. Nonetheless, the trends are similar everywhere in the industrialised world, including Central and Eastern Europe.

The proportion of children living in one-parent households in the United States rose by a factor of 2.5 between 1960 and 1986; by 1986 nearly one child in four was living with only one parent, the highest proportion in the industrialised countries. By the mid-1980s, of all families with children, 17 per cent were one-parent families in Sweden, 15 per cent in Canada, 14 per cent in Denmark and the United Kingdom, around 13 per cent in France and Germany, between 10 and 12 per cent in Belgium, Luxembourg and the Netherlands, between 5 and 10 per cent in Ireland, Italy, Portugal and Spain, around 7 per cent in Japan and less than 5 per cent in Greece (US Bureau of Census, 1990; Kiernan and Wicks, 1990; Kamerman and Kahn, 1989). In Czechoslovakia the figure was close to 11 per cent (Kroupovà, 1988).[4]

If the rate of separation and divorce is the main factor in the increase in the proportion of lone parent families in recent years,[5] the growth of the proportion of children born outside marriage is an important secondary factor. With the exception of the Mediterranean countries, the number of children born to unmarried mothers has increased substantially in recent decades:[6] for example, in the United Kingdom one-third of all births are to unmarried mothers, in Ireland one in six. The proportion is also high in the United States and in the Scandinavian countries, although in the latter a substantial proportion are born to cohabiting parents (Roussel, 1989; Commission of the European Communities, 1994). It is also noticeable that the likelihood of lone parenthood at some stage appears greater where there has been early child-bearing, whether in or out of marriage.

In the late 1980s, lone parent families were estimated to represent 10-15 per cent of all families with dependent children in the OECD countries, with the exception of Ireland, Japan and Spain, where the proportion was below 10 per cent (OECD, 1990). However, the proportion of all families which pass through a lone-parent phase is higher. Over 90 per cent of non-widow, lone-parent families are headed by the mother. Lone-parent families may, therefore, be more accurately defined as lone-mother families.

In all countries lone mother families tend to be poorer than two-parent families, notwithstanding that in most countries the proportion of lone mothers holding a job is higher than that of married women in two-parent households. The greater risk of poverty experienced by lone parent families arises from a number of factors:

– Firstly, there is only one adult to provide the care and income which in two-parent households are provided by two. This renders it more difficult for the lone parent to balance the demands of caring and work, constraining the range of employment options. This is particularly the case if child-care services are scarce, of low quality or too costly. Lone-parent families, in fact, are a new and specific kind of one-earner family, different from two-parent ones.

– Secondly, no-longer or never-cohabiting fathers often contribute only a fraction of the cost of children, irrespective of their own income level. There is a strong tendency for absent fathers not to acknowledge their financial obligations towards their children after their relationship with the mother has ended (Festy, 1988; Seltzer, 1994).

– Thirdly, lone mothers' chances in the labour market are often constrained not only by their present need to balance caring and income demands, but by their past investment in marriage and child-raising, and by the persistence of occupational segregation on the basis of gender (De Singly, 1987).

The higher risk of poverty incurred by lone parents thus arises largely from the gender division of labour and responsibilities within marriage, and from the expectations this encourages at the level of social behaviour and at the level of labour market and social policies. At the same time, it is also a "side-effect" of the growth of dual-earner families, in so far as marital instability is highest where the proportion of women in the labour force is higher. The highest proportion of lone-parent families which experience poverty, however, and risk to remain poor for a longer time, is found among unmarried mothers who do not cohabit with the father of their children (OECD, 1990). In this case, poverty is not only the consequence of lack of child support and of the difficulty in balancing caring and work responsibilities, but often also of lack of education and training, which render it more difficult for mothers to find jobs which are suitable both from the point of view of income and from that of time schedules, as well as to find adequate and affordable child care.

Even where poverty can be avoided, lone mothers face other disadvantages. They must carry the dual responsibility of being the main breadwinner and the main carer in a labour market where breadwinners are usually perceived as being free from caring responsibilities, and in relation to other social organisations which often continue to take for granted the flexibility and availability of a mother's time (e.g. the time schedule of schools, the offer of child-care services, the time schedule of shops, public offices, etc.).

There also appears to be a general weakening of the father-child tie with growing marital instability. In contemporary societies, while the mother-child bond seems to become stronger, the father-child bond is on the contrary becoming weaker, in so far as many fathers seem to remain attached to children, and to feel obligations towards them, only when they live with their mother. Thus, it seems more likely that a man will feel obligations towards the children of his new companion rather than towards his biological children (Jensen, 1992; Seltzer, 1994; Marsiglio, 1995; Arendell, 1995). This phenomenon is related to the gender division of labour and responsibilities within marriage, in so far as fathers define their responsibilities towards their children mainly in terms of bread-winning, not of caring, and allow their relationship with their children to be mediated by their mother.[7]

Marital instability and the growth of lone-parent families confront social policies with two questions in relation to family and governmental obligations towards children: who should care for the children? and who should support them? Answers differ between countries, both with regard to the degree, and manner to which government is willing to help lone mothers to shoulder the dual responsibility as breadwinner and as carer (offering income support, or care support, or both), and with regard to the degree to which government either enforces or substitutes for fathers' obligations. These differences directly affect the welfare of children involved, as well as that of their mothers.

Reduced fertility

In most industrialised countries the fertility rate is well below replacement level. In some countries where the level of fertility is now lowest it continues to decrease, as in Italy, Japan, Portugal and Spain, while in others, such as France and Sweden, which were first to fall below replacement level in recent years, a reversal of this trend is seen. Up until the 1970s, the level of fertility was negatively related to the level of women's participation in the labour force and their level of education. Within the last twenty years, this association has been almost reversed in inter-country comparisons: the fertility rate is now lowest in countries where women's participation in the labour force is lowest[8] and some countries which have a high level of labour participation by women, such as Sweden, also have the highest levels of fertility. This must be due not only to cultural differences, but also to the different ways in which national policies deal with family obligations and have responded to the growth in female employment.

Notwithstanding these national differences in trends, in all industrialised countries reduced fertility, together with the lengthening of life, has changed the experience of childhood on the one hand, and the form of inter-generational ties on the other. There are more grandparents than grandchildren. Children now have a greater chance of having two or three generations of adults in their family network than of having two or three siblings or cousins in their own generation.

This phenomenon is usually debated either from the point of view of inter-generational redistribution, through the pension system, or from the point of view of the cost of children and policies aimed at supporting fertility. It is less debated from the point of view of the redefinition of children's experience in growing up. The fact that children are likelier to have very few other children in their immediate kin network should prompt a reflection on child-care services and on the role of the school in socialisation. Child-care services can no longer be viewed only in terms of support to working mothers. They are also a means of allowing both parents and children to share experiences which otherwise may no longer be found easily within the kin network. Particularly, they offer children the experience of a peer group where children at slightly different stages of development are present: an experience once common within families with three or more children, but now increasingly rare. Analogous arguments may be offered in the case of the school, which for children and adolescents has become the main social space in which they can meet, compare and share experiences.

Another consequence of reduced fertility which is not sufficiently reflected in policy debates is that the next generation of elderly people, if and when it becomes frail, will be less likely to have daughters and daughters-in-law available to provide care: partly because more women are in the labour force, but mainly because they will simply be less numerous. Even in those countries, such as Japan, where many elderly people still live with the next generation, the new cohorts entering old age may find that their own fertility behaviour has restricted dramatically the pool of children among whom to choose to live, or by whom to be chosen.

This imbalance will be all the greater as the number of the elderly is increasing in absolute and not just relative terms, due to the lengthening of life. At the same time increasing marital instability is weakening expectations of continuity in inter-generational relationships: sons- and daughters-in-law may no longer feel an obligation to support parents-in-law when their own marriage has ended.

AGEING OF THE POPULATION

Demographic ageing arises from reduced fertility rather than from rising life expectancy. Yet, longer average life has a great impact on inter-generational relationships within the family.

On the one hand, higher life expectancies mean that more elderly people live longer and better lives. This implies that the elderly must not be conceptualised as implicitly needy or burdensome. On the contrary, just as longer life and better health in older age are prompting a redefinition of the ageing process in relation to employment, so it should with regard to family relations (see Laslett, 1989). The elderly may be and often are a resource for younger generations, both in terms of supporting their children well into adulthood, and in terms of offering care for their fewer grandchildren.

Dependence typically arises only in a few years of the period of life which we call "old age", and affects only a small proportion of the elderly at any one time. Yet when it occurs it is highly costly in terms of health care and professional services, and in demands on social care and relationships. Recent research in Italy has indicated that 16.4 per cent of all the elderly suffer from some kind of disability (ISTAT, 1994). There is in all industrialised countries a general belief that children have an obligation to care for their needy elderly parents, even if they are not on good terms (Leseman and Martin, 1993), although this obligation is only expressed in law in a few. Moreover, in all industrialised countries, not only the most "family-centred" family members are the main providers of care (Sundström, 1994; Moen and Forest, 1995). The presence of frail elderly relatives has a considerable impact on the family network, imposing constraints both on economic and time resources (although the degree to which all or part of the provision or cost of care is assumed by central or local government makes a great difference).

Research has indicated that family care-givers are mostly women (Finch and Groves, 1983; Finch, 1989; Ungerson, 1989; Facchini and Scortegagna, 1993): daughters, daughters-in-law, grand-daughters, nieces, but particularly wives. Given the age differential between spouses, and the greater life expectancy of women, family care-giving to a frail elderly person is largely performed by an elderly wife (although there are also a smaller number of elderly husbands providing care). "Family care", through a spouse, is therefore more available to frail elderly men than to frail elderly women. In Italy, for instance, 58.6 per cent of men aged over 80 live with a spouse, while 20.8 per cent live alone, compared to 12 per cent of women aged over 80 who live with a spouse and 50.4 per cent who live alone. Policies which assume that "families" will be available to provide care may therefore overlook the burden they are allocating to elderly women.[9] Moreover, elderly women are and will be likely to be exposed to higher risks of not receiving needed care. Given the interplay between the gender division of labour, women's greater life expectancy and the gender age differential within marriage, elderly women, in fact, are more likely than older men to be widowed and to have lower incomes. This might change with the cohorts which are not young; but it will be true for a number of cohorts entering old age in the near future.

When a spouse is not available, caring is performed mostly by other female kin. Since in all the industrialised countries, with the partial exception of Japan, the most common family form has for some time been the nuclear family, elderly couples and elderly single people often live by themselves out of their own choice. If and when they become frail, caring by kin involves a number of changes, negotiations and arrangements which are underestimated by policies which stress the primacy of family obligations. Adult daughters and daughters-in-law are now fewer in number, and have their time divided between their own family and work obligations, and also normally live in a different household, and often in a different town or city, from that of the elderly person needing care. A study in Italy has shown that 45 per cent of all lone elderly receive help from kin in the form of health and body care, as well as household chores, compared to about 15-20 per cent of all the elderly receiving this kind of support (ISTAT, 1994). Even when the person needing care now lives in the same household, this has often necessitated the reorganisation of the caring person's household and family life, and of the cared-for person's life, sense of privacy and autonomy and social relationships.

Research has indicated that in countries where family obligations are more binding, the family network of elderly people is more dense, but that their overall social network is reduced (Hollinger and Haller, 1990; Lecchini et al., 1995). The frail elderly in these countries may be able to rely more on their kin, but are more exclusively dependent upon them. Where they have no kin available, they are left with few social resources.

FAMILY OBLIGATIONS AND SOCIAL POLICIES

There are variations between countries in the way the trends described above have been experienced, and variations in the ways that national policies have responded. These are accounted for partly by differences in national labour markets and economies, and partly by differences in religious, political and family cultures. Particularly relevant are the assumptions concerning gender relations and inter-generational solidarity that are implied in the different social arrangements and national welfare regimes: we might say in national concepts and embodiments of social citizenship.

Assumptions about gender relations in social policies

Gender relations have until recently been absent from most analyses of welfare policies and welfare models.[10] The concept of social rights which informed the development of welfare states, and which stemmed from the labour and social-democratic tradition, was focused more on men as (full-time, stable) workers, enabling them to exercise civil and political rights, than it was on overcoming the social and economic inequalities which derived from the gender division of labour. In this section I consider the effect of in-built gender assumptions in three social policy areas: child care and parental leave; care for disabled and frail elderly people; and the design of social security systems.

Child care and parental leave policies

Even social policies which have addressed women specifically, such as maternity leave and child care, have their origins in the view that, one the one hand, the ability to give birth is a weakness in the ideal worker, and, on the other hand, that the mother's exclusive responsibility for caring for her children is part of the natural order of things.

These assumptions are mirrored in social arrangements and policies in most industrialised countries. For example, a study in 1988 of 12 EU countries showed that, with one national exception, fathers of children under 4 years old were taking almost no part in child care, irrespective of the mother's working status. Only in Denmark was "a high degree of joint responsibility towards children" reported (Phillips and Moss, 1988, p. 4). Given this lack of fathers' involvement, it is therefore the availability of good and inexpensive child care that affects the labour market participation of mothers with pre-school children.

One conclusion to the 1988 study was that "the single biggest child-care problem in the Common Market is simply the lack of it.[11] Most European working parents cannot choose to go out to work in the secure knowledge that their children will be well cared-for" (op. cit., p. 15). However, the term "mothers" should be substituted for "parents": fathers are rarely hampered from entering the labour market because of a lack of child-care services. Mothers, on the other hand, may be accused of "abandoning" their children to child-care services, and of shifting their duties and the resulting costs to the collectivity. Their social rights, as workers and as citizens, are therefore less institutionalised and legitimate than the long-acknowledged workers' rights to sick pay and health care. The situation is no better in the United States and Canada, where only 5 per cent and 1 per cent respectively of the under two-year olds and 2 per cent and 35 per cent of the three- to four-year-olds are in publicly-funded child care. The figures for Australia are 2 per cent and 26 per cent (Kamerman and Kahn, 1991, 1994a, 1994b; Gornick et al., 1996). In these latter countries, and in the United Kingdom, most child care is provided outside the state sector. In Australia there are low-income subsidies and in the United Kingdom a "free area" within the in-work benefit Family Credit, both designed to support access to child care, as a different strategy to direct provision.

Policies concerning maternity and parental leave differ widely between countries, as do the degree of, and criteria for, compensation for lost wages. A study of EU countries published in 1989 found that the Netherlands, Portugal and the United Kingdom had the shortest statutory ante-natal and post-natal leave, while Italy had the longest, followed by France, Spain and Luxembourg (Commission of the European Communities, 1989). Since then there has been an extension of rights in some countries, including the United Kingdom, following the EU's Pregnant Worker's Directive. However, even in Italy, which appears very generous on the statutory level, many working mothers have in fact no entitlement, either because they work in the informal labour market or because they are self-employed, and some full-time employees, such as housekeepers and domestic servants, have less leave entitlement and very reduced compensation. Australia and Canada also have mandatory paid leave, although in Australia it covers only a fraction of working women (about 10 per cent). In the United States it is not mandatory and it covers about 25 per cent of working women (Gornick et al., 1996).

Some form of parental leave entitlement was identified in 12 out of 14 EU countries studied in 1993. In Ireland and the United Kingdom, however, there is no provision for workers' parental duties and family responsibilities beyond those around birth (Pillinger, 1992, pp 26-29). Since this lack is coupled with a general scarcity of child-care provisions, mothers in these two countries are particularly hard-put to maintain any continuity of employment while their children are young.[12] In the United States entitlement either to parental (extended) or to paternity leave is not present, although labour contracts may provide them. The same occurs in Canada. In Australia both extended leave and paternity leave are available, although only for those who are covered under publicly-mandated maternity benefits (Gornick et al., 1996).

The level of labour-market participation by women reflects not simply the age and number of children and availability of child-care services, but the entire specific national mix of cultural patterns, social behaviours and available alternative forms of child care. A 1992 study proposed that the European Union countries fall into four categories in this respect:

- Those in which having children does not influence the mothers' activity rate, because women are expected to be in the labour market and there is a high provision of child-care services. This is the case in the Scandinavian countries.

- Those in which having children has a minimal impact on the female activity rates. This is the case with France, where the level of employment of mothers does not fall noticeably until the third child. The same is true of Italy in recent years, although with overall lower activity rates of employment as well as much lower fertility rates. In Italy it would appear that young women are reducing their fertility to a minimum, in order to enter and remain in the labour force.[13]

- Those in which the difficulties of combining family life and career result in part-time work. This is the case with Germany[14] and the United Kingdom.

- Those in which women's activity rate drops with the birth of the first child, as in Ireland and the Netherlands.

The activity rate of lone mothers, as shown in Table 3.1, appears to depend even more than that of married mothers on both cultural assumptions and social policy provisions. It is lower in those countries such as Australia, Germany, the Netherlands, the United Kingdom and, to a lesser extent, the United States, where income support policies suggest that it is legitimate for mothers to stay at home to take care of their children, and to receive, therefore, economic support when in need. All these countries have income support policies specifically designed to help low-income lone mothers. It should be pointed out, however, that in recent years in these same countries there has been a growing concern about the development of long-term benefit dependence, leading to more or less dramatic shifts in policies: through limiting the number of years a lone mother may benefit from income support, as in the Netherlands and the new United States welfare reform bill, or through promoting education and training programmes which should help these women to enter the labour market, as in Australia and Germany, or through changes in benefit rules in order to encourage working while avoiding the poverty trap, as in Australia and the United Kingdom.

In a recent overview of the institutional framework of family obligations in the European Union, Millar and Warman (1996) suggest that, even in countries in the first of the above categories, there has been a recent shift to home child care rather than care in centres, as a cost-containment measure. In Denmark, a home-care supplement has been introduced and extended parental leave provided for parents who give up work to care for children at home. Similar provisions apply in Sweden and Finland. Since it is mostly women who take up this opportunity, particularly within the least-skilled groups, concern has developed about the implications of such a trend for gender equality. These provisions, as so often with measures supporting mothers, may be read either as a measure enabling women to deal more flexibly with their work and family obligations or, on the contrary, as a measure encouraging women to remain at home (Fagnani, 1994).

Care for disabled and frail elderly people

A similar analysis may be developed with regard to the provision of care for disabled or frail elderly people. Informal care, and particularly more intensive informal care, is predominantly provided by women in all industrialised countries. However, the level of public obligation differs quite substantially between countries and has a considerable impact on the resources and rights of those needing care and on the constraints on women as family carers. More generally, it has been pointed out that informal family care of the ill or infirm is a tremendous social resource; yet, the absence of policies or institutional supports for the "hidden patient", i.e. the caregivers of older or chronically ill relatives, may have the effect of draining this very resource (Moen and Forest, 1995).

Millar and Warman (1996), for instance, have proposed a four-way categorisation of EU countries on the basis of how they conceptualise family obligations to care for disabled adults and the frail elderly:

- In the first group, which includes Italy, Portugal and Spain, there are wide-reaching legal obligations between kin-members to support each other in both economic and caring terms. Thus, in Italy home-help is provided by the municipality under a dual test of means, such that it is provided only to disabled or frail individuals with both a low income and no close kin, particularly female kin, available to provide care.[15]

- In the second group, which comprises Austria, Belgium, France, Germany, Greece and Luxembourg (to which may be added Japan outside the EU), there are legal obligations on the next generation to support the elderly. In some of these countries, however, the costs of long-term care which are not covered by health insurance can be paid through local social assistance if the individual cannot meet these costs.[16] However, recent changes in Austria and Germany, where the social insurance systems now include compulsory "care insurance", have reduced these obligations, partly in response to growing public expectations of welfare services.

- In the third group, comprising Ireland and the United Kingdom (to which may be added the United States), there are no legal obligations on kin to provide or pay for the care of frail or disabled adults. However, access to nursing homes is means-tested against the disabled or elderly person's assets, and other family members may feel obliged to meet some of these costs themselves. As Millar and Warman (1996) observe, this causes discontent, as public attitudes are different from countries in the first two groups, such that "(...) paying for the care of even elderly parents is not generally accepted as being 'natural' in the United Kingdom". The view that providing constant care is a role for welfare services rather than the family may also grow in countries where family obligations traditionally have been deeper. There is evidence of this process happening in the past in, for example, Norway (Daatland, 1990).

- The fourth group comprises the Scandinavian countries and the Netherlands, in which public obligations to adults with care needs are made explicit and where support is directed to the individual rather than the family. Although even in these countries adult children, and particularly daughters, are the primary informal care-givers, older people regard access to public services as an entitlement, independent from their family situation, while help received from family members is seen as an extra contribution deriving from choice.

This pattern has been somewhat complicated in recent years by the growth of payments for care (Evers *et al.*, 1994). There are differences between countries where payments go to care-givers and countries where they go to care-receivers. However, there is a more fundamental difference between situations in which payments for care are a substitute for other, more expensive, forms of service,[17] and situations where payments have the aim of granting more rights to care-givers and care-recipients, while promoting more family involvement.[18] Yet, in all payment-for-care schemes, it is mostly women who are called upon to act as paid care-givers. This form of support may therefore reinforce the traditional gender division of family caring obligations precisely at the moment when there are fewer daughters available to care.

It should be pointed out that while payments for care performed by kin are being introduced in many countries, time off for caring for handicapped or frail elderly kin has difficulty in finding its way in social security and leave policy, although various countries have started some usually very limited experimentation, mostly confined to public sector employees.

The design of social security systems

The way in which social security systems are linked to status in the labour force and to family status has a strong influence on women's participation in the labour market and on their degree of economic autonomy.

Many national pension systems, such as those of Belgium, Italy, the Netherlands and the United Kingdom, in the past adopted different statutory pensionable ages for men and women. It indicates the tendency of pension systems originally to be designed around an assumption about the "normal" age differential between husband and wife, and of the wife's dependence on the wage-earner. It also indicates the wider tendency of pension systems to be designed largely to protect the future income status of full-time regular employees. Equal opportunities legislation, as, for instance, within the EU, has initiated a process of equalising pension ages.

Women remain less likely to be able to earn an occupational pension. Women's interrupted employment patterns, and the fact that more women than men are employed in the irregular labour force, reduce their chances of having a significant "second tier" pension from their employment. In some private pension regimes, for example the United Kingdom, women with rights to an occupational pension who become widowed must decide which pension to take: their own, or a survivor's pension deriving from their husband's contributions and work record. Many working women therefore pay contributions from which they will not benefit.

Since in most industrialised countries there is no universal non-contributory flat-rate public pension irrespective of work history, many women in old age at present must rely either on a social assistance pension, which is often very low, or on a survivor's pension. Given the increasing instability of marriage the latter, however, can become unavailable when it is too late for a woman to start her own contributory record. At the same time, in countries where the survivor's pension is paid to the surviving spouse irrespective of her or his income and contributory history, there may be women (as well as, to a lesser degree, men) who may benefit from two pensions.[19]

Income supplementation for those of working age is normally also paid in a way that reinforces the economic dependence of women. In most industrialised countries income supplements are paid on a family base and to a family head – that is, there is no individual entitlement to income support. Women therefore do not have access to an individual income even when the family unit is entitled to social assistance. At the same time, they are discouraged from seeking paid employment, as this will be taken into account when testing the family's entitlement to support. It has been argued by Holland (1993) that "the institution of the family payment – one payment for the entire family, comprising a payment for the main claimant and his (in a few cases her) dependents – is probably the single greatest testament to the state's unwillingness to provide an independent income to women when they are married".

The obligation to provide for children

The increasing presence of working mothers also raises a different, although intertwined, social policy issue, which, together with gender relations, is central to the debate about the boundaries between the family and the State: that of the formal obligations of parents towards their children.

In all countries parents are defined as the main, and natural, responsible actors towards their children. Yet, the specific boundaries and contents of these obligations vary quite widely both at the level of social values and at the level of legislation. In addition, there is great variation in the degree to which government may enforce, or substitute for, parental obligations.

Values differ in relation to public responsibilities towards children. The offer of public child-care services could be viewed as an interference with family autonomy and responsibility; alternatively, an effective absence of such services could be viewed as indicating a degree of social irresponsibility towards children and parents, or even neglect of the individual rights of the child. These varying responses reflect different underlying ideas about parental responsibilities and the rights of children, but also about the operation of the principle of subsidiarity by the State.

Subsidiarity in state-family relations may be interpreted as government having the right to intervene only in exceptional cases in which the family is demonstrably inadequate or unfit to care for its dependent members; alternatively, it may be seen as indicating an obligation on government to provide support for families to enable them to fulfil their obligations. The latter interpretation may in turn be used to justify a range of specific policy options, *e.g.* enabling women with young children to stay at home; enabling women to reconcile employment and family responsibilities; or enabling both parents to share in child-care responsibilities.

In the industrialised countries, parents' duties of guardianship and care for children generally cease at the latest at the age of 18-19, when children are deemed "adults". But while in some countries, *e.g.* the Scandinavian countries, the United Kingdom and the United States, this also marks the end of any legally-enforced financial obligation, in other countries the parent's legal financial obligations can continue until the child is "self-supporting", and in some countries may continue indefinitely. In Austria, Belgium, Germany, Italy[20] and Luxembourg, for instance, a child unable to support him or herself, even if able-bodied, can claim support from his parents throughout his or her life. This means that, for example, if adult children claim social assistance, the parents may be legally required to contribute.[21] On the contrary, in Denmark, Finland and Sweden, students are entitled to financial support in their own right, and without any account being taken of parental income, at 18-20 years of age, when their parents lose entitlement to child allowances.

A further distinction arises between countries in which parents' financial obligations are actively supported by government, and those in which they are only expected and enforced. Thus, in the majority of EU countries, government shoulders a part of the cost of a child up to a certain age (legal majority, or the end of full-time schooling), through child allowances or child benefit schemes. In other countries, such as Greece, Italy, Spain and the United States, public support is only provided to parents in low-income groups.

Bradshaw *et al.* (1993) ranked the industrialised countries using an index of average income support offered to families with children (including child allowances, housing allowances, health care costs, etc.). This indicated that countries are clustered in identifiable groups which do not always correspond to those used in comparisons of welfare state regimes (see also Wilensky, 1990). As Table 3.2 indicates, three clusters may be identified by declining order of average level of financial support to families:

– Belgium, France and Luxembourg cluster with the Scandinavian countries as the most generous;

– Germany and the Netherlands are grouped with Australia and the United Kingdom;

– Greece, Ireland, Italy, Portugal and Spain are grouped with Japan and the United States.

It is noticeable that those countries in which the subsidiarity principle seems to be interpreted as low direct public support are also those in which both women's labour market participation and (with the exception of Ireland) rate of fertility are lowest.

Table 3.2. **Average ranking of selected OECD countries on the basis of family supports**

	Before housing expenses		After housing expenses
Sweden	3.6	France	3.7
Luxembourg	3.7	Luxembourg	3.8
Norway	4.3	Norway	4.8
France	4.5	Belgium	5.1
Belgium	4.8	Sweden	5.3
Denmark	7.2	Denmark	7.0
Germany	7.6	United Kingdom	7.6
United Kingdom	9.3	Germany	8.0
Australia	9.7	Netherlands	9.4
Netherlands	10.1	Australia	9.6
Portugal	11.1	Italy	10.3
Italy	11.4	Portugal	11.3
Japan	11.8	Spain	12.8
United States	12.1	Ireland	13.1
Ireland	13.0	Japan	13.4
Spain	14.1	Greece	14.3
Greece	14.1	United States	14.9

Note: Rankings have been obtained taking the average of 36 rankings for each of 36 family types. Each ranking goes from 1 for the most generous country to 17 for the less numerous. Thus, when household expenses are taken into account France is ranked first, with an average ranking of 3.7, while the United States is 17th, with an average ranking of 14.9.

Source: Bradshaw *et al.* (1993).

A further indicator of public responsibility towards children is the degree and type of regulation of child support when one parent, usually the father, is absent. It is a particularly crucial issue given the increasing fragility of marriage and of the father-child relationship. Policies in this respect have developed along two, sometimes alternative, sometimes integrated directions: first, that of strengthening and enforcing of fathers' responsibilities, and, secondly, that of partial substitution of public support for that of the absent father.

Legislation and practice in many countries tend to encourage, or enforce, the father's responsibility towards his children, irrespective of his relationship with the mother. Thus, in the event of separation and divorce, joint custody may be preferred, or even enforced (e.g. in France and California), rather than custody by one parent. This policy is supported by the need to sustain a continuing relationship between father and children, and by the belief that, if fathers are given direct responsibility for their children, they are more likely to continue freely to support them. Research in the United States (Seltzer, 1991) generally confirms this, indicating that joint legal custody encourages similarities between the way divorced fathers and fathers in two-parent households invest in their children. Although qualitative research finds that occasionally fathers with joint custody fail to contribute to the child's support above that which they spend on "their" share of custody, irrespective of the mothers' economic situation (Arendell, 1995),[22] the overall positive outcome of this arrangement should not be undervalued.

A different way to enforce the father's responsibility is that recently adopted in Australia and the United Kingdom, where recent legislation has defined the father's financial obligations and a public agency has taken on the task of enforcing it (Stuart, 1991; Scheiwe, 1994). This approach may be criticised as being more focused on coercing fathers to do their duty (and obliging mothers to denounce "failing fathers", with possible conflict as a result), than on providing adequate support when fathers fail to do so. Yet, the question of how to enforce and support fathers' responsibility may not easily be overlooked.

The second policy line, that of partial substitution, does not deny the parents' (and specifically fathers') responsibility, but aims to extricate this issue from the personal relationship between the parents, and to focus directly on the need for material support, rather than on the identity of the ideal supporter(s). Therefore, in some countries, e.g. France, the Scandinavian countries and the United States, government provides material support where the father does not or cannot. The collection of the non-cohabitant parent's share of support is a public responsibility (either in all cases or in particularly conflictual cases). Further, in the United States objective criteria have been developed – first experimentally in Wisconsin and then extended to other states – to get the level of child support as a percentage of the noncohabitant parent's income. Thus, the level of child support is no longer left to negotiation between parties or to judges' discretion.

As Millar and Warman (1996) have concluded, "In examining the relationship between parents and children it is clear that there is no simple continuum from interventionist to non-interventionist approaches. Much seems to depend on whether the context for intervention is primarily one of family privacy or one of family support".

A NEW APPROACH TO FAMILY POLICIES

Family policies (or, more accurately, family-relevant policies) draw different boundaries between families, between individuals and families, and between the state and families. It has been seen that, in Italy, Spain and Portugal, legally-enforced obligations cross household boundaries to include a substantial number of family members (including those through marriage), while in France and Germany these obligations involve only the nuclear family (with the partial exception of parents and adult children, whose reciprocal obligations are deemed as lasting through life); and, in the Scandinavian and most Anglophone countries, most reciprocal family obligations cease once a young person reaches adulthood, and children may be perceived as having rights of their own, irrespective of their family membership (Therborn, 1993).

The precise role of government within each of these three broadly similar situations varies from country to country. It may positively enforce family obligations through legal means, or simply require them to be met by not providing any alternative supports, or offer positive help in meeting them. To see legal frameworks, public policies and social expectations as merely reflecting deeply-rooted national values is to overlook the political conflicts and negotiations which underlie them, and the specific policy history which has resulted in each current set of national conditions.

The industrialised countries are faced by the task of re-drawing these arrangements in the face of three-fold pressure:

- pressure from changing social values, *e.g.* about gender relations, and about trans-generational obligations;
- pressure from the increasing fragility of traditional forms of support, be this from marital and family arrangements or from the social security system;
- pressure from budget constraints.

Countries approach this task from different vantage points, with regard to the nature of their labour markets, and with regard to their political and social cultures, with the family values and expectations that these include. From this perspective, it is not surprising that those countries which have most relied on extended family solidarity and on a gendered division of labour, and which now experience severe budget constraints and higher unemployment rates, seek a solution in appealing to strengthened family solidarity. However, this approach may constrain family, and particularly female, choices, and perhaps therefore also constrain fertility, hence further aggravating the demographic imbalance. Alternative solutions appear difficult to articulate in these countries in a way which may gain the necessary social consensus for redesigning the social policy framework.

This "familistic" approach is less feasible in countries where extended family obligations are less supported by law and by social practice, and where gender relations are less asymmetrical. There are some tendencies in these countries towards a re-familisation of social obligations, *e.g.* with the growth of payments for care, but the strong culture of individual social rights and of gender equality necessitates that any re-definition of boundaries and obligations be carefully negotiated.

It has been proposed that a useful way of analysing welfare states is to assess to which degree economic and social rights are granted to individuals of all ages and family conditions or are *vice versa* contingent on family membership and circumstances. From this perspective, some authors have suggested that the concept of "de-familisation" might be useful, indicating "the terms and conditions under which people engage in families, and the extent to which they can uphold an acceptable standard of living independently of the (patriarchal) family" (McLaughlin and Glendinning, 1994, p. 65). As family obligations typically now rest on a smaller circle of family members, and on more fragile family ties, the extent of de-familisation may be as crucial for the welfare of individuals and families as is the strength of family obligations themselves.

De-familisation in this perspective does not imply a breaking of family bonds. On the contrary, it might be conceived as a means to support them by allowing individuals to undertake family responsibilities without being trapped in them; while at the same time avoiding the individual's life chances being all staked in his or her family circumstances or resources. To quote McLaughlin and Glendinning again, "The issue is not whether people are completely 'de-familised', but rather the extent to which packages of legal and social provisions have altered the balance of power between men and women, between dependents and non-dependents, and hence the terms and conditions under which people engage in familial or caring arrangements" (*op. cit.*, p. 66).

This focuses on the question of what "supporting the family" might mean. If it means enabling the family and its members to take care of each other, to shoulder the obligations they freely choose to enter, without at the same time creating power imbalances, over-dependence and closed exits, a degree of de-familisation could become a basis on which new forms of contract between the individual, the family and the state may be negotiated. By contrast, over-familisation of responsibilities and rights may result in over-burdening, thus causing further social problems, or in a growing refusal to assume family obligations, through (un)reproductive behaviour when young and through reluctance to fulfil obligations towards the elderly when older. From this perspective, Moen and Forest (1995, p. 827) suggest that the underlying goal of family policies should be "to foster competence and independence", allowing families and their individual members "to actively negotiate resources to develop their own adaptive strategies and retain maximum independence and autonomy at all stages of the life-course".

Within this approach, particular attention should be given to children and to families with children. Not only for demographic reasons, it is apparent that investment in the future and protection from the risk of poverty during the life-course due to lack of education, of needed professional and social skills, require that resources be invested in a sustained way in the younger generation, from early childhood on. This might require a shift in the balance of the social budget towards younger cohorts and younger families.

Finally it should be pointed out that families and governments are not the only relevant actors in this redrawing of boundaries and responsibilities. The labour market, enterprises, and trade unions also have a role in shaping a society which is more friendly to individuals – women, as well as men – with family responsibilities. From this point of view, the flexibilisation of the working time and of the working life might be perceived and negotiated as a means of meeting the needs both of workers and of enterprises.

NOTES

1. Together with this feminisation of employment there has been a feminisation of unemployment. In 1986 women accounted for 46 per cent of the unemployed in the EC countries, rising to 52 per cent in 1989 (Pillinger, 1992, p. 17). Women also account for a great share of the under-employed, the "casually employed" and the part-time employed (Women of Europe, Supplement 1992). Women are therefore more exposed than men to the vagaries of the market, and have greater economic dependence, either within their families or upon the welfare state.

2. Within services, as within industry, women remain segregated from men and concentrated in a narrow number of jobs. They are also likely to work in jobs which are lower skilled than men's and are often clustered in those manual and assembly line jobs which are most vulnerable to restructuring (Pillinger, 1992, pp. 46-47).

3. One exception is Japan, where one consequence of modernisation, up to the late 1970s, was increased marital stability, given the different rules concerning marriage and divorce applying in the past. But separation and divorce are now also increasing in Japan (Kumagai, 1983; Preston and Kono, 1988; Goode, 1993).

4. All these data must be read with caution, since different countries use different criteria both to define "a child's presence" in the family (on the basis of age) and to define one-parent households (see for instance Ermisch, 1990; Hantrais and Mangen, 1994).

5. Very recently, the average duration of marriages which end in divorce has been declining, so that the age of children involved tends to be lower. The likelihood of children being involved in a marriage break-up has diminished, as a larger share of marriages ending in divorce are now childless (Barbagli, 1990; Goode, 1993).

6. Unmarried mothers tend to be younger women, often teenagers. 10-18 per cent of all 15-19 year old females become pregnant in Czechoslovakia, Hungary and the United States, the countries with the highest teenage pregnancy rates in the industrialised world.

7. An indirect demonstration of this can be seen in the finding that the more fathers have been involved in child care during marriage or cohabitation, the less estranged they become once their relationship with their children's mother ends (Arendell, 1995).

8. With the exception of Ireland, which has both a low activity rate and the highest fertility in Europe, at about two children per woman.

9. It may also happen, as in Finland with the introduction of Informal Care Allowances, that caring elderly spouses are *de facto* excluded from receiving cash allowances for care. Finnish regulations require that an "informal care-giver" shall be under 65 (Millar and Warman, 1996).

10. A first attempt at comparing European welfare regimes from the point of view of women's experience may be found in Lewis (1993).

11. Services for children under 3 years old are particularly lacking, although in some countries, such as Portugal and the United Kingdom, services for older pre-school children are also scarce. For instance, in Italy more than 80 per cent of pre-school children aged three years and above are in kindergarten, while less than 10 per cent of those under 3 years old are in day care; there are wide local variations (Saraceno, 1990).

12. In 1992, 59 per cent of women employed worked part-time in the Netherlands, 33 per cent in the United Kingdom (Commission of the European Communities, 1994).

13. It should be kept in mind that in Italy there is a wide geographical variation both in fertility rates and in women's labour force participation: the fertility rate is lowest, and the labour force participation is highest, in the Centre-North, where child-care services are most numerous.

14. The former East and West Germanies had very different approaches to women's work and support for families. Child-care places for under-threes were available for less that 3 per cent of children in former West Germany but for 56 per cent of children in former East Germany, largely provided by the employer. Following unification,

child-care services in the eastern regions are being run-down, and the Western Germany model of child care for children under three – by the mother – is becoming predominant (Ostner, 1994).

15. It should be added that in some, at least, of these countries, totally disabled people receive an accompanying person indemnity which is not means tested, together with a means-tested public pension.

16. The same is true in some regions in Italy, if they formally renounce their rights to retrieve costs from "liable kin".

17. For example, social insurance benefits paid to care-receivers in Austria and Germany to allow them to buy support, or payments made to family care-givers in certain Italian regions on the condition they host an elderly relative.

18. For example, the case of the Swedish and Norwegian schemes, which employ family members, thus conferring rights such as pension contributions and sick leave, and where this recruitment of family members is integrated into a high level of service provision.

19. It is, for instance, the case of Italy, where in the late seventies the Constitutional Court declared it against the principle of equality that only male contributions could count towards building up survivors' benefits.

20. In Italy legally enforced financial obligations extend to adult children, parents, parents-in-law and siblings (including adult siblings).

21. Legally prolonged financial obligations towards children may be purely symbolic, if entrance to the labour market is not difficult and if the cost of higher education is low, *i.e.* heavily subsidised by local or central government. But when both youth unemployment and education costs are high, this obligation may increase substantially the cost of raising children. This seems to be the case, for instance, with Austria, Ireland, Italy, Portugal and Spain.

22. There is, however, some evidence that enforcing on principle joint custody may have perverse effects when one of the parents is abusive, or violent, thereby restricting the opportunity for the other parent to create a viable, independent life for (usually) herself and the children (Arendell, 1995).

BIBLIOGRAPHY

ANDERSON, M. (1985), "The emergence of the modern life cycle in Britain", *Social History*, Vol. 10:1, pp. 69-87.

ARENDELL, T. (1986), *Mothers and Divorce*, University of California Press, Berkeley.

ARENDELL, T. (1995), *Fathers and Divorce*, Sage, Thousand Oaks, California.

BARBAGLI, M. (1990), *Provando e riprovando*, il Mulino, Bologna.

BAWIN-LEGROS, B., GAUTHIER, A. and GUILLAUME, J.F. (1991), "Intérêt de l'enfant et paiement des pensions alimentaires après divorce en Belgique", *Population*, Vol. 4, pp. 855-890.

BRADSHAW, J., DITCH, J., HOLMES, H. and WHITEFORD, P. (1993), *Support for Children: A Comparison of Arrangements in Fifteen Countries*, HMSO, London.

BRADSHAW, J. et al. (1996), *The Employment of Lone Parents: A Comparison of Policy in 20 Countries*, Family Policy Studies Centre, London.

BURKHAUSER, R.V. and DUNCAN, G.J. (1989), "Economic risks of gender roles: income loss and life events over the life course", *Social Science Quarterly*, Vol. 70, pp. 3-23.

CARMIGNANI, F. and PRUNA, M.L. (1991), "Le donne nel mercato del lavoro. Vecchi problemi e nuove opportunità", *Sociologia del lavoro*, Vol. 43, pp 137-148.

CARNEY, L.S. and O'KELLY, C.G. (1990), "Women's work and women's place in the Japanese economic miracle", in K. Ward (ed.), *Women Workers and Global Restructuring*, ILR Press, Cornell University, Ithaca, N.Y.

COMMISSION OF THE EUROPEAN COMMUNITIES (1989), *Employment in Europe*, Luxembourg.

COMMISSION OF THE EUROPEAN COMMUNITIES (1990a), *Employment in Europe*, Luxembourg.

COMMISSION OF THE EUROPEAN COMMUNITIES (1990b), "The impact of the completion of the internal market on women in the European Community", Report prepared by P. Conroy-Jackson for the Equal Opportunities Unit, Brussels.

COMMISSION OF THE EUROPEAN COMMUNITIES (1993), *Employment in Europe*, Luxembourg.

COMMISSION OF THE EUROPEAN COMMUNITIES (1994), *Employment in Europe*, Luxembourg.

DAATLAND, S.O. (1990), "What are families for? On family solidarity and preference for help", *Ageing and Society*, Vol. 10, pp. 1-15.

DE SINGLY, F. (1987), *Fortune et infortune de la femme mariée*, PUF, Paris.

DUNCAN, G.J. and RODGERS, W. (1990), "Lone-parent families and their economic problems: transitory or persistent?", *Lone-parents Families: The Economic Challenge*, OECD, Paris, pp. 43-68.

ERMISCH, J.F. (1990), "Demographic aspects of the growing number of lone-parent families", *Lone Parents: The Economic Challenge*, OECD, Paris, pp. 27-42.

EUROPEAN PARLIAMENT (1990), Report of the Committee of Social Affairs, Employment and the Working Environment on the communication from the Commission on its Action Programme relating to the implementation of the Community Charter of fundamental social rights for workers – priorities for the period 1991-92, Brussels.

EUROSTAT (1985), *Labour Force Survey*, Statistical Office of the EC, Luxembourg.

EVERS, E., PIJL, M. and UNGERSON, C. (eds.) (1994), *Payments for Care: A Comparative Overview*, Avebury/Ashgate, Aldershot, United Kingdom.

FACCHINI, C. and SCORTEGAGNA, R. (1993), "Italy: alternatives to institutionalization and women's central role", in Leseman and Martin (eds.), pp. 33-69.

FAGNANI, J. (1994), "A comparison of family policies for working mothers in France and West Germany", in Hantrais and Mangen (eds.).

FESTY, P. (1988), "Après la séparation: diversité et stabilité des comportements", *Population*, Vol. 3, pp. 517-536.

FINCH, J. (1989), *Family Obligations and Social Change*, Routledge & Kegan Paul, London.

FINCH, J. and GROVES, D. (eds.) (1983), *A Labour of Love: Women, Work and Caring*, Routledge & Kegan Paul, London.

GARFINKEL, I. and McLANAHAN, G.B. (1990), *Single Mothers and their Children: A New American Dilemma*, Urban Institute Press, Washington, DC.

GARFINKEL, I. and McLANAHAN, S. (1990), "The effects of child support provisions of the Family Support Act of 1988 on child well-being", *Population Research and Policy Review*, Vol. 9, pp. 205-234.

GOODE, W. (1993), *World Changes in Divorce Patterns*, Yale University Press, Ann Arbor.

GORNICK, J.C., MEYERS, M.K. and ROSS, K.E. (1996), "Enabling the employment of mothers. Policy variations across fifteen welfare states", Luxembourg Income Study (LIS) Working Paper, June.

HANTRAIS, L. and MANGEN, S. (eds.) (1994), "Family policy and the welfare of women", *Cross-national Research Papers*, University of Loughborough, United Kingdom.

HOLLAND, S. (1993), "The European imperative: economic and social cohesion in the 1990s", Spokesman, Nottingham, United Kingdom.

HÖLLINGER, F. and HALLER, M. (1990), "Kinship and social networks", *European Sociological Review*, Vol. 6:2, pp. 103-124.

ISTAT (1994), *Indagine multiscopo sulle famiglie – La condizione degli anziani*, Rome.

JALLINOIA, R. (1989), "Women between family and employment", in K. Boh, M. Bak and C. Clason (eds.), *Changing Patterns of European Family Life: A Comparative Analysis of 14 European Countries*, Routledge, London, pp. 95-122.

JENSEN, A.M. (1992), "Changing gender roles as reflected in children's families", Paper presented at IUSSP Seminar on Gender and Family Change in Industrialized Countries, January 1992, Rome.

JOSHI, H. (1989), "The cash opportunity costs of childbearing: an approach to estimation using British data", *Population Studies*, Vol. 6.

KAMERMAN, S.B. (1995), "Gender role and family structure changes in the advanced industrialised west: implications for social policy", in K. McFate et al. (eds.), *Poverty, Inequality and the Future of Social Policy*, Russell Sage Foundation, New York, pp. 231-256.

KAMERMAN, S.B. and KAHN, A.J. (1989), "Single parent, female-headed families with children in Western Europe. Social change and response", *International Social Security Review*, Vol. XLII:1, International Social Security Association, Geneva.

KAMERMAN, S.B. and KAHN, A.J. (1991), "Government expenditure for children and their families in advanced industrialized countries, 1960-85", UNICEF, Innocenti Occasional Papers No. 20, Florence, Italy.

KAMERMAN, S.B. and KAHN, A.J. (1994*a*), *A Welcome for Every Child: Care, Education and Family Support for Infants and Toddlers in Europe*, Arlington, VA.

KAMERMAN, S.B. and KAHN, A.J. (1994*b*), *Social Policy and the Under 3s, Six Country Case Studies: A Resource for Policy Makers, Advocates and Scholars*, Gross National Studies Research Program, Columbia University, New York.

KIERNAN, K. and WICKS, M. (1990), *Family Change and Future Policy*, Family Policy Studies Centre, London.

KROUPOVÀ, A. (1988), "Perspectives of Czechoslovakia's family formation", *Childhood Implications for Child Care Policies,* Seminar report, European Center for Social Welfare Training and Research, Gananoque, Ontario, Canada, June 29-30.

KUMAGAI, F. (1983), "Changing divorce in Japan", *Journal of Family History*, Vol. 1, pp. 85-108.

KURZ, D. (1995), *For Richer, For Poorer: Mothers Confront Divorce*, Routledge, New York.

LANGAN, M. and OSTNER, I. (1991), "Gender and welfare: towards a comparative framework", in G. Room (ed.), *Towards a European Welfare State?*, School for Advanced Urban Studies, Bristol, pp. 127-150.

LASLETT, P. (1989), *A Fresh Map of Life: The Emergence of the Third Age*, Weidenfeld and Nicolson, London.

LECCHINI, L., MARSIGLIA, D. and BOTTAI, M. (1995), "Anziani e reti di relazioni sociali", *Continuità e discontinuità nei processi demografici. L'Italia nella transizione demografica*, SIS, Università degli Studi di Calabria, Cosenza, pp. 575-588.

LESEMAN, F. and MARTIN, C. (eds.) (1993), *Les personnes âgées. Dépendance, soins et solidarités familiales. Comparaisons internationales*, La Documentation française, Paris.

LEWIS, J. (ed.) (1993), *Women and Social Policies in Europe: Work, Family and the State*, Edward Elgar, Cheltenham, United Kingdom.

MACLEAN, M. (1990), "Lone-parent families: family law and income transfers", in OECD (1990), pp. 91-100.

MARSIGLIO, W. (1995), *Fatherhood. Contemporary Theory, Research and Social Policy*, Sage, Thousand Oaks, CA.

MARTIN, C. (1996), "Father, mother and the welfare state. Family and social transfers after marital breakdown", in *Journal of Social Policy*, Vol. 5:1, pp. 43-63.

MARTIN, V. (1996), "Protection sociale et protection par la famille en Europe du Sud: quelles specificités?", Paper presented at conference on "Comparing Southern Welfare States" organized by MIRE, Florence, February 1996.

MCLAUGHLIN, E. and GLENDINNING, C. (1994), "Paying for care in Europe: is there a feminist approach?", in L. Hantrais and S. Mangen (eds.).

MILLAR J. and WARMAN, A. (1996), *Defining Family Obligations in Europe. The Family, the State and Social Policy*, Report to the Joseph Rowntree Foundation, York, United Kingdom.

MOEN, P. and FOREST, K.B. (1995), "Family policies for an ageing society: moving to the twenty-first century", *The Gerontologist*, Vol. 35, No. 6, pp. 825-830.

OECD (1990), *Lone-parents Families: The Economic Challenge*, Social Policy Studies No. 8, Paris.

OECD (1994), *Caring for Frail Elderly People – New Directions in Care*, Social Policy Studies No. 14, Paris.

OECD (1995), *Employment Outlook*, Paris.

OSTNER, I. (1994), "Back to the fifties: gender and welfare in unified Germany", in *Social Politics*, Vol. I:1, pp. 32-60.

PHILLIPS, A. and MOSS, P. (1988), *Who Cares for Europe's Children?*, Report of the European Childcare Network, Commission of the European Communities, Brussels.

PILLINGER, J. (1992), *Feminising the Market*, MacMillan, London.

PRESTON, S.H. and KONO, S. (1988), "Trends in the well-being of children and the elderly in Japan", in J.L. Palmer, T. Smeeding and B. Torrey (eds.), *The Vulnerable*, Urban Institute Press, Washington, D.C.

ROUSSEL, L. (1989), *La famille incertaine*, Éditions Odile Jacob, Paris.

SARACENO, C. (1990), "Child poverty and deprivation in Italy: 1950 to the present", Innocenti Occasional Papers No. 6.

SARACENO, C. (1992), "Trends in the structure and stability of the family from 1950 to the present: the impact on child welfare", Innocenti Occasional Papers No. 27.

SARACENO, C. (1993), "Elementi per un' analisi delle trasformazioni di genere nella società contemporanea e delle loro conseguenze sociali", *Rassegna italiana di sociologia*, Vol. XXXIV:1, pp. 19-56.

SARACENO, C. (1994), "The ambivalent familism of the Italian welfare state", *Social Politics*, Vol. I:1, pp. 32-59.

SCHEIWE, K. (1994), "Labour market, welfare state and family institutions: the links to mothers' poverty risks", *Journal of European Social Policy*, Vol. 4, No. 3, pp. 201-234.

SELTZER, J.A. (1991), "Legal custody arrangements and children's economic welfare", *American Journal of Sociology*, Vol. 96:4, pp. 895-929.

SELTZER, J.A. (1994), "Consequences of marital dissolution for children", *Annual Review of Sociology*, Vol. XX, pp. 235-266.

SORENSEN, A. (1991), "Divorce and its consequences: the distribution of risk between women and men", in W. Heinz (ed.), *Life Course and Social Change: Comparative Studies in Labour Market and Social Policy*, Deutschen Studien Verlag, Veinheim.

STUART, A. (1991), "Australia's new child support scheme", *Journal of Divorce and Remarriage*, pp. 139-151.

SUNDSTRÖM, G. (1994), "Care by families: an overview of trends", in OECD (1994), pp. 15-55.

THERBORN, G. (1993), "The politics of childhood: the rights of childhood in modern times", in F.G. Castles (ed.), *Families of Nations: Patterns of Public Policy in Western Democracies*, Dartmouth, Aldershot, United Kingdom.

UNGERSON, C. (ed.) (1989), *Gender and Caring: Work and Welfare in Britain and Scandinavia*, Harvester Wheatsheaf, London.

US BUREAU OF CENSUS (1990), "Children's well-being: an international comparison", *International Population Reports Series*, P-95, No. 80, U.S. Department of commerce, Bureau of Census, Washington, DC.

WILENSKY, H.L. (1990), "Common problems, divergent policies. An 18-nation study of family policy", *Public Affairs Reports*, Institute of Government Studies, University of California at Berkeley, Vol. 3, No. 31.

WOMEN OF EUROPE (1992), "The position of women on the labour market. Trends and developments in the twelve Member states of the European Community. 1983-1990", *Women of Europe: Supplement No. 36*, European Commission, Brussels.

EMPLOYMENT AND SOCIAL PROTECTION: ARE THEY COMPATIBLE?

by

Robert Haveman
University of Wisconsin-Madison, United States

INCOME PROTECTION SYSTEMS AMONG OECD COUNTRIES

Among the larger and more industrialised OECD countries, a large and financially costly system of income protection is in place. While the levels of coverage, generosity and accessability of these systems differ substantially over the countries, the following characteristics tend to be common to all or nearly all of them:[1]

- An *unemployment benefit programme* seeks to replace earnings losses due to the involuntary separation of a worker from a job. These programmes tend to replace a substantial proportion of earnings losses – from 30 to 80 per cent – among the OECD countries. Moreover, in many countries unemployment benefits can be received for a long period of time, often a year or more. In some of the countries, the expiration of unemployment benefit eligibility triggers eligibility for an alternative benefit programme, such as disability benefits.

- A *disability benefits programme* provides earnings replacement to workers who become handicapped during their working years, either on or off the job. These programmes tend to replace a substantial proportion of the lost earnings, but again the replacement rates vary substantially across the countries. Receipt of benefits is typically of long duration.

- *Provision for early retirement norm* from the work force is available in most of the countries; this provision is often a transition from the receipt of unemployment or disability benefits to the receipt of retirement pensions. The replacement of earnings in early retirement schemes is typically less than if retirement is delayed until the normal retirement age, but in several countries the replacement rate reaches up to 70 per cent after age 60.

- All of the countries have in place a *safety-net welfare system* that provides cover for working-age individuals and families headed by such individuals. Benefit levels in these programmes range widely across the countries, and in some cases vary significantly across various regions within a country. Many OECD countries have welfare-programme benefit levels that provide recipients with an income level around one-third to one-half of the median income level in the country.

- Many of the countries have a legal *minimum wage policy* that requires employers to pay a minimum wage rate (or a minimum weekly wage for full-time workers) to employees irrespective of their education, skill, training, or productivity. This policy typically applies to all workers, including school leavers without work experience and recipients of unemployment and disability benefits should they decide to return to work. Other countries achieve an effective minimum wage arrangement through more or less comprehensive collective bargaining agreements. In a few countries, some groups of workers are not covered by minimum wage laws; in others (*e.g.* the Netherlands) wages below the minimum are permitted for some groups of workers (*e.g.* young workers).

- Many of the countries have *employment regulations* that limit the ability of employers to alter the size of their work force in response to changes in the demand for their output; hence, an employment contract translates to a fixed cost to the employer, generating caution in taking on permanent workers to the enterprise. Such regulations also lead to disguised unemployment in periods or places of slack demand, as employers are prevented from laying-off workers, even if there is insufficient demand to justify keeping them on.

THE PROS AND CONS OF A GENEROUS AND ACCESSIBLE SOCIAL PROTECTION SYSTEM

The constellation of policies yielding full cover and a generous and accessible safety net of social protection has both positive and negative economic impacts. Both positive and negative consequences are positively related to the comprehensiveness, generosity and accessibility of the system, however, only negative effects arise from administering the system in a loose or open-ended manner.

As a result of a comprehensive and generous social safety net, income poverty is reduced and disparities between high- and low-income families that results from the unfettered operation of labour markets are moderated. In the process, workers are protected from severe income losses due to illness, disability, unemployment, and retirement, and homemakers experiencing divorce or child-bearing out of marriage have their incomes and those of their children supported. The security against adverse events that these policies afford is of value to both those who are directly protected by them, and to others on whom burdens would fall were it not for this protection. Moreover, many of these programmes provide employment protection which fosters long-term employer-employee relationships and the training-productivity benefits that are inherent in such relationships. Similarly, the provision of income support during periods of short-term unemployment may foster the search for jobs and good employment matches.

However, these policies can also have distinctly negative effects on economic performance to the extent that they:

- reduce the demand for labour (especially low-wage, low-skilled labour), and encourage the substitution of temporary employees for permanent workers. The latter effect reduces the level of job training offered by firms to employees, and erodes the benefits from establishing long-term employer-employee relationships;

- reduce the willingness to work, and the incentive to look for work in those who are recipients of income support benefits which may be available for a long duration, *e.g.* unemployment and disability benefits. Such working-people, living at relatively low levels of assistance are described as being in a "poverty trap" or a "joblessness trap";

- increase the overheads of enterprises that are required to pay taxes to cover the costs of the benefits or higher-than-market wages; in the open economies that characterise many of the OECD countries, these costs reduce the demand from foreign markets for the goods and services produced;

- create rigidities in the labour market, preventing wage rates from equilibrating and labour demand from expanding to its true potential;

- erode the incentive for diligence and effort for current job holders, as the possibility of job loss is reduced by employment regulations, and the alternative available income support from public transfer programmes provides income protection in the face of job loss.

These negative economic effects are considered by many to prejudice the rate of productivity growth, inhibiting employment and economic growth, increasing joblessness among low-wage, low-experience and low-skilled workers, and create a low-income or joblessness trap for many individuals and families who receive income support benefits. It is in this context that analysts, advocates and policy makers propose reforms of welfare state policies, typically with the objective of reducing these adverse economic effects of social protection.[2]

These adverse effects of generous and accessible income protection policies are even more serious if the income protection policies are loosely structured, poorly integrated or ill-managed.

Numerous examples of programmes with defects of either design or administration have been documented in the social welfare literature. They include:[3]

- failure to make sure whether beneficiaries of unemployment-benefit programmes are continuing to look for work;

- failure to detect voluntary job-leaving as the basis for benefit claims, or undeclared employment among beneficiaries of unemployment programmes;

- benefit reduction (marginal tax) rates equal to or approaching 100 per cent in some assistance programmes;

- lax administration of income support programmes financed by central government rather than by local authorities;

- acquiescence in unlimited duration unemployment-benefit programmes either through legislation or by allowing people to alternate between receiving benefit and participating in active labour market programmes;

- arrangements which encourage a shift from unemployment benefits to disability benefits and to early retirement programmes.

If the incidence of such problems is as widespread as anecdotal evidence suggests, the availability of income protection benefits can increase programme costs, inflate apparent unemployment rates beyond the true rates, promote the demand for benefits and the resulting joblessness and undermine the effectiveness of active labour market policies. Such programme structures or administrative practices exaggerate the adverse effects that stem directly from the provision of income support in the absence of employment.

TRENDS IN EMPLOYMENT, INEQUALITY AND SOCIAL PROTECTION WITHIN THE OECD COUNTRIES

The first page of a recent volume, *Reducing Unemployment* (Higgins, 1994), summarised the global unemployment problem as follows:

"While unemployment will ebb somewhat as countries recover from the recent global recession, millions are likely to remain jobless for a variety of structural reasons. Moreover, there is a disturbing trend in many industrialised countries toward long-term unemployment, especially among low-skilled workers. This trend has had less effect on measured unemployment in the United States than in Europe in part because United States workers have greater incentives to accept low-wage jobs. Nonetheless, virtually all industrialised countries face a jobs problem that impairs living standards and threatens a breakdown in social cohesion."

This description contains two key points. The first is the emphasis on structural barriers to the reduction of unemployment (or non-employment) in OECD countries – namely, high minimum wages, generous and accessible income protection programmes, and stringent labour market regulations. The second is the contrast in unemployment, joblessness and inequality among OECD countries, especially between North America and Europe.

While the relative demand for low-skilled workers has fallen in all higher-income, industrialised economies, countries in these two regions have tended to respond in quite different ways. The differences in policy and employment experiences between the United States and Europe suggest a trade-off between a *North American package* consisting of:

- low minimum wages;

- a relatively modest social protection system, with relatively low levels of income support;

- few institutional barriers to hiring, firing and geographic mobility.

These policies have been accompanied by:

- rapid employment growth, especially for low-wage workers;

- high and rising wage inequality;

– slow wage growth.

This contrasts with a *European-style package* of:

– generous and accessible social benefit programmes;

– high minimum wage levels;

– relatively stringent labour market regulations and constraints.

This policy stance has been accompanied by:

– high unemployment and joblessness;

– slow employment growth;

– low and steady wage inequality;

– relatively high wage growth.

Whether or not the trade-off between social policy and economic performance is as explicit as this characterisation, high levels of available income support to working-age people through unemployment, disability, sickness and early retirement programmes – combined with relatively high and rigid minimum wages – do appear to contribute to a "poverty-trap" or "jobless trap" for low-skilled workers. When confronted with the choice between continued employment at relatively modest wage rates and a life without a job supported by public benefits equal to a relatively high proportion of potential net earnings, many choose the non-work/recipiency option. Similarly, facing high minimum wages, employers tend to find the hiring of low-skilled workers an unprofitable option. Conversely, low minimum wages and the availability of relatively low social protection benefits encourage high levels of employment and job growth, but with the side effect of high and growing wage inequality and poverty.

A few statistics will make the comparison between the North American and European experiences clear.

Employment growth

Relative to other industrialised regions, North America has been a "job creation machine."[4] From 1960 to the present, employment in North America has doubled, while the number of jobs in European Community has increased by less than 20 per cent. Over the decade of the 1980s, the number of new jobs created in North America and Australia was well above 20 per cent of the level of 1979 employment. That for the remainder of the OECD country groupings ranges from essentially zero to about 10 per cent (OECD, 1994).

Unemployment levels and changes

This differential pattern of job growth is also reflected in the unemployment experience among countries. In North America, the standardised unemployment rate in the 1990s (1990-93) was 6.9 per cent, which is about 110 per cent of its level over the period from 1960-90. By contrast, the 1990s unemployment rate in the European Community (9.2 per cent) was equal to its value in the 1980s, but more than 300 per cent of its level during the 1960s and 1970s.[5]

Joblessness levels and changes

Much the same pattern is seen if one focuses on joblessness, rather than unemployment. Among males aged 25-54, a group that excludes those who have chosen early retirement or continued schooling in the face of poor labour market prospects, the male jobless rate in the United States has gone from about 9 per cent in the 1970s to about 12 per cent in the 1990s, an increase of about one-third. For the European Community, however, the male jobless rate for workers in this age range has doubled from about 7 per cent in the 1970s to 14 per cent in the 1990s.[6]

Generosity and accessibility of unemployment benefit programmes

These differential changes in unemployment and jobless patterns between North America and Europe appear to be related to changes in the generosity and accessibility of public income support programmes. For example, among the 12 European Community countries, 6 increased the maximum period for which unemployment benefits are available over the 1961 to 1991 period; there was no increase in this benefit accessibility indicator in North America.[7]

A composite indicator of overall unemployment benefit generosity provides an even clearer comparison of this differential pattern. A simple average of this generosity indicator across the European Community countries (excluding Luxembourg) stood at 17.4 in 1961. By 1991, the index had increased to 31.5, representing an increase of more than 80 per cent. For the European Free Trade Association (EFTA) countries, the increase was from 8.3 to 34.5, or an increase of more than four-fold. By contrast, the simple average indicator for North America stood at 19.5 in both 1961 and 1991.[8]

Generosity and accessibility of other income protection programmes

As well as unemployment benefits, other income support programmes also enable working-age individuals to opt for non-work/recipiency status. Early-retirement and disability-benefit programmes are two such alternatives. A calculation of the simple average of replacement rates of the disability benefit programmes among the European Community countries shows a slight increase from the mid-40s to the upper 40s from 1974 to 1993. For North America, the replacement rate increased from a level of about one-half of that in the European Community in 1974 to about 30 per cent in 1993. Although the absolute increase is about the same in the two regions, the difference in the average level of the replacement rates is notable.[9]

Minimum wage levels

Whereas the European Community countries tend to support the income of non-working people at a substantially higher level than in North America, where statutory minimum wages do exist, these too are higher in Europe than in North America.[10] For example, in the early-1990s the minimum wage in the Netherlands and France stood at over 50 per cent of the average wage, while in the North American countries the minimum wage was about 35 per cent of the average wage.

The trend in average earnings

Consistent with the patterns of income support, unemployment and joblessness, one would expect the pressures for productivity improvements to be greater in those countries with the higher social protection and minimum wage levels, than in those with more flexible and less constrained labour markets. As a result, wage growth in the latter countries (*e.g.* North America) would be expected to be lower than in the former (*e.g.* the European Community).

In a quite distinct break from the early post-war period in the United States, when the real wage of the average worker grew about 2 per cent per year, the real hourly earnings of the average worker has been virtually constant since the early 1970s. The basic cause of the sharp decline in average earnings growth is the fall in the rate of productivity growth, to which gains in average compensation are ultimately tied. From 1948 to 1973, output per worker in the United States business sector increased nearly 2.9 per cent per year; since 1973, the average gain has been about 1 per cent per year. While this pattern explains why average earnings growth has been so anaemic, it does not explain why the rate of productivity growth has stagnated since the early 1970s. Since 1970, the 10 per cent real wage growth of the United States contrasts with real wage growth of nearly 60 per cent in the European Community; conversely, over the same period the nearly 60 per cent employment increase in the United States compares with a small 10-15 per cent increase in the European Community.

The level and trend in earnings and income inequality

In most OECD countries, there has been a widening of wage rate and earnings differentials since the late-1970s, although the patterns among countries vary widely. In North America, Australia, Japan, and the United Kingdom, the relative wage of low-skilled workers fell from 10 to 25 per cent during the 1980s. On the other hand, the relative wage of low-skilled workers in most continental European countries was about the same at the beginning of the 1990s as it was in 1980 (OECD, 1994). This pattern probably reflects the higher relative minimum wage established either through legislation or bargaining in Europe relative to North America and the United Kingdom.

The high and accessible level of income protection benefits and high minimum wages in Europe have successfully maintained a relatively low level of income inequality, even in the face of rising unemployment and joblessness. Figures for the late-1980s indicate that the simple average Gini coefficient for North America (Canada and the United States) equalled 31.5, while that for the European Community countries (excluding Denmark, Spain, Portugal, and Greece) was 27.9, and that for the primary EFTA nations stood at 22.[11]

The level and trend in poverty

Poverty rates among OECD countries vary widely. North America and Australia all have poverty rates well above the average, whereas the continental European countries of Austria, Belgium, Germany, Luxembourg and the Netherlands have the lowest rates. France, Ireland, Italy, Sweden and the United Kingdom have rates close to the average, with France and Sweden falling at the low end of this group.[12]

Evidence on changes in poverty rates is not available for most of these countries. For the United States, however, the level of official income poverty has risen substantially since the early-1970s, from an already high level. At the beginning of the 1970s, the rate of poverty defined by the United States government stood at about 11 per cent; by 1992, over 14.5 per cent of the nation's population lived in poverty. Between 1973 and 1992, the number of people officially classified as poor increased from 23 million to 37 million persons. This pattern is consistent with the growing earnings inequality that has occurred during the past two decades, and again reflects the implications of the lack of generosity and accessibility of income protection programmes, and the relatively low minimum wage.

In Europe, then, wage rates at the bottom of the range have been maintained by a variety of measures, including policies and collective bargaining arrangements that result in a high effective minimum wage (as a percentage of the average wage). Moreover, income protection policies (*i.e.* unemployment benefits, disability benefits, early retirement policies, and welfare benefits) are more accessible and generous in Europe than in North America. As a result, the declining relative European demand for new labour market entrants and other lower-skilled workers has been revealed in high unemployment and joblessness rates, and in the increasing prevalence of long-term unemployment. Given the pattern of growth in labour demand, the structure of income protection programmes in the European countries has tended to create a "poverty trap" or a "joblessness trap" for workers with low potential earnings.

In North America, on the other hand, a lower minimum wage, less generous and accessible social benefits, and fewer other barriers to employment creation have encouraged job growth for low-skilled workers. The overall unemployment rate has not shown an upward trend – unlike that in Europe. As a result, a high percentage of all workers occupy minimum wage, low-earning jobs in North America. Wage rates and earnings have fallen substantially for low-skilled, low-education, young and minority-group workers, and as a result wage rate and earnings inequality has grown substantially. While the growth in earnings inequality has been effectively checked in Europe by a comprehensive set of social protection programmes, this is not the case in North America. This, among other factors, has led to a rapid increase in the poverty rate in the United States of over 30 per cent, and an increase by more than 60 per cent in the number of poor people.

However, in nearly all OECD nations, unemployment and joblessness have become increasingly concentrated among the young and other low-skilled workers. While the incidence of joblessness and part-time work (especially for younger and minority-group male workers) has increased substantially in North America since 1973, both of these indicators have increased more in the European Community.

IS THERE NO ALTERNATIVE APPROACH?

The patterns described above prompt the question of whether there are alternative approaches to social policy that could simultaneously address the problems of both:

- high aggregate unemployment, growing joblessness and poverty traps in the (mainly European) countries with generous, accessible, and in some cases ill-managed income protection programmes; and

- stagnant wages, high rates of non-employment among low-skilled workers, and increasing inequality and poverty that characterise the (mainly North American and Australian) countries with relatively modest income protection programmes.

I would suggest that for both of these quite different sets of labour-market problems, a common prescription could attain the following objectives:

- provide a minimum income floor for all individuals and families, equal to, say, one-third of the per capita median income;

- eliminate the serious disincentives to work implicit in existing social policies, and create positive incentives for increases in the labour supply of low-skilled workers; and

- stimulate the demand of private and public employers for the services of low-skilled workers.[13]

A wide variety of individual measures have been proposed to further these objectives. They range from simple retrenchment of the eligibility conditions and benefit generosity of existing programmes, to substituting a costly universal, high-level Basic Income Guarantee (BIG) programme for the existing constellation of often poorly-integrated measures. Other measures also proposed as improvements for categorical systems which are difficult to administer the Negative Income Tax (NIT) and Credit Income Tax (CIT) programmes (to replace existing categorical measures), earnings supplementation plans (e.g. earned income tax credits), and wage rate and employment subsidies operating on both the demand and supply sides of the low-wage labour market.[14]

Taken alone, each of these individual measures could make a contribution to the effectiveness of social policy, especially in the high-benefit welfare states. However, a review and assessment of them leads to one clear conclusion:

"No single approach is capable of both assuring adequate income support to those without sufficient earnings (i.e. poverty reduction) and attaining the employment objectives cited above. The "iron law" of income support dictates that an income guarantee, assuring all citizens an "adequate" level of living, requires a structure of marginal tax rates on both benefit recipients and taxpayers that may imply substantial work disincentives. And, the higher the minimum income guarantee, the more severe the work disincentives."

This conclusion suggests that a combination of measures is necessary to achieve the goals set out above. For example, a CIT or an NIT could be an effective instrument for i) providing a minimum income floor below which no individual or family would fall; and ii) reducing the serious disincentives to work that are implicit in some existing social policies (e.g. unemployment, disability, and welfare income support policies with relatively high benefit levels and few restrictions on duration). However, these policies would be unlikely to induce a sizable increase in the supply or demand for the services of low-skilled workers, or in overall employment levels.

Conversely, work-conditioned policies – earnings supplements, wage rate subsidies, and employer-based marginal employment subsidies – can i) increase the return to labour supply and work; ii) increase the effective demand for the services of low-skilled workers; and iii) contribute to reducing poverty through increasing the rewards of working. Such measures, however, are not effective in providing a minimum income floor for all individuals and families.

These conclusions suggest that a judicious combination of a moderate minimum income guarantee, supply- and demand-side labour market programmes, and measures to tighten programme monitoring and administration could be implemented simultaneously to achieve these employment and income support goals. The stimuli to the demand for, and the supply of, low-skilled labour are designed to increase the employment and earnings of this high joblessness/high unemployment group. The minimum income guarantee would eliminate economic destitution, but without being high enough to seriously diminish the attractiveness of earnings from work. The increased stringency of programme administration would seek to ensure that those able to work would not fail to seek labour market options.

The following section provides a rough outline of one possible combination of income support and labour market reform policies. Such a draconian package of changes should be viewed as illustrative of a general strategy designed to both reduce poverty and promote self-sufficiency. It is intended to stimulate discussion leading to policy changes with this goal, and not to argue that this prototypical approach is better than alternatives with a similar purpose.

Employment-centered social policy: a stylised reform strategy[15]

The strategy proposed is designed to be relevant to *both* those OECD countries with generous and accessible income protection systems (*e.g.* many of the European Community and EFTA countries) *and* those with less generous and accessible arrangements (such as those in North America and Australia). While the former group of countries tends to have more severe unemployment and poverty-trap problems caused by generous and easily accessible public benefits than countries with less fulsome benefit arrangements, the latter group of countries has problems of increasing wage inequality and poverty. The proposed reform is designed to mitigate both sets of drawbacks. The core policy changes that could comprise this "blueprint" include the following.

Adoption of a two-pronged employment subsidy programme for low-skilled workers[16]

The proposal offered here is two-pronged, and is aimed both at disadvantaged workers and those who hire them. Its effect would be to alter the terms on which workers could be hired – in effect, to make hiring low-skilled workers a more profitable and attractive proposition than it is now. Both prongs of the policy are designed to offset restrictions on labour demand from market rigidities, to increase the employment of less-skilled workers, and to increase the returns to them from the work that they do. In the process, business costs would tend to fall, while output would tend to increase.[17]

An employer-based marginal employment subsidy

This prong of the programme would provide financial incentives to employers to hire more low-skilled workers than they would otherwise. One possible form of marginal employment subsidy targeted on enterprises might work as follows: the government would provide a tax credit (or other financial subsidy) to any enterprise equal to (say) 50 per cent of the first (say) $10 000 of wages paid to the (say) 50 workers hired in a firm above (say) 102 per cent of the firm's previous year's employment. Hence, the subsidy would be marginal in nature, affecting the decisions of firms regarding both the level of inputs to hire and their composition. While this arrangement does not distinguish among workers by their unemployment or poverty status, the subsidy (and hence the incentive to hire workers) is a higher percentage of the wages of low-skilled than it is for more skilled workers. By attempting directly to expand the demand for the services of low-wage workers, this form of employment subsidy seeks to reduce poverty and unemployment by directly changing the structure of the labour market.[18]

A *wage rate subsidy*

The second prong of this programme focuses on the low-skilled workers themselves. An employee-based wage rate subsidy programme would be instituted for disadvantaged workers and those with long-term and persistent unemployment problems. Some portion of the wage rate of low-wage workers would be subsidised by the government, giving the worker a labour market advantage, and hence an incentive to seek work. Workers would have incentive to exercise job-seeking initiative on their own behalf.

Such a wage rate subsidy programme would require the establishment of a socially determined threshold hourly wage. For any worker earning less than this threshold, a per-hour subsidy is paid equivalent to some percentage (the subsidy rate) of the difference between the threshold wage rate and the actual wage rate. For example, if the target wage rate were set at $8.00 per hour while the subsidy rate was 0.5, a worker earning $5.00 per hour would receive a subsidy of $1.50 per hour worked ($1.50 is 0.5 of the difference between the target wage rate of $8.00 per hour and the actual $5.00 per hour wage). The "take-home" hourly wage of that person would then be $6.50.

A wage rate subsidy is but one example of what have become known as "in-work benefits", all of which are characterised by the provision of support only when accompanied by market work. Other examples include the Family Credit in the United Kingdom, the subsidisation of work in markets which are intensive in employing low-skilled labour (*e.g.* home cleaning, lawn maintenance and garden work), as is currently being pursued in Denmark and the Netherlands, and an earnings subsidy, one variant of which is the Earned Income Tax Credit of the United States.

The United States Earned Income Tax Credit (EITC) provides a supplement to earnings below $8 000 per year in 26.3 per cent for families with one child and of 30 per cent for families with more than one child. Over $8 000, the supplement ($2 038 for one child; $2 528 for two children) remains constant until earnings reach $11 000, and it is then phased out at a rate of about 16 to 17 per cent. The credit is totally phased out by an earnings level of about $24 000. Clearly, the EITC acts as a strong work incentive for lower-income families – especially those experiencing the "negative" marginal tax rate. However, the EITC reduces work incentives for families (with two children) who are earning more than $11 000, and it is in this region of the earnings distribution that the density of the population becomes high. The positive work effect of the incentive to move from joblessness to employment offsets this disincentive effect.[19]

The new labour market environment generated by a two-pronged supply-side and demand-side policy proposal will improve the employment prospects of disadvantaged workers by generating ongoing job creation pressures at reasonable cost. By targeting the additional employment on segments of the labour market with the most severe unemployment problems and the greatest susceptibility to "poverty trap" problems created by existing tax and transfer programmes, employment and output could be increased without significant inflationary pressure. This two-pronged labour market programme will fundamentally alter the wage structure in private labour markets, raising the take-home pay of low-skilled workers relative to those with more secure positions in the labour market. It would reduce inequality in employment and earnings in a way that encourages independence, work and initiative.

Establishment of a Credit Income Tax (CIT) programme

In this programme, a family's income would be defined comprehensively, and a tax credit would be awarded to each living unit (or taxpaying unit) according to how large it is and who lives in it (for example, the adult/child composition of the unit). This credit would guarantee to taxpaying units a minimum income that would be set at a modest level, perhaps two-thirds of the explicit or implicit poverty line in the country. Units with no other means of support would receive the full amount of the credit as a grant; those with some other income would receive smaller net payments; better-off families would receive no net payment, and would pay positive taxes. This programme would be integrated with the positive income tax, so as to yield a smooth marginal tax rate pattern.

As a result of this low-guarantee plan, "hard-core" poverty would be eliminated, as the tail of the nation's income distribution would be amputated. However, the minimum income which is ensured by this base income support plan is low (as a percentage of median income) relative to accepted benefit levels for unemployment, disability and retirement pension programmes (and safety-net welfare programmes) in those OECD countries with large and generous transfer systems.[20]

A central advantage to be gained from this component of the proposed arrangement is the substantial increase in work incentives relative to those inherent in the existing high benefit-reduction rates of the income-support programmes of most of the larger OECD nations. A universal CIT would also strip away the complexity of the mix of current programmes, and eliminate much of the stigma associated with welfare programmes; however, the moral problem associated with such support would still exist. With a CIT integrated with the standard income tax structure, incomes would be taxed and support provided in a simple, open, universal and just manner.[21]

Elimination of existing programmes for disability income transfers, unemployment compensation benefits and welfare benefits

Eliminating or scaling back the benefit levels in these programmes, and establishing them as supplements to the Credit Income Tax described above would free budgetary resources to support the new programmes, and would eliminate or moderate the effects of those aspects of these programmes in many OECD countries that contribute to high work disincentives and the poverty/joblessness trap.

OBSTACLES TO AN EMPLOYMENT-CENTERED SOCIAL POLICY REFORM

The objective of this proposed new direction is to provide income support to the poor families of a nation and, at the same time, to encourage work effort and individual initiative, consistent with the objectives stated above. As in any proposed change that represents a major policy adjustment, this new direction also confronts several obstacles.

One concern with this approach is that the income guarantee level that lies at the base of the "blueprint" lies well below the implicit income minimum provided by existing programmes in those OECD countries with the most generous and accessible benefits. Clearly, a minimum income guarantee of this level could not be sustained were universal income support measures (e.g. a CIT or NIT) to be substituted for a set of individual of categorical benefit programmes. Were a general CIT or NIT to provide an income guarantee level as high as even 50 per cent of per capita median income in these countries, the marginal tax rate imposed on *all* earnings would be intolerably high for the policy reform to be budget neutral (OECD, 1994). While the poverty-unemployment trap would be reduced for current benefit recipients, severe work disincentives would be imposed on the remainder of the population. Such a policy substitution seems economically unworkable.

Two options seem possible. First, OECD countries which wish to eliminate the poverty trap and to increase work incentives and employment for low-skilled workers must face the fact that the replacement rates and eligibility standards now in force in some of their programmes need to be scaled back if incentives to retain or to seek work are to exist for lower-skilled workers. While this is a bitter political pill to swallow, the "iron law" of income-support policy described above indicates that high guaranteed incomes and strong work incentives are incompatible objectives.[22]

There is also a second option. Governments could set the level of the income guarantee in a CIT or NIT at a rather low level (say, one-third of per capita median income), and this guarantee would extend to all citizens. However, people included in restricted categories (e.g. the disabled or the unemployed) could be eligible for supplementary-benefits programmes designed for them.

With such a two-tiered arrangement, a comprehensive and universal income support system supplemented by categorical programmes could be financially feasible and workable. A modest income floor would be established for all working-age families, and work incentives would be maintained. However, workers receiving benefits from programmes in the special categories would not face the desirable work incentives that confront the remainder of the population; for them, something of a poverty trap will persist. If this strategy is implemented, it would be essential for eligibility restrictions on benefits from these programmes to be tightly enforced, to monitor whether recipients assessed as fit for work are moonlighting and engaged in job search activities and that programme administration be geared to returning beneficiaries to the work force. Moreover, it could be a good idea to whittle down the seriousness of the trap by incrementally reducing the replacement rates incorporated into these programmes and simultaneously restricting the eligibility criteria for benefits.

Discussion of this obstacle to an employment-centered social policy raises the question: "If such an employment-centered reform strategy is so attractive, why have countries not adopted such large-scale changes?". One answer to this question highlights yet another obstacle to a sizable employment-centered social policy reform – namely, the losses that would be experienced by those individuals now receiving benefits in the unemployment, disability and early retirement programmes of countries with high replacement rates and easily accessible benefits (and people who would expect to be benefi-ciaries in the future) would be adversely affected by the change. There is no easy way to assess the strength of this potential political obstacle, though efforts to retrench social benefit programmes by reducing replacement rates or tightening eligibility standards inevitably generate heated opposition from those who reflect the interests of beneficiaries, or who otherwise support the *status quo*.

Another obstacle to an employment-centered strategy rests on the argument that generous and accessible systems (especially if tightly administered) do provide the security that the future incomes of all citizens are not liable to the risk of shrinkage. A corollary of this argument is the observation that systems which do provide transfer support to otherwise well-off classes tend to have strong systems of social protection that ensure low levels of poverty and inequality. While such arrangements may, indeed, reduce both poverty and inequality, they do so at the cost of reduced overall work effort and lower measured national income. Perhaps the only way to blunt the force of such arguments in favour of generous and accessible systems is to make as clear as possible the large efficiency toll that the incentives in such systems impose on the society as a whole. Such arguments, unfortunately, tend not to be persuasive in the face of those private interests that benefit from the generous systems in place. Here, then, may lie the ultimate dilemma.

NOTES

1. The following description focuses on the programmes providing support to the working-age population, and hence does not discuss the work incentives implicit in the social security retirement programmes. Descriptions of the nature of welfare and labour market policies among Member countries are available in several OECD publications. A basic description of the eligibility and coverage provisions of several of the programmes is US Social Security Administration (1995). The effects of benefit programmes, employment protection and minimum wage programmes on employment, joblessness, wage adjustment and economic growth are discussed in OECD (1994), Chapters 5, 6, 8, and 9.

2. Edmund Phelps has analysed the effect of these distortions in the framework of "natural unemployment rate" theory, concluding that their impact is to drive up the natural rate (Phelps, 1994b). The theoretical underpinning of Phelps' natural rate model has been challenged by a number of reviewers; these challenges are alluded to in Phelps, 1995. See also Layard *et al.* (1991), and Lindbeck (1996). A helpful discussion of the implications of alternative theoretical frameworks in analysing the effects of the welfare state on economic welfare is found in Atkinson, 1995. This analysis makes it clear that the nature of the impact suggested above remains the same irrespective of the labour market assumptions made, although the anticipated magnitude of the effects may vary.

3. These examples, and numerous others, are discussed in OECD (1994), Chapter 8. The study concludes as follows: "[If] unemployment is to be kept low, it is vital to limit entitlements to benefit and refuse benefit to people who are not available for work" (p. 213).

4. A good summary of recent trends in the United States labour market is found in Auer (1995).

5. Calculations from data in Martin (1994).

6. If the jobless rate for males aged 20 to 64 had been shown, the difference between North America and Europe would have been even larger; youth joblessness and early retirement has grown in both regions, but more in Europe than America.

7. Three of the four EFTA countries increased the maximum benefit period over this time period, and Sweden adopted a procedure that enabled a virtually permanent extension of unemployment benefit eligibility.

8. For the United States alone, the indicator fell from 17 to 11. These calculations are from data in OECD (1994).

9. In the EFTA countries, the replacement rate of disability benefits was a very high 66 per cent in 1981; by 1993, it had fallen slightly to 61 per cent. A regression fit over the OECD countries relating the per cent of those aged over 55 receiving disability benefits and the generosity of disability benefits, as measured by the replacement rate, has a regression coefficient of 0.48, a standard error of 0.2, and an R^2 value of 0.3. Data in this paragraph are from Blondal and Pearson (1995).

10. Among the larger OECD countries, statutory minimum wages exist in the United States, Canada, Japan, France, the Netherlands, Spain and Portugal. Several other countries have established *de facto* wage minima through tripartite and other collective arrangements, but not through legislation. Data is available only on statutory wage minima. In a number of countries, primarily in Europe, an effective wage floor is established by benefit levels in social protection programmes. These wage floors tend to be a higher proportion of the average wage than is the minimum wage in the North American countries. (For Germany and Australia, however, evidence suggests that the minimum wage is effective for adults, but not for young people.)

11. Calculations from OECD (1994). Evidence necessary to indicate differential trends in income inequality between North America and Europe is not available.

12. The data on comparative poverty rates are from Forster (1994). The criterion for measuring poverty is the percentage of people living in households with disposable income adjusted for family size (using an equivalence scale with an elasticity of 0.55) which is less than 50 per cent of the median household income in the country.

13. A more full-bodied statement of these objectives might read as follows:

1) ensure that public programmes that guarantee income support do not inhibit the willingness of people to work at prevailing market wages, and limit the duration of support for which workers qualify;

2) increase employment opportunities for low-skilled labour and stimulate the willingness of workers to accept work at prevailing wages in a manner that encourages investments in education and training; and

3) increase the monitoring of recipients in terms of unreported work and job search efforts, and improve aspects of programme integration and administration.

14. Elsewhere, I have discussed these various approaches as potential reforms for existing, high-benefit welfare state systems, and assessed their advantages and disadvantages. See Haveman (1996).

15. A recent Australian comprehensive reform package contains many of the elements highlighted in the prototype presented here. They include: subsidies to youth, the long-term unemployed and those at risk of long-term unemployment for job search, employment and training; employer subsidies for hiring/training people in these categories; reform of income support (unemployment benefit) programmes so as to provide incentives for job search and work; intensive case management and a "compact" between workers and the public sector indicating mutual obligations. See Commonwealth of Australia (1994).

16. This component of the blueprint rests on the view that most OECD countries face a situation where minorities, young people, older workers, disabled workers, and single mothers – all characterised by low levels of skill and education – face relatively bleak labour market opportunities. Given prevailing wage standards, union wage contracts, and the fringe benefits and payroll taxes that businesses are required to pay for every standard worker, hiring low-skilled workers simply does not generate much additional output or profit for employers. These restrictions on labour market flexibility contribute to the labour market disadvantage of the low-skilled.

17. The case for such a labour market strategy is made in Haveman (1996), Appendix to Chapter 7. See also the paper by Betson and Bishop in Haveman and Palmer (1982). Phelps estimates that wage incomes of $7 000 or less could be topped up to about $11 000 with an employment subsidy programme that would cost about $100 billion per year for the United States. The empirical basis for this assertion is unclear (see also Phelps, 1994a).

18. A possible structure for this programme is the New Jobs Tax Credit that was in place in the United States during the late-1970s. Evaluations of the New Jobs Tax Credit programme concluded that it was a potent and cost-effective measure to increase the employment of low-skilled workers. A wide variety of modifications could be made to its structure to increase its employment generating potential. For evidence on the effect of the New Jobs Tax Credit on employment levels, see Haveman and Bishop (1979), and Perloff and Wachter (1979).

19. The design and effects of the Earned Income Tax Credit in the United States have been analysed in Scholz (1994). An earnings supplementation plan can easily be integrated with a credit income tax (see below). Haveman (1996) discusses this option and its advantages and disadvantages.

20. As a result, if these programmes were to be replaced with only the universal CIT (see below), poverty rates would be increased, even though "hard core" poverty would be eliminated. As an alternative, income losses by recipients of existing generous programmes could be offset either by increased earnings associated with improved incentives for labour supply and the employment subsidies which are also part of this proposal (see above), or by adopting supplemental categorical unemployment, disability and retirement programmes.

21. Reform proposals with a negative income tax or a credit income tax at their heart have been recently debated in the United Kingdom. Nobel Laureate James Meade (1995) suggests such an arrangement in his recent volume. Similarly, Roger Douglas (1995), former Finance Minister of New Zealand, has also proposed a Guaranteed Minimum Family Income as the basis of his reform suggestions. In a commentary on these proposals, Samuel Brittan (1995) states that: "Meade has always insisted that if people are to be priced into work, whether through free market forces or direct intervention, there must be an adequate safety net for those whose earnings in the market place do not provide a reasonable standard of living". This sentiment motivates the employment-centered social policy reform that the "blueprint" represents. A basic income guarantee for the non-elderly population, conditional on "participation" (defined to include work, sick though employed, unemployed though seeking work, in education or training, and caring for young, elderly and disabled), has also been proposed by Atkinson (1996).

22. Viewed in this way, the policy strategy suggested above would seem more feasible for those OECD countries with benefit levels and replacement rates set at lower percentages of median income (such as the United States) than for countries with higher rates (such as some of the Northern European countries).

BIBLIOGRAPHY

ATKINSON, A. (1995), "The welfare state and economic performance", *National Tax Journal*, Vol. XLVIII, No. 2, pp. 171-198.

ATKINSON, A. (1996), "The distribution of income: evidence, theories, and policy", *The Economist*, Vol. 144, No. 1, pp. 1-21.

AUER, P. (1995), "The American employment miracle", *InforMISEP*, Employment Observatory Policies, Employment in Europe, European Commission, Directorate-General for Employment, Industrial Relations and Social Affairs, No. 49, spring, pp. 18-27.

BLONDAL, S. and PEARSON, M. (1995), "Unemployment and other non-employment benefits", *Oxford Review of Economic Policy*, Vol. 11, No. 1.

BRITTAN, S. (1995), "No, not the next budget", *Financial Times*, November 9.

COMMONWEALTH OF AUSTRALIA (1994), *Working Nation: Policies and Programmes*, Australian Government Publishing Service, Canberra.

DOUGLAS, R. (1995), *Unfinished Business*, New Zealand Random House, Wellington.

FORSTER, M. (1994), "Measurement of low incomes and poverty in a perspective of international comparisons", OECD Labour Market and Social Policy Occasional Paper No. 14, Paris.

HAVEMAN, R. (1996), "Reducing poverty while increasing employment: a primer on alternative strategies, and a blueprint", *OECD Economic Studies*, Paris.

HAVEMAN, R. and BISHOP, J. (1979), "Selective employment subsidies: can Okun's law be repealed?", *American Economic Review*, Vol. 69, May, pp. 124-130.

HAVEMAN, R. and PALMER, J. (1982), *Jobs for Disadvantaged Workers: The Economics of Employment Subsidies*, Brookings Institution, Washington, DC.

HIGGINS, B. (1994), " Symposium summary", *Reducing Unemployment: Current Issues and Policy Options*, A symposium sponsored by the Federal Reserve Bank of Kansas City.

LAYARD, R., NICKELL, S. and JACKMAN, R. (1991), *Unemployment: Macroeconomic Performance and the Labour Market*, Oxford University Press, Oxford.

LINDBECK, A. (1996), "The West European employment problem", Seminar paper No. 616, Institute for International Economic Studies, August.

MARTIN, J.P. (1994), "The extent of high unemployment in OECD Countries", *Reducing Unemployment: Current Issues and Policy Options*, A symposium sponsored by the Federal Reserve Bank of Kansas City.

MEADE, J. (1995), *Full Employment Regained*, Cambridge University Press, Cambridge.

OECD (1994), *The OECD Jobs Study: Evidence and Explanations*, Paris.

PERLOFF, J.M. and WACHTER, M. (1979), "The New Jobs Tax Credit: an evaluation of the 1977-78 wage subsidy program", *American Economic Review*, Vol. 69, May, pp. 173-179.

PHELPS, E.S. (1994a), "Low-wage employment subsidies versus the welfare state", *American Economic Review*, No. 84, May, pp. 54-58.

PHELPS, E.S. (1994b), *Structural Slumps: The Modern Equilibrium Theory of Unemployment, Interest, and Assets*, Harvard University Press, Cambridge, Mass.

PHELPS, E.S (1995), "The structuralist theory of employment", *American Economic Review*, No. 85, May, pp. 226-231.

SCHOLZ, J.K. (1994), "The Earned Income Tax Credit: participation, compliance, and antipoverty effectiveness", *National Tax Journal*, No. 47, March, pp. 59-81.

US SOCIAL SECURITY ADMINISTRATION (1995), "Social security programmes throughout the world", Social Security Administration Publication No. 13-11805, Research Report No. 64, Office of Research and Statistics, Washington, DC, July.

THE CHALLENGE OF POVERTY AND EXCLUSION

by

Bea Cantillon
Centre for Social Policy, Belgium

INTRODUCTION

In many countries there has been talk of "new poverty". In the Anglo-Saxon countries, the alleged rise in poverty is frequently associated with the emergence of a so-called "underclass", while in Europe there is a tendency to perceive "new poverty" as one manifestation of the wider problem of "social exclusion". The concept of "new poverty" is somewhat imprecise, and is used in rather different ways in various countries (Room, 1990). Nonetheless, it is claimed, or the impression is created, that "new poverty" is on the increase, and this assertion is supported with reference to high and/or increasing levels of unemployment; growing numbers of people depending on social assistance; and the growing number of homeless people on city streets.

The principal aim of this chapter is to set the scope for a discussion of various aspects of the "new poverty" concept. However, the present state of the art does not yet make it possible to conduct a comprehensive quantitative cross-country analysis in this area. Inevitably, therefore, this chapter starts with presenting direct evidence on trends in financial poverty in a number of OECD countries. More specifically, this analysis addresses three questions. *First*, have overall levels of poverty increased, decreased or remained stable? *Second*, has the incidence of poverty shifted from certain demographic groups to others? *Third*, how have social income transfer systems coped in their task of protecting people from poverty? Answers to these questions will be sought by analysing the Luxembourg Income Study (LIS) database which brings together data from a large number of household income surveys (Smeeding *et al.*, 1990), from some other cross-country studies such as Gottschalk and Smeeding (1995), and de Vos and Zaidi (1993*a-c*, 1994*a-d*), and from some national studies. Furthermore, we will consider the impact of socio-demographic and labour market change on poverty, relying mostly on published research plus some additional analysis.

The last part of this chapter draws together the evidence on financial poverty and the emerging discussion on the context of the "new poverty concept", so as to set the stage for a discussion on the challenges posed to social policy. This chapter is inevitably somewhat superficial in that its scope does not allow for in-depth analysis of underlying causes of developments, or a discussion of changes in social policy in the several countries. This chapter merely sets the stage for further research.[1]

FINANCIAL POVERTY: LEVELS AND TRENDS

The overall extent of financial poverty

Direct cross-country comparative evidence on the evolution of poverty remains relatively scarce. Despite the considerable efforts that have been made over recent years, comparative time series remain rather incomplete and the periods to which the data refer rarely span the complete time-period of interest. Also, the use of standardised datasets which facilitate cross-country analysis over time permits only the use of a rather arbitrary statistical measure of financial poverty. People are said to be in financial poverty if they live on an equivalent income (household income adjusted for family size) that is less than half of average equivalent income.

Country rankings are generally fairly well reproduced when applying slightly different poverty measures to the same datasets (Table 5.1). Using average equivalent income instead of median equivalent income results in significantly higher poverty rates, especially in countries with a higher degree of income inequality. A relatively flat equivalence scale tends to produce higher poverty rates in the Scandinavian countries, probably because of the relatively high frequency of single person households.[2] Other cross-country differences, which can be quite significant such as for the Netherlands and France, may derive from a different treatment of missing data and negative incomes.

Our principal focus, however, is the evolution of financial poverty. Unless indicated otherwise, we cite findings on the basis of our analysis of the LIS-datasets, which probably provide the most comprehensive cross-country comparative time-series to date. Because not all countries of interest are covered we will also refer to other authors, who use a slightly different method (a different equivalence scale or a poverty threshold based on median rather than mean income) so that the results cannot be considered strictly comparable. In the context of overall poverty rates, the poverty line is set at the same percentage of average equivalent income in each year (see Table A.2*a* in Appendix 2 at the end of this chapter). The trend in "absolute" poverty is measured by translating the relative poverty line in a reference year to the other years, using the consumer price index, thus keeping the poverty line constant in terms of purchasing power (Table A.2*b*). Poverty rates are given in terms of households, as well as in terms of individuals. The aggregate poverty gap, whether measured in terms of households or individuals as a percentage of aggregate disposable income (as estimated from survey data) is also shown.

With respect to relative poverty the following general findings can be drawn (for country specific findings we refer to Box 1). First, there is considerable cross-country variation in the extent of relative poverty (Table A.2*a*): the highest levels are found in North America, Australia and the United Kingdom, whereas the lowest levels are found in the Scandinavian and the Benelux countries. Different measurement procedures produce slight differences in relative cross-country levels, but country rankings are generally fairly well reproduced. Second, no single country has achieved the total eradication of relative poverty. In some countries, this is despite levels of social protection expenditure that would be sufficient to fill the poverty gap several times over (see below). Even in Sweden and Norway, undisputedly among the most elaborate welfare states, some 6 per cent of the population remain poor. Third, on the basis of the time-series available, typically spanning the 1980s period, there is no evidence at all of a consistent rise in relative poverty across the OECD area. There is only evidence of a fairly sharp increase in relative poverty (among individuals) in Ireland (1973-87) and in the United Kingdom during the late 1980s. Moderate, but probably significant increases are found for Australia (1981-89),

Table 5.1. **Extent of financial poverty in OECD countries, using two different measures of poverty**

	Persons below 50 per cent of mean equivalent income ("steep" equivalence scale)		Persons below 50 per cent of median equivalent income ("flat" equivalence scale)	
	Level	Country rank	Level	Country rank
Australia (1985)	15.7	2	12.6	2
Belgium (1985)	5.8	10	4.8	10
Canada (1987)	13.8	3	12.1	3
Finland (1987)	5.5	11	6.9	8
France (1984)	11.9	5	7.3	7
Germany (1983)	8.0	7	6.9	9
Netherlands (1987)	8.3	6	3.0	11
Norway (1986)	6.4	8	7.8	6
Sweden (1987)	6.3	9	8.1	5
United Kingdom (1986)	13.0	4	8.4	4
United States (1986)	22.6	1	17.7	1

Sources: Left column from author's calculations.
Right column from Gottschalk and Smeeding (1995).

Box 1. **Trends in overall poverty rates and poverty gaps**

Australia appears to have experienced a significant increase in the incidence of poverty over the 1980s. Moreover, the poverty gap increased significantly. The rise in poverty appears to have occurred fairly consistently across the three demographic groups. Noteworthy is the strong increase in the poverty gap among elderly households. These findings are fairly consistent with those reported by Saunders (1994), although he reports a stronger increase in the incidence of poverty among the elderly.

In **Belgium**, the extent of relative poverty appears to have remained stable – at a comparatively low level – in the period 1985 to 1992 (Cantillon *et al.*, 1993). Furthermore no important changes in the distribution of poverty across broad demographic groups appears to have occurred. When the poverty line is kept at its 1985 level in terms of purchasing power, the extent of poverty falls by about one third.

In **Canada**, a consistent and significant decrease in relative poverty appears to have occurred during the period 1975 to 1991, especially at the household level. The decline is particularly strong when the poverty line is kept at the same real level. Our figures suggest a remarkable decline in poverty among the elderly, which appears to account for the entire overall decline, since child poverty and poverty among the non-elderly remained stable at a relatively high level. These results are in agreement with those of Hanratty and Blank (1992), who have compared trends in poverty in Canada and the United States between 1970 and 1986 among the non-elderly population, using official low-income cut-offs. They find that in the early seventies, the main source of a decline in Canadian poverty was a decline in pre-transfer poverty. In the eighties, however, a further decline in poverty was due to transfers becoming more generous.

In **Denmark**, important changes appear to have happened. Poverty rates fell considerably at the 50 per cent and 60 per cent thresholds, but much less at the 40 per cent line. It appears that poverty has fallen in particular (by about three-quarters) for the elderly. Further analysis has shown that this is a result of a large number of elderly people who were just below the poverty line in 1987, and being just above it in 1992. Since, in real terms, average equivalent income hardly changed between 1987 and 1992, the "absolute" poverty rates behave in much the same way as the relative ones.

In **Finland**, relative poverty increased somewhat between 1987 and 1991. Poverty increased, particularly among the elderly. This finding contrasts with that of Ritakallio (1994), who reports that relative poverty went down in Finland in the period 1985 to 1990. Finland experienced a sharp economic downturn in 1991, which account for the difference. If our findings are correct, they would constitute a break in the trend of decreasing relative poverty in Finland between 1966 and 1985 (Gustafsson and Uusitalo, 1990). When the poverty line is kept at its 1987 level, the extent of poverty diminishes in Finland in the period studied.

In **France**, the results from tax surveys indicate a decline in relative poverty between 1979 and 1984. The decrease is even larger when the poverty line is kept at the same real level. The decline in the overall poverty rate is mainly due to a large reduction in the incidence of poverty among the elderly; among non-elderly persons the poverty rate remains stable. For the subsequent period 1984/85 to 1989, de Vos and Zaidi (1994*b*) report an increase in relative poverty rates. Poverty increased particularly among children, and also among non-elderly adults. When a constant poverty line is used, overall poverty rates remain virtually stable. For reasons given in Appendix 2, the LIS data are not comparable with those of de Vos and Zaidi.

For **Germany** during the period 1978 to 1983, we find stable relative poverty rates in terms of persons and falling poverty rates in terms of households. This indicates that poverty has shifted from small to large households. The poverty rate has indeed increased somewhat among children, and fallen for other persons, though the changes are modest. By contrast, Hauser and Becker (1994, Table 8), using data from the same surveys, report a modest increase in the number of persons with less than half of average equivalent income (from 6.9 per cent to 7.9 per cent). The reasons for this discrepancy are not clear. When the poverty line is kept at the same real value, German poverty rates fell during the period 1978 to 1983. If the results of de Vos and Zaidi (1993*a*) are comparable to ours (data from the survey and the same poverty line definition were used, but the income concept may have been different), relative poverty in Germany went up between 1983 and 1988. Poverty among children would seem almost to have doubled, whereas there would have been modest increases in poverty among adults. However, Hauser and Becker (1994, Table 8; figures also shown in Table 5.3 in this chapter), report a fairly stable number of people with less than half of average equivalent income during the period 1983-90 (around 8 per cent). Those results are based on the German Socio-Economic Panel.

(continued on next page)

(continued)

For **Greece**, de Vos and Zaidi (1994*c*) report that relative poverty increased slightly between 1982 and 1988. This rise is located solely among the elderly. "Absolute" poverty has gone up a little more.

In **Ireland**, the number of persons in relative poverty increased considerably, both in the period 1973 to 1980, as well as between 1980 and 1987 (Callan *et al.*, 1989). The proportion of households in poverty has remained virtually stable, however, indicating that the incidence of poverty has shifted from smaller to larger households. Table A.3 reveals that there has been a dramatic change in the demographic composition of the poor: poverty among the elderly has fallen by more than two-thirds, while poverty among children has almost doubled.

The findings for the **Netherlands** are somewhat confusing. Between 1983 and 1987, poverty appears to have declined somewhat. (This statement is true both for relative and "absolute" poverty.) This result is mainly due to the apparent virtual eradication of poverty among the elderly in 1987 – consider the poverty gap in particular. There is no evident reason why such a large decline should have occurred, and it may well be a data artefact. The 1991 survey may well be more representative of the population than the 1983 and 1987 surveys, but it is almost certainly not comparable with the latter. The SCP (1994, p. 205) reports that the number of poor households doubled between 1979 and 1983, from 4 per cent to 8 per cent. After 1983, it stabilised to 7 per cent, as measured in 1987 and 1991. The SCP uses a political poverty line, which is equal to the staturtory minimum income guaranteed by social assistance. In the period of 1983 to 1991, this level has declined in real terms in some years, and it certainly has fallen behind the so-called "modal income".

In **Norway**, the extent of relative poverty appears to have been fairly stable in the period 1979 to 1991. At the 50 per cent line, there is a peculiar jump in the poverty rate in 1986. As this jump is not replicated at the other lines, nor is reflected in the poverty gaps, it is probably due to a data quirk. The same quirk (if it is that) appears in the poverty rate for the elderly in 1986; the trend in the poverty gap among the elderly is always downward. No changes in relative poverty of any importance are measured for children and non-elderly adults. Since Norwegians appear to have enjoyed a considerable general improvement in living standards, "absolute" poverty has been more than halved in the period from 1979 to 1991.

For **Portugal**, de Vos and Zaidi (1994*d*) report a modest decline in relative poverty rates between 1980 and 1989. The decline appears to have been greatest among children. When the poverty line is kept at a constant real value, poverty rates have come down by more than a third. Also, de Vos and Zaidi (1993*b*) indicate a small decline in relative as well as "absolute" poverty in **Spain** between 1980 and 1988. Table A.3 shows that poverty seems to have come down considerably among the elderly, but to have remained stable among the non-elderly. The 1988 survey is, however, probably not entirely comparable to the 1980 one.

In **Sweden**, the general picture that emerges is that the extent of relative poverty was more or less stable between 1975 and 1981, then increased in the period up to 1987 (though from a rather low level) and stabilised again between 1987 and 1991. The small decline in measured poverty in the first period is due to the apparently virtual elimination of poverty among the elderly in 1981, and it is unclear whether this is realistic. Nonetheless, over the period 1975-91 as a whole, relative poverty declined among the elderly, whereas it increased for non-elderly adults, and perhaps also for children. When the poverty line is kept at the same real value across years, there is an almost continual decrease in poverty rates, though the pace of decline was somewhat slower between 1987 and 1991 than in the other periods. Gustafsson and Uusitalo (1990, p. 258), using a "political administrative" poverty line, which is based on guidelines for the level of social assistance, report a somewhat different trend in poverty rates in Sweden between 1967 and 1985. "Poverty declined very rapidly until 1975, and continued to decline although with a somewhat slower pace until 1980, when it was at its lowest level. (...) In the beginning of the 1980s, poverty rates increased, except for 1985, when there was a decrease."

For the **United Kingdom**, we present data on trends in poverty from three sources which all use Family Expenditure Survey data, and which appear to be in broad agreement which each other: LIS, de Vos and Zaidi (1993*c*), and Goodman and Webb (1994). During the seventies, there was a modest decline in poverty. In the early 1980s, there was an increase in poverty rates, which accelerated in the second half of the 1980s. As a result, in 1991 the poverty rate was more than three times what it was in 1978. An important reason for this steep rise in relative poverty was that those at the very top experienced very large increases in income, while the incomes of those at the very bottom were rising only slowly (Good-

(continued on next page)

(*continued*)

man and Webb, 1994, p. 25). When the poverty line is kept at the same level in terms of purchasing power, we indeed observe downward, rather than upward, trends in poverty rates. However, by 1991 even the absolute poverty rate seems to have increased (based on an after-housing cost measure); in that year 20 per cent more people were receiving less than half of 1979 average income than in 1979 itself (Hills, 1995, p. 32). "Absolute poverty" decreased by around 10 percentage points between 1979 and 1992/93 when measured on basis of a before-housing cost measure. The trends in relative poverty have not been the same for all demographic groups. During the 1970s, and even in the beginning of the 1980s, there was a strong decline in the poverty rate among the elderly (in 1982 it was only a third of what it was in 1973), while poverty remained stable, or even rose a little, among children and non-elderly adults. In 1988, however, the poverty rate for the elderly rose quickly back to its 1973 level, and it has continued to rise since that year. At the same time, poverty among the non-elderly has nearly tripled.

In the **United States**, relative poverty appears to have increased significantly, although by no means linearly, over the period 1974 to 1991. An initial decrease during the late 1970s was reversed during the early 1980s, after which poverty stabilised at a relatively high level. The "absolute" level of poverty (reference year 1986) remained virtually stable throughout the whole period. A rather dramatic increase in the incidence of relative poverty among children and a significant increase among non-elderly adults appear to have occurred, especially during the early 1980s. These increases were only partly counterbalanced by a decrease of the incidence of relative poverty among the elderly. These findings are broadly consistent with trends in the official American poverty rate. Overall official poverty among individuals increased rather more moderately than relative poverty. However, the changes in the structure of official poverty are very similar to those in relative poverty: *i.e.* a striking increase in poverty among children and a significant decrease among the elderly (SSA, 1995).

Finland (1987-91) and Sweden (1981-87) and for the United States, especially during the early 80s. Our findings further suggest relative stability in Belgium (1985-92), Germany[3] (1978-83 as well as 1983-90), Greece (1982-88), the Netherlands (1983-87) and Norway (1979-91). Our findings further suggest that relative poverty decreased in Denmark (1987-92), and in Portugal (1980-89) and Spain during the 1980s. Finally, only Canada appears to have experienced a marked decline in relative poverty over the late 1970s and during the 1980s. Furthermore, all but a few countries have enjoyed marked declines in absolute poverty (Table A.2*b*), except for Greece (1982-88), Australia (1981-89) and the United States (1974-91) at the individual level.

Trends in the structure of financial poverty

In Table A.3 (in Appendix 2) the relevant poverty indicators are shown for three demographic groups: children (*i.e.* persons below 18 years), elderly persons (*i.e.* adults aged 65 or over) and non-elderly adults.[4] The evidence seems to suggest that many countries have made considerable progress in eradicating financial poverty among the elderly (*e.g.* the Netherlands and Sweden), and the evidence on Canada suggests that a similar eradication took place over a short period of time. During the time periods for which we have data, relative poverty among the elderly appears to have declined in Belgium, Canada, Denmark, France (1979-84), Germany (1978-83), Ireland, Spain and the United States. In the United Kingdom, it would appear that the elderly experienced a marked improvement of their relative position during the late 1970s and early 1980s, however this improvement was reversed during the late 1980s (Goodman and Webb, 1994, Figure 3.13). In a number of countries, such as the Netherlands, Norway and Sweden, the picture is rather confusing because of not readily explainable fluctuations which may be due to the fact that a high proportion of the elderly live on an income that is very near to the poverty threshold. Finally, in Australia, Finland and Greece, the relative plight of the elderly appears to have deteriorated rather than improved. The level of cross-country differences in the incidence of financial poverty among the elderly still remains considerably greater than the differences in the overall incidence of financial poverty. Relative poverty among the elderly remains very high, typically around or over 30 per cent, in southern Europe, as well as in Australia, the United States and the United Kingdom.

In most advanced economies the incidence of relative poverty among non-elderly individuals appears to have remained more or less stable, although in Australia, Canada, Ireland and Sweden the trend seems to be, though hesitantly, towards increasing vulnerability (Table A.3 in Appendix 2). Only in the United Kingdom and the United States, our findings suggest, have non-elderly adults clearly become more exposed to poverty. Moreover, we find a considerably more consistent increase in pre-transfer poverty among prime-aged adults (Table A.4). This trend is probably in part a reflection of increased dependence on social transfers, particularly following the (partly intentional) expansion of early retirement programmes during the 1980s. However, this trend is probably also in part an indication of decreasing self-sufficiency in the wake of family dissolution and deteriorating labour market conditions for particular segments of the workforce.

Arguably one of the more consistent trends across the OECD area is that of a rising incidence of relative poverty among children (Table A.3). There is evidence of rises in child poverty in Australia, Belgium, Canada, France, Germany, Ireland, the Netherlands, the United Kingdom and the United States. In the last two countries, as well as in Ireland, the rise was even fairly significant. Moreover, Table A.4 suggests even greater increases in pre-transfer poverty among children, even in countries which experienced only modest or no increases in actual child poverty. Most notably, this is the case for Sweden. To some extent, this trend is bound to be a consequence of family dissolution, and the rising number of lone-parent families in particular. However, the changing socio-demographic composition of the population does not appear to provide the full explanation. In the United Kingdom and the United States, countries where the most significant increases in child poverty appear to have occurred, poverty rates rose most strongly among couples with children rather than among single parents.

The "feminisation of poverty" thesis is not unambiguously supported (Table A.5). Effectively, poverty rates are consistently higher for female-headed households than for male-headed households. At about the late 1980s, female-headed households were about three times more likely to be in relative poverty in Australia, Finland, Germany, Norway, the United Kingdom or the United States. In other countries, the "gender gap" is less striking, for example in Belgium or Sweden, but also in southern Europe, where relative poverty rates are very high for male- and female-headed households alike. However, for most countries the available time-series appears to suggest a decline in relative poverty among female-headed households. Also, the share of female-headed households among poor households as a whole appears to have remained stable in most countries, with the notable exception of Norway, where 60 per cent of poor households were female headed in 1991 compared to under 50 per cent in 1979.

An analysis of poverty trends by age reveals marked increases in relative poverty among households headed by persons aged between 16 and 24 in Australia, Belgium, Canada, Denmark, Finland, France (1979-84), Netherlands (1983-87), Norway, Portugal, Spain, Sweden, the United Kingdom and the United States (Table A.6). There is no comprehensive satisfactory explanation for this finding. Increasing youth unemployment may be a factor in some countries. However, relative youth poverty started to increase in Norway and Sweden prior to the increase of youth unemployment, and despite a high youth unemployment rate, youth poverty is relatively low in France. Similarly, in some countries low-skilled youngsters were hit by feeble real wage growth, or real wage decline, *e.g.* the United States over the 1980s, which probably contributed to the rise in relative youth poverty, but does not fully explain its increase.

The duration of poverty

Longitudinal research suggests that there is extensive movement into and out of relative poverty; only a very small number of people stay poor in the long run, whereas a surprisingly high number are confronted with relative income poverty within a period of a few years. The temporarily poor are not very different from the population as a whole, but those who escape poverty do not generally make large gains. An eight-country comparative study (Canada, France, Germany, Ireland, Luxembourg, the Netherlands, Sweden and the United States) by Duncan *et al.* (1995) suggests that there exists considerable cross-country variation in the duration of financial poverty.[5] A rapid escape (after one year) from financial poverty seems to be more likely in countries with low poverty rates (like the Netherlands and Sweden) than in countries with high poverty rates (like Canada and the United States). In other words, there appears to exist a marked inverse relationship between the incidence of poverty and escape rates. To a certain extent, this is related to poverty thresholds typically occurring higher up the income distribution in high poverty countries. Hence, the greater the income increase required to escape poverty. A different approach, which examines escape from the bottom decile reveals essentially similar patterns of economic mobility across countries, although comparison of different national studies reported in Jarvis and Jenkins (1995) suggests that mobility out of the bottom income decile may be greater in the United Kingdom than in Germany, Sweden or the United States. However, the limited number of countries in these studies and sometimes small samples do not allow for a generalisation of results.[6]

THE IMPACT OF SOCIAL EXPENDITURE

This section considers whether social security transfers (including social assistance) have succeeded in dampening possible poverty enhancing effects of increasing unemployment and other economic and social developments, or whether, conversely, rising poverty rates are the result of a reduction in the effectiveness of social security transfers as regards minimum income protection (Box 2). The analysis is limited to the effectiveness of transfers to beneficiaries as a means of poverty alleviation.[7] Therefore the results we obtain may not adequately cover the social protection provided by countries that put a greater emphasis on in-kind transfers or third-party subsidies. The results are also likely to be sensitive to data issues related to aspects such as housing assistance. [For an extensive discussion of the money and transfer concepts and other methodological issues, refer to Appendix 1 and to Atkinson in OECD (1995*c*). For this analysis, only results from LIS are available and are shown in Table A.4.]

During the 1980s and early 1990s – ignoring cyclical and other variations – social expenditure remained relatively stable in the majority of OECD economies, ending up slightly higher in most countries. Marked increases occurred in Canada, Finland, Norway, Italy, Spain and the United Kingdom. No single country experienced substantial reductions, although expenditure came down from above average levels in Belgium and Germany during the mid- and late 1980s (OECD, 1996*a*).

There is considerable cross-country variation in the effectiveness of social expenditure (these figures relate to the mid-1980s, so as to also include France and Germany). Cash transfer systems in Belgium and Sweden, our findings suggest, succeeded in lifting more than 80 per cent of pre-transfer poor individuals from poverty. In Denmark, Finland, the Netherlands and Norway the corresponding effectiveness rate was well over 70 per cent, and in France, Germany and the United Kingdom over 60 per cent. By contrast, in Canada just under 50 per cent of pre-transfer poor persons were lifted from poverty, in Australia just under 40 per cent and in the United States well under 25 per cent. Similarly, transfer systems in countries like Belgium and Sweden achieved an almost 95 per cent reduction of the poverty gap, compared to about 80 per cent France and Germany, and, at the other end of the spectrum, to about 55 per cent in the United States. The most significant reduction in the poverty gap is generally realised among the elderly (typically 90 per cent or more with the exception of the United States, where only slightly more than 80 per cent of the elderly poverty gap is reduced by social transfers).

Analytically speaking, one can think of the adequacy of social security as being determined by the extent and the structure of need, the level of social protection expenditure and the efficiency of the transfer system. Differences in poverty rates across countries appear to be, at least to some extent, a reflection of differing welfare effort: poverty rates are generally lower in countries with higher levels of social expenditure. In the mid-1980s, social expenditure as a percentage of GDP varied from well over 30 per cent in Sweden, to about or over 25 per cent in Belgium, Denmark, Finland, France, Germany,

Box 2. **The impact of social expenditure: country-by-country trends**

In **Australia** over the 1980s, social transfers did not fully compensate for the apparent increase in pre-transfer poverty among children and non-elderly adults, resulting in an increase of post-transfer poverty. However, in terms of reduction of the poverty gap, the effectiveness of social transfers remained virtually unchanged. It also appears that there has been a slight deterioration in the effectiveness of social transfers in lifting the elderly from poverty, as a result of which poverty increased slightly.

In **Belgium**, no important changes in the impact of social security transfers on poverty are measured between 1985 and 1992. If anything, the effectiveness of social transfers appears to have improved a little.

In **Canada** in the period 1975 to 1991, the effectiveness of social transfers in lifting people from poverty appears to have improved substantially. The marked increase in pre-transfer poverty among children and non-elderly appears to have been dampened quite substantially by social transfers. Most remarkable, however, is the dramatic improvement in the effectiveness of social transfers *vis-à-vis* the elderly.

In **Denmark**, the effectiveness of social security in alleviating poverty seems to have improved considerably between 1987 and 1992. For the elderly, the dramatic fall in the poverty rate appears to be wholly attributable to a greater impact of social transfers. Among children and non-elderly adults pre-transfer poverty rates have gone up, while post-transfer poverty rates have remained stable.

For the elderly in **Finland**, 1987-92, the pre-transfer poverty rate went down, whereas the post-transfer poverty rate went up; for children, however, the performance of social transfers in fighting poverty appears to have improved, as post-transfer poverty rates went down slightly.

For **France**, the figures indicate that the poverty-alleviating impact of social security transfers for the elderly has improved considerably between 1979 and 1984. Also, for children and non-elderly adults, social transfers reduced the poverty gap in 1984 to a greater extent than in 1979.

Few changes are registered in **Germany** between 1978 and 1983. Overall, the pre-transfer poverty rate increased a little, while the post-transfer poverty rate remained stable. For all demographic groups, somewhat larger poverty gap reduction rates were measured in 1983 than was the case in 1978. Among children, social security transfers did not quite succeed in relieving an increase in the pre-transfer poverty rate.

Results for the **Netherlands** are dominated by the seemingly virtual elimination in 1987 of poverty among the elderly. Between 1983 and 1987 the impact of social security transfers also reduced poverty gaps for non-elderly adults and children, although the post-transfer poverty rate among children rose slightly. The results for 1991 are probably valid in themselves, but not comparable to those for 1983 and 1987 (see Appendix 2).

Results for **Norway** do not indicate a clear trend in the period 1979 to 1991 (the seemingly dramatic rise in the poverty rate among the elderly in 1986 is probably a data quirk). Yet, in the period 1979 to 1991 as a whole, the post-transfer poverty rate among the elderly went up despite a drop in the pre-transfer poverty rate and a slight improvement in the poverty gap which reduced the impact of social security transfers. Among children and non-elderly adults, slight increases in the pre-transfer poverty rate did not produced higher post-transfer poverty rates.

The poverty-alleviating effectiveness of social security transfers appears to be high in **Sweden**, and steadily improved over the 1975-1992 period. Among the elderly, the poverty gap had already been virtually completely eliminated in 1975, although post-transfer poverty rates declined between 1975 and 1992. Among children and non-elderly adults, strongly rising pre-transfer poverty rates (doubled for children) led only to quite modest increases in post-transfer poverty rates.

Results for the **United Kingdom** are ambiguous: on the one hand, the large decline in the poverty rate for the elderly between 1974 and 1986 appears to have been wholly due to an improved performance by social security transfers. However, social transfers have not succeeded in preventing the large rise in pre-transfer poverty rates among children and non-elderly adults, resulting in increases in post-transfer poverty rates, although they have dampened it considerably. Unfortunately, we have no data about the performance of social security transfers in the period after 1986, when financial poverty increased in the United Kingdom.

In the **United States**, in the period 1974 to 1991, the effectiveness of social transfers in lifting people from poverty appears to have remained more or less stable relative to the incidence of pre-transfer poverty. The marked increase in post-transfer poverty among non-aged adults and especially among children occurred because of a significant rise in pre-transfer poverty. The decline in the incidence of poverty among the elderly during the 1980s seems mainly attributable to a decrease in the extent of pre-transfer poverty rather than to the improved effectiveness of pensions.

the Netherlands, Norway and Finland, well under 25 per cent in Canada, Ireland, Italy and Spain and, at the other extreme, to below 15 per cent in Australia and the United States. Evidently, poverty rates are much lower in the high spending Scandinavian and Benelux countries compared to southern Europe, North America and Australia. There is no complete agreement, however, on the extent to which the level of social expenditure actually matters.

Förster (1993) reports a significant relationship between the level of social expenditure and the overall level of poverty among non-elderly households in OECD countries. Similarly, Deleeck et al. (1992) in a study involving seven European countries found a significant relationship between welfare effort and outcome. Mitchell (1991) has claimed on the basis of extensive cross-national research involving the major OECD countries that welfare effort is a rather poor predictor of outcome, whether measured in terms of head-count or poverty gap. Welfare effort and pre-transfer need, Mitchell (1995) claims, account for around 60 per cent of the differences in outcomes. However, if efficiency factors are included, the explanatory performance increases to about 90 per cent. She concludes that need, effort and efficiency all contribute approximately in equal measure to explaining differences in welfare outcomes. Our findings suggest relatively little cross-national variation in transfer efficiency, if measured as the proportion of social transfers used to fill the poverty gap. Only Australia appears to direct a significantly higher proportion of social transfers to the poor. Apparently, even systems that are fairly narrowly focused on poverty prevention fail to keep spillovers to below 40 per cent of total expenditure.

Overall, two main conclusions emerge. First, without social security transfers, the extent of poverty, even among the non-elderly, would be much larger than it actually is. Social transfers succeed in lifting out of poverty more than 60 per cent of pre-transfer poor individuals in Belgium, Sweden, Denmark, Finland, the Netherlands, Norway, France, Germany and the United Kingdom. In Canada just under 50 per cent of pre-transfer poor are lifted from poverty, in Australia just under 40 per cent and in the United States under 25 per cent. In all countries, the most significant reductions in poverty gaps have been achieved for the elderly. Second, there is no evidence that the impact of social security on the extent of poverty has diminished. On the contrary, in all countries, except Australia and Finland, the trend in the proportion of the pre-transfer poverty gap that is filled by social security transfers is upward, rather than downward. In some countries [Canada, Denmark, France (1979-84) and the United Kingdom] large reductions in the poverty rate among the elderly can be attributed to an improved performance by social transfers. In a number of countries [Canada, Denmark, France (1979-84), Norway, Sweden and the United Kingdom] increases in pre-transfer poverty among children and/or non-elderly adults have been compensated or considerably dampened by social security transfers. There is no country where the proportional reduction in the poverty gap among children due to social transfers has become smaller, and only one (Finland) where the impact of social transfers on the poverty gap among non-elderly adults has declined. Social security transfers appear to be as important in preventing poverty as ever.[8]

SOCIO-DEMOGRAPHIC CHANGE AND POVERTY

The past few decades have been marked by a major socio-demographic transition.[9] Family dissolution and the rise of lone-parenthood in particular appear to be associated with an increased need for social protection. In contrast, the proliferation of the two-earner household appears to have been associated in most cases with enhanced income security at the household level, but this trend also appears to be associated with the emergence of a "new" social risk: lack of a second household income.

Single-person households

The proportion of single-person households has risen fairly consistently across the OECD. Figures by the European Commission (1995) suggest that in the majority of EU countries, the number of single-person households increased by about 40 to 50 per cent in the period 1971-91. This trend, which is part of a general trend towards smaller household units, has a direct impact on the distribution of welfare because of the economies of scale associated with income pooling and shared consumption; two individuals living separately typically enjoy a lower standard of living compared to two individuals with identical incomes living under one roof and sharing consumption. In virtually all countries, poverty rates among single-person households in the active age-group are several times higher than poverty rates among couples, but our findings suggest relative stability over time in most countries (Table A.7). More importantly, it is the continuing rise in the relative share of single person households that may push the poverty rate upward.

Lone parenthood

The rise in lone-parent households has been the focus of much attention over the past 10 years or so (OECD, 1990b and OECD, 1993). Despite the amount of research that has been done on this topic, estimates on the incidence of lone parenthood still differ rather considerably. Bradshaw et al. (1995), in a recent and comprehensive survey, find that lone-parent families currently represent almost 30 per cent of families with children in the United States. Their relative share amounts to about 20 per cent in Denmark, Germany, Ireland, the United Kingdom, Australia and Norway and to nearly 15 per cent in France and the Netherlands. Lone parenthood is still relatively uncommon in Belgium, Luxembourg and Italy and, probably, in most other Mediterranean countries.

In the mid-1980s, Förster (1993) reports, single parents were typically three times more likely to be in poverty than other non-elderly families: in North America and in Australia about 50 per cent of single-parent households lived in poverty,[10] in Germany, Ireland and the United Kingdom about 30 per cent, in France, the Benelux countries and Norway in between 10 and 20 per cent. Overall, our own findings provide a very similar picture: lone parents are at an extraordinarily high risk of being in poverty in Australia, Canada and the United States, especially if compared to the plight of lone mothers in the Scandinavian countries.[11] However, our findings suggest relative stability of relative poverty rates among single parents. Exceptions include the Netherlands but, as noted in Appendix 2, the 1987 and 1991 datasets are not comparable. There is a similar problem with respect to the comparability of the United Kingdom 1974-79 datasets. However, the increase in poverty among lone parents in Australia over the 1980s probably reflects a real development.[12]

In some countries, lone parenthood is at the forefront of political debate over welfare reform, while in other countries it is a marginal issue or no issue at all. Most concern tends to be expressed in countries where lone parenthood is associated with massive and often long-term dependence on social assistance. Bradshaw et al. (1995) report that around 1992, 73 per cent of lone mothers in the United Kingdom were receiving social assistance, 49 per cent in the United States and 61 per cent in Australia, compared to about 30 per cent in Finland, Norway or the Netherlands. Moreover, Duncan et al. (1995) find that, during the mid-1980s, assistance spells involving lone-parent families were substantially longer than spells involving two-parent families. The proportion of lone parents still receiving social assistance after three years ranged from 26 per cent in Germany, to about 35 per cent in the United States, 58 per cent in Canada and 84 per cent in the United Kingdom. Long-term dependence on social assistance is in some countries perceived to be associated with a culture of dependency. In fact, a major cause of poverty and chronic welfare dependence among lone mothers with modest earning capacity is their inability to combine their role as breadwinner and child-rearer, typically because of a shortage of suitable and affordable child care facilities (OECD, 1993).

Dual earnership

The past few decades were also characterised by a marked increase in female labour market participation. Probably, dual-earnership is the most important reason why drops in individual income and increases in unemployment have not resulted in corresponding increases in poverty and income inequality. Dual-earnership is also associated with enhanced income security at the household level, i.e. a reduced need for social transfers in the case that one of the household members loses his or her labour income (Cantillon, 1994). Evidence so far suggests that dual-earnership (married women's earnings) has so far been mainly associated with a reduction in inequality among couples. Analyses of the income distribution in countries that have experienced a considerable increase in inequality have concluded that overall women's earnings still have an equalising effect (Machin and Waldfogel, 1994, for the United Kingdom; Cancian *et al.*, 1993, for the United States; Bjorkland, 1992, for Sweden; Saunders, 1993, for Australia; Cantillon *et al.*, 1993, for Belgium). For other countries, the evidence is rather mixed, with a majority of studies concurring on equalisation (Saunders *et al.*, 1994). However, some recent studies suggest that women's earnings have had less equalising effect in recent years (Blackburn and Bloom, 1994).

However, despite the overall equalising effect of double earnership, inequality between two-income families and one-income families appears to have increased, with one-earner families regressing towards the bottom end of the distribution. Consequently, the inability to secure a second household income is increasingly associated with financial vulnerability, particularly since the relative poverty threshold is increasingly a function of the dual-earner living-standard. Single-income households, especially those with dependent children, often experience great difficulties in making ends meet. For example, O'Connor and Smeeding (1995) found that, during the mid-1980s, a large fraction of prime-aged poor households contain an all year-round, full-time working head. Similarly, in a study of seven European countries, Deleeck *et al.* (1992) found that some 40 per cent of poor households contained at least one fully employed person.

Moreover, the traditional division of labour between men and women appears to be giving way to a division of labour that is more strongly based on education and skills. These two trends could be mutually reinforcing in their effect on the distribution of welfare; *i.e.* households consisting of well qualified members accumulate the advantages of stable, well-paying jobs while, at the other extreme, households consisting of unskilled members are much more likely to be accumulating disadvantage. Possibly, inequality is further increased by the sociological phenomenon of homogamy, *i.e.* partners frequently sharing similar educational and economic backgrounds. Consequently, poverty and disadvantage may well become increasingly concentrated among the less skilled, not only because of their losing ground in the labour market as individuals, but also because they typically live with a partner who is also low skilled. However, this hypothesis remains to be tested in cross-country analysis.[13]

EMPLOYMENT AND POVERTY

Most people of working age depend for their living either exclusively or primarily on labour market income. Moreover, most social protection arrangements in the advanced economies critically assume that the market takes care of most needs from the moment that one leaves school until retirement. Consequently, it is of prime importance to ascertain whether the labour market is, as is often alleged, becoming less adequate in providing a decent standard of living to those who are institutionally assumed to be virtually self-reliant. As documented in the previous sections, our findings suggest that poverty may be shifting from the elderly to the non-elderly. Moreover, "need", as posited by pre-transfer poverty, appears to have risen fairly consistently, and in some cases quite significantly among non-elderly adults and children. We will first review some key developments in labour markets and then look at the relationship between labour market performance and poverty at the aggregate level.

Developments in OECD labour markets

In the OECD area as a whole, the share of the population at working age holding a job has remained virtually unchanged over the past 25 years. This picture of overall stability obscures widely different trajectories across countries. In the United States, employment increased by about 50 per cent between 1970 and 1990, versus a rise of merely 10 per cent in Europe (EU), only just keeping up with the growth of the working age population and clearly lagging behind the growth of the labour force. However, feeble job growth in Europe was compensated by a strong increase in real wages, which occurred in a majority of countries on the European continent pretty much across the board. In the United States, in contrast, real wages remained virtually stagnant and a considerable minority experienced real wage decline (OECD, 1994*a*).

Virtually all major OECD countries, with the notable exception of the United States and more recently the United Kingdom, have experienced a continuing rise in unemployment since the early 1970s, a trend which was only temporarily reversed in the second half of the 1980s. During the early 1990s, dramatic increases in unemployment occurred in previously low-unemployment countries like Sweden and Finland. Typically, about half of the unemployed in Europe are long-term unemployed versus around 10 per cent in the United States and Canada, and few European countries have experienced a sustained drop in long-term unemployment. More important, however, were the marked increases in the incidence of unemployment among certain social categories.

Firstly, over the 1980s, there were striking increases in female unemployment, which more than doubled in Germany, the Netherlands and Ireland and almost tripled in Spain[14] (OECD, 1991). Presumably, this was an important development in an era in which the lack of a second income within the household was increasingly associated with financial need. The increase in female labour force participation has remained significant, especially in countries with traditionally low female participation rates. The inflow in the years to come will consist mainly of relatively less skilled women, for whom unemployment rates are already very high in most continental European countries.

Secondly, in the early 1980s youth unemployment was typically two to three times the average, with the notable exception of Germany. Youth unemployment has risen faster than average in a number of European countries, most notably in France, Ireland and in southern Europe. In contrast, the United Kingdom, Australia and the United States saw a decline in youth unemployment (OECD, 1991).

Thirdly, the 1995 *Employment Outlook* reports that about one-third to half of all the unemployed in the OECD live in households in which no other person has a job. This proportion increased almost universally across OECD countries between the mid-1980s and the early 1990s. Moreover, a growing proportion of the unemployed living in these "jobless" households are long-term unemployed (OECD, 1995a).

Finally, in many countries, the trend in unemployment understates the rise in joblessness. Participation rates of older men have been dropping precipitously in many European countries. In addition, taking into account discouraged workers and involuntary part-time workers, the majority of whom are women, would increase the unemployment rate in most countries by another 2 to 9 percentage points, involuntary part-time unemployment being by far the most important factor (OECD, 1995a). There is much current concern over increasing insecurity of employment, but lack of comparative data makes it difficult to document this alleged trend.

Many countries appear to have experienced a shift in demand away from relatively unskilled jobs to jobs that require more skills. In most countries, including the high-employment-generating countries, the fastest growth in employment has been in the more highly-skilled professional and administrative occupations rather than in the relatively unskilled occupations, such as sales and service staff. The relative proportion of production workers has declined sharply. Data on educational qualifications also suggest that a general upskilling of the workforce has been taking place (OECD, 1994a). In Europe, where wages are relatively inflexible and minimum protection arrangements are more generous, both relative employment and unemployment rates have generally deteriorated.[15] In countries with relatively flexible wages (United States, Canada and Australia) the relative employment and unemployment rates have remained more or less stable, but low-paid (male) workers experienced a real decline in wages, especially in the United States. There are some indications pointing to an intensification over the 1980s (OECD, 1994a). However, there is no firm evidence at present that unemployment and real wage decline are in effect two distinct manifestations of one underlying trend: *i.e.* the deterioration of the relative earnings-capacity of the least skilled (Blank, 1995).[16]

Finally, it should be noted that there is evidence of an accumulation of labour market disadvantage at the household level. To illustrate this, whereas one would expect women living with an unemployed man to have a greater incentive to work, one actually observes participation in employment for wives of the unemployed to be significantly and consistently lower than for wives of working men (Giannelli and Micklewright, 1995). This effect appears to be stronger in benefit regimes where wive's earnings are taken into account in allocating benefits (Dex *et al.*, 1995).

Employment and poverty: an exploratory analysis

Although unemployment is widely regarded as one of the major causes of poverty among the non-elderly population, a strong and consistent positive correlation between unemployment and poverty at the aggregate level is not immediately apparent (Chart 5.1). Arguably, one can discern four distinct clusters of countries. A first cluster, comprising Norway, Sweden and Switzerland enjoyed at around the mid-1980s a very low level of unemployment with moderately low levels of financial poverty among the non-elderly population. A second set of countries, comprising the United States, Canada and Australia, combine moderately low levels of unemployment with high levels of poverty. A third cluster comprises most continental European countries, which all combine relatively high levels of unemployment with average to low levels of poverty. The Netherlands and Belgium, for example, appear to enjoy relatively low poverty rates despite above average levels of unemployment. Finally, only Ireland appears to meet the general expectation in that a very high level of unemployment is actually linked with a high level of poverty.

Frequent but short spells of unemployment may entail fewer social costs than less frequent but much longer spells without work. But, again, a strong positive relationship between the aggregate long-term unemployment rate and number at working age in poverty is not immediately evident (Chart 5.2). A similar clustering of countries occurs, even more distinctly. Clearly, some countries do combine high long-term unemployment rates with comparatively low levels of poverty. Of course, this finding does not refute the hypothesis that for individuals long-term poverty has far more serious consequences than a temporary lack of work.

Reducing poverty remains one of the principal motivations behind the efforts of many governments to increase the number of people holding a job. But a higher share of the working-age population employed is not *ipso facto* associated with less people in poverty (Chart 5.3). Only Switzerland, Sweden

◆ Chart 5.1. **Unemployment and poverty**

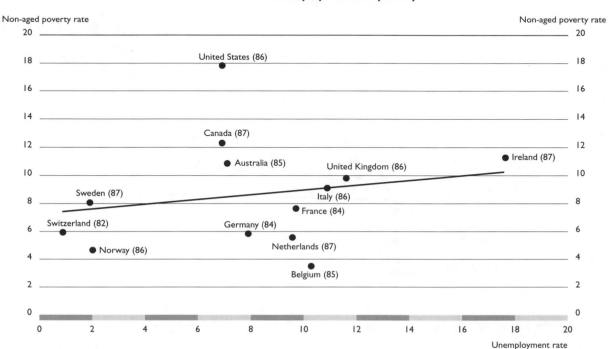

Note: Data for mid-1980s.
Sources: OECD (1995*b*), Table 7.2, and OECD (1995*c*), Table 2.15.

◆   Chart 5.2. **Long-term unemployment and poverty**

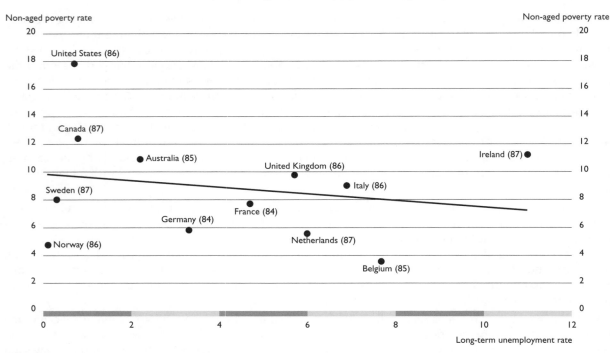

Note: Data for mid-1980s.
Sources: OECD (1995*b*), Table 7.2, and OECD (1995*c*), Table 1.18.

◆   Chart 5.3. **Employment and poverty**

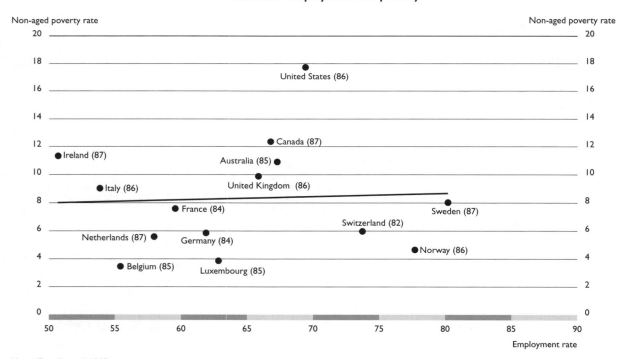

Note: Data for mid-1980s.
Sources: OECD (1995*b*), Table 7.2, and OECD (1995*c*), Table 2.14.

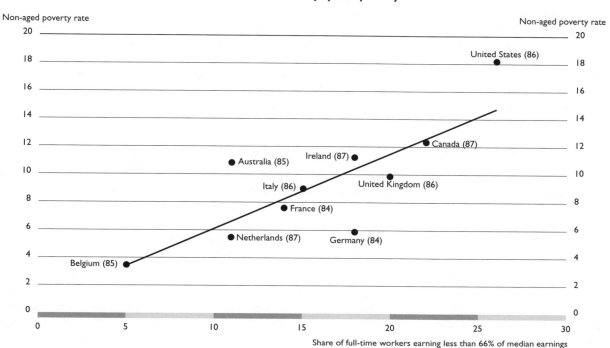

◆ Chart 5.4. **Low pay and poverty**

Non-aged poverty rate (left and right axes, values 0 to 20)

Share of full-time workers earning less than 66% of median earnings (horizontal axis, 0 to 30)

Data points:
- United States (86)
- Canada (87)
- Ireland (87)
- Australia (85)
- United Kingdom (86)
- Italy (86)
- France (84)
- Netherlands (87)
- Germany (84)
- Belgium (85)

Note: Data for mid-1980s.
Sources: OECD (1995*b*), Table 7.2, and OECD (1995*c*), Table 1.11.

and Norway, of which at least the latter two countries have pursued active full employment policies, combine very high employment levels (over 75 per cent) with moderately to low levels of poverty.[17] By contrast, the United States, Australia, Canada and the United Kingdom, countries which rely more heavily on freely operating markets with decentralised wage setting to achieve high employment rates (between 65 and 70 per cent), find themselves confronted with high levels of poverty. At the other extreme, European countries like Belgium, the Netherlands and Germany enjoy moderate to low poverty rates despite comparatively high levels of non-employment.[18]

Part of the explanation for this finding may rest in a possible trade-off between employment and low-pay. In the countries achieving the highest non-subsidised employment rates, most notably the United States and Canada, one also encounters by far the highest levels of wage differentials and the highest proportion of workers working for relatively low pay. Moreover, in a number of major countries (United States, Canada and Australia), employment growth has been accompanied by a real decline in the wages of low-paid workers or with a relative deterioration of their earnings, as in the United Kingdom. At present, there is mostly *prima facie* evidence for a trade-off between low wages and employment. Glynn (1995) reports a significant correlation between real wage cost growth for the low-paid and employment, and Freeman (1995*a*) also claims to have found evidence in support of the trade-off hypothesis.[19] Conversely, simple cross-country correlation analysis presented in OECD (1996*b*) suggests no significant tendency for employment to be lower in countries where there are relatively few low-paid jobs available. Clearly, this matter requires further research, especially since a rather strong positive correlation appears to exist between the proportion of people working for low pay and the overall level of poverty among the non-elderly population. It is important to point out that this finding, presented in Chart 5.4, is based on the limited data available and on a limited number of countries. However, it is worthwhile noting in this context that the decline in real wages for men has been identified as the single most important cause of the persistent high poverty rates in the United States

(Blank, 1993). Again, it remains unclear to what extent real wage decline in the United States is actually a reflection of structural shifts affecting all advanced economies, or whether specific circumstances (e.g. immigration) account for most of the decline in real wages. It remains uncertain, therefore, whether a move towards labour market deregulation, decentralised wage setting and reduced social protection expenditure would necessarily result in real wage decline and increases in poverty in other countries. Further research in this area is needed, but it is reasonable to suspect that bringing down unemployment, or non-employment for that matter, through deregulation (e.g. abolishing or lowering minimum wage protection) has its limitations as an anti-poverty strategy.[20]

FINANCIAL POVERTY AND SOCIAL EXCLUSION: "NEW POVERTY"

So far our analysis has necessarily focused on financial aspects of poverty and the determination of those factors which appear to be correlated to being in poverty as defined above. However, it is often argued that the concept of poverty should not be restricted to a single dimension, i.e. a low standard of living, but should also encompass a number of other dimensions: a "new poverty concept". In Anglo-Saxon countries, particularly the United States, this discussion has focused on the term "underclass", whereas the term "social exclusion" is more prevalent in continental Europe.

Perhaps the most developed conception of the underclass, is that of Wilson who describes the underclass as a population living in the ghetto, "whose primary predicament is joblessness reinforced by growing social isolation" (Wilson, 1991, p. 641).[21] Economic, political and social (race discrimination) factors have triggered an increase in the concentrations of poor people in certain urban neighbourhoods. Successful people have moved out of these neighbourhoods, depriving those who stayed behind of conventional role models and social networks linking them to the wider society, resulting in their social isolation. This does not imply that the ghetto poor adopt a different system of values, but that they only come into contact with people like themselves, and the nature of these contacts amplifies the effect of living in a highly concentrated poverty area.

"What distinguishes members of the underclass from those of other economically disadvantaged groups is that their marginal economic position or weak attachment to the labour force is uniquely reinforced by the neighbourhood or social milieu" (Wilson, 1991, p. 663). Indeed, Peterson (1991) remarks of Wilson's theory that it applies to only a small portion of the poverty population: less than 9 per cent. The underclass appears to be a group of people where the problems of poverty are compounded by a number of other social and economic disadvantages. This makes their situation rather impregnable for standard anti-poverty policies. However, Jencks (1992) has challenged on empirical grounds the claim that declining economic opportunities have created a new "underclass". He argues that, while economic opportunities for less-skilled workers in the United States began to deteriorate in the 1970s, most of the other problems associated with the "underclass" followed different trajectories. He also points out that in the United States welfare dependency has not increased since the early 1970s, and that illiteracy, teenage motherhood and violence have declined somewhat.

The continental European debate is more focused on the concept of "social exclusion". Social exclusion typically refers to the multi-dimensional character of disadvantage and exclusion in modern market economies, i.e. in the areas of work and income, but also in housing, health, access to social services, and, characteristically, culture.[22] The concept of social exclusion is, in itself, of course rather vague and broad, and encompasses much more than just poverty, in the traditional sense of the word. Nevertheless, some authors, in particular the Dutch sociologist Engbersen (1991), have defined poverty in terms of social exclusion. Engbersen (1991, p. 12) writes that modern poverty can roughly be described as "the structured exclusion of citizens from social participation, coupled with permanent dependence on the state". Modern poverty can so be characterised by seven elements: financial strain (low income, debts); social isolation (fewer visits to friends and relatives, etc.); little benefit from some government services (such as education); bureaucratic control of private life (for some); heterogeneity among the poor; geographic concentration (in particular in old neighbourhoods of large cities); and certain cultural adaptations (accepting a situation of exclusion and dependence). Thus, poverty in a modern welfare state is more than just a low standard of living or a low level of resources – although that is a necessary condition to be in poverty.

The essential feature of "new" poverty is social exclusion, from informal social networks, as well as from formal institutions (work, education, etc.). This implies multiple deprivation, or "cumulative misery" (Schuyt and Tan, 1988, p. 44): no work, low income, low education, bad health, etc. In Europe there is less evidence of strong spatial concentration of the poor in certain neighbourhoods. There is probably not a single characteristic that the "socially excluded" have in common, except, perhaps, not having a stable well-paying job which is also reflected by the increasing numbers of long-term unemployed in many countries. The "socially excluded" are not a single group, but are composed of diverse sorts of people who are "under": *i.e.* people "who suffer from an accumulation of disadvantage which cannot be reached by macro-policies" (Dahrendorf, 1990, p. 151). One might add, that many of these people are difficult to reach by any kind of policy (Engbersen, 1991, p. 19).

Yet, despite its heterogeneity and its wide scope, the term "social exclusion" in its broadest possible meaning does not appear to encompass some conditions and persons that plausibly might be called "poverty" and "poor". These are, for instance, regularly working people with low earnings, single earners with large families to support, and some elderly people with low pensions. They have in common that their standard of living is (temporarily or permanently) low, but they do not necessarily suffer from other clear disadvantages, and they are not necessarily excluded from society. Their situation may be characterised as "invisible hardship", in contrast to the "visible hardship", by which social exclusion is characterised (Schuyt and Tan, 1988, p. 40). Although they suffer real deprivations, this may not be easily recognisable for outside observers.[23]

Rising social assistance dependence is frequently taken as evidence for "new poverty" (Funken and Cooper, 1995). A comprehensive survey by Eardley *et al.* (1996) shows that there have been very significant increases in the number of social assistance recipients in OECD countries during the 1980s and early 1990s. In Belgium, for example, the number of social assistance (MINIMEX) increased from about 25 000 in 1980 to over 62 000 in 1994. In Canada, the estimated number of social assistance beneficiaries doubled from 1.4 million in 1980s to over 3 million in 1994, and in the western *Länder* of Germany, the increase in general assistance recipients rose from 1.3 million in 1980 to almost 2.9 million in 1990. Improvements in benefit levels and extension of eligibility explain some of these increases, but much will reflect real increases in family distress.

Homelessness is one of the most visible faces of poverty. While there is a general feeling that the number of homeless people in many countries has risen, reliable statistics are difficult to come by. Estimates are made on different definitions in different countries. A Council of Europe report on homelessness (1993) reports that in the reunified Germany in 1991, for example, about 1 million people are homeless. This number includes single homeless people, persons in (shared) temporary accommodation, migrants and asylum seekers. About 200-400 000 persons were reported to be using makeshift housing in France in 1987.

The extension of the poverty concept to a wider category of persons than those that are "socially excluded" implies, however, that it does not cover all problems which can push people into social exclusion, but only one particular deprivation: a low standard of living. A low standard of living belongs to the core of the common-sense meaning of "poverty", even though it may not cover all the connotations of the word.

NEW POLICY AVENUES

Summary of the main findings

Our research, as that of others, suggests that cross-national differences in the extent of relative income poverty are quite significant. Different measurement procedures do produce mild variation in cross-national differences but country rankings are generally fairly well reproduced and similar clusters of high-poverty and low-poverty countries emerge. The evidence on mobility trends out of poverty is not yet conclusive: the poor in high poverty countries may experience more difficulties in escaping from poverty than is the case in low-poverty countries. As for poverty trends, here too we find considerable variation across countries. The overwhelming impression, however, is that poverty levels are generally rather stable; responsiveness to changes in economic growth or unemployment appear to be mild at most. We have not found evidence of a consistent rise in poverty across the OECD area, but limited data availability may account at least in part for this finding.

There are in fact few countries where sharp increases in poverty are evident, with the notable exception of the United Kingdom over the late 1980s. The incidence of poverty appears to have risen moderately in a number of countries including Australia (1981-89) and in the United States during the 1980s. The countries mentioned so far also happen to be the countries where much of the debate on "polarisation" and "new poverty" originates. It would appear, therefore, that the international debate is unduly influenced by what is happening in a limited number of countries. The findings reported in this paper suggest relative stability, or mild increases at most, in Belgium (1985-92), Finland (1987-91), Germany (1978-83 and 1983-90), the Netherlands (1983-87), Norway (1979-91), Sweden (1975-92). Poverty appears to have decreased significantly in Canada (1975-91) and moderate decreases were found for Denmark (1987-92), Portugal (1980-89) and Spain (1980-88).

Second, without social transfers the extent of poverty would be much greater than it actually is. As with financial poverty, there is considerable variation in the effectiveness of social transfers across countries, due to differences in expenditure effort, the extent and structure of need and the efficiency of the distribution system. However, there is no agreement yet on the relative importance of need, effort and efficiency. It is evident, however, that countries with higher levels of social expenditure generally enjoy lower levels of financial poverty. It is equally clear that no country with a below average level of social expenditure enjoys a low or moderate level of financial poverty. A lower level of expenditure can be compensated by a higher level of transfer efficiency, but only to a fairly limited extent. The overall effectiveness of social transfers on preventing financial poverty has remained more or less stable over time. There is even evidence of significant improvements in a number of countries. Hence, there is no evidence at all of welfare states disintegrating, either in terms of welfare effort – welfare spending actually increased in a majority of countries – or in terms of the adequacy of social protection transfers. But it is equally true that even countries with extremely high levels of social expenditure have failed to achieve a total eradication of poverty.

Third, poverty appears to be shifting from the elderly to the non-aged, and to families with children in particular. Moreover, there is an even more consistent rise in pre-transfer poverty among the non-elderly population. In part this seems related to certain deliberate policy interventions (e.g. expansion of early retirement). The rise in pre-transfer poverty is probably also due to both socio-demographic change – family breakdown – and labour market change. Single-person households and lone-parent households are significantly more likely to be in poverty relative to other household configurations, except in one or two countries. The relative proportion of these financially precarious household configurations continues to rise virtually all across the OECD area. However, socio-demographic change cannot be the sole explanation for the upward trend in financial vulnerability among the non-elderly. In countries where poverty increased most strongly, the most significant increases occurred among couples with and without children rather than among single-parent households or single-person households. Presumably, then, the rise in need must also be seen in the context of adverse labour market conditions for particular groups. The relationship between labour market change and poverty remains rather elusive, especially because of the wide diversity in household income packaging strategies compensating for weak or deteriorating individual labour market positions.

However, the highest levels of financial poverty among the non-elderly population are found in countries which enjoy the highest levels of non-subsidised employment. The least productive, it appears, succeed in gaining a job, or holding on to one, by accepting wages that are frequently insufficient to acquire a standard of living above the relative poverty threshold. Many European countries appear to have maintained lower poverty levels, despite higher non-employment levels, through a stronger emphasis on minimum wage protection combined with relatively generous transfer policies. While welfare state dependence is a concern, there appears to be, at the margin, an even stronger concern for the plight of those who are genuinely unemployable at a "reasonable" wage. It remains uncertain, however, whether an increase in European employment levels would necessarily require an expansion of the low-wage sector and a general reduction in social protection. Moreover, it remains uncertain to what extent enhanced labour market flexibility can solve the employment problem. The Nordic countries suggest a third way, requiring a comprehensive set of macroeconomic, labour market and welfare policies that maintain high employment and low poverty.

The continental European "two track" paradigm of high wages for those in work and relatively generous benefits for many of the non-employed appears to have succeeded relatively well in keeping poverty down. However, there is much concern over the "socially excluded" since they are forced into virtual total idleness which many tend to experience as degrading, and which, moreover, tends to reinforce their outsider status by bringing about a progressive erosion of skills. Still, poverty is widespread among households living exclusively on a replacement income. Arguably, their plight cannot be substantially improved simply by means of increasing benefits. A single household income, and *a fortiori* a single replacement income is generally insufficient to acquire a decent standard of living in context where the double-earner living standard sets the tone. Europe is facing a non-employment problem: 40 per cent of the population at working age are not on the labour market. There is a massive lack of jobs to provide the second household income that many prime-age households require to stay out of poverty.[24] Undoubtedly, this is at least in part a consequence of the very strong emphasis on protecting household living standards through the breadwinner, by means of high (minimum) wages, job security regulation and mandatory social benefits. It may be argued therefore that financial poverty is currently not so much a problem of the breadwinner having a wage that is too low, but rather a problem of the partner being unable to acquire the necessary second household income.

Consequently, the double deficiency of the continental European paradigm is that of self-reinforcement and social exclusion on the one hand and inadequate income protection *vis-à-vis* some categories of non-employed on the other. Little progress can be expected by expanding the predominantly passive income protection policies that have been instrumental in compensating the social consequences of massive labour market exclusion. Clearly, increasing minimum wage protection for those in work and handing out more benefits to those without a job is not going to bring Europe much social progress in any meaning of the word. It would appear that only a work-oriented strategy can offer a solution to both the problems of social exclusion and poverty deriving from involuntary non-employment.

However, at least one major case suggests strongly that a stronger emphasis on job creation alone may not suffice. Social policy in the United States has been characterised by a distinct preoccupation with ensuring that, first and foremost, people have access to a job, thus enabling them to be self-reliant, to participate and to be upwardly mobile.[25] Unemployment and, more broadly, involuntary exclusion from the labour market are primarily considered an economic disequilibrium problem, rather than a social or political problem, as tends to be the case in Europe. Effectively, compared to Europe, the American job creation record is impressive. Clearly, the problem is that relative poverty appears to have increased further, from an already high level, despite a massive supply of new jobs, many of which yield average or above average earnings. A major problem is that the lowest paid men have experienced considerable real decreases in hourly wages, while much of the rest enjoyed little or no increase in wages. To a considerable extent, the effect of declining male earnings on poverty has been dampened by income packaging strategies at the household level, in particular working women's earnings compensating for stagnating male earnings. The American labour market succeeded in meeting the demand for additional household income, but on the whole, the results have not been really satisfactory from a social perspective.

And just as in Europe, those who do enjoy minimum income protection are confronted with a problem of social exclusion. In essence, therefore, the major problem with both European and American welfare systems is identical, namely incompatibility between social protection and work. The failure of the welfare system (Aid for Families with Dependent Children) to provide lone mothers on social assistance with adequate incentives to work remains at the centre of the American social policy debate, even though the overall levels of benefit dependence are modest compared to those in Europe. Moreover, the general perception that the system fosters dependence and that it adversely affects family formation has severely eroded public and political support for the welfare system. Much as in Europe, there is a broad consensus that measures have to be taken to reduce passive dependence. However, welfare reform aimed at stimulating, even forcing people to move out of dependence and into the labour market is almost certainly destined to fail, at least from a social perspective, unless there are initiatives to increase earnings-capacity of the least skilled, to facilitate the combination of work an care, especially for lone parents, and to increase the rewards from work.[26]

Hence, both the continental European and the American social policy paradigm appear to be "exhausted" in the sense that neither of the two is capable of achieving substantial social progress by way of incremental expansion along the policy lines that have been pursued for over so many years now. Arguably the principal challenge consists of finding a social policy paradigm that achieves a synthesis between labour market participation (social inclusion) and income protection. Increasingly, it appears, solutions are required that build on the principle of complementarity between work and social protection.[27]

Rethinking social policy

The apparent rise in need among the non-elderly population is an important development since social protection regimes in most advanced economies rest on the critical assumption that the market takes care of most needs of those at working age, except for a small minority of permanently disabled people and a limited number of workers struck by misfortune. Socio-demographic change (family decomposition and the rise in lone-parenthood) and economic change (structural unemployment and widening earnings differentials) are challenging this critical assumption. There are indications that poverty and need (as measured by pre-transfer poverty) are shifting towards those who are institutionally and culturally assumed to be self-sufficient. These developments present governments with closely interrelated challenges in keeping with incentive effects as well as sustainability concerns in a budgetary sense:

- the challenge of maintaining and improving the effectiveness of social protection arrangements. Our findings suggest that the effectiveness of social protection has remained more or less stable in a majority of countries despite a fairly general rise in need. From this perspective at least, the need for a drastic reorientation of social policy should not be overstated. However, need deriving from low pay or precarious employment, lone parenthood or long-term unemployment, and social non-participation sometimes pose new challenges to social protection arrangements. A "redesigning" of such arrangements may be needed to avoid undermining preparedness for work or adversely influencing family formation;

- the important challenge of improving and sustaining the legitimacy of social protection arrangements so that they keep the "non-deserving" from benefiting and avoid moral hazard type problems (*e.g.* reluctance to move out of dependence or to make efforts to be able to do so).

Virtually all advanced economies are faced with the challenges of improving effectiveness, maintaining affordability and enhancing legitimacy. However, in view of the huge cross-country diversity across the OECD-area it is virtually impossible to formulate a single set of policy recommendations. Some countries are predominantly faced with a poverty challenge, whereas others are primarily faced with a problem of labour market exclusion or budgetary or economic sustainability. Values differ: some countries traditionally put great emphasis on equality, whereas other countries are much more oriented towards maximising economic performance and promoting individual self-reliance.

Targeting

The challenge for each individual country is to find a balance that is optimal from the social (poverty prevention), economic (income stabilisation) and budgetary perspectives. Obviously, countries may want or may have to attach a different weight to each of these objectives. The appeal of targeting crucially depends on how broadly or narrowly the objectives of social policy are assessed. It is striking that in countries that rely most on targeted welfare provision, one tends to find most voices arguing for a more universal provision of welfare services (for example health care insurance or child benefits) while many continental European countries are moving in exactly the opposite direction. Mainly driven by budgetary concerns, governments seem to be looking for ways to target social expenditure on the most needy. In social insurance systems especially there is probably scope for increasing both "expenditure efficiency" and adequacy by reducing benefit levels for two-earner house-holds and increasing the level of protection for single-earner and single-parent households. Targeting could be implemented through direct means-testing, categorical selectivity (adjusting benefit levels to household type), or taxing benefits.

However, there are limits to the effectiveness of targeting. First, it may be financially irrational to take low-paid jobs, at least if possible future gains and the non-pecuniary benefits of work are left out of the calculation. Second, there probably exist organisational and administrative limits to designing and implementing highly selective systems of social protection, which may even disadvantage the least advantaged groups, in that they may lead to non-take up among those most in need.[28] Third, political support for targeted welfare provisions tends to be weaker. Different patterns of welfare provision on the public-private dimension cannot be regarded as functional equivalents. A shift from state to private and occupational welfare is likely to imply less vertical redistribution and hence an increase in inequality.

The challenges

One of the principal challenges facing policy makers is to make work and income protection more compatible, in a way that is economically sustainable. Effective education and training policies are essential components of any long-term strategy to increase overall living standards and reduce poverty. Similarly, the need to promote steady, sustainable growth through macroeconomic and other policies is widely agreed upon. But other measures seem to require arbitration between conflicting objectives. Demonstrably, direct income transfers play a critical, if not decisive role in preventing poverty, one that is, moreover, unlikely to diminish in the foreseeable future. Social transfers evidently represent a budgetary burden, but there seems to be little actual evidence that maintaining a social expenditure level that ensures a moderately low level of poverty is in any way economically impractical or unsus-tainable. In view of budgetary constraints, it may be necessary, however, to reconsider benefit and tax policies *vis-à-vis* the elderly, in order to meet rising need among the non-elderly population, children in particular. Although it is preferable to reduce dependence, an over-emphasis on promoting self-reliance is likely to have adverse social consequences; particular segments of society face in effect great difficulties in acquiring an adequate standard of living without direct or indirect income support. But because it is imperative to avoid the definite harmful effects of long spells of labour market exclusion it is essential to find new ways of integrating work and income protection.

We list some target groups and propose possible courses of action. But, as Freeman (1995*a*) has rightly pointed out, advanced welfare states are complex, tightly coupled systems. The specific context in which a policy initiative is embedded matters; it may enhance but also dampen its effectiveness. What we propose therefore are options, not prescriptions.

Alleviation of poverty amongst the working poor

In the United States, the EITC (Earned Income Tax Credit) incorporates the principle of comple-mentarity between work and income support. This programme provides a refundable tax credit for every dollar earned, up to a certain limit. It has, in principle, a number of important advantages. First, it provides an incentive to work, while at the same time providing income support. Second, it does not have any direct job-destroying side-effects, unlike, for example, minimum wage increases. Third, it helps intact families and not just, as in the case of AFDC, single mothers. In the United Kingdom, there exists an income support scheme (Family Credit) with a similar rationale, *i.e.* to provide income support for working, low-paid families with children. This programme was implemented to overcome the problems of high marginal tax rates in work facing those on means-tested income support. Family Credit aims to encourage labour market participation by entitling families with children to income support when they work a minimum number of hours. While there is a need to alleviate immediate financial hardship among the working poor, longer term policy should be also aimed at increasing the earnings capacity of the least skilled through education and training policies.

Combat child poverty

Few contest the absolute need to guarantee children a minimum standard of living and to provide them with access to adequate health and educational resources, especially since the adverse impact of poverty on child development and on children's ability to acquire an adequate education can be quite significant (Huston, 1991; Gottschalk *et al.*, 1994).

As lack of work and low earnings are among the principal causes of child poverty it is evident that policy initiatives are required in these areas. However, additional measures are probably desirable. In a number of countries, universal child allowances, tax allowances, lump sum payments at birth, and paid maternity or parental leave provide usually modest, but significant, levels of financial support. Special payments to single-parent families can also help to avoid financial hardship, as the example of France shows. Emphasis on labour market integration is important, but direct financial support, especially when children are very young, seems to be the surest way of preventing poverty.

Activate socially excluded long-term unemployed

In other parts of Europe, various new programmes have been implemented to "activate" the long-term unemployed, by encouraging them to work while retaining income support; unemployment benefits are being "activated" – turned into wage subsidies; and targeted subsidies are offered to employers (mostly time-limited reductions in social security contribution rates). In addition, providing the long-term unemployed with more marketable skills through education and training, and provision of job-search assistance or financial aid for the self-employed may be effective. For an evaluation of the effectiveness of such programmes, see Fay (1996).

As Haveman (Chapter 4 in this volume) rightly points out, a combination of supply and demand measures is required to *i*) increase the effective demand for low-skilled workers, through judicious deregulation in combination with targeted reductions in non-wage labour costs or employment subsidies; and *ii*) make work attractive, through simultaneously tightening benefit accessibility and expanding tax and cash credits increasing the rewards from working.

Activate socially excluded lone parents

Complementarity between labour income and social protection could also take the form of indirect, non-wage support. The particular vulnerability of lone-parent households, for example, is to a considerable extent due to an inability to combine work and care responsibilities. In fact, many women with children are unable to complement the household income because child care facilities are in short supply or too expensive. Therefore, indirect income support through public or subsidised child care provision can contribute significantly to alleviating poverty, as the example of the Scandinavian countries suggests. The low level of poverty among lone parents in Sweden, for instance, is not so much due to generous direct income support as to policies creating the conditions under which lone parents can maximise their earnings potential.[29]

Increasing dual earnership (invisible hardship)

Moving away from "breadwinner bias" in labour market regulation and adapting social security to non-standard work patterns (part-time work, irregular careers) can help to stimulate dual earnership. Likewise, individualising social security rights and tax reform can increase effective labour supply, but may have adverse consequences on living standards of single-income households if jobs remain scarce. Workers can be helped to cope with the dual demands of work and family through accessible and affordable childcare facilities, parental leave programmes, and pension crediting of periods of absence.

Recognising the particular employment problems of the least skilled, some countries are deploying initiatives to boost the demand for social and personal services, for example by means of selective reductions in social security contribution or so-called "service cheques". Institutional reform intended to permit greater earnings spread and wage flexibility could constitute a more comprehensive solution, but the risks in terms of a general deterioration of wages and living standards also seem to be higher.

Redistribution of work (shorter work time, paid leave) is an appealing option, especially because it seems that it could be beneficial both for those in need of a job as for those seeking an alternative for a lifelong, full-time career. There exist rather persuasive theoretical and empirical arguments against work redistribution as a sustainable and comprehensive solution for the unemployment problem. However, the time has probably come to re-evaluate the notion of work and to consider broadening the range of activities that are deemed valuable to society, and also to reflect on ways of supporting and putting a value on periods dedicated to caring for children or frail elderly people.

Reaching the difficult to reach (homeless)

The homeless on city streets constitute a relatively small but rather heterogeneous and highly problematic group (Council of Europe, 1993). They are generally among the most underprivileged in terms of education and occupational skills. Many are people whose life has been a succession of extreme difficulties in family, school, marriage and work. Some suffer from psychiatric disorders or drug addiction. In addition, there are the political refugees and immigrants from Eastern Europe and other regions. Reception centres providing shelter, information and administrative assistance are necessary to provide immediate relief. But because the rather diverse and often complex nature of the problems, specialised measures are required.

We advocate gradual reform. Some will contend however that, in order to overcome fundamental trade-offs, a radical reorientation is needed. It can be argued, for example, that a gradual shift towards redistribution through work could solve the labour market exclusion problem, but that the adverse incentive problems remain basically the same. Employees in subsidised employment, or low-wage workers receiving supplements (cash or in kind) are probably less motivated to acquire training and to make efforts to move up; employers have less incentive to invest in innovations that increase productivity. An unconditional income for every citizen, proponents argue, would offer a route towards a synthesis between efficiency and equity; everyone would enjoy a minimum income and would still be fully motivated to work and to seek higher earnings (e.g. van Parijs, 1992). Moreover, it is argued that people would be more inclined to take entrepreneurial risks. Such proposals for radical reform are definitely worth discussion and analysis, but it is probably unwise to jeopardise the very real achievements of present systems for the uncertain and indeed doubtful gains of a complete overhaul.

NOTES

1. We thank our colleagues at the Centre for Social Policy for their help and comments, in particular Rudi Van Dam for superb research assistance. We also thank Koen Vleminckx at the Luxembourg Income Study (LIS).

2. For more elaborate sensitivity analyses we refer to OECD (1995c) and to Buhmann et al. (1988).

3. Throughout this chapter "Germany" refers to the Federal Republic of Germany before re-unification.

4. Unfortunately, in some LIS datasets it was not possible to distinguish between elderly and non-elderly persons on the individual level. In these cases, the elderly are defined as individuals living in a household where the head is 65 or over. In order to retain comparability of results across years, this definition was also used for all other surveys for the same country. This change of the definition of elderly persons had only a minor effect on measured poverty rates and poverty gaps.

5. Duncan et al. (1995) also examine linkages between poverty entries and unfavourable events, and results show that employment events correlate much more strongly with entries into poverty than divorce or separation. It is reported that loss of work and reduction in work time together accounted for more than half of all poverty entries in Canada, the United States and Luxembourg, and at least one-quarter of entries in all other countries. Divorces and separations figured less prominently in the United States than in most other countries. Finally, the termination of social insurance benefits is tied to between 10 and 20 per cent of the poverty entries.

6. For national studies of income mobility, see Bane and Ellwood (1994), Deleeck et al. (1992), Duncan et al. (1984), Duncan et al. (1993), Gottschalk et al. (1994), and Jarvis and Jenkins (1995).

7. The broader objectives of social security systems, including the aim of encouraging independence, are not discussed, nor are the implications of transfers for poverty alleviation on government control over public expenditure.

8. A number of countries have managed to sustain high levels of social expenditure without clearly discernible adverse effects on economic growth. The empirical evidence on the adverse incentive effects of social protection arrangements is frequently remarkably ambiguous and inconclusive, which is in part a consequence of the methodological difficulties one encounters in attempting to establish causal links with any degree of certainty. Atkinson asserts: "To dismantle the welfare state on the grounds that it causes disincentives would risk losing the very definite redistributive advantages for the sake of an uncertain pay-off in terms of improved economic performance" (Atkinson and Mogensen, 1993, p. 297). On this issue also see Atkinson in OECD (1995c); Cantillon (1995); Schmähl (1995).

9. For an overview of socio-demographic change across the OECD see Saraceno, Chapter 3 in this volume.

10. Families below 50 per cent of median income.

11. In many countries, poverty among lone parents is first and foremost a problem of lone mothers, as is evident from the tables in Esping-Andersen's contribution (Chapter 2 of this volume) exposing the extreme financial vulnerability of lone mothers in Australia, Canada and the United States, especially those who are relatively young.

12. Esping-Andersen's figures (Chapter 2 of this volume) suggest that poverty among lone parents in Australia has in fact declined between 1985 and 1989. However, the findings presented in Saunders (1994, Table 9.2) are in agreement with ours, i.e. they indicate a strong and consistent increase in poverty among sole parents between 1981 and 1989.

13. The findings of Cantillon and Marx (1995a) for Belgium, Juhn and Murphy (1996) for the United States and those of Blackburn and Bloom (1994) for a number of OECD countries are at least in part consistent with this hypothesis, as are the findings by Gregg and Wadsworth (1996) which suggest a growing polarisation between work-rich and work-poor households.

14. Although some countries with relatively good unemployment records (Switzerland, Austria, Japan) had relatively moderate increases in female labour force participation, the general pattern was for countries with the smallest increase in unemployment to have substantial rises in participation (Nordic countries, North America) (Elmeskov and Pichelmann, 1993).

15. Nickell and Bell (1995) dispute the thesis that there has been a substantial shift in demand away from the unskilled. They argue that most European countries have experienced increases in skilled unemployment as well as in unskilled unemployment.

16. Still, it is forcefully argued that the labour market position of the low-skilled is structurally deteriorating. Wood (1994), for example, claims that global trade is having a major impact (consistent with the Stolper-Samuelson-theorem) while Esping-Andersen (1993) argues that deindustrialisation and the concentration of the least skilled in the low-wage services sector cause a relative deterioration of their income position (consistent with the Baumol theorem). However, whether or not an intensification of international trade is adversely affecting the low-skilled remains a strongly contested issue (see, for example, Krugman and Lawrence, 1993; OECD, 1994a). Indeed, there is not a great deal of consensus on the whole issue of labour market inequality and its causes (Freeman and Katz, 1994; Gottschalk and Joyce, 1995; Nickell and Bell, 1995).

17. For an extensive comparison and interpretation of cross-national employment trajectories see Esping-Andersen (1990, 1993, and Chapter 2 in this volume).

18. During the 1970s and 1980s many countries, particularly on the European continent were confronted with a labour market crisis which led to an expansion of early retirement or even invalidity programmes so as to take the pressure off labour markets. Hence, in these European countries, this policy has produced high levels of dependence well before the normal age of retirement. In countries like Belgium and the Netherlands, the number of households receiving a replacement income from social security amounts to between 40 and 50 per cent of the total population. It would appear, therefore, that lower levels of benefit dependence are feasible without eroding social protection.

19. Freeman (1995b) also points out that low-paid American men had relatively poor employment prospects despite falling real wages. Similarly, Schmitt and Wadsworth (1994) argue that non-employment rates among low-skilled men remained fairly high in the United Kingdom during the 1980s despite a distinct increase in wage-dispersion.

20. Recent research suggests however that the relationships between labour market flexibility, economic performance and job growth are probably not as straightforward as is often assumed (see Blank, 1994).

21. The concept of the underclass has gained renewed prominence in recent years (in particular through the books of Auletta, 1982; Murray, 1984; Wilson, 1987). The underclass is sometimes defined in plainly moralistic terms. Murray et al. (1990) write that the term "underclass" refers to "a certain type of poor person defined not by his condition [...] but by his deplorable behaviour in response to that condition" (p. 68). The deplorable behaviour takes three main visible forms: illegitimacy, violent crime, and drop-out from the labour force (p. 4). A more specific description is that the underclass is a subset of the poor, including only those "whose poverty was somehow attributable to their behaviour" (Jencks, 1992, p. 145; see also Jencks, 1991). The latter description links the "underclass" with the "culture of poverty" approach of the 60s and 70s (Lewis, 1968).

22. The debate on the problem of social exclusion remained for a long time almost exclusively confined to the French-speaking countries and, to a considerable extent, this still remains the case (Xibberas, 1993; Paugam, 1994).

23. The main reason for the inclusion of these situations of "invisible hardship" in the concept of poverty is that the welfare state, the main institution for the prevention of poverty in western societies, casts its net considerably wider than those who are "excluded" by any definition. It provides benefits for temporary periods of income loss, due to unemployment or sickness. It supports wage-earning families with many children. It seems undeniable that the objective of ensuring a minimum standard of living comes into effect at some point considerably before people have reached the rather hopeless state of being socially excluded.

24. Belgium, for example, has pursued to extreme limits the strategy of high wages and job security for those in work and generous benefits for most of the unemployed and the early retired. The proportion of people at working age enjoying one or another type of benefit is matched by few OECD countries, as is the level of non-employment (about 44 per cent). Non-employed (typically low-skilled) women now constitute the single most important social category at risk of poverty. Of course, the chronic lack of a second household income is not one of the conventional "social risks" covered by social security (Cantillon and Marx, 1995b).

25. Discussion based on Bane and Ellwood (1994); Blank (1993); Danziger et al. (1994); Jencks (1992).

26. Especially since there is evidence of earnings-capacity poverty having increased (Haveman and Buron, 1993).

27. Some argue that in order to overcome the inherent trade-off between efficiency and equity, a radical new approach is needed. One that is increasingly attracting attention is a basic income (van Parijs, 1992).

28. On the issue of non-take up, see van Oorschot (1995).

29. For the interesting case of Sweden see Gustafsson (1995) and for Scandinavia as a whole see Leira (1992). For a comparison of female labour market participation in Belgium and the Netherlands and the impact of child care facilities see Henkers et al. (1993). For a broader cross-national perspective we refer to Phipps (1993); Gustafsson and Stafford (1994); Kamerman (1995); Gornick and Ross (1996); Gornick et al. (1996) and Saraceno (Chapter 3 in this volume).

METHODS OF POVERTY MEASUREMENT

Poverty measurement entails choices involving a number of more or less technical issues. Here we do not want to attempt a full discussion of these matters. (The interested reader is referred to Ruggles, 1990, for an extensive discussion.) We will merely indicate the choices made, and the main reasons for making them.

INCOME OR EXPENDITURE

In this study, disposable household income will be used as the preferred measure of economic resources to assess poverty status. This choice may seem fairly obvious, as income is a good index of a household's command over market goods and services. Nevertheless, Eurostat (1990) and a number of other studies, including de Vos and Zaidi (1993*a-c*, 1994*a-d*), have opted for household expenditure. The main reason is a practical one: in the Household Budget Surveys, which these studies use, income does not seem to be well measured and is seriously under-reported in number of countries (Hagenaars *et al.*, 1992, p. 5). In addition, there are theoretical arguments in favour of using expenditure, as stressed by Slesnick (1993) and others. According to these authors, short periods (*e.g.* one year) of low income may not lead to low consumption, if households have sufficient resources to bridge over the slump in income. In fact, this argument points to the potential importance of taking household wealth into account when assessing poverty status. Unfortunately, in most surveys, wealth appears not to have been measured. In any case, as yet unpublished results for Belgium suggest that few households among the poor have any appreciable cash reserves.

INDIVIDUAL, HOUSEHOLD OR FAMILY

Poverty is assumed to be a household phenomenon, *i.e.* members of a household share resources in such a way that either all, or none are poor. While there is clear evidence of unequal divisions of power and income within some households and families (Jenkins, 1991), it is extremely difficult to measure within-household distributions: not all data sources provide this information, even though the household is the preferred level of poverty analysis. In a number of surveys, families or tax-units are the unit of measurement. Moreover, definitions of what constitutes a family differ across countries; *e.g.* in the Netherlands and Sweden, persons of 18 years or older who are living with their parents are regarded as separate families, and in these cases, there is no choice but to use the unit imposed by the database. For the determination of trends in poverty it is obviously important that the unit of measurement remains the same over the years. This will usually be the case when the same kind of survey is used for all years in any single country.

Even though poverty status assessment is carried out on the level of the household or the family, the number of poor can be counted either in terms of households or in terms of persons and both procedures are used in this paper.

THE POVERTY LINE AND THE EQUIVALENCE SCALE

The literature describes various methods to identify poverty lines (for reviews see, van den Bosch, 1993, and Callan and Nolan, 1991). However, most methods (*e.g.* budget, subjective, food-ratio) require information that is not available in several or all Luxembourg Income Study datasets. Therefore, in the present context, the only feasible approach is a relative one, where the poverty line is set at a certain percentage of mean or median equivalent income. The percentage chosen is largely arbitrary, but 50 per cent (of the mean) is frequently used.

The choice of an equivalence scale is, in effect, almost equally arbitrary. As shown by the reviews of Whiteford (1985) and Buhmann *et al.* (1988), *inter alia*, a very wide range of scales is used or presented in the literature. In O'Higgins and Jenkins (1990) and Eurostat (1990), the scale recommended by the OECD (1982) has been used, which assigns a factor of 1 to the first adult in a household, 0.7 to each additional adult, and 0.5 to each child (the equivalence scale value for the household is found by summing the individual factors, and the equivalent income of a household is calculated by dividing disposable income by the equivalence scale value). Compared with almost all other equivalence scales, the OECD-scale is very steep (Buhmann *et al.*, 1988), *i.e.* the assumed needs of households increase very strongly with the number of household members. Several authors have questioned its appropriateness for developed western countries (van den Bosch *et al.* 1993; Haveman, 1990; and Deleeck *et al.*, 1992). Therefore, following Hagenaars *et al.* (1992) and de Vos and Zaidi (1994a), we will use a "modified" OECD-scale with factors of 1 for the first adult, 0.5 for each additional adult, and 0.3 for each child. This scale is situated at about midway between flat and steep scales.

The use of country-specific poverty lines implies that poverty is regarded as a country-specific phenomenon. This choice seems appropriate for a study where the focus is on trends in poverty rates within individual countries. If the aim had been to compare poverty rates across countries, or to determine the evolution of poverty in the European Union as a whole, it may be used to extrapolate to a "Union-wide" poverty line, as was done in Eurostat (1990). In the present study, such a "Union-wide" approach would make little sense in that it produces poverty rates of up to 70 per cent (in Portugal, Eurostat, 1990), which are of no relevance within a national context.

One consequence of using relative poverty lines is that a nationwide improvement in incomes which leaves the relative positions of households unchanged, has no effect on the poverty rate. Without entering into the difficult debate on the relativity of poverty, it must be granted that a situation where the lowest incomes fall while average income remains stable, is worse than a development where low-income households do not share an increase in average income. Yet, both may result in an increase in relative poverty. For this reason, we will also present poverty rates that are estimated from "absolute" poverty lines, which are kept at the same real level across years.

A practical problem in using the number of people below the poverty line (*i.e.* the so-called head-count) as a measure of the extent of poverty is that it can be rather sensitive to the precise level of the poverty line. It is possible that large numbers of households have incomes that are just below, or above, the poverty line. In such cases, a poverty line defined as 51 per cent of average income may yield a totally different picture of the trend in poverty, compared to a line set at 49 per cent. For this reason, in addition to the results from the 50 per cent threshold, we will also present poverty rates derived from poverty lines set at 40 per cent and 60 per cent of average equivalent income. We will also use the poverty gap, which is less sensitive to the level of the poverty line, as a measure of the extent of poverty. The poverty gap is defined as the aggregate income shortfall of all poor households relative to the poverty line.

THE IMPACT OF SOCIAL SECURITY TRANSFERS

The impact of social security transfers on the extent of poverty is measured by comparing poverty rates and poverty gaps before and after transfers are granted. That is, every household's poverty status is evaluated on the basis of disposable income (*i.e.* after transfers) and on the basis of disposable income minus income transfers (*i.e.* before transfers). This method has already been applied by Deleeck *et al.* (1992) and Hausman (1993). It differs from the most common procedure to measure the impact of income transfers on income inequality and poverty, where the distribution of gross income (market income plus transfers before taxes and social security contributions are paid) is compared with the distribution of net disposable income (Mitchell, 1991). One reason for not adopting the latter method is that gross income is an administrative concept rather than an economic one. The level of gross income depends to a considerable degree on the division of social security contributions between employees and employers. Employee contributions are part of gross income, while those of employers are not, but a good argument can be made that in an economic sense both are in fact borne by employees.

Consequently, cross-country comparisons of the redistributional impact of social security transfers where gross income is used as the baseline may be quite misleading. The same can be true for comparisons across time within a single country if contribution rules have changed. A practical advantage of the method used here is that it can be used even when the variable gross income is not available, as is the case in a number of LIS surveys. An implication of the approach is, obviously, that we only consider the impact of social security benefits, not at that of social security contributions or taxes.

Australian analysts have criticised international comparisons using the LIS database on methodological grounds. They have argued that concentrating on income statistics as opposed to other measures of well being is not appropriate for social policy analysis and may misrepresent the overall progressive nature of welfare systems. More specifically, it is argued that the impact of social wage services (in-kind benefits such as housing, medical care, education, child care and transport) is not adequately taken into account. Moreover, it is pointed out that poverty among the elderly is overestimated, because we fail to take into account the benefits of home ownership, which is comparatively widespread in Australia. These points of criticism are valid and they apply to all the countries included in our study. We are not convinced however that failure to account fully for in-kind benefits and home ownership puts Australia in a particularly unflattering light. In-kind benefits, such as the ones listed are also extremely important in low-poverty countries such as the Scandinavian and the Benelux countries. The poverty rate among the elderly in Australia is still much as higher compared to Belgium, for example, despite the fact that home ownership is almost equally widespread.

Appendix 2

COMPARABILITY OF THE LUXEMBOURG INCOME STUDY (LIS) DATASETS

The comparability of data across countries is of crucial importance: it is not sufficient to use the same poverty line, it is also necessary to ensure comparability of the surveys from which the data are taken. The countries for which the LIS database contains data for two or more years are listed in Table A.1. Three conditions were considered to evaluate the comparability of the surveys across years within each country: the surveys should be all of the same type; the unit of measurement should remain the same across years; the trend in average household income per head of the population as calculated from LIS data should be roughly equal to the same trend as calculated from national account statistics. Three indicators of total household income were taken from the OECD *National Accounts*, Table 8 ("Accounts for households and private unincorporated enterprises"): Total Current Receipts (TCR), Final Consumption Expenditure (FCE) and the sum of Final Consumption Expenditure and Net Saving (FCE+S). In order to obtain amounts per head, these numbers were related to total population, as given in United Nations Demographic Yearbooks. The third concept probably comes closest to the LIS definition of the disposable income of households. Nevertheless, it must be stressed that none of the *National Accounts* income concepts perfectly matches the LIS concept, and therefore some discrepancies are to be expected. The results of this comparison are presented in Table A.1. Income data are shown in current prices and as percentages of the amount for the year 1985, or the year closest to 1985 (the consumer price index is also given). The remainder of this section will provide a brief country-by-country description of whether the LIS surveys can be considered to be comparable across years.

For ***Australia***, there is consistency both in the survey organisation and the unit of analysis. The trend in average per capita income deduced from the LIS dataset is virtually identical to the trend deduced from the *National Accounts*.

For ***Belgium***, there is consistency both in the survey organisation and in the unit of measurement. The increase in average income is somewhat below that indicated by *National Accounts* data. One reason for this may be that income from financial assets, which is not measured well in this survey (as is the case in most income surveys), has risen more than other kinds of income. Another reason is that the fieldwork of the 1985 survey was carried out at the end of that year, while the 1992 survey was mainly done in the first quarter of 1992.

For ***Canada***, there is consistency in the survey organisation and virtual consistency in the unit of measurement, with the exception of 1981 when the results refer to the economic family rather than the household. The trend in average per capita income deduced from the LIS dataset is very similar to the trend deduced from the *National Accounts*.

In ***Denmark***, according to the Income Tax Survey, average income declined a little in real terms between 1987 and 1992. Nevertheless, the trend does not diverge very widely from that according to *National Accounts* statistics. For ***Finland***, the survey findings seem to overestimate the rise in average income between 1987 and 1991, but not to such an extent that the surveys can not be considered comparable. For ***France*** there are no problems. We will also use results published by de Vos and Zaidi (1994*b*), which are based on the French household budget surveys of 1984/85 and 1989.

Germany (the former Federal Republic only) is represented by five datasets in LIS, derived from three kinds of surveys: the Income and Consumer Survey (in effect the German household budget survey), the Transfer Income Survey, and the German Socio-Economic Panel. All three surveys use the household as the unit of measurement. The average income results indicate that the first of these is not comparable to the other two. One of the reasons for this may be that the Income and Consumer Survey covers only households with a head of German nationality. The trend in average income between 1984 and 1989, according to the Socio-Economic Panel, is not too divergent from that according to the *National Accounts*. However, LIS staff recommended that the 1989 dataset should not be used. For this reason, only results from the Income and Consumer Survey will be presented below. They will be supplemented by published figures from de Vos and Zaidi (1994*a*), who used the 1988 German Income and Consumer Survey, and from Hauser and Becker (1994).

For **Italy**, use of the Bank of Italy Income Surveys results in a wildly exaggerated increase in average income. These datasets will not be used below. For the **Netherlands**, the change from one kind of income survey to another leads to an increase in average income between 1987 and 1991 that is far too high compared with the *National Accounts* indicators. No national account figures for 1983 are available, but other sources indicate that average household income did not change in the period 1983 to 1987, as the LIS data suggest. The 1983 and 1987 surveys are therefore assumed to be comparable. The 1991 survey is clearly not comparable with the others, but the findings of this survey will nevertheless also be presented, for what they are worth.

For **Norway**, the 1979 survey used tax units as the unit of measurement, whereas the 1986 and 1991 surveys recorded income on the level of the household. Yet, the trend in average income according to these surveys agrees well with *National Accounts* statistics, and changes in other variables also seemed plausible. With some reservations therefore, all Norwegian surveys are judged to be comparable. All four **Swedish** surveys are of the same kind, and all (as far as is known) use tax units as the unit of measurement. Regarding the trend in average income, the survey data agree well with *National Accounts* figures, although the increase between 1987 and 1992 has been somewhat overestimated.

In the **United Kingdom**, all datasets are derived from the Family Expenditure Survey (FES). However, average income (in current prices) in the 1974 survey is only slightly below that in the 1979 survey, which, given the rate of inflation during this period, would imply a dramatic fall in real living standards. This is clearly unrealistic, and it is probably caused by using a different unit to record income. There are no apparent problems of comparability between the 1979 and 1986 FESs. Results from the 1974 dataset are used, although they may not be comparable with those for later years. In addition, we will use published results by de Vos and Zaidi (1993*c*) and by Goodman and Webb (1994), which are also based on the FES.

The **United States** data have been derived from the March Current Population Survey and the household consistently serves as unit of measurement. The trend in average income is more than sufficiently consistent with what emerges from the *National Accounts* to serve for cross-temporal comparisons.

To sum up, the Austrian and the Italian LIS datasets are not considered to be comparable across years, and no results for these countries are used. For Germany only the 1978 and 1983 Income and Consumer Survey datasets will be used. The Dutch 1991 survey is probably not comparable to the other Dutch surveys. In the following tables (Tables A.1 to A.7), this is indicated by a blank space between the Netherlands 1987 and 1991 rows. The same applies to the United Kingdom 1974 dataset. Within the other countries, all datasets are regarded as comparable.

De Vos and Zaidi (1993*b*, 1994*c-d*) also estimated trends in poverty, using Household Budget Survey data, for three countries which are not (yet) included in LIS, *i.e.* Greece, Portugal and Spain. These will be presented, where possible, along with the other results. Because income is under-reported in several of the Household Budget Surveys, de Vos and Zaidi (1994*a*, pp. 2-8) prefer expenditure to income as the measure of economic resources to assess poverty status. A comparison of the trends in average expenditure per capita according to the surveys with those according to *National Accounts* statistics shows that there are no apparent problems of comparability across years, except possibly for Spain.

Table A.I. **Comparability of LIS surveys across years within countries**

Country	Year	Name of Luxembourg Income Study (LIS) survey	Unit of measurement	Indicators of trend in average income per capita				Price index
				TCR	FCE	FCE + S	DPI (LIS)	
Australia	1981	Australian Income and Housing Survey	Household	68.8	69.1	69.3	71.4	73.7
	1985	Australian Income and Housing Survey	Household	100.0	100.0	100.0	100.0	100.0
	1989	Australian Income and Housing Survey	Household	151.9	142.7	137.4	140.3	136.5
Austria	1987	Austrian Microcensus	Family	100.0	100.0	100.0	100.0	100.0
	1991	Austrian Microcensus	Household	125.5	122.9	124.3	89.1	111.5
Belgium	1985	Panel Survey of the Centre for Social Policy	Household	100.0	100.0	100.0	100.0	100.0
	1988	Panel Survey of the Centre for Social Policy	Household	113.5	112.6	114.6	109.5	104.1
	1992	Panel Survey of the Centre for Social Policy	Household	149.0	141.1	152.6	133.2	117.3
Canada	1975	Survey of Consumer Finances	Household	33.8	34.0	35.4	36.3	42.3
	1981	Survey of Consumer Finances	Econ. Family	71.9	68.8	73.8	70.5	72.3
	1987	Survey of Consumer Finances	Household	100.0	100.0	100.0	100.0	100.0
	1991	Survey of Consumer Finances	Household	125.3	120.4	122.7	121.6	120.9
Denmark	1987	Income Tax Survey	Household	100.0	100.0	100.0	100.0	100.0
	1992	Income Tax Survey	Household	127.8	116.0	129.1	116.1	118.1
Finland	1987	Income Distribution Survey	Household	100.0	100.0	100.0	100.0	100.0
	1991	Income Distribution Survey	Household	138.3	127.3	131.8	142.8	124.0
France	1979	Survey of Individual Income Tax Returns	Tax Unit	56.2	55.7	58.8	54.8	59.0
	1984	Survey of Individual Income Tax Returns	Tax Unit	100.0	100.0	100.0	100.0	100.0
Germany	1978	Income and Consumer Survey	Household	72.5	72.6	73.1	91.9	76.9
	1981	Transfer Income Survey	Household	89.1	87.5	89.7	91.7	89.8
	1983	Income and Consumer Survey	Household	94.8	95.4	94.8	120.0	97.6
	1984	German Socio-Economic Panel Study	Household	100.0	100.0	100.0	100.0	100.0
	1989	German Socio-Economic Panel Study	Household	122.8	120.1	121.5	113.6	106.5
Italy	1986	Bank of Italy Income Survey	Household	100.0	100.0	100.0	100.0	100.0
	1991	Bank of Italy Income Survey	Econ. Family	164.3	163.1	162.0	218.7	132.3
Netherlands	1983	Additional Enquiry on the Use of Public Services	Household	–	–	–	100.0	100.0
	1987	Additional Enquiry on the Use of Public Services	Household	100.0	100.0	100.0	100.0	100.0
	1991	Socio-Economic Panel of the Central Bureau of Statistics	Household	119.2	117.3	116.9	147.2	107.9
Norway	1979	Survey of Norwegian Tax Files	Tax Unit	47.3	44.0	48.9	41.0	54.5
	1986	Income and Property Distribution Survey	Household	100.0	100.0	100.0	100.0	100.0
	1991	Income and Property Distribution Survey	Household	136.9	122.7	133.5	139.3	130.6
Sweden	1975	Income Distribution Survey	Unknown	27.4	29.9	32.3	32.8	38.0
	1981	Income Distribution Survey	Tax Unit	60.5	57.2	62.0	63.4	76.2
	1987	Income Distribution Survey	Tax Unit	100.0	100.0	100.0	100.0	100.0
	1992	Income Distribution Survey	Tax Unit	146.0	139.7	154.8	167.3	133.1

Table A.1. **Comparability of LIS surveys across years within countries** *(cont.)*

Name of Luxembourg Income Study (LIS) survey		Unit of measurement	Indicators of trend in average income per capita				Price index
			TCR	FCE	FCE + S	DPI (LIS)	
United Kingdom	1974 Family Expenditure Survey	Unknown	21.5	22.1	22.7	49.5	28.0
	1979 Family Expenditure Survey	Family	48.3	48.9	52.4	53.2	57.8
	1986 Family Expenditure Survey	Family	100.0	100.0	100.0	100.0	100.0
United States	1974 March Current Population Survey	Household	38.1	37.6	38.8	38.8	45.0
	1979 March Current Population Survey	Household	61.7	61.6	61.9	60.3	66.2
	1986 March Current Population Survey	Household	100.0	100.0	100.0	100.0	100.0
	1991 March Current Population Survey	Household	128.7	130.1	128.1	123.0	124.3

Notes: TCR: Total Current Receipts of Households per head of the population from *National Accounts.*
FCE: Final Consumption Expenditure of Households per head of the population from *National Accounts.*
FCE + S: Final Consumption Expenditure plus Net Saving of Households per head of the population from *National Accounts.*
DPI: (LIS) Disposable Income per head of the population according to LIS survey.
Price index: price index of private household consumption.
All figures are expressed as a percentage of corresponding amount for year which is nearest 1985.

Sources: TCR, FCE, FCE + S: calculated using aggregate amounts from OECD *National Accounts,* Table 8, various editions, and population figures from United Nations Demographic Yearbook, various editions.
DPI: calculated from results out of Luxembourg Income Study database. Price index: *OECD Main Economic Indicators,* various editions.

Table A.2a. **Extent of poverty in a number of OECD countries, using relative poverty lines**

		Households below line at:			Persons below line at:			Poverty gap[1]	Index line[2]	Measure of resources	Source
		40%	50%	60%	40%	50%	60%				
		of average equivalent income									
Australia	1981	6.6	18.0	26.3	6.4	14.4	22.2	1.9	102.5	Income	LIS
	1985	6.3	19.4	28.9	6.3	15.7	24.7	2.0	100.0	Income	LIS
	1989	8.0	19.7	28.9	7.7	16.1	24.8	2.3	103.3	Income	LIS
Belgium	1985	2.5	6.2	14.0	2.2	5.8	13.8	0.7	100.0	Income	LIS
	1988	2.5	6.9	15.1	2.3	6.2	14.4	0.7	111.0	Income	LIS
	1992	2.4	6.4	13.6	2.1	5.5	11.8	0.6	118.0	Income	LIS
Canada	1975	13.3	20.1	26.8	10.2	16.0	23.0	3.1	87.3	Income	LIS
	1981	10.6	17.8	25.9	9.0	15.3	22.8	2.5	94.5	Income	LIS
	1987	8.9	15.1	24.0	8.1	13.8	22.0	2.1	100.0	Income	LIS
	1991	9.4	15.4	24.2	7.6	13.2	20.5	2.1	95.2	Income	LIS
Denmark	1987	5.8	12.8	21.9	3.8	8.9	15.9	1.5	100.0	Income	LIS
	1992	5.1	8.2	17.0	3.3	5.5	12.0	1.1	97.0	Income	LIS
Finland	1987	4.2	8.7	17.1	2.6	5.5	11.6	0.8	100.0	Income	LIS
	1991	4.6	10.4	17.9	2.8	6.4	12.1	0.9	114.0	Income	LIS
France	1979	6.3	14.0	23.9	6.6	13.2	23.2	1.8	95.0	Income	LIS
	1984	5.6	11.5	22.4	5.7	11.9	22.9	1.6	100.0	Income	LIS
	1984/85	6.9	13.2	21.6	6.0	12.4	21.1		100.0	Expend.	DV93a
	1989	7.5	14.9	24.5	6.9	14.7	25.0		109.0	Expend.	DV93a
Germany	1978	6.2	12.3	20.2	3.7	8.2	15.5	1.1	98.0	Income	LIS
	1983	4.4	10.9	19.4	3.1	8.0	16.2	0.9	100.0	Income	LIS
	1988	6.0	13.6	22.6	4.5	10.6	19.1		108.0	Income	DV93b
	1978					6.4				Income	Becker
	1983					8.7				Income	Becker
	1988					8.9				Income	Becker
	1983[3]					8.3				Income	Hauser
	1987[3]					7.7				Income	Hauser
	1990[3]					8.8				Income	Hauser
Greece	1982	10.6	18.5	28.4	9.5	17.4	27.6		100.0	Expend.	DV93c
	1988	12.6	19.9	29.0	10.7	17.9	26.9		97.0	Expend.	DV93c
Ireland	1973[4]	8.5	17.9	27.0	7.5	15.9	26.4			Income	Callan
	1980[4]	8.6	17.6	27.9	9.3	17.4	27.6			Income	Callan
	1987[4]	8.9	18.5	30.5	10.5	21.2	32.2			Income	Callan
Netherlands	1983	6.1	8.5	15.7	6.5	9.3	17.4	2.7	100.0	Income	LIS
	1987	5.0	7.9	13.6	4.4	8.3	15.6	1.9	100.0	Income	LIS
	1991	3.9	8.0	20.8	3.7	7.7	18.1	1.5	134.0	Income	LIS
Norway	1979	3.8	6.2	19.0	2.7	4.8	13.3	0.9	81.0	Income	LIS
	1986	3.4	11.0	19.0	2.1	6.4	11.8	0.8	100.0	Income	LIS
	1991	3.4	8.9	17.1	2.1	5.3	11.2	0.8	105.0	Income	LIS

Table A.2a. **Extent of poverty in a number of OECD countries, using relative poverty lines** *(cont.)*

		Households below line at:			Persons below line at:			Poverty gap[1]	Index line[2]	Measure of resources	Source
		40%	50%	60%	40%	50%	60%				
		of average equivalent income									
Portugal	1980	17.5	27.3	36.7	16.1	26.4	35.8		100.0	Expend.	DV93d
	1989	17.3	26.5	35.2	15.5	24.5	33.3		123.0	Expend.	DV93d
Spain	1980	10.9	18.7	27.7	9.7	17.5	26.7		100.0	Expend.	DV93e
	1988	8.8	16.2	25.8	8.2	15.7	25.4		97.0	Expend.	DV93e
Sweden	1975	4.0	7.8	16.9	2.5	5.2	11.5	0.9	90.0	Income	LIS
	1981	3.8	5.6	10.2	2.9	4.6	8.3	0.8	86.0	Income	LIS
	1987	6.0	9.4	15.3	3.8	6.3	10.5	1.3	100.0	Income	LIS
	1992	5.9	9.2	15.3	3.8	6.0	10.5	1.3	126.0	Income	LIS
United Kingdom	1974	6.3	15.4	24.4	4.5	11.4	19.6	1.2	185.0	Income	LIS
	1979	4.4	13.6	25.2	4.1	10.8	19.5	1.2	93.0	Income	LIS
	1986	5.3	12.7	24.2	5.9	13.0	23.2	2.3	100.0	Income	LIS
	1985	3.2	13.1	27.7	3.7	13.2	24.7		100.0	Income	DV93f
	1988	9.0	22.4	32.2	8.8	19.0	28.1		120.0	Income	DV93f
	1978[5]				1.8	6.8	16.4			Income	Goodman
	1982[5]				2.5	7.8	18.2			Income	Goodman
	1985[5]				2.7	10.7	22.9			Income	Goodman
	1988[5]				7.4	18.3	28.1			Income	Goodman
	1991[5]				10.6	20.4	29.7			Income	Goodman
United States	1974	13.8	20.6	27.7	12.8	18.8	26.0	3.7	95.6	Income	LIS
	1979	13.3	19.8	26.8	12.3	18.6	25.8	3.3	93.5	Income	LIS
	1986	15.8	22.4	29.6	16.0	22.6	29.8	4.1	100.0	Income	LIS
	1991	15.2	22.7	30.1	15.2	22.6	30.7	3.9	97.7	Income	LIS

1. Aggregate poverty gap using 50 per cent poverty line, as a percentage of aggregate disposable income.
2. Real value of line as a percentage of poverty line in year closest to 1985.
3. These poverty rates for Germany are based on equivalence scale with factors 1 for the first adult, 0.8 for other adults and varying from 0.45 for young children to 0.9 for children aged 16 to 21.
4. Results for Ireland are based on equivalence scale with factors 1, 0.6, 0.4.
5. These poverty rates for the United Kingdom are based on equivalence scale with factors 0.61 for the first adult, around 0.4 for other adults and varying from 0.09 for young children to 0.36 for children aged 16 or over; income is income before housing costs.

Sources : LIS: Luxembourg Income Study.
DV93a: de Vos et Zaidi (1994b).
DV93b: de Vos et Zaidi (1993a).
Becker: Becker, I., *Stabilität in der Einkommensverteilung – Ergebnisse für die Bundesrepublik Deutschland bis zur Wiedervereinigung*, EVS-Projekt Arbeitspapier n° 6, Johann Wolfgang Goethe-Universität, Frankfurt.
Hauser: Hauser et Becker (1994), tableau 8.
DV93c: de Vos et Zaidi (1994c).
Callan: Callan, Nolan et al. (1989), pp. 70-71.
DV93d: de Vos et Zaidi (1994d).
DV93e: de Vos et Zaidi (1993b).
DV93f: de Vos et Zaidi (1993c).
Goodman: Goodman et Webb (1994).

Table A.2b. **Poverty rates in a number of OECD countries, using "absolute" poverty lines**

Country	Year	Households below line at:			Persons below line at:			Reference year	Measure of resources	Source
		40%	50%	60%	40%	50%	60%			
		of equivalent income in reference year								
Australia	1981	6.9	18.6	26.9	6.7	15.0	22.8	85	Income	LIS
	1985	6.3	19.4	28.9	6.3	15.7	24.7	85	Income	LIS
	1989	7.4	18.5	27.6	7.7	16.1	24.8	85	Income	LIS
Belgium	1985	2.5	6.2	14.0	2.2	5.8	13.8	85	Income	LIS
	1988	2.1	5.7	13.1	1.8	5.2	12.4	85	Income	LIS
	1992	1.7	3.9	9.8	1.6	3.3	8.3	85	Income	LIS
Canada	1975	17.2	24.7	32.2	13.4	20.8	29.0	87	Income	LIS
	1981	11.4	19.1	27.0	9.6	16.3	23.9	87	Income	LIS
	1987	8.9	15.1	24.0	8.1	13.8	22.0	87	Income	LIS
	1991	9.6	15.8	24.8	7.8	13.6	21.1	87	Income	LIS
Denmark	1987	5.8	12.8	21.9	3.8	8.9	15.9	87	Income	LIS
	1992	5.4	9.3	18.9	3.5	6.3	13.5	87	Income	LIS
Finland	1987	4.2	8.7	17.1	2.6	5.5	11.6	87	Income	LIS
	1991	2.8	6.3	12.0	1.7	3.8	7.5	87	Income	LIS
France	1979	8.5	17.0	27.0	7.9	16.1	26.9	84	Income	LIS
	1984	5.6	11.5	22.4	5.7	11.9	22.9	84	Income	LIS
	1984/85	6.9	13.2	21.6	6.0	12.4	21.1	84/85	Expend.	DV93
	1989	6.1	12.5	22.0	6.0	12.7	22.5	84/85	Expend.	DV93
Germany	1978	6.5	12.8	21.1	3.9	8.7	16.4	83	Income	LIS
	1983	4.4	10.9	19.4	3.1	8.0	16.2	83	Income	LIS
Greece	1982	10.6	18.5	28.4	9.5	17.4	27.6	82	Expend.	DV93
	1988	13.7	21.3	31.0	11.9	19.2	28.9	82	Expend.	DV93
Netherlands	1983	6.1	8.5	15.7	6.5	9.3	17.4	87	Income	LIS
	1987	5.0	8.0	13.7	4.5	8.4	15.8	87	Income	LIS
Norway	1979	6.0	20.7	31.3	4.7	14.8	25.8	86	Income	LIS
	1986	3.4	11.0	19.0	2.1	6.4	11.8	86	Income	LIS
	1991	3.2	7.0	14.6	1.9	4.1	9.4	86	Income	LIS
Portugal	1980	17.5	27.3	36.7	16.1	26.4	35.8	80	Expend.	DV93
	1989	10.4	17.9	25.5	9.2	16.0	23.5	80	Expend.	DV93
Spain	1980	10.9	18.7	27.7	9.7	17.5	26.7	80	Expend.	DV93
	1988	9.5	17.7	27.8	5.6	11.8	19.8	80	Expend.	DV93
Sweden	1975	5.5	13.0	23.6	3.5	8.6	17.0	87	Income	LIS
	1981	4.8	9.5	18.8	3.9	7.7	15.4	87	Income	LIS
	1987	6.0	9.4	15.3	3.8	6.3	10.5	87	Income	LIS
	1992	4.3	5.8	8.4	2.7	3.7	5.4	87	Income	LIS

Table A.2b. **Poverty rates in a number of OECD countries, using "absolute" poverty lines** (cont.)

		Households below line at:			Persons below line at:			Reference year	Measure of resources	Source
		40%	50%	60%	40%	50%	60%			
		of equivalent income in reference year								
United Kingdom	1979	6.2	18.0	28.7	5.5	13.9	22.8	86	Income	LIS
	1986	5.3	12.7	24.2	5.9	13.0	23.2	86	Income	LIS
	1985	3.2	13.1	27.7	3.7	13.2	24.7	85	Income	DV93
	1988	3.2	10.7	22.0	3.5	10.1	18.7	85	Income	DV93
United States	1974	16.7	24.2	32.5	15.4	22.3	31.3	86	Income	LIS
	1979	15.4	22.5	30.2	14.3	21.4	29.5	86	Income	LIS
	1986	15.8	22.4	29.6	16.0	22.6	29.8	86	Income	LIS
	1991	15.7	23.2	30.8	15.7	23.2	31.4	86	Income	LIS

Sources: See Table A.2a.

151

Table A.3. **Poverty rates and poverty gaps for persons, by age**

		Poverty rates				Poverty gaps				Source
		All persons	Children	Elderly 65+	Adults –65	All persons	Children	Elderly 65+	Adults –65	
Australia	1981*	14.4	16.4	29.9	10.5	1.9	2.0	2.7	1.7	LIS
	1985*	15.7	17.0	33.4	11.3	2.0	2.0	3.4	1.8	LIS
	1989*	16.1	18.3	32.5	11.8	2.3	2.3	3.9	1.9	LIS
Belgium	1985	5.8	4.7	11.3	5.2	0.7	0.5	1.4	0.6	LIS
	1988	6.2	4.9	10.6	5.8	0.7	0.4	1.5	0.6	LIS
	1992	5.5	4.9	10.6	4.7	0.6	0.4	1.4	0.5	LIS
Canada	1975*	16.0	16.5	34.5	12.4	3.1	2.2	6.5	2.9	LIS
	1981*	15.2	17.9	24.6	12.3	2.5	2.3	3.3	2.4	LIS
	1987*	13.8	18.1	14.3	11.9	2.1	2.1	1.7	2.1	LIS
	1991*	13.7	17.5	8.6	13.1	2.1	2.0	0.7	2.4	LIS
Denmark	1987	8.9	4.0	25.9	6.5	1.5	0.4	2.6	1.6	LIS
	1992	5.5	3.6	6.3	5.9	1.1	0.4	1.6	1.3	LIS
Finland	1987	5.5	3.4	10.1	5.4	0.8	0.3	1.0	0.9	LIS
	1991	6.4	3.1	14.4	6.0	0.9	0.3	1.4	1.1	LIS
France	1979*	13.2	12.8	16.0	12.7	1.8	1.3	2.0	2.0	LIS
	1984*	11.9	13.1	7.3	12.4	1.6	1.3	0.8	1.9	LIS
	84/85	12.4	12.9	24.8	10.0					DV94
	1989	14.7	16.6	24.3	11.9					DV94
Germany	1978	8.2	4.9	20.9	7.2	1.1	0.4	3.3	1.1	LIS
	1983	8.0	6.5	18.8	5.8	0.9	0.5	2.5	0.6	LIS
	1988	10.6	11.0	19.4	7.8					DV93a
Greece	1982	17.4	15.9	33.7	14.5					DV94
	1988	17.9	15.0	37.8	14.4					DV94
Ireland	1973[1]	14.8	15.7	33.8	14.4					Callan
	1980[1]	16.2	18.5	24.4	15.2					Callan
	1987[1]	19.8	26.0	9.7	17.3					Callan
Netherlands	1983*	9.3	7.0	6.4	10.8	2.7	1.5	1.5	3.5	LIS
	1987*	8.3	8.9	2.7	9.2	1.9	1.1	0.1	2.5	LIS
	1991*	7.7	9.2	7.2	7.3	1.5	1.5	1.0	1.6	LIS
Norway	1979*	4.8	4.4	6.7	4.6	0.9	0.5	1.7	0.9	LIS
	1986*	6.4	3.9	16.4	4.4	0.8	0.5	1.1	0.8	LIS
	1991*	5.3	3.9	9.5	4.5	0.8	0.4	0.6	1.0	LIS
Portugal	1980	26.4	27.9	42.3	22.1					DV94
	1988	24.5	22.9	42.9	20.7					DV94
Spain	1980	17.5	16.9	32.3	15.0					DV94
	1988	15.7	16.5	24.7	13.6					DV94

THE CHALLENGE OF POVERTY AND EXCLUSION

Table A.3. **Poverty rates and poverty gaps for persons, by age** (cont.)

		Poverty rates				Poverty gaps				Source
		All persons	Children	Elderly 65+	Adults –65	All persons	Children	Elderly 65+	Adults –65	
Sweden	1975*	5.2	2.1	8.6	5.5	0.9	0.2	0.6	1.3	LIS
	1981*	4.6	4.5	0.9	5.9	0.8	0.4	0.0	1.2	LIS
	1987*	6.3	3.1	4.3	8.1	1.3	0.3	0.3	2.0	LIS
	1992*	6.0	2.6	4.9	7.6	1.3	0.3	0.5	2.0	LIS
United Kingdom	1974	11.4	10.8	34.4	6.8	1.2	0.9	4.2	0.8	LIS
	1979	10.8	10.7	25.9	7.2	1.2	1.1	2.0	1.1	LIS
	1986	13.0	17.4	13.3	11.0	2.3	2.4	1.2	2.5	LIS
	1985	13.2	19.2	16.7	9.9					DV93b
	1988	19.0	22.3	36.7	13.4					DV93b
	1973[2]	9.7	7.2	29.6	4.8					Goodman
	1978[2]	6.8	7.6	10.6	3.9					Goodman
	1982[2]	7.8	9.0	8.7	5.8					Goodman
	1985[2]	10.7	13.1	12.7	7.0					Goodman
	1988[2]	18.3	19.3	31.2	11.6					Goodman
	1991[2]	24.0	26.9	37.0	15.1					Goodman
United States	1974*	18.8	22.8	31.4	14.0	3.7	3.8	6.7	3.0	LIS
	1979*	18.6	24.1	28.9	13.7	3.3	3.4	6.1	2.7	LIS
	1986*	22.6	30.7	28.3	17.7	4.1	4.7	5.7	3.4	LIS
	1991*	22.7	30.3	26.1	18.4	3.9	4.3	5.0	3.5	LIS

Notes: * Elderly are defined as persons in households where the head is 65 or over; adults –65 are similarly defined as persons over 16 in households where the head is younger than 65.
1. Results for Ireland are derived using an equivalence scale with factors 1, 0.66 and 0.33.
   Figures shown for the elderly are poverty percentages for households headed by an elderly person.
   Figures shown for adults are for all adults, regardless of age.
2. These poverty rates for the United Kingdom are based on equivalence scale with factors 0.61 for the first adult, around 0.4 for other adults and varying from 0.09 for young children to 0.36 for children aged 16 or over; income is income before housing costs.
   Figures shown for children are poverty percentages for persons living in households with children.
   Figures shown for the elderly are for pensioners; figures shown for adults are for non-pensioners living in households without children.
   For measure of economic resources see Table A.2a.
Sources: See Table A.2a.

Table A.4. **Impact of social security transfers on poverty rates and poverty gaps by age of persons**

		Poverty rates before and after social transfers								Reduction in poverty gap due to social transfers				
		All persons		Children		Elderly 65+		Adults –65		All persons	Children	Elderly 65+	Adults –65	Transfer efficiency
		Before	After	Before	After	Before	After	Before	After					
Australia	1981[1]	24.0	14.4	22.6	16.4	70.7	29.9	16.3	10.5	78.4	61.8	92.9	68.1	59.1
	1985[1]	25.9	15.7	23.6	17.0	66.4	33.4	18.2	6.3	77.8	64.9	89.7	70.2	61.4
	1989[1]	27.0	16.1	26.5	18.3	70.6	32.5	18.5	11.8	76.9	61.7	89.5	68.5	64.0
Belgium	1985	33.6	5.8	24.0	4.7	88.9	11.3	27.6	5.2	95.0	90.5	97.4	93.5	44.4
	1988	35.1	6.2	24.1	4.9	86.8	10.6	28.7	5.8	95.0	91.0	97.1	93.4	44.1
	1992	34.5	5.5	24.4	4.9	92.0	10.6	26.7	4.7	96.4	92.6	97.9	95.3	49.2
Canada	1975[1]	24.6	16.0	24.3	16.5	64.7	34.5	17.7	12.4	61.0	55.0	79.7	44.7	44.7
	1981[1]	24.2	15.2	24.2	17.9	62.4	24.6	17.3	12.3	66.0	52.3	88.2	49.4	45.3
	1987[1]	26.5	13.8	26.2	18.1	67.5	14.3	19.0	11.9	73.9	60.2	94.2	58.7	44.2
	1991[1]	29.5	13.7	29.4	17.5	66.3	8.6	23.6	13.0	76.6	68.2	97.3	63.1	42.0
Denmark	1987	32.0	8.9	20.1	4.0	84.5	25.9	23.7	6.5	88.9	90.1	94.3	82.5	41.7
	1992	36.6	5.5	27.1	3.6	83.3	6.3	28.3	5.9	93.0	94.4	96.6	89.6	47.6
Finland	1987	21.8	5.5	17.6	3.4	56.6	10.1	16.9	5.4	85.9	86.5	95.2	77.0	32.1
	1991	23.0	6.4	20.7	3.1	50.9	14.4	18.3	6.0	84.1	90.0	92.2	76.4	30.2
France	1979[1]	35.9	13.2	33.3	12.8	80.8	16.0	25.1	12.7	85.0	73.4	95.8	67.4	44.7
	1984[1]	38.4	11.9	34.9	13.1	88.1	7.3	28.8	12.4	88.1	78.1	98.5	76.1	44.6
Germany	1978	24.5	8.2	12.3	4.9	73.8	20.9	20.3	7.2	87.6	79.8	90.6	85.8	44.4
	1983	26.2	8.0	15.9	6.5	72.2	18.8	18.5	5.8	90.4	80.6	92.4	89.0	42.6
Netherlands	1983[1]	33.5	9.3	24.0	7.0	77.3	6.4	28.8	10.8	85.2	83.7	96.9	78.8	53.1
	1987[1]	34.3	8.3	26.9	8.9	77.7	2.7	28.4	9.2	90.0	87.5	99.7	85.7	53.7
	1991[1]	30.2	7.7	22.9	9.2	75.8	7.2	23.1	7.3	89.4	78.3	97.5	85.8	49.8
Norway	1979[1]	23.2	4.8	14.1	4.4	78.5	6.7	12.8	4.6	91.4	84.1	96.1	80.7	49.3
	1986[1]	22.3	6.4	10.5	3.9	75.0	16.4	11.4	4.4	91.7	72.2	97.2	78.0	45.4
	1991[1]	25.6	5.3	16.0	3.9	73.6	9.5	15.1	4.5	91.8	87.7	98.2	80.9	41.9
Sweden	1975[1]	30.4	5.2	15.3	2.1	93.9	8.6	18.1	5.5	93.5	91.0	99.0	80.2	44.2
	1981[1]	38.6	4.6	23.8	4.5	98.2	0.9	25.3	5.9	95.7	88.9	99.9	87.5	44.2
	1987[1]	40.0	6.3	22.7	3.1	98.2	4.3	26.7	8.1	94.1	93.2	99.7	81.0	48.2
	1992[1]	43.3	6.0	29.6	2.6	97.1	4.9	31.3	7.6	94.1	95.6	99.3	85.3	48.3
United Kingdom	1974	20.1	11.4	15.2	10.8	72.0	34.4	11.7	6.8	81.0	55.4	87.3	75.4	51.1
	1979	27.5	10.8	23.4	10.7	78.5	25.9	17.4	7.2	87.8	76.8	95.0	79.9	45.4
	1986	37.2	13.0	37.7	17.4	76.7	13.3	27.6	11.0	83.9	77.6	96.9	75.2	49.4

Table A.4. **Impact of social security transfers on poverty rates and poverty gaps by age of persons** (cont.)

		Poverty rates before and after social transfers								Reduction in poverty gap due to social transfers				
		All persons		Children		Elderly 65+		Adults –65		All persons	Children	Elderly 65+	Adults –65	Transfer efficiency
		Before	After	Before	After	Before	After	Before	After					
United States	1974[1]	26.2	18.8	26.7	22.8	66.9	31.4	17.6	14.0	57.9	39.5	79.9	42.6	50.7
	1979[1]	26.0	18.6	27.6	24.1	64.1	28.9	16.9	13.7	59.2	42.8	79.5	42.2	46.8
	1986[1]	29.6	22.6	33.3	30.7	60.4	28.3	21.1	17.7	54.9	38.1	78.9	39.6	47.8
	1991[1]	31.6	22.7	35.3	30.3	61.2	26.1	22.9	18.4	58.5	44.4	81.2	43.3	46.8

1. Elderly are defined as persons in households where the head is 65 or over; adults –65 are similarly defined as persons over 16 in households where the head is younger than 65.
Source: LIS, and author's calculations.

Table A.5. **Poverty rates and composition of the poor by sex of the head of household**

		Percentage in poverty		Percentage of all poor		Measure of resources	Source
		Female head	Male head	Female head	Male head		
Australia	1981	39.4	12.4	45.1	55.0	Income	LIS
	1985	42.1	13.6	44.6	55.4	Income	LIS
	1989	42.5	13.4	46.7	53.3	Income	LIS
Belgium	1985	9.0	5.7	23.1	76.9	Income	LIS
	1988	13.8	5.7	31.6	68.4	Income	LIS
	1992	9.9	5.5	30.8	69.2	Income	LIS
Canada	1975	42.7	14.0	45.4	54.6	Income	LIS
	1981	35.4	12.3	47.2	52.8	Income	LIS
	1987	27.8	11.6	39.8	60.2	Income	LIS
	1991	26.9	11.6	43.4	56.6	Income	LIS
Denmark	1987	20.2	9.9	43.8	56.2	Income	LIS
	1992	13.7	6.5	45.3	54.7	Income	LIS
Finland	1987	15.9	5.8	52.0	48.0	Income	LIS
	1991	20.7	6.1	58.8	41.2	Income	LIS
France	1979	23.4	11.4	35.3	64.7	Income	LIS
	1984	15.1	10.5	28.7	71.3	Income	LIS
	1984/85	21.0	11.0	35.3	64.7	Expend.	DV93a
	1989	22.6	12.5	36.5	63.5	Expend.	DV93a
Germany	1978	28.7	6.6	60.2	39.8	Income	LIS
	1983	22.1	6.5	56.7	43.3	Income	LIS
	1988	23.5	8.5	58.6	41.4	Income	DV93b
Greece	1982	27.2	16.9	23.1	76.9	Expend.	DV93c
	1988	27.6	18.0	27.6	72.4	Expend.	DV93c
Netherlands	1983	11.6	7.7	29.2	70.8	Income	LIS
	1987	10.9	6.9	36.3	63.7	Income	LIS
	1991	12.1	6.8	35.0	65.0	Income	LIS
Norway	1979	10.7	4.4	48.2	51.8	Income	LIS
	1986	26.7	5.2	65.7	34.3	Income	LIS
	1991	17.6	4.9	62.1	37.9	Income	LIS
Portugal	1980	35.4	24.8	30.7	69.3	Expend.	DV93d
	1989	33.9	23.9	32.3	67.7	Expend.	DV93d
Spain	1980	30.0	16.9	22.0	78.0	Expend.	DV93e
	1988	23.7	14.7	24.6	75.4	Expend.	DV93e

Table A.5. **Poverty rates and composition of the poor by sex of the head of household** (cont.)

		Percentage in poverty		Percentage of all poor		Measure of resources	Source
		Female head	Male head	Female head	Male head		
Sweden	1975	13.9	5.8	45.2	54.8	Income	LIS
	1981	5.2	5.7	27.4	72.6	Income	LIS
	1987	13.1	7.9	40.4	59.6	Income	LIS
	1992	14.7	6.8	48.1	51.9	Income	LIS
United kingdom	1974	36.7	9.8	49.6	50.4	Income	LIS
	1979	25.7	10.1	42.8	57.2	Income	LIS
	1986	15.7	11.7	29.9	70.1	Income	LIS
	1985	18.2	11.5	33.6	66.4	Income	DV93f
	1988	42.7	16.4	43.6	56.4	Income	DV93f
United States	1974	43.0	13.8	49.0	51.0	Income	LIS
	1979	36.8	13.0	53.1	46.9	Income	LIS
	1986	41.8	15.4	49.7	50.3	Income	LIS
	1991	40.0	16.2	51.8	48.2	Income	LIS

Notes and sources: See Table A.2a.

Table A.6. **Poverty rates by age of head of household, using 50 per cent relative poverty line**

		Percentage in poverty			Distribution of sample			Source
		16-24	25-64	65+	16-24	25-64	65+	
Australia	1981	17.0	13.2	37.5	7.3	74.2	18.5	LIS
	1985	20.2	13.6	40.3	5.9	73.8	20.3	LIS
	1991	22.5	14.1	39.9	5.9	74.2	20.0	LIS
Belgium	1985	11.5	4.9	10.5	3.1	76.0	20.9	LIS
	1988	20.4	4.8	11.7	2.0	74.4	23.6	LIS
	1992	16.4	4.4	11.1	3.5	73.3	23.2	LIS
Canada	1975	27.1	13.8	42.1	10.9	72.1	17.0	LIS
	1981	26.3	13.8	30.4	9.4	73.5	17.1	LIS
	1987	29.2	13.5	17.3	6.0	75.8	18.2	LIS
	1991	38.3	14.7	10.2	6.3	75.3	18.4	LIS
Denmark	1987	28.0	5.4	26.2	10.3	65.7	24.1	LIS
	1992	35.4	5.0	7.4	9.5	66.3	24.2	LIS
Finland	1987	30.6	5.0	13.6	7.8	73.0	19.2	LIS
	1991	34.0	5.7	18.8	7.4	72.8	19.8	LIS
France	1979	14.8	12.3	18.6	3.5	71.1	25.4	LIS
	1984	17.5	12.2	8.2	4.3	73.1	22.6	LIS
	1984/85	13.6	9.3	26.6	5.1	73.9	21.0	DV94
	1989	11.3	11.3	26.1	4.5	70.9	24.6	DV94
Germany	1978	24.8	6.3	24.8	1.9	67.5	30.6	LIS
	1983	17.4	6.4	21.1	3.8	68.9	27.3	LIS
	1988	33.5	10.2	20.4	2.6	69.9	27.6	DV93
Greece	1982	10.4	13.7	35.6	2.5	75.4	22.1	DV94
	1988	8.2	13.8	38.8	2.7	72.2	25.2	DV94
Netherlands	1983	32.9	7.4	5.9	5.7	73.5	20.8	LIS
	1987	36.6	6.8	1.6	7.2	72.7	20.2	LIS
	1991	32.7	6.8	6.8	4.8	73.2	22.0	LIS
Norway	1979	19.1	4.4	7.4	6.4	66.2	27.3	LIS
	1986	30.4	4.6	21.8	6.7	65.8	27.6	LIS
	1991	35.9	4.4	13.9	6.4	67.7	26.0	LIS
Portugal	1980	27.9	20.7	50.2	5.7	73.2	21.0	DV94
	1989	33.8	19.0	49.5	5.4	72.7	22.0	DV94
Spain	1980	11.5	14.2	37.5	2.5	78.0	19.5	DV94
	1988	18.8	13.0	27.2	1.1	76.4	22.5	DV94
Sweden	1975	21.0	3.9	9.8	14.7	61.4	23.8	LIS
	1981	20.6	4.1	1.1	13.6	60.6	25.8	LIS
	1987	31.4	5.3	5.7	15.3	58.8	25.9	LIS
	1992	38.1	3.3	6.5	14.5	60.5	25.0	LIS

Table A.6. **Poverty rates by age of head of household, using 50 per cent relative poverty line** (cont.)

		Percentage in poverty			Distribution of sample			Source
		16-24	25-64	65+	16-24	25-64	65+	
United Kingdom	1974	7.4	7.7	39.0	4.5	70.8	24.7	LIS
	1979	13.7	8.2	27.9	4.8	68.9	26.3	LIS
	1986	16.7	11.7	14.5	5.4	68.7	25.8	LIS
	1985	26.2	10.8	17.0	4.2	68.7	27.0	DV94
	1988	32.5	14.8	40.1	4.9	68.4	26.8	DV94
United States	1974	28.2	15.4	36.8	8.1	72.3	19.6	LIS
	1979	23.2	15.3	33.8	8.1	71.5	20.5	LIS
	1986	36.5	18.5	32.8	5.2	73.7	21.1	LIS
	1991	42.9	19.0	30.6	4.7	73.3	21.9	LIS

Notes: See Table A.2a.

Table A.7. **Poverty rates for households whose head is at active age, by household-type**

		Poverty rates				Distribution of sample				Unit of measurement	Source
		Single person	Lone parent	Couple no children	Couple with children	Single person	Lone parent	Couple no children	Couple with children		
Australia	1981	20.1	40.9	7.0	10.4	21.9	6.3	26.1	45.7	Household	LIS
	1985	18.3	43.3	8.1	10.6	25.4	6.8	25.9	41.9	Household	LIS
	1989	20.4	46.7	7.7	10.8	23.0	7.2	28.9	40.9	Household	LIS
Belgium	1985	11.4	14.9	4.6	3.8	14.7	3.0	43.1	39.2	Household	LIS
	1988	13.2	7.8	4.5	4.3	16.2	3.2	43.8	36.8	Household	LIS
	1992	10.6	8.4	5.6	4.1	17.5	5.1	36.9	40.4	Household	LIS
Canada	1975	27.4	43.4	6.4	10.0	26.6	5.3	22.2	45.8	Econ. family	LIS
	1981	22.7	41.3	6.5	10.9	28.0	6.8	24.3	41.0	Household	LIS
	1987	20.9	40.8	7.5	11.7	25.8	6.1	28.5	39.7	Household	LIS
	1991	24.7	42.1	7.9	10.4	32.1	7.0	26.5	34.4	Household	LIS
Denmark	1987	16.6	4.7	3.7	3.6	38.6	5.8	25.1	30.4	Household	LIS
	1992	14.3	3.8	2.0	2.0	39.9	6.5	27.5	26.1	Household	LIS
Finland	1987	16.3	3.7	2.4	2.9	34.7	5.1	27.1	33.1	Household	LIS
	1991	17.7	5.7	3.6	2.5	35.2	5.6	27.3	31.9	Household	LIS
France	1979	17.9	24.9	11.1	10.7	18.2	3.9	28.7	49.2	Household	LIS
	1984	18.0	19.4	12.3	11.2	21.7	4.5	29.6	44.1	Household	LIS
Germany	1978	26.2	24.2	8.2	3.1	31.0	2.6	31.0	35.4	Tax unit	LIS
	1983	19.3	21.3	6.8	4.1	34.8	4.2	28.2	32.8	Tax unit	LIS
Netherlands	1983	17.6	9.0	6.7	7.5	18.8	4.3	31.5	45.4	Household	LIS
	1987	17.6	10.0	4.6	6.9	29.5	4.5	28.6	37.4	Household	LIS
	1991	18.5	26.2	5.7	7.2	26.6	4.5	34.3	34.6	Household	LIS
Norway	1979	12.4	9.6	3.4	2.9	24.8	11.6	14.8	48.8	Tax unit	LIS
	1986	15.8	14.2	1.2	1.8	32.1	9.2	22.0	36.7	Household	LIS
	1991	14.7	9.5	0.6	2.0	39.7	11.7	19.3	29.4	Household	LIS
Sweden	1975	15.0	2.4	2.6	2.2	42.7	5.0	22.1	30.1	Unknown	LIS
	1981	12.2	5.4	3.0	3.9	46.1	5.9	20.8	27.2	Tax unit	LIS
	1987	19.6	4.7	3.0	2.9	48.8	5.4	20.6	25.1	Tax unit	LIS
	1992	18.9	2.4	1.9	2.6	48.2	6.7	21.0	24.1	Tax unit	LIS
United Kingdom	1974	16.4	27.2	2.7	5.8	15.5	5.3	29.5	49.6	Unknown	LIS
	1979	13.1	19.9	4.8	7.4	18.0	6.3	27.9	47.8	Household	LIS
	1986	11.0	16.2	8.1	14.8	22.5	7.9	29.9	39.7	Household	LIS
United States	1974	22.2	52.1	8.2	11.9	19.7	9.2	25.7	45.3	Household	LIS
	1979	19.2	46.3	6.6	11.8	24.4	11.0	25.0	39.6	Household	LIS
	1986	20.8	52.2	8.8	17.6	24.9	10.5	27.3	37.3	Household	LIS
	1991	22.1	51.3	9.5	17.9	27.0	11.0	26.3	35.7	Household	LIS

Notes: See Table A.2a.

BIBLIOGRAPHY

ATKINSON, A. (1993*a*), "On targeting social security: theory and Western experience with family benefits", Discussion Paper 99, LSE Welfare State Programme.

ATKINSON, A. (1993*b*), "The welfare state and economic performance", Discussion Paper 109, LSE Welfare State Programme.

ATKINSON, A. and MOGENSEN, G. (eds.) (1993), *Welfare and Work Incentives: A North European Perspective*, Clarendon Press, Oxford.

ATKINSON, A., GARDINER, K., LECHÊNE, V. and SUTHERLAND, H. (1993), "Comparing poverty in France and the United Kingdom", Discussion Paper WSP/84, Suntory-Toyota International Centre for Economics and Related Disciplines, London.

AULETTA, K. (1982), *The Underclass*, Random House, New York.

BANE, M.J. and ELLWOOD, D. (1994), *Welfare Realities: From Rhetoric to Reform*, Harvard University Press, Cambridge, MA.

BARR, N. (1992), "Economic theory and the welfare state: a survey and interpretation", *Journal of Economic Literature*, Vol. XXX, pp. 741-803.

BERGHMAN, J. and CANTILLON, B. (1993), *The European Face of Social Security, Essays in Honour of Herman Deleeck*, Avebury, Aldershot.

BJORKLUND, A. (1992), "Rising female labour force participation and the distribution of family income – The Swedish experience, *Acta Sociologica*, Vol. 35, pp. 299-309.

BJORKLUND, A. and FREEMAN, R. (1994), "Generating equality and eliminating poverty: the Swedish Way", NBER Working Paper 4945, NBER, Cambridge, MA.

BLACKBURN, M. and BLOOM, D. (1994), "Changes in the structure of family income inequality in the United States and other industrialised nations during the 1980s", Working Paper No. 118, Luxembourg Income Study, Luxembourg.

BLANK, R. (1993), "Why were poverty rates so high in the 1980s?", in D. Padadimitriou and E. Wolff (eds.), *Poverty and Prosperity in the USA in the Late Twentieth Century*, Macmillan, New York.

BLANK, R. (1994), *Social Protection versus Economic Flexibility: Is there a Trade-off?*, University of Chicago Press, Chicago.

BLANK, R. (1995), "Changes in inequality and unemployment over the 1980s: a comparative cross-national perspective", *Journal of Population Economics*, Vol. 8, pp. 1-21.

BOSCH, VAN DEN, K. (1993), "Poverty measures in comparative research", in Berghman and Cantillon (1993), pp. 3-23.

BOSCH, VAN DEN, K. *et al.* (1993), "A comparison of poverty in seven European countries and regions using subjective and relative measures", *Journal of Population Economics*, Vol. 6, pp. 235-259.

BRADSHAW, J. *et al.* (1995), *Why and how do Lone Parents Work outside the Home? – A Comparison of 20 Countries*, Social Policy Research Unit, York.

BUHMANN, B., RAINWATER, L., SCHMAUS, G. and SMEEDING, T. (1988), "Equivalence scales, well-being, inequality, and poverty: sensitivity estimates across ten countries using the Luxembourg Income Study (LIS) database, *Review of Income and Wealth*, Vol. 34, No. 2, pp. 115-142.

CALLAN, T. and NOLAN, B. (1991), "Concepts of poverty and the poverty line", *Journal of Economic Surveys*, Vol. 5, No. 3, pp 243-261.

CALLAN, T., NOLAN, B. *et al.* (1989), "Poverty, income and welfare in Ireland", General Research Series Paper No. 146, The Economic and Social Research Institute, Dublin.

CANCIAN, M., DANZIGER, S. and GOTTSCHALK, P. (1993), "Working wives and family income inequality among married couples", in S. Danziger and P. Gottschalk (eds.), *Uneven Tides: Rising Inequality in America*, Russell Sage, New York, pp. 195-221.

CANTILLON, B. (1994), "Family, work and social security", in S. Baldwin and J. Falkingham (eds.), *Social Security and Social Change: New Challenges to the Beveridge Model*, Harvester Wheatsheaf, London.

CANTILLON, B. (1995), "Dependence on social security and the impact of incentive measures", *Social Security Tomorrow: Permanence and Change*, International Social Security Association (ISSA), Geneva.

CANTILLON, B. and MARX, I. (1995a), *Naar een sociaal doelmatig tewerkstellingsbeleid,* Koning Boudewijnstichting, Brussels.

CANTILLON, B. and MARX, I. (1995b), "Armoedebestrijding en sociale zekerheid: mogelijkheden en beperkingen", in M. Despontin and M. Jegers (eds.), *De sociale zekerheid verzekerd?*, VUBPress, Brussels.

CANTILLON, B., MARX, I., PROOST, D. and DAM van, R. (1993), *Indicateurs Sociaux 1985 – 1992, Revue Belge de la Sécurité Sociale*, Vol. 36, No. 2, pp. 497-549.

COMMISSION OF THE EUROPEAN COMMUNITIES (1981), *Final Report from the First Programme of Pilot Schemes and Studies to Combat Poverty*, Brussels.

COUNCIL OF EUROPE (1993), *Homelessness*, Strasbourg.

DAHRENDORF, R. (1990), *The Modern Social Conflict – An Essay on the Politics of Liberty,* University of California Press, Berkeley and Los Angeles.

DANZIGER, S., SANDEFUR, G. and WEINBERG, D. (1994), *Confronting Poverty: Prescriptions for Change*, Harvard University Press, Cambridge, MA.

DELEECK, H., van den BOSCH, K., DE LATHOUWER, L. (1992), *Poverty and the Adequacy of Social Security in the EC, A Comparative Analysis*, Avebury, Aldershot.

DEX, S., GUFSTAFSON, S., SMITH, N. and CALLAN, T. (1995), *Cross-national Comparison of the Labour Force Participation of Women Married to Unemployed Men*, Oxford Economic Papers, Vol. 47, pp. 611-635.

DUNCAN, G. et al. (1984), *Years of Plenty. The Changing Economic Fortunes of American Workers and Families,* Institute for Social Research, Michigan.

DUNCAN G. et al. (1993), "Poverty dynamics in eight countries", *Journal of Population Economics*, Vol. 6, pp. 215-234.

DUNCAN, G., GUSTAFSSON, B., HAUSER, R., SCHMAUS, G., JENKINS, S., MESSINGER, H., MUFFELS, R., NOLAN, B., RAY, J.C. and VOGES, W. (1995), "Poverty and social assistance in the United States, Canada, and Europe", in K. McFate, R. Lawson and W.J. Wilson (eds.), *Poverty, Inequality and the Future of Social Protection*, Russell Sage Foundation, New York.

EARDLEY, T., BRADSHAW, J., DITCH, J., GOUGH, I. and WHITEFORD, P. (1996), *Social Assistance in OECD Countries*, HMSO, London.

ELMESKOV, J. and PICHELMANN, K. (1993), "Unemployment and labour force participation – Trends and cycles", in Economics Department Working Paper, No. 130, OECD, Paris.

ENGBERSEN, G. (1990), *Publieke Bijstandsgeheimen*, Stenfert Kroese, Leiden en Antwerpen.

ENGBERSEN, G. (1991), "Moderne armoede: feit en fictie", *Sociologische Gids*, Vol. 37, No.1, pp. 7-23.

ESPING-ANDERSEN, G. (1990), *The Three Worlds of Welfare Capitalism*, Polity Press, Cambridge.

ESPING-ANDERSEN, G. (1993), *Changing Classes: Stratification and Mobility in Post-industrial Societies*, Sage, London.

EUROPEAN COMMISSION (1995), *The Demographic Situation in the European Union: 1994,* Brussels.

EUROSTAT (1990), *Poverty in Figures. Europe in the Early 1980s*, Office for Official Publications of the European Communities, Luxembourg.

FAY, R.G. (1996), "Enhancing the effectiveness of active labour market policies: evidence from programme evaluations in OECD Countries", Labour market and social policy occasional papers No. 18, OECD, Paris.

FÖRSTER, M. (1993), "Comparing poverty in 13 OECD countries: traditional and synthetic approaches", Luxembourg Income Study Working Papers, Luxembourg.

FREEMAN, R. (1995a), "The large welfare state as a system", *AEA Papers and Proceedings*, Vol. 85, No. 2, pp. 16-21.

FREEMAN, R. (1995b), "The limits of wage flexibility to curing unemployment", *Oxford Review of Economic Policy*, Vol. 11 (1), pp. 63-72.

FREEMAN, R. and KATZ, L. (1994), *Changes and Differences in Wage Structures*, University of Chicago Press, Chicago.

FUNKEN, K. and P. COOPER, (1995), *Old and New Poverty: The Challenge for Reform*, Rivers Oram Press, London.

GIANNELLI, G. and MICKLEWRIGHT, J. (1995), "Why do women married to unemployed men have low participation rates?", *Oxford Economic Papers*, Vol. 47, pp. 471-486.

GLYNN, A. (1995), "The assessment: unemployment and inequality", *Oxford Review of Economic Policy*, Vol. 11 (1), pp. 63-72.

GOODIN, R. (1988), *Reasons for Welfare: the Political Theory of the Welfare State*, Princeton University Press, Princeton.

GOODIN, R. and LEGRAND, J. (1986), *Not only the Poor. The Middle Classes and the Welfare State*, Allen and Unwin, London.

GOODMAN, A. and WEBB, S. (1994), *For Richer, For Poorer – The Changing Distribution of Income in the United Kingdom, 1961-91*, Commentary No 42, The Institute for Fiscal Studies, London.

GORNICK, J. and ROSS, K. (1996), "Supporting the employment of mothers: policy variation across fourteen welfare states", Luxembourg Income Study, Working Paper No. 139, Luxembourg.

GORNICK, J., MEYERS, M. and ROSS, K. (1996), "Public policies and the employment of mothers: a cross-national study", Luxembourg Income Study, Working Paper No. 140, Luxembourg.

GOTTSCHALK, P. and JOYCE, M. (1995), "The impact of technological change, deindustrialisation, and international-isation of trade on earnings inequality: an international perspective", in K. Mcfate, R. Lawson and W. Wilson (eds.), *Poverty, Inequality, and the Future of Social Policy: Western States in the New World Order*, Russell Sage, New York.

GOTTSCHALK, P. and SMEEDING, T. (1995), "Cross-national comparisons of levels and trends of inequality", Luxembourg Income Study, Working Paper No. 126, Luxembourg.

GOTTSCHALK P., MCLANAHAN, S. and SANDEFUR, G. (1994), "The dynamics and intergenerational transmission of poverty and welfare participation", in S. Danziger, G. Sandefur and D. Weinberg (eds.), *Confronting Poverty. Prescriptions for Change*, Harvard University Press, Cambridge, MA, pp. 85-108.

GREGG, P. and WADSWORTH, J. (1996), *It Takes Two: Employment Polarisation in the OECD*, Centre for Economic Performance Discussion Paper No. 304, CEPR, London School of Economics, London.

GUSTAFSSON, S. (1995), "Single mothers in Sweden: why is poverty less severe?", in K. Mcfate, R. Lawson and W. Wilson (eds.), *Poverty, Inequality, and the Future of Social Policy: Western States in the New World Order*, Russell Sage, New York.

GUSTAFSSON, S. and STAFFORD, F. (1994), "Three regimes of childcare: the United States, the Netherlands, and Sweden", in R. Blank (ed.), *Social Protection vs. Economic Flexibility: Is There a Trade-off?*, Chicago University Press, Chicago.

GUSTAFSSON, S. and UUSITALO, H. (1990), "The welfare state and poverty in Finland and Sweden from the mid-1960s to the mid-1980s", *The Review of Income and Wealth*, Vol. 36, No. 3, pp. 249-266.

HAGENAARS, A., de VOS, K. and ZAIDI, M. (1992), *Statistiques relatives à la pauvreté, basées sur des microdonnées – Résultats pour neuf Etats membres des Communautés européennes*, Erasmus University, Rotterdam.

HANRATTY, M. and BLANK, R. (1992), "Down and out in North America: recent trends in poverty rates in the United States and Canada", *Quarterly Journal of Economics*.

HAUSER, R. and BECKER, I. (1994), "The development of the income distribution in the Federal Republic of Germany during the seventies and eighties", Arbeitspapier No 1, EVS-Projekt, Johann Wolfgang Goethe-Universität, Frankfurt.

HAUSMAN, P. (1993), "The impact of social security in the European Community", in Berghman and Cantillon (1993), pp. 109-122.

HAVEMAN, R. (1990), "Poverty statistics in the European Community: assessment and recommendations", in Teekens and van Praag (1990), pp. 459-467.

HAVEMAN, R. and BURON, L. (1993), "Escaping poverty through work: the problem of low earnings capacity in the United States, 1973-1988", *Review of Income and Wealth*, Vol. 39:2, pp. 141-157.

HENKERS, K., SIEGERS, J. and van den BOSCH, K. (1993), "Married women on the labour market: a comparative study of Belgium and the Netherlands", in G. Beets, R. Cliquet, G. Dooghe and J. de Jong Gierveld (eds.), *Population and Family in the Low Countries 1992: Family and Labour*, Swets and Zeitlinger, Amsterdam.

HILLS, J. (1995), *Inquiry into Income and Wealth, Volume 2 – A Summary of the Evidence*, Joseph Rowntree Foundation, York.

HUSTON, A. (1991), *Child Poverty: Child Development and Public Policy*, Cambridge University Press, Cambridge.

INTERNATIONAL SOCIAL SECURITY ASSOCIATION (1995), *Social Security Tomorrow: Permanence and Change*, ISSA, Geneva.

JARVIS, S. and JENKINS, S. (1995), "Do the poor stay poor? New evidence about low income dynamics from the BHPS", ESRC Research Centre on Micro-social Change Occasional Paper 95/2, London.

JENCKS, C. (1991), "Is the American underclass growing?", in C. Jencks and P. Peterson (eds.), *The Urban Underclass*, The Brookings Institution, Washington, DC, pp. 28-102.

JENCKS, C. (1992), *Rethinking Social Policy: Race, Poverty and the Underclass*, Harvard University Press, Cambridge (MA) and London.

JENCKS, C. and PETERSON, P. (1991), *The Urban Underclass*, The Brookings Institution, Washington, DC.

JENKINS, S. (1991), "Poverty measurement and the within-household distribution: agenda for action", *The Journal of Social Policy*, Vol. 20, No. 4, pp. 457-483.

JUHN, C. and MURPHY, K. (1996), "Wage inequality and family labour supply", NBER Working Paper No 5459, NBER, Cambridge, MA.

KAMERMAN, S. (1995), "Gender role and family structure changes in the advanced industrialized West: implications for social policy", in K. Mcfate, R. Lawson and W. Wilson (eds.), *Poverty, Inequality, and the Future of Social Policy – Western States in the New World Order*, Russell Sage, New York.

KRUGMAN, P. and LAWRENCE, R. (1993), "Trade, jobs and wages", NBER Working Paper No. 4478, NBER, Cambridge, MA.

LEIBFRIED, S. (1991), *Towards an European Welfare State? On Integrating Poverty Regimes in the European Community*, ZeS -Arbeitspapier No. 2/91, Zentrum für Sozialpolitik, Bremen.

LEIRA, A. (1992), *Welfare States and Working Mothers: The Scandinavian Experience*, Cambridge University Press, Cambridge.

LEWIS, O. (1968), "Culture of poverty", in D. Moynihan (ed.), *On Understanding Poverty: Perspectives from the Social Sciences*, Basic Books, New York.

LINDBECK, A. *et al.* (1994), *Turning Sweden around*, MIT Press, Cambridge, MA.

LODEMEL, I. (1992), "European poverty regimes", Paper for presentation at the International Research Conference on Poverty and Distribution, Oslo, 16 and 17 November.

MACHIN, S. and WALDFOGEL, J. (1994), "The decline of the male breadwinner: changing shares of husbands' and wives' earnings in family income in the UK", Working Paper WSP/103, Welfare State Programme, London School of Economics, London.

MITCHELL, D. (1991), *Income Transfers in Ten Welfare States*, Avebury, Aldershot.

MITCHELL, D. (1995), "Is there a trade-off between the efficiency and effectiveness goals of income transfer programs?", *Journal of Income Distribution*, Vol. 5 (1), pp. 111-135.

MITCHELL, D. and GRUEN, F. (1995), "The role of targeting in rethinking social security", *Social Security Tomorrow: Permanence and Change*, International Social Security Association, Geneva.

MOYNIHAN, D. (1968), *On Understanding Poverty: Perspectives from the Social Sciences*, Basic Books, New York.

MURRAY, C. (1984), *Losing Ground, American Social Policy, 1950-1980*, Schuster, New York.

MURRAY, C. *et al.* (1990), *The Emerging British Underclass*, The IEA Health and Welfare Unit, London.

NICKELL, S. and BELL, B. (1995), "The collapse in demand for the unskilled and unemployment across the OECD", *Oxford Review of Economic Policy*, Vol. 11 (1), pp. 40-62.

O'CONNOR, T. and SMEEDING, T. (1995), "Working but poor: a cross-national comparison of earnings adequacy", *Journal of Income Distribution*, Vol. 5 (1), pp. 91-110.

O'HIGGINS, M. and JENKINS, S. (1990), "Poverty in Europe: estimates for the numbers in poverty in 1975, 1980, 1985", in Teekens and van Praag (1990), pp. 187-212.

OECD (1982), *OECD List of Social Indicators*, Paris.

OECD (1990a), *Labour Market Policies for the 1990s*, Paris.

OECD (1990b), *Lone-parent Families: The Economic Challenge*, Social Policy Studies No. 8, Paris.

OECD (1991), *Employment Outlook*, Paris.

OECD (1993), "Breadwinners or child rearers: the dilemma for lone mothers", Labour Market and Social Policy Occasional Papers No. 12, Paris.

OECD (1994a), *OECD Jobs Study: Evidence and Explanations*, Paris.

OECD (1994b), *New Orientations for Social Policy*, Social Policy Studies No 12, Paris.

OECD (1995a), *Employment Outlook*, Paris.

OECD (1995b), *Historical Statistics, 1960-1993*, Paris.

OECD (1995c), *Income Distribution in OECD Countries*, Social Policy Studies No. 18, Paris.

OECD (1996a), "Social expenditure statistics of OECD Member countries – Provisional version", Labour Market and Social Policy Occasional Papers No. 17, Paris.

OECD (1996b), *Employment Outlook*, Paris.

OORSCHOT van, W. (1995), *Realizing Rights: A Multi-level Approach to Non-take-up of Means-tested Benefits*, Avebury, Aldershot.

PAPADAKIS, E. (1993), "Class interests, class politics and welfare state regime", *British Journal of Sociology*, Vol. 2, pp. 249-270.

PARIJS van, P. (1992), *Arguing for Basic Income: Ethical Foundations for a Radical Reform*, Verso, London.

PAUGAM, S. (1994), *Précarité et exclusion en France*, Paris.

PETERSON, P. (1991), "The urban underclass and the poverty paradox", *Political Science Quarterly*, Vol. 106, No. 4, winter, pp. 617-638.

PIERSON, P. (1995), *Dismantling the Welfare State. Reagan, Thatcher and the Politics of Retrenchment*, Cambridge University Press, Cambridge.

PHIPPS, S. (1993), "International perspectives on income support for families with children", Luxembourg Income Study, Working Paper No. 103, Luxembourg.

RITAKALLIO, V.-M. (1994), "Finnish poverty: a cross-national comparison", Luxembourg Income Study, Working Paper No. 119, Luxembourg.

ROBINSON, P. (1995), "The decline of the Swedish model and the limits to active labour market policies", Centre for Economic Performance Working Paper, London.

ROOM, G. (1990), *New Poverty in the European Community*, Macmillan, Basingstoke.

ROOM, G. (1995), "Poverty in Europe: competing paradigms of analysis", in *Policy and Politics*, Vol. 2, pp. 103-113.

ROSEN, S. (1995), "Public employment, taxes and the welfare state in Sweden", NBER Working Paper No. 5003, NBER, Cambridge, MA.

RUGGLES, P. (1990), *Drawing the Line, Alternative Poverty Measures and their Implications for Public Policy*, The Urban Institute Press, Washington, DC.

SAUNDERS, P. (1993), *Married Women's Earnings and Family Income Inequality in the Eighties*, Australian Bulletin of Labour, Vol. 19, pp. 199-217.

SAUNDERS, P. (1994), *Welfare and Inequality: National and International Perspective on the Australian Welfare State*, Cambridge University Press, Cambridge.

SAUNDERS, P., O'CONNOR, I. and SMEEDING, T. (1994), "The distribution of welfare: inequality, earnings capacity, and household production in comparative perspective", Luxembourg Income Study, Working Paper No. 122, Luxembourg.

SCHMÄHL, W. (1995), "Social security and competitiveness", *Social Security Tomorrow: Permanence and Change*, International Social Security Association (ISSA), Geneva.

SCHMITT, J. and WADSWORTH, J. (1994), "The rise in economic inactivity", in A. Glynn and D. Miliband (eds.), *Paying for Inequality: The Economic Costs of Social Injustice*, London.

SCHUYT, C. and TAN, A. (1988), "De Maatschappelijke Betekenis van Armoede. Deel II", *Op zoek naar armoede en bestaansonzekerheid langs twee sporen*, Nationale Raad voor Maatschappelijk Welzijn, Rijswijk, pp. 34-54.

SCP (1994), *Sociaal en Cultureel Rapport 1994*, Sociaal en Cultureel Planbureau, Rijswijk.

SLESNICK, D. (1993), "Gaining ground: poverty in the postwar United States", *Journal of Political Economy*, Vol. 101, No. 1, pp. 1-38.

SMEEDING, T., RAINWATER, L. and O'HIGGINS, M. (1990), *Poverty, Inequality and the Distribution of Income in an International Context: Initial Research from the Luxembourg Income Study* (LIS), Wheatsheaf, London.

SSA (1995), *Annual Statistical Supplement to the Social Security Bulletin*, Social Security Administration, Washington, DC.

TEEKENS, R. and PRAAG, van B. (1990), *Analysing Poverty in the European Community*, Eurostat News Special Edition, Office for Official Publications of the European Communities, Luxembourg.

VOS, de K. and ZAIDI, M. (1993a), *Research on Poverty Statistics Based on Micro-data, Results for Germany,* Erasmus University and Economics Institute, Rotterdam and Tilburg.

VOS, de K. and ZAIDI, M. (1993b), *Trend Analysis of Poverty in Spain* (1980-88), Erasmus University and Economics Institute, Rotterdam and Tilburg.

VOS, de K. and ZAIDI, M. (1993c), *Trend Analysis of Poverty in the United Kingdom* (1985-88), Erasmus University and Economics Institute, Rotterdam and Tilburg.

VOS, de K. and ZAIDI, M. (1994a), *Objective Monetary Poverty, Study on Trends in the 1980s*, Erasmus University and Economics Institute, Rotterdam and Tilburg.

VOS, de K. and ZAIDI, M. (1994b), *Trend Analysis of Poverty in France* (1984/85-89), Erasmus University and Economics Institute, Rotterdam and Tilburg.

VOS, de K. and ZAIDI, M. (1994c), *Trend Analysis of Poverty in Greece* (1982-88), Erasmus University and Economics Institute, Rotterdam and Tilburg.

VOS, de K. and ZAIDI, M. (1994d), *Trend Analysis of Poverty in Portugal* (1980-89), Erasmus University and Economics Institute, Rotterdam and Tilburg.

WHITEFORD, P. (1985), "A family's needs: equivalence scales, poverty and social security", Research Paper No. 27, Development Division, Department of Social Security, Australia.

WILSON, W.J. (1987), *The Truly Disadvantaged, The Inner City, The Underclass and Public Policy*, University of Chicago Press, Chicago/London.

WILSON, W.J. (1991), "Another look at the truly disadvantaged", *Political Science Quarterly*, Vol. 106, No. 4, winter, pp. 639-656.

WOOD, A. (1994), *North-South Trade, Employment and Inequality*, Clarendon Press, Oxford.

XIBBERAS (1993), *Les théories de l'exclusion*, Méridiens Klincksieck, Paris.

CAN WE AFFORD TO GROW OLD?
Adjusting Pension Policies to a more Aged Society

by

Lans Bovenberg and Anja van der Linden
Bureau for Economic Policy Analysis, the Netherlands

INTRODUCTION

OECD countries will experience rapid ageing of the population in the near future. These demographic trends will constitute serious challenges to the systems of social insurance, pensions and health care, particularly in the second quarter of the next century. This paper focuses on the consequences of ageing for the systems of income support in old age, including pension design and retirement policies, rather than for health care, housing, and social care services. The first section explores the strengths and weaknesses of various pension systems. The second section illustrates the major uncertainties surrounding the relative performance of various pension systems by providing scenarios for the main future trends affecting old-age income support. To spread the risks, OECD countries should act on several fronts in order to prepare their economies for the ageing of their populations. The third section outlines various possible policy measures. Whereas several of these measures involve social insurance and pension systems, other suggested policies concern the economy more generally.

STRENGTHS AND WEAKNESSES OF VARIOUS PENSION SYSTEMS

Depending on the type of financing, three types of pension schemes can be distinguished: Pay-as-you-go (PAYG), defined-benefit (DB), and defined-contribution (DC) schemes.

PAYG systems pay retirement benefits out of premiums collected on the labour income of the young. In the absence of capital funding, these schemes typically imply substantial inter-generational transfers. Depending on the benefit and premium formula used, PAYG systems generally redistribute resources also within generations. In particular, we can distinguish between, on the one hand, highly redistributive PAYG schemes that provide flat benefits (but link premiums to earnings) and, on the other hand, less redistributive systems that relate benefits to salary levels or premiums paid. Table 6.1, which provides an overview of pension schemes in OECD countries, shows that many larger countries (including Germany, France, Italy, the United States) tend to feature less redistributive PAYG systems than the smaller countries (including the Netherlands, Denmark, New Zealand). In particular, the first group of countries provide earnings-related schemes that link benefits to average salary levels. The second group, in contrast, provides flat benefits.

In contrast to PAYG plans, DC schemes are not redistributive – either *within* or *across* generations. Indeed, individual retirement benefits are directly related to individual contributions. At any point in time, the accumulated capital corresponds to the discounted value of future retirement benefits.

DB schemes can be viewed as a mixture of PAYG and DC schemes. These schemes are typically provided as occupational schemes by firms. Just like DC schemes, DB systems employ capital funding. However, in contrast to DC schemes, benefits are based on salary levels in the period preceding retirement[1] rather than on the discounted value of individual life-time contributions. Indeed, besides accumulating capital, the funds levy premiums on the younger working members of the scheme to finance benefits of the older workers and the retired.[2] In this way, the plans, in fact, employ a mixture of capital funding and pay-as-you-go financing.

Table 6.1. **Pension schemes in selected OECD countries**

	Germany	France	Italy	Denmark	Netherlands	Switzerland	United Kingdom	Canada	New Zealand	United States	Japan
Statutory retirement age (M/F)	65	60	65	67	65	65/62	65/60	65	62	65	60/55
First pillar											
Type of benefit[1]	AS	AS	AS	LS	LS	LS/AS	LS/AS	AS	LS	AS	LS/AS
Financing method	PAYG	PAYG	PAYG	PAYG	PAYG	PAYG	PAYG	PAYG	PAYG	PAYG+fund	PAYG+fund
Coverage[2]	E	E/S	E/S	R	R	R/E/S	R/E	R/E/S	R	E/S	R/E
Typical replacement rate (full career)	70	±40	max 80				max 50	40		41	LS +30% AS
Guaranteed minimum pension[3]		#	#			#		#			
Vesting period (in years)	5		16	3		1	0-1	10	10	10	25
Second/third pillar											
Type of benefit[1]	AS	AS	DC	AS/DC	FS	DC	FS	FS	DC/FS	FS	FS
Financing method	Book reserves	PAYG	Funded	Funded	Funded	Funded	Funded	Funded	Funded	Funded	Funded
Coverage	E	E	E	E	E	E	E	E	E	E	E
Extent of coverage[3]	+	+	–	+	+	+	+			+	
Typical replacement rate[4]	70	70			70			80			
Vesting period	10			0-5	1		2	0-5		max 5	

1. AS = Linked to average salary, FS = Linked to final salary, DC = Defined contribution, LS = Lump sum.
2. R = Residents, E = Employees, S = Self-employed.
3. + = Extensive, – = Uncommon, # = Available.
4. The typical replacement rate includes the first pillar.

Sources: OECD (1993a), OECD (1993b), OECD (1993c), OECD (1995), Missoc (1994), Social Security Administration (1995), Clifford Chance (1993).

Box 1. **Strengths and weaknesses of various pension systems**

	Pay-As-You-Go (PAYG)		Defined Benefit (DB)	Defined-Contribution (DC)
	Flat benefits	Benefits based on contribution or salary		
Insurance against				
– inter-generational inequities	+	+	+	–
– demographic shocks	–	–	0	+
– low return on human capital	–	–	+	+
– low return on financial capital	+	+	0	–
– political risks	–	–	0	+
Strong incentives to:				
– save	–	–	0	+
– work	–	0	0	+
– invest in human capital	–	0	+	0
Efficient allocation of labour (portability of claims)	+	+	–	+
Poverty alleviation	+	–	–	0
Low administrative costs	+	+	+	0
Individual choice of participation and pension level	–	–	–	+

The rest of this section explores the strengths and weaknesses of the various types of pension schemes. Box 1 summarises the discussion.[3]

Inter-generational risk

The main potential strength of PAYG and DB schemes is inter-generational risk-sharing in the face of major long-term macroeconomic risks, including depressions, wars, natural disasters, financial crisis, etc. In PAYG schemes, and to a lesser extent in DB schemes, these risks can in part be shifted to the young in the form of changes in the premium rate. This inter-generational risk-sharing, aimed at protecting the incomes of the elderly, can be efficient because the young are generally better able to adapt to changes in wealth than are the elderly.

In DC schemes, the elderly are fully exposed to investment risks. How serious this is depends not only on investment risks, but also on whether efficient financial markets allow investors to hedge against these risks. Moreover, the government may provide some insurance through the tax system (see below).

Political risk

Whereas PAYG systems are less vulnerable to investment risk than are DC schemes, they are likely to be more vulnerable to political risk. In particular, the implicit inter-generational contract associated with PAYG schemes may break down as individualisation erodes inter-generational altruism and as ageing makes inter-generational solidarity more expensive to maintain.

DC schemes are less vulnerable to political risk, because they feature well-defined property rights on individual pensions. However, also these schemes may be affected by distributional and political conflicts arising from fiscal imbalances associated with ageing because these conflicts may result in excessive taxes (including inflation taxes) on pension wealth.

DB schemes may suffer from political risk, as individual property rights on assets tend to be ill-defined. Indeed, DB schemes tend to feature implicit rather than explicit contracts, as the benefit promise is backed up not only by financial assets, but also by the reputation and market power of the firm and the solidarity of future workers. Hence, DB schemes seem particularly attractive in corporatist settings in which workers trust firms to carry out commitments in implicit contracts. Ageing makes the commitment of firms to DB schemes (and age-related pay schemes in general) less credible, because an older labour force makes these schemes more expensive.

Individual choice and administrative costs

PAYG schemes, and to a lesser extent DB schemes, require compulsory participation under rather uniform conditions. If individuals were free to opt out or select their own pension packages, adverse selection would erode intra- and inter-generational risk-sharing and redistribution. The limitations on individual choice amount to an implicit tax and generate welfare losses.

DC schemes leave more scope for individual choice and can cater better to the specific needs and preferences of each individual participant. However, individual choice implies higher transaction costs. Indeed, there is a trade-off between, on the one hand, exploiting economies of scale and scope (in uniform pension plans), and on the other hand, tuning pensions to specific needs through product differentiation.

Insurance, poverty alleviation and incentives

The inter-generational transfers associated with inter-generational risk-sharing imply that PAYG benefits are not actuarially fair. The distortions implied by the associated tax or subsidy depend on the precise pension and contribution formulas. In setting these formulas, policy makers face a trade-off between efficiency (by keeping marginal tax rates low) and intra-generational equity (by alleviating old-age poverty).

The objectives of poverty alleviation and old-age insurance may conflict, depending on income heterogeneity *within* generations compared to heterogeneity *across* generations. These objectives do not conflict much if the old are a homogeneous group that is poorer than the young. However, if incomes become more heterogeneous within (rather than across) generations, age is not a good indicator for poverty. Hence, the government has to supplement information about age with information about incomes to determine who is poor. This imposes additional administrative costs, may cause limited take-up due to stigmatising effects, and distorts saving and labour supply. Accordingly, poverty alleviation becomes more expensive.

Voluntary DC schemes distort neither saving nor labour supply because they do not redistribute across and within generations. DC schemes are particularly attractive if society does not attach a high priority to (intra- and inter-generational) redistribution and risk-sharing.

Employers often adopt occupational schemes of the DB type to address labour market failures associated with asymmetric information and lack of commitment. In particular, long vesting periods, limited indexation of pension rights for those who end participation before retiring, and linking retirement benefits to the final wage motivates workers not to shirk (when effort is costly to monitor) and binds workers to the firm. This reduces costs associated with monitoring, training, hiring, and firing. Moreover, a stronger commitment of the worker to the firm encourages the stockholders of the firm (*e.g.* shareholders and workers) to invest in firm-specific (human) capital.

These positive incentive effects come at a price. In particular, limited portability impedes labour mobility across firms, which renders the allocation of labour less efficient and may discourage gradual retirement (see below).[4] Accordingly, DB schemes seem to be particularly attractive if firm-specific investments make a stable workforce desirable, and if the need for flexible adjustment of the allocation of labour in response to unexpected shocks can be met within firms. By focusing on stable firm-worker relations, DB schemes tend to favour the rich (who tend to have stable jobs and fast careers) rather than the poor (who tend to suffer from high rates of job turnover).

Demographic shocks and the Aaron condition

The Aaron condition (see Aaron, 1966) shows how the rate of return, the growth rate of labour productivity, and the growth rate of the labour force affect the relative merits of PAYG versus funded schemes. The long-run return to PAYG schemes depends on the growth rate of labour income determining the growth of the contribution base. The return on funded schemes, in contrast, depends on the rate of return on financial assets. Hence, in the long run, funding can offer higher retirement benefits if the rate of return on financial capital exceeds the growth rate of labour income (*i.e.* the sum of the growth rate of labour productivity and the growth rate of employment).

Table 6.2 compares the average real growth rate of wages with the average real return on capital during the 1970s and 1980s. In contrast to the real interest on government bonds, the return on shares substantially exceeded the growth rate of wages during this period.

Ageing of the population reduces the attractiveness of PAYG by decreasing the growth rate of employment. However, ageing is also likely to make labour scarcer relative to physical capital. This may raise wage growth and depress the rate of return on capital. Accordingly, the overall effect of ageing on the Aaron condition is ambiguous. Moreover, non-demographic trends may impact the Aaron condition. To illustrate, the World Bank (1994) expects that enhanced international capital mobility will boost the return on capital, thereby making funding more attractive. Indeed, whereas labour mobility (*i.e.* inward migration) may sustain PAYG schemes in ageing countries, capital mobility (*i.e.* capital exports) may help funded schemes in these countries to maintain high returns. In particular, by investing capital in non-OECD countries with relatively young populations and abundant labour, funded schemes can exploit the phasing differential in ageing between the ageing OECD countries and the non-OECD countries, which can be expected to age only later.

Summing up

Depending on the particular objective, one type of pension scheme may perform best. In particular, alleviating old-age poverty is best accomplished by a nationwide public PAYG system that provides a minimum standard of living in old age. This welfare system should be mandatory, redistributive, and can be financed from current tax revenues. Another objective is relatively uniform insurance against longevity and income risks in old age. To avoid moral hazard involving means-tested benefits, adverse selection in annuity markets, and to facilitate inter-generational risk-sharing, this function may require some compulsory insurance. Those high-income workers who want to go beyond the mandatory level of pension insurance can use supplementary private pension plans, which will tend to be of the DC type. These schemes will be particularly important in heterogeneous societies with rather diverse needs.

Table 6.2. **Real wage growth contrasted with real returns on capital, selected OECD countries, 1971-90**

	Real wage growth	Real average annual return on equities	Real average annual return on government bonds
Canada	1.1	5.0	1.1
Denmark	2.5	9.4	4.5
France	4.0	9.6	1.3
Germany	3.6	9.3	2.6
Japan	3.0	11.2	0.0
Netherlands	1.4	8.6	1.8
Switzerland	1.8	4.7	1.7
United Kingdom	2.4	10.8	1.6
United States	0.1	5.9	1.2

Source: World Bank (1994).

Many OECD countries, including Germany, France, and Italy, have integrated the first two functions into a single comprehensive public pension system (see Table 6.1). In other OECD countries, including Switzerland, Denmark, the Netherlands, and New Zealand, the second function of old-age insurance is performed by privately-funded schemes.

SCENARIOS

Another important reason for adopting a mix of pension systems is to diversify macroeconomic risks. Workers should not put all their eggs in one basket to avoid excessive exposure to the substantial political, investment, and human-capital risks. Each country should determine its own mix depending on its political preferences (*e.g.* for inter- or intra-generational risk-sharing) and the functioning of capital and labour markets. The selected mix should depend also on expectations regarding future trends.

To illustrate the uncertainty and the importance of the returns on physical and human capital for the performance of the various pension systems, we construct two scenarios. These scenarios are called the *market* scenario and the *inter-generational solidarity* scenario, respectively. These scenarios are differentiated with regard to the relative economic performances of the OECD region versus the non-OECD region affecting the determinants of the Aaron condition.[5]

In the *market scenario*, non-OECD countries rapidly catch up with OECD countries. Increased international capital mobility allows investors in OECD countries to benefit from high returns on investment outside the OECD. At the same time, older and smaller labour forces slow economic growth in OECD countries. In the *inter-generational solidarity scenario*, in contrast, the OECD region benefits from rapid productivity growth as scarce labour encourages labour-saving technological progress. Growth in the non-OECD suffers from inward-looking policies. Poor investment opportunities in the non-OECD and scarce labour in the OECD depress the rate of return on capital in the OECD.

The two scenarios show diverging economic performance of the OECD versus the non-OECD because they are constructed so as to yield extreme values for the relative return on human capital versus financial capital in the OECD countries.[6] According to the Aaron condition, this relative return is an important determinant of the attractiveness of PAYG versus funded schemes.

These scenarios should not be interpreted as suggesting that the economic performance of the OECD necessarily differs from that of the non-OECD countries. Indeed, one could easily imagine two other scenarios involving, respectively, low and high growth rates in the entire world (see Box 2). The low-growth scenario, which could be called *global crisis*, features low interest rates and slow wage growth. Hence, the returns on both human and financial capital would be low. In the high-growth scenario, called *rapid growth*, the situation would be reversed. We will not explore these two latter scenarios any further because they do not yield extreme values for the Aaron condition. Table 6.3 contains the inputs for the two scenarios. In the so-called market scenario, the economy is dynamically efficient in that the real rate of return on capital (*i.e.* 4 per cent) substantially exceeds the real growth of labour productivity (*i.e.* 1 per cent). In the inter-generational solidarity scenario, the Aaron condition is reversed. Whereas

Box 2. **The main features of the scenarios**

	Growth performance:		OECD returns on:	
	OECD	Non-OECD	Physical capital	Human capital
Market	–	+	+	–
Inter-generational solidarity	+	–	–	+
Rapid growth	+	+	+	+
Global crisis	–	–	–	–

Table 6.3. **Input scenarios**

	Market		Intergenerational solidarity	
	1990	2075	1990	2075
Retirement age	65	65	67	67
Participation rate 55-65	51.4	60.9	51.4	60.0
Effective retirement age	61.6	62.0	61.6	64.0
	Average growth rate per annum			
Nominal rate of return on capital		7		5
Nominal labour productivity growth		4		6
Rate of increase of consumer prices		3		4

Source: Authors' calculations.

labour productivity grows by 2 per cent in real terms, the real rate of return amounts to only 1 per cent. Rapid wage growth and low rates of return encourage the elderly to delay their retirement. Accordingly, the effective retirement age gradually rises from 61.6 in 1990 to 64 in 2075. In the market scenario, the effective retirement age remains constant.

We focus on the consequences of the various assumptions for the development of the premium level over time. To clearly identify the performance of the various schemes, we do not take into account endogenous changes in the mix of the pillars. Indeed, the scenarios assume that the three pillars, PAYG, DB, and DC, each account for a third of pension benefits. We present the results for the three pillars separately. Hence, the consequences of different mixes of pillars can be computed easily by attaching different weights to the results for the various pillars.

The various pillars are modelled as follows.[7] The pension level at retirement amounts to 60 per cent of final salary. Each of the three pillars pays one-third of the total pension level. After retirement, nominal benefits rise with the rate of inflation. DC and DB benefits are linked to employment history. PAYG benefits, in contrast, are paid to all citizens, irrespective of employment history. Since PAYG benefits are paid also to those outside the labour force, aggregate PAYG benefits exceed benefits paid by the other two pillars.

Tables 6.4 and 6.5 present the contributions and retirement benefits as a percentage of the wage sum. In the market scenario, pension benefits are a higher percentage of the wage sum, because real

Table 6.4. **Market scenario**

In percentage of gross wage

	1990	2000	2025	2050	2075
Contribution rates					
PAYG	6.6	6.7	9.6	12.4	11.7
DC	3.2	3.3	3.5	3.8	3.8
DB	3.2	4.3	4.2	5.2	4.1
Total	13.0	14.3	17.3	21.4	19.6
Pension levels					
PAYG	16.9	17.0	17.3	17.0	17.0
DC	12.8	11.8	11.6	12.3	13.6
DB	12.8	12.8	13.2	13.7	13.9
Total	42.5	41.5	42.0	43.1	44.5

Source: Authors' calculations.

Table 6.5.   **Intergenerational solidarity scenario**

In percentage of gross wage

	1990	2000	2025	2050	2075
Contribution rates					
PAYG	4.9	5.0	7.1	9.2	8.6
DC	7.7	8.0	8.6	9.4	9.4
DB	5.9	9.1	9.3	11.1	9.6
Total	18.5	22.1	25.0	29.7	27.6
Pension levels					
PAYG	16.2	16.2	16.5	16.1	16.1
DC	12.9	12.3	12.7	11.8	13.2
DB	12.9	12.9	13.5	14.1	14.5
Total	42.0	41.4	42.7	42.0	43.8

Source: Authors' calculations.

wage growth is relatively slow. Accordingly, compared to the incomes of the young, the incomes of elderly are relatively high. In the market scenario, the PAYG system is much more expensive than the funded systems. In the inter-generational solidarity scenario, in contrast, PAYG is relatively cheap. Indeed, the PAYG scheme offers higher benefits at lower premiums. Moreover, the rise in the PAYG premium as a result of an increase in the old-age dependency ratio is mitigated by an increase in the age of retirement. In the inter-generational solidarity scenario, DB schemes adopt an expected nominal rate of return of 6 per cent, which exceeds the realised return of 5 per cent. Accordingly, initially, premiums can be relatively low. However, as expected investment returns are not realised, the benefit promise needs to be backed up by higher premiums. Indeed, DB turns out to be a mixture of PAYG and DC in this case.[8]

POLICIES TO INSURE AGAINST AGEING

The scenarios illustrate that the future is fundamentally uncertain, especially in the long-term. To diversify risks, policy makers in OECD countries should take action on several fronts. The use of several instruments is attractive not only from the point of view of risk-sharing but also for political reasons: costs and benefits are spread over various groups. Indeed, a package of reforms facilitates the building of consensus about reforms. Box 3 summarises the various policy measures suggested in this chapter.

Investing in human capital

To prepare for ageing, society can invest in human capital of either the elderly or the young. Investing in the elderly reduces the need for inter-generational transfers. Investing in the young, in contrast, increases this need so that the elderly can share in the fruits of the investments in the young.

Human capital of the elderly

Over the last two decades, the effective retirement age has dropped substantially in the European OECD countries (see Tables 6.6 and 6.7). In these countries, various policies encouraged older workers to leave the labour market in order to alleviate the adverse social effects of industrial restructuring and to preserve employment opportunities for younger workers. By reducing the supply of experienced labour, early retirement is an increasingly costly and short-sighted way to address unemployment. Maintaining adequate levels of social insurance in the face of an ageing population requires the labour supply to rise rather than fall, so that the contribution base is maintained.

Indexing the retirement age to life expectancy is the most natural way to insure society against a longer average life of its citizens, so that people spend part of their extended life in work and part in

Box 3. **Policies to insure against ageing**

INVESTING IN HUMAN CAPITAL

Human capital in general

- alleviate moral hazard in social security provision;
- tighten requirements for disability and unemployment;
- enhance efficiency of social security administration;
- reduce social security benefits;
- reduce marginal tax wedge on labour income;
- strengthen link between contributions and benefits by reforming PAYG and DB pension schemes or by moving to multi-pillar systems with a larger role for DC schemes;
- reduce perverse redistribution in pension schemes;
- shift tax burden to those outside the labour force (*e.g.* by shifting to consumption taxes);
- maintain cash-flow income tax treatment of pension saving;
- broaden the tax base by reducing tax privileges for the more affluent elderly;
- mitigate tax arbitrage through a more neutral system of capital income taxation.

Human capital of the elderly

- raising effective retirement age;
- make pensions more actuarially fair;
- encourage lifelong learning;
- reconsider age-related pay schemes and final-pay pension schemes;
- deregulate labour markets and sheltered sectors of the economy;
- alleviate moral hazard in social security provision.

Human capital of the young
- raise participation rate of women;
- enhance child care;
- reduce disincentives to work originating in the tax system.

INVESTING IN PHYSICAL CAPITAL

Public saving

- cut budget deficit.

Private saving

- provide tax incentives;
- (gradually) reduce the relative importance of PAYG benefits;
- make pension saving compulsory;
- issue indexed government bonds.

(continued on next page)

(continued)

Investment inside the OECD

– develop stock markets;
– improve corporate governance;
– enhance competition;
– pursue stable macroeconomic policies.

Investment outside the OECD

– enhance efficiency of financial sectors in non-OECD;
– improve accounting standards;
– promote trade liberalization;
– relax regulatory constraints on foreign investments in OECD.

---

retirement. Several countries, including Germany, Italy, Japan and the United States, have announced gradual increases in the retirement ages for their public schemes. Other countries have limited early access to public pension benefits. A higher retirement age implies that the human capital embodied in the elderly is used more intensively. This raises the return on effort and schooling, thereby facilitating lifelong training ("permanent education"). In this way, the pattern of the use of time over the lifecycle becomes more flexible as education, work and leisure are distributed more uniformly over various age groups. By redistributing human capital more equally over various generations, a higher retirement age

Table 6.6. **Participation rates and effective retirement age[1]
in the EC, Japan and the United States, 1990**

	Participation rates					Retirement age	
	50-54	55-59	60-64	65-69	70-74	Effective	Statutory
Belgium	54.0	34.2	12.1	1.9	0.4	59.5	65/60
Denmark	84.1	72.7	37.5	16.4	2.3	62.6	67
France	74.8	51.6	16.3	4.5	1.4	59.9	60
Germany	73.2	58.7	21.4	4.6	1.7	60.8	65
Greece	61.9	50.8	33.1	14.6	4.1	63.1	65/60
Ireland	57.4	49.3	35.2	15.4	6.8	63.9	66
Italy	59.0	42.0	21.1	7.8	1.6	61.1	65
Luxembourg	57.4	35.4	13.2	0.0	0.0	59.2	65
Netherlands	61.3	46.3	17.1	6.4	2.3	60.8	65
Portugal	66.0	54.8	37.7	23.3	8.1	64.0	65/62
Spain	57.5	48.8	31.0	6.5	1.1	62.5	65
United Kingdom	79.0	67.0	38.0	10.7	3.3	62.4	65/60
Austria	73.1	53.3	15.1	2.6	2.1	59.9	65/60
Finland	77.9	58.3	28.6	3.4	2.8	60.9	65
Sweden	92.6	82.8	56.4	9.8	3.1	63.1	65
EC average	69.5	53.8	25.5	7.3	2.3	61.3	65
Japan	82.0	71.5	54.7	24.4	23.9	64.8	60/55
United States	80.0	66.1	44.2	11.5	6.3	62.8	65

1. The effective retirement age is calculated as follows:

$$\frac{(P_{55-59} - P_{50-54})^*55 + (P_{60-64} - P_{55-59})^*60 + (P_{65-69} - P_{60-64})^*65 + (P_{70+} - P_{65-69})^*70 + P_{70+}{}^*72}{P_{50-54}}$$

with p_i equal to the activity rate of the age category i.

Source: Besseling and Zeeuw (1993).

Table 6.7. **Participation rate, effective retirement age and life expectancy, 1950-80**

	Participation rate age group 55-64		Effective retirement age		Life expectancy at birth	
	1950	1980	1950	1980	1950	1980
Belgium	46.0	38.3	63.8	61.2	67.5	73.7
Denmark	59.6	58.5	64.2	62.7	71.0	74.5
France	57.7	45.7	64.4	61.0	66.5	74.7
Germany	49.8	43.1	63.7	61.0	67.5	73.9
Greece	48.9	43.3	65.2	63.1	65.9	74.7
Ireland	55.4	50.2	65.8	64.1	66.9	73.1
Italy	45.5	31.7	63.9	60.3	66.0	74.6
Luxembourg	50.0	28.6	64.4	59.9	65.9	73.3
Netherlands	50.9	40.9	64.6	62.2	72.1	76.0
Portugal	47.3	44.7	65.4	63.1	59.3	72.2
Spain	49.2	41.2	65.5	62.9	63.9	75.8
United Kingdom	53.9	61.9	64.4	62.8	69.2	74.0
EC average	51.3	45.1	64.3	61.8	67.0	74.4
Japan	63.0	64.5	64.7	64.0	63.9	76.9
United States	57.2	55.8	64.4	63.0	69.0	74.5

Sources: ILO (1986); United Nations (1989); authors' calculations.

attacks at the root the potential fiscal and social problems of ageing. The elderly rely less on the solidarity of the young and more on their own human capital. Indeed, by keeping older workers employed for longer, governments reap a double dividend: a cut in social spending and a broader contribution base.

Raising the effective retirement age requires a stronger labour market position of elderly workers. Employers can be encouraged to employ elderly workers not only by increasing the skills of the elderly, but also by reducing wage costs. To achieve this, age-related pay schemes may have to be reconsidered so that wages can be better adjusted to individual productivity levels. More generally, wages of elderly workers may have to decline relative to wages of younger workers, especially when younger workers become relatively scarce. This requires deregulation of the labour market and the promotion of wage flexibility. Moreover, it calls for modification of social insurance schemes. For example, occupational pension systems that link pension benefits to final pay discourage gradual retirement through occupational downgrading with lower rates of pay.

A gradual transition from work to retirement can keep many older people employed longer. The growth of self-employment and part-time work in several OECD countries may help retirement to become a less abrupt process. Both self-employment and part-time work may be stimulated by deregulating not only the labour market but also sheltered sectors, especially those sectors that experience little technological change but can employ experienced older workers. To illustrate, sectors providing services to and caring for the very old seem to offer considerable scope for employing low-skilled elderly who want to retire part-time. The same holds true for child care, as women with children participate more in the labour market. When labour becomes increasingly scarce and demand for these non-tradable services grows, elderly men and women face increasing incentives to keep supplying labour longer, provided that markets for labour, goods and services are allowed to function efficiently.

Different people may want to leave the labour force at different times and in different ways. To facilitate efficient decision-making by workers with diverse needs and preferences, pension systems should confront potential retirees and their employers with the social costs of retirement. Hence, early and late retirement benefits should be actuarially fair.

Reforming social insurance

Various routes for withdrawing from the labour force are substitutes. Accordingly, in confronting workers with the social costs of their labour-supply decisions, governments should pursue a comprehensive approach. Various conditional social insurance benefits, such as unemployment and disability benefits, are subject to moral hazard. As the workforce ages, these moral hazard problems become more serious as older workers are subject to higher disability and unemployment risk.

The Central Planning Bureau's study, "Scanning the future", distinguishes two possible directions for social insurance reform aimed at reducing moral hazard (see CPB, 1992). The first direction aims to preserve the European legacy of social equity as much as possible by reducing improper use of social insurance. This can be done by tightening the requirements for social benefits (*e.g.* stricter evaluations of disability, making unemployment benefits conditional on retraining or accepting less desirable jobs), tightening checks on improper use of social benefits, and enhancing the efficiency of the organisations administering social benefits. However, privacy arguments may be a stumbling block to avoiding moral hazard. Moreover, an increasingly heterogeneous society with flexible and diverse lifestyles complicates this strategy.

The second direction focuses on reducing the level of insurance. It simplifies social insurance and widens the income gap between working and non-working. At the extreme, a negative income tax could replace social insurance altogether. In this way, the government would give up social insurance for events such as unemployment, disability, and age and leave this insurance to the market. Indeed, the government would use only income information in redistributing resources.

Both strategies may be combined, in part to diversify risks. Moreover, the second strategy aids the first: lower benefits help to prevent improper use of social insurance. Furthermore, within the first strategy of making social insurance more efficient, market-oriented reforms can play a useful role. The government, while prescribing the level of insurance, may leave the administration of the insurance to the private sector.

A *lower marginal tax wedge*

As workers become more flexible in selecting how and when to retire and, more generally, supply labour to the formal and informal sectors, lowering the marginal tax wedge becomes a more important instrument to ensure efficient decisions on labour supply. In this connection, the strong link between individual contributions and benefits in DC schemes facilitates more efficient retirement decisions. In several countries with earnings-related public schemes (*e.g.* France, Italy and Sweden), benefits are being more closely linked to contributions. However, the scope to raise actuarial fairness and reduce marginal tax rates is reduced by the desire to redistribute resources within generations (*i.e.* protect the needy and alleviate poverty) and across generations (inter-generational risk-sharing). To improve the trade-off between efficiency, redistribution and risk-sharing, governments should ensure that redistribution is transparent. Moreover, perverse redistribution should be eliminated if it does not enhance incentives.

One way to tighten the link between benefits and contributions without harming equity is to separate pension schemes into one part focusing on poverty alleviation and another part dealing with old-age insurance (see World Bank, 1994).[9] Such a reform could prevent ageing from raising payroll taxes, which tend to bear relatively heavily on low-skilled workers with an increasingly weak labour market position. In particular, the public scheme dealing with poverty alleviation is explicitly redistributive and should be financed not by payroll taxes but by other taxes, such as progressive income taxes and commodity taxes on consumption. Replacing payroll taxes by consumption taxes (such as VAT) alleviates the tax burden on workers by shifting part of this burden to those outside the labour force, including the retired. Progressive income taxes move the tax burden from workers with low incomes to those with higher incomes and, if pensions are taxed on a cash-flow basis (see below), to retirees with high incomes. Increasing the burden on higher incomes may raise the marginal tax rate. However, by more closely linking pension premiums and benefits in the insurance part of the pension system, the government may be able to reduce the overall marginal tax rate.

Shifting from PAYG schemes with a weak link between contributions and benefits to DC schemes with a strong link creates a transition problem, as current workers have to pay for two pensions, *i.e.* that of those already retired and that for themselves. The temporarily high premium may raise wage costs and reduce employment. However, the government may use debt policy in such a way that the premiums are smoothed over time and all generations benefit from the efficiency gains produced by reducing labour market distortions (see Kotlikoff, 1995). In particular, by financing part of the reform by issuing public debt, future generations, who reap the efficiency gains associated with a better functioning labour market, pay part of the costs of the reform.

Cash-flow treatment of pension saving under the income tax

Most OECD countries treat pensions on a cash-flow basis under personal income tax. Consequently, pension premiums are tax deductible, whereas pension benefits are subject to income tax. This implies that the government delays the collection of the income tax until retirement. In this way, the government, in effect, participates in the pension funds. The return on this public investment amounts to the taxes the government eventually collects on the retirement benefits (see Bovenberg and Petersen, 1992).

This cash-flow treatment has a number of important advantages. In particular, the cash-flow treatment broadens the tax base when ageing boosts public spending. Moreover, by including retirement benefits in the income tax base, tax deferral provides the government with an additional instrument to ensure an equitable distribution *between* generations without adversely affecting the distribution *within* generations.

By participating in the pension funds, the government shares in the investment risk. The government can alleviate the investment risk further by letting the tax rate on the investment income of pension funds rise with the average return. Alternatively, the government may issue indexed bonds. In this way, pension funds are protected against the risk of inflation, but still bear real interest-rate risk. By issuing longer maturities, the government can absorb part of the latter risk as well.

Human capital of the young

Increasing labour market participation

One way to help sustain inter-generational solidarity in an ageing society is to increase the participation of the young in the labour market. This creates a stronger base for financing retirement benefits. Increasing the rewards of work by tightening social insurance benefits and reducing the tax wedge (see above) may stimulate the labour supply of not only older, but also younger workers.

Following the drop in fertility, many women have moved from the informal into the formal sector. However, in many OECD countries, there is still considerable scope for women to increase their labour supply. When labour becomes increasingly scarce, women will face stronger financial incentives to increase their labour market participation, provided the tax system does not blunt these incentives. Improved child care, which could be provided by elderly workers, may also enhance the labour market participation of young women with young children. This trend toward a higher female participation rate strengthens the labour skills and human capital of women. This allows them to rely less on public transfers when old – an added benefit from the point of view of reducing the claim of old-age pensions on the budget.

More human capital

Helping the young to accumulate more human capital is another way to strengthen the contribution base for PAYG and DB schemes. However, raising productivity growth may actually worsen the financial problems of pension systems if pension benefits are indexed to wages. Indeed, if the elderly share fully in productivity gains, increased labour productivity will raise pension costs. Accordingly, raising productivity growth by investing in the human capital of the young makes PAYG and DB schemes more sustainable only if pensions are not indexed to wages so that retirees do not share fully in productivity growth. Hence, while the elderly enjoy a higher standard of living in absolute terms, their relative income position worsens.

Numerical illustration

Table 6.8 illustrates how increased labour supply can contain the rise in the retiree/worker due to ageing. The present average retirement age in the OECD is 62 years. The younger age brackets feature a participation rate of 72.4. These figures imply a worker/retiree ratio of about 3. If the retirement age and the participation rate were to remain at present levels, demographic developments would cause the worker/retiree ratio to drop to 1.5 in the course of the next 50 years (see the first column of the table). As a direct consequence of this 50 per cent reduction, the PAYG contribution rate would have to double to keep the replacement rate (i.e. the pension level as a percentage of wages) at a constant level. However, if the actual retirement age were to rise by one year each decade and the participation rate in the younger age brackets to rise gradually to 85 per cent, the worker/retiree ratio would change much less (see the diagonal in Table 6.8). Accomplishing such an increase in overall labour supply would require fundamental reforms, including alleviating disincentives to work by tightening social insurance benefits, reducing the tax wedge, and making pensions more actuarially fair.

Investing in physical capital

To reduce the risk of ageing, countries can shift resources inter-temporally by saving more, either through the public or private sector.

Public saving

Public sectors providing extensive public pension schemes or other sizeable benefits to the elderly could raise public saving (or reduce dissaving) in order to prepare for ageing. This yields several advantages. First, inter-temporal tax smoothing may enhance efficiency. If governments expect tax rates to rise or otherwise give rise to increasing distortion over time, they may want to avoid high tax rates in the future by moderately raising tax rates now. Increasing public saving may also benefit inter-generational equity if future generations are expected to be harmed by poor growth or worsening environmental conditions. Moreover, increasing public saving through a trust fund (as in Canada, Sweden and the United States) provides a clear signal that the babyboom generation is willing to contribute to its own retirement. This may help to sustain the inter-generational contract between generations when the babyboom generation retires.

Table 6.8. **Ratio of number in employment to the number of retired in OECD countries under alternative assumptions**

Average retirement age[1]	62	63	64	65	66	67	68
Activity rate[2]	72.4	75.1	77.5	79.7	81.7	83.4	85.0
1990	3.01						
2000	2.78	3.10					
2010	2.47	2.79	3.13				
2020	2.03	2.28	2.55	2.84			
2030	1.66	1.86	2.07	2.31	2.57		
2040	1.51	1.67	1.85	2.03	2.24	2.47	
2050	1.48	1.64	1.80	1.98	2.18	2.39	2.62

1. Activity rates for those aged 55 and over, such that they retire on average at the specified age.
2. Average activity rate for the population aged 15-54.
Source: Authors' calculations.

Raising public saving also implies some risks. First, lower public debt (or higher pension reserves) may tempt governments to spend more, thereby raising the overall tax level. In any case, higher public saving is likely to require higher current tax rates, thereby discouraging labour supply in the short run. The pay-off in terms of lower future tax rates and higher welfare of future generations may be quite low if the interest rate turns out to be low compared to the growth rate. By making labour scarcer relative to capital, the return on financial capital may well fall below that on human capital. Moreover, if growth rates are high, future generations will be better off than the babyboom generation. This weakens the case for raising public saving on the grounds of inter-generational equity (see Cutler *et al.*, 1990).

Private saving

Governments can stimulate private saving through various channels. By an early announcement of a gradual reduction in the relative importance of PAYG benefits, they may stimulate private funded schemes.[10] Furthermore, to prevent private agents from exploiting means-tested benefits to the elderly, governments may want to make some pension saving mandatory. Private pension saving can be enhanced also by making collective bargaining agreements on occupational pension schemes compulsory. Finally, providing a proper legislative framework, including an independent supervisory authority, facilitates the introduction and growth of private pension funds.

Table 6.9 shows how a funded system could be introduced in a country that presently relies only on PAYG pensions. As of 1995, all employees start to pay 4 per cent of their gross wage in a DC scheme. These schemes will mature gradually, thereby allowing for a gradual decline in the PAYG replacement ratio. In particular, PAYG benefits at retirement are not fully indexed to wages, but rather lag these wages by one percentage point per year from 1995 until 2030. Moreover, the statutory retirement age will gradually increase to 67 years. These numbers imply that the reduction in PAYG benefits slightly exceeds the phased-in benefits from the DC scheme. Initially, contribution rates are somewhat higher. The additional savings prevent the contribution rates from rising rapidly. In fact, starting in 2010, the overall contribution rate is lower than in the benchmark scenario.

Fiscal privileges for pension saving

Most OECD countries grant tax preferences to pension saving. These privileges do not originate in the deductibility of pension premiums as such but rather in two other aspects of the tax treatment of pension saving. First, the marginal tax rates at which pension contributions can be deducted typically exceed the marginal rates applied to the benefits during retirement. Indeed, many countries tax the elderly at concessionary rates or grant other special tax privileges to the elderly.

The second reason most tax systems favour pension saving is that no income tax is levied on the investment income of pension funds. Accordingly, the increase in the value of pension rights that corresponds to this capital income escapes the income tax, whereas the return on other types of saving is, at least in principle, subject to income tax.[11]

The tax privileges for pension saving have been supported by several arguments. In particular, tax advantages encourage individuals to provide for sufficient retirement incomes, thereby reducing the

Table 6.9. **Contribution rate with comprehensive package**

As percentage of gross wage

	1990	2000	2025	2050	2075
Without reform	17.7	18.0	25.6	32.7	31.1
With reform	17.7	21.2	20.0	21.3	19.1
Difference	0	3.2	5.6	11.4	12.0

Source: Authors' calculations.

use of means-tested benefits during retirement. Furthermore, they may correct the short horizon of young workers.

However, fiscal privileges for pension saving suffer from a number of disadvantages. They provide opportunities for tax arbitrage transactions, which change the composition of private saving without raising its level. Indeed, the non-neutral treatment of various types of saving distorts the allocation of saving towards institutional saving. Furthermore, the tax advantages benefit mostly high-income earners, although the arguments supporting them apply primarily to low-income earners.

Rather than providing tax breaks, governments can require individuals to save part of their income for retirement. However, compulsory schemes may reduce labour supply by distorting the labour market. In particular, forcing low-skilled workers to save may raise wage costs, thereby further weakening the labour market position of these workers.

Investing in OECD countries

Investing pension savings domestically yields several advantages. First, investing pension savings as equity in domestic firms makes the elderly stakeholders in the functioning of the domestic economy and raises the wages of the young. This is likely to foster inter-generational solidarity. Second, concentration of ownership of firms by pension funds may facilitate monitoring of management, thereby raising the return. Third, domestic investment strengthens the base for financing public spending.

Financial innovation can make funded schemes more attractive by raising the return, reducing transaction costs, and lowering investment risk. Developing the stock market and improving corporate governance allow pension schemes to take advantage of higher returns on equity investments. Also deregulating and enhancing competition in goods markets may raise returns. Stable and disciplined macroeconomic policies encourage long-term planning. Increased pension saving may set in motion a virtuous circle by encourageing financial innovation, improving corporate governance, and building the political support for stable and disciplined macroeconomic policies.

Investing in non-OECD countries

International financial markets can play a key role in enhancing the risk-return trade-off on pension saving in OECD countries. In particular, by allowing OECD savings to be invested in the emerging markets of the younger economies of the non-OECD countries, international financial markets can help to maintain a high return on OECD savings. International capital markets can also help by diversifying risk and shifting risk to those who can best bear it. In particular, by investing their savings in the emerging economies, the elderly in the OECD countries are insured against adverse country-specific shocks in their own countries. Moreover, by investing in the non-OECD countries, the ageing OECD countries become stakeholders in the growth performance of the emerging countries. This can facilitate international co-operation, thereby further reducing political risks and ensuring stable property rights and rules of the game.

To reap the full potential of international capital flows, the competitiveness and competence of financial sectors in non-OECD countries should be enhanced. Also OECD countries can facilitate mutually beneficial capital flows by relaxing regulatory constraints on foreign investment by institutional investors.

CONCLUSIONS

This chapter has provided a broad overview of policy options available to OECD countries in preparing their systems of old-age income support for the demands of an ageing society. It has stressed that not only demographic developments but also non-demographic trends will substantially affect the appropriate systems of old-age insurance. The scenarios described illustrate the considerable uncertainty surrounding these non-demographic trends. Accordingly, the most appropriate strategy involves diversification of various policy measures.

No regret strategies

Some policies are part of "no regret" strategies because they work out well in all scenarios.

Higher effective retirement age

The most robust policy conclusion is that the effective retirement age should rise with life expectancy. A higher retirement age reduces the need not only for fiscal transfers, but also inter-temporal transfers in the form of financial savings. Indeed, labour income can be regarded as a fourth pillar of old-age income insurance. Gradual retirement is consistent with a more uniform distribution of education, work and leisure over the lifecycle.

Broad-based tax system

Since the elderly lead longer, healthier lives, they are in a position to be net contributors to the budget for a longer time. Ensuring that net contributions to the budget decline less rapidly with age is a major instrument in alleviating the fiscal transfer problem associated with ageing. In this connection, broadening the tax base by reducing tax privileges to the elderly and by making the tax treatment of capital income more neutral are important elements. Indeed, as differences within the elderly population increase, the net contribution to the budget should be based less on age and more on income. To illustrate, old-age poverty alleviation could be financed through broad-based taxes paid by the entire population, rather than through narrow-based taxes that hit only the wages of the workforce.

More efficient markets

A well-functioning market mechanism is a major instrument in adjusting production to new needs originating in demographic and other trends. For example, it can induce workers to delay retirement so that the human capital of elderly citizens is employed to meet newly emerging needs. Moreover, efficient markets can contribute to a higher participation rate of not only the elderly, but also the young, thereby mitigating the decline in the worker/retiree ratio on account of ageing. Indeed, clear market signals become more important as people can more flexibly allocate their time to various activities. On the international level, efficient international markets for capital, commodities, and services allow countries exhibiting different demographic developments to exploit their relative advantages.

Social insurance reform

A reform of the social insurance system is essential to improve the efficiency of the labour market. Moreover, it helps to raise the effective retirement age and the net contribution of the elderly to the budget, because the elderly are especially vulnerable to moral hazard involving social insurance benefits. Tightening the requirements for social insurance benefits can improve the trade-off between equity and efficiency. Moreover, in addition to lower marginal tax rates, a reduced level of insurance may also have to contribute to more efficient retirement and other labour market decisions.

Diversifying risks

To spread their risks, the elderly may want to draw on a mix of assets. In particular, they can rely on human capital of the young, not only through the inter-generational contracts implicit in PAYG and DB schemes, but also through explicit financial claims in DB and DC schemes. In addition, they may want to become stakeholders in foreign economies by investing their savings abroad. Finally, they can rely on their own human capital.

Pooling risks

Another major instrument to reduce risks is the tax system. By including the elderly in the tax system, the tax system can play a major role in intra- and inter-generational risk-sharing. In this way, it can pool risks and shift the risks to those who can best bear it.

Private pension provision

Another way to alleviate the burden of the elderly on the budget is to stimulate private pension provision. Indeed, countries that currently rely heavily on public PAYG systems, may gradually reduce the benefits these systems offer to higher incomes. This would stimulate privately-funded pension plans. The government could stimulate DC systems by providing inflation-indexed bonds and by conducting inter-generational risk-sharing through the tax system.

Choices and trade-offs facing countries

Whereas some policy responses are robust to the major trends, others are more appropriate in specific scenarios. We now turn to some of the major trade-offs facing countries.

The level of saving

The first trade-off involves the level of saving. This can be illustrated with the transitional problem associated with the move from public PAYG to private funded schemes. Without an increase in the budget deficit, a rapid transition requires a substantial increase in national saving. This may carry a high price tag in terms of a high burden on current generations and a short-term decline in employment due to high labour costs and lower labour supply. Hence, a trade-off between saving and employment emerges. Tax incentives for private pension saving may reduce the burden on current generations. However, these incentives may result in tax arbitrage.

The composition of saving

Countries face a trade-off in selecting not only the *level* but also the *composition* of saving. Saving is not limited to financial assets, but can also involve human capital. Investing in the human capital of the elderly allows them to remain in the work force for longer, thereby reducing the need for fiscal transfers. Investing in the human capital of the young (through *e.g.* public education or public infrastructure) raises wages, thereby broadening the tax base and allowing higher PAYG benefits. However, in contrast to investments in the human capital of the elderly, investments in the human capital of the young do not mitigate the need for fiscal transfers. Moreover, relying on the human capital of the young (and the implicit inter-generational contract) may impose substantial political risks on the elderly. To mitigate these political risks, the elderly can also invest in young workers by investing their financial assets in their own country. In this way, they acquire an explicit rather than implicit claim on younger workers employed in domestic firms.

Issues for discussion

The major choices countries face are the following:

– Up to what income level should the government provide old-age insurance? Should the government concede tax privileges to the old? What role should the government and other institutions play in providing old-age insurance to the middle-class? Should it be provided (in part) through public PAYG schemes or (compulsory?) private schemes? At what level of income should individuals be free to make their own decisions on pensions?

– How can pensions become more actuarially fair while also meeting distributional objectives? In particular, should low-skilled workers be forced to contribute to their own pensions?

- Should governments affect the choice between DB and (occupational or personal) DC schemes? Should governments allow firms to meet labour market objectives by limiting the portability of DB schemes? Should governments discourage final-pay DB schemes and age-related pay? Should they stimulate DC schemes by providing inter-generational risk-sharing arrangements (*e.g.* through the tax system or by issuing inflation-indexed government bonds?)

- How much of its income should a society save? How should a society save? Should public or private saving be increased? Should savings be invested in human capital (of the young or elderly?) or in financial capital? Should financial capital be invested at home or abroad?

We can afford to grow old

Can we afford to grow old? Fortunately, the answer is an unambiguous yes! Growing old raises the potential return on human capital by providing the opportunity to employ human capital over a longer time scale. Moreover, by leading longer, healthy lives, citizens are in a position to contribute more to society in general and to the budget in particular. Finally, ageing allows OECD countries to exploit the comparative advantages that come with age (such as experience and financial capital) by trading with younger societies.

However, like other trends that affect our society, ageing requires countries to adapt their economies. This chapter shows that countries have various ways to do just that. Since ageing is a rather predictable trend, countries still have time to act. Gradually phasing in policy measures at an early stage, avoids abrupt painful policy corrections that cannot be anticipated. Hence, early actions allow policy makers to reconcile flexibility and stability, thereby protecting the confidence and trust in the democratic institutions that hold our societies together.

NOTES

1. This period can be the entire career (so-called average-pay systems) or the year(s) immediately preceding retirement (so-called final-pay systems).

2. In particular, wage increases result in considerable additional pension obligations with respect to older workers. The costs of these so-called backservice obligations are spread over all workers.

3. By using signs, Box 1 summarises the arguments with a broad brush. The main text discusses some of the gradations of the various arguments.

4. Governments may impose regulations on DB schemes (e.g. shortening vesting periods or requiring indexation of vested rights) to improve portability, thereby enhancing insurance against job mobility. However, these regulations may induce employers to replace DB pension schemes by alternative instruments to achieve their labour-market objectives.

5. The names of the scenarios originate in the implications of the scenarios for the relative attractiveness of inter-generational solidarity. In the market scenario, high capital returns make individual pensions supplied by the capital market relatively attractive. In the inter-generational solidarity scenario, in contrast, high wage growth implies that the return on PAYG schemes is relatively high. One could rename the two scenarios on the basis of the diverging relative economic performances of the OECD and the non-OECD. In particular, following the names in CPB (1992), the market scenario could be relabelled as *global shift* and the inter-generational solidarity scenario as *OECD Renaissance*.

6. The scenarios assume the same demographic projections, which are based on the population projections of the United Nations for the OECD countries (see United Nations, 1994).

7. The model used is an extended version of that used in Besseling and Zeeuw (1993).

8. Also when in the market scenario the expected nominal rate of return equals the realized return, DC and DB rates differ slightly, because DB rates adjust slowly to demographic changes.

9. In the academic literature, the first function is associated with *tax-transfer* approach. The second function corresponds with the *insurance* approach. The *annuity-welfare* model links the welfare and insurance functions. The World Bank (1994) argues in favour of seperating these two functions, whereas others disagree (see the discussion in Diamond *et al.*, 1996). Table 6.1 shows that many larger OECD countries have integrated the two functions. Indeed, combining the two functions may yield economies of scale and scope. Moreover, integrating the insurance function with the welfare function gives income earners with middle and higher incomes a direct interest in the public scheme. This may strengthen political support for the welfare function.

10. For example, governments may link PAYG benefits to prices rather than wages, thereby gradually reducing the replacement rate. It may also announce a gradual increase in the retirement age. Another option is to focus the PAYG scheme more on poverty alleviation by reducing benefits to those earning higher incomes. This encourages high-income earners to save more. To spread the costs of such a transition over various generations, the government may finance part of its existing PAYG obligations through public debt issue (see above). In that case, lower public saving offsets some of impact of more private saving on national saving. The gradual reduction in the replacement rate in the public PAYG scheme implies that elderly without additional pension incomes are likely to fall below the poverty line. This boosts public spending on means-tested benefits aimed at poverty alleviation.

11. Also other major categories of saving, such as housing, typically enjoy fiscal privileges. Furthermore, some countries have moved away from a comprehensive income tax towards a schedular income tax on capital income. Under these schedules taxes, capital income is taxed at a flat rate below the top marginal rate on labour income.

BIBLIOGRAPHY

AARON, H.J. (1966), "The social insurance paradox", *Canadian Journal of Economic and Political Science*, Vol. 32.

BESSELING, P.J. and ZEEUW, R.F. (1993), *The Financing of Pensions in Europe: Challenges and Opportunities*, CPB research Memorandum No. 111, The Hague.

BOVENBERG, A.L. and PETERSEN, C. (1992), "Public debt and pension policy", *Fiscal Studies*, Vol. 13., No. 3, pp. 1-14, London.

CLIFFORD CHANCE (1993), *Pensions in the European Community*.

CPB (1992), "Scanning the future", Sdu Publishers, The Hague.

CUTLER, D.M., POTERBA, J.M., SHEINER, L.N. and SUMMERS, L.H. (1990), *An Ageing Society: Opportunity or Challenge?*, Brookings Papers on Economic Activity, Vol. 1, pp. 1-73, Washington, DC.

DIAMOND, P.A., LINDEMAN, D.C. and YOUNG, H. (1996), *Social Security: What Role for the Future?*, National Academy of Social Insurance, Washington, DC.

INTERNATIONAL LABOUR OFFICE (1986), *Economically Active Population*, Volumes I and II, Geneva.

KOTLIKOFF, L.J. (1995), "Privatization of social insurance: how it works and why it matters", NBER Working Paper No. 5330, Cambridge, Massachussets.

MISSOC (1994), "Social protection in the member states of the European Union", Luxembourg.

OECD (1993*a*), *Private Pensions in OECD Countries – The United States*, Social Policy Studies No. 10, Paris.

OECD (1993*b*), *Private Pensions in OECD Countries – New Zealand*, Social Policy Studies No. 11, Paris.

OECD (1993*c*), "Pension liabilities in the seven major economies", OECD Working Paper No. 142, Paris.

OECD (1995), *Private Pensions in OECD Countries – Canada*, Social Policy Studies No. 15, Paris.

SOCIAL SECURITY ADMINISTRATION (1995), "Social insurance programs throughout the world 1995", Washington, DC.

UNITED NATIONS (1989), "Long range world population projections", New York.

UNITED NATIONS (1994), "Long range world population projections", New York.

WORLD BANK (1994), *Averting the Old Age Crisis – Policies to Protect the Old and Promote Growth*, Oxford University Press, Oxford.

DEVELOPING HEALTH AND LONG-TERM CARE FOR A MORE AGED SOCIETY

by

Riyoji Kobayashi
Tokyo Metropolitan University, Japan

INTRODUCTION

Trends in ageing

OECD countries share the characteristics of ageing societies, including an increase in the number of people aged 65 and over, a rapid increase in those aged 80 and over, and a subsequent increasing demand for the care of the very frail within these age groups. Population ageing also coincides with a changing social structure whereby a weakening of family ties and an increase in women's participation in the labour market can be seen as just two of the factors influencing a decreasing ability to care for disabled old parents.

Policies for the care of the aged, in particular long-term care policies, are becoming a central issue for governments to address. They impose an increasing financial burden on public expenditure during a period of serious budget constraints and sluggish economies worldwide.

A basic philosophy or policy objective for care of the aged which has been accepted across countries has been termed "Ageing in place". This proposes that elderly people, including those in need of care and support, should, whenever possible, be enabled to continue living in their own house, and that, where this is not possible, they should be enabled to live in a sheltered and supporting environment that is as close to their community as possible, in both social and geographical senses (OECD, 1994). Though this a common objective, the way in which it is being implemented differs according to the particular social and economic context underlying the aged-care strategy.

In 1990, Sweden, with 17.8 per cent of the population in the age group 65 years and over, had the highest proportion of elderly people in the population of all OECD countries, followed by Norway with 16.3 per cent and the United Kingdom with 15.6 per cent. Australia (11.1 per cent), Canada (11.2 per cent) and Japan (12 per cent) had the lowest proportion of elderly people. However, population projections suggest that by 2020 Japan will have the highest proportion (25 per cent), followed by Italy (23 per cent) and Greece (22 per cent), while the lowest proportions of the elderly in the population will be in Australia, the United States and Canada (all with around 16-17 per cent). In general, the Scandinavian countries have the most experience in preparing for a more aged society. However, the picture over the next 20 years will change dramatically (Japan Ministry of Health and Welfare, 1995a).

The speed of ageing is also an important issue to be considered in understanding aged care policy. It is well known that the Japanese society is ageing remarkably quickly compared with other industrialised countries. It took 114 years for the proportion of the elderly in France to increase from 7 per cent to 14 per cent, 82 years for Sweden, 69 years for the United States, 45 years for Western Germany and Great Britain, and 35 years for Australia. In Japan it only took 25 years (Japan Ministry of Health and Welfare, 1995b). The rate at which a nation's society is ageing seems to exert a profound influence on the extent of its government's policy preparation and implementation.

There is an understanding across OECD countries that both the number and the proportion of the "old-old" (those aged 80 and over) will have a direct influence on aged care policy. In OECD countries in 1980, Japan had the lowest proportion of the population aged 80 and over (1.39 per cent), preceded by Turkey (1.46 per cent) and New Zealand (1.7 per cent) (see Table 7.1 and OECD, 1994). Sweden had the highest proportion (3.17 per cent), followed by Norway (2.96 per cent) and Denmark (2.78 per cent). By 2020 it is projected that Japan will have the highest proportion of the old-old (7.1 per cent), followed by Portugal (6.13 per cent) and Belgium (5.55 per cent). The projections for the Scandinavian countries suggest a comparatively gradual development in the proportion of old-old population.

Family structure has become an important issue in a number of OECD countries in relation to care for the disabled elderly. The proportion of elderly living alone is highest in northern European, particularly Scandinavian countries, and co-residence between generations in these countries is low. The situation is the reverse in countries such as Italy, Spain and Poland. In remarkable contrast to other OECD countries, 65 per cent of the population aged 65 and over in Japan in 1990 still lived with their offspring, while only 11 per cent lived alone. However, there are indications that these figures are changing rapidly (Table 7.2).

Shared living with adult children helps elderly parents stay longer in their home. However, family carers often feel great stress as a result of the care work required, particularly once heavy care becomes a necessity. Governments need to acknowledge the contributions from family carers and intervene carefully.

Another factor that will exert a heavy influence on care structures is the participation rates of women in the labour market. It is sometimes suggested that the universalistic welfare service system in Scandinavian countries was a response to women's greater participation in the labour market. Based on women's participation rates in 1994, of those aged 45 to 64, the highest participation rates were in the Scandinavian countries, followed by a group of countries including the United States, Japan and the United Kingdom. The lowest rates were in Italy, Ireland, Spain and the Netherlands (Table 7.3).

Although the data on government intervention in the care of the elderly cannot be strictly compared across countries because of national differences in definitions and data collection methods, they nevertheless give an interesting picture of aged care policy.

Table 7.4 shows that for 19 OECD countries around 1990, rates of the elderly living in residential care varied from 2 per cent in Portugal to 9.1 per cent in the Netherlands. For home help service utilisation, countries can be classified into three groups: the high utilisation group, comprised of Scandinavian countries, had a 16 to 24 per cent utilisation rate, the five north European countries had a 6 to 8 per cent rate, whilst the remaining 11 countries had a rate of only 1 to 4 per cent. It should be noted that urban and rural area service utilisation rates differ considerably within any given country.

Table 7.1.   **Percentage of elderly people aged over 80 in the whole population**

	1980	1990	2000	2020
Australia	1.74	2.18	2.99	4.12
Austria	2.68	3.69	–	–
Belgium	2.69	3.47	3.65	5.55
Canada	1.85	2.37	3.53	5.06
Denmark	2.78	3.67	4.10	4.29
Finland	1.81	2.88	3.34	4.35
Japan	1.39	2.39	3.60	7.10
New Zealand	1.70	2.29	2.79	3.73
Norway	2.96	3.76	–	–
Portugal	1.71	2.73	3.09	6.13
Spain	1.94	2.87	3.43	4.46
Sweden	3.17	4.30	5.01	4.83
Switzerland	2.66	3.69	3.93	4.83
Turkey	1.46	1.46	–	–
United Kingdom	2.70	3.67	4.08	4.55
United States	2.28	2.79	3.49	4.11

Source: OECD (1996).

Table 7.2. **Percentage of elderly people over 65 living alone or with the family in the whole population**

	Living alone		Living with the family	
	Per cent	Year	Per cent	Year
Australia	21	1986	25	1987
Austria	35	1990	–	–
Belgium	24	1986	–	–
Canada	25	1986	–	–
Denmark	53	1988	4	1988
Finland	38	1987	14	1987
France	28	1982	20	1982
Western Germany	41	1985	14	1987
Hungary	20	1980	–	–
Iceland	32	1988	23	1987
Ireland	23	1986	–	–
Italy	31	1990	39	1990
Japan	11	1990	65	1985
Netherlands	31	1986	8	1987
New Zealand	28	1991	–	–
Norway	35	1990	11	1988
Poland	20	1988	28	1988
Portugal	18	1981	–	–
Spain	19	1989	37	1985
Sweden	39	1990	5	1986
Switzerland	35	1986	16	1986
Turkey	16	1988	–	–
United Kingdom	36	1985	16	1980
United States	32	1984	15	1987

Source: OECD (1996).

Nevertheless, corresponding rates across countries may provide some clues for investigating aged care policy from a comparative viewpoint.

Other variables such as social security expenditure, national health service expenditure, saving rates and the rate of owner-occupiers can be utilised in considering the factors that will influence aged care policies in all nations.

Table 7.3. **Percentage of women aged 45-60 in the labour market**

	1980	1990
Australia	35.3	44.7
Canada	44.5	53.5
Finland	79.6	85.0
France	49.6	48.0
Western Germany	40.6	44.5
Ireland	21.8	23.4
Italy	22.9	22.1
Japan	55.0	58.8
Netherlands	21.8	32.5
New Zealand	51.0	54.2
Norway	60.9	67.7
Portugal	38.3	44.3
Spain	24.6	25.4
Sweden	68.4	79.0
United Kingdom	53.2	56.4
United States	50.7	59.2

Source: OECD (1996).

Table 7.4. **Percentage of elderly people over 65 in residential care and receiving elderly home help services**

	Residential care		Receiving home help services	
	%	Year	%	Year
Australia	6.2	1991	7	1988
Austria	4.6	1988	3	1991
Belgium	5.2	1991	6	1990
Canada	7.1	1991	2	1990
Denmark	5.4	1992	22	1990
Finland	7.0	1991	24	1990
France	5.1	1992	7	1985
Western Germany	5.4	1992	3	1992
Ireland	5.0	1991	3	1990
Italy	2.4	1988	1	1988
Japan	6.4	1990	1	1990
Netherlands	9.1	1990	8	1990
New Zealand	6.7	1991	1	1993
Norway	6.5	1992	16	1992
Portugal	2.0	1992	1	1992
Spain	2.4	1988	1	1985
Sweden	5.3	1990	16	1991
United Kingdom	5.1	1990	7	1992
United States	5.2	1990	4	1990

Source: OECD (1996).

A typology of service provision

OECD countries can be divided into three groups, according to their aged care and long-term care policies. The first type, based on the Scandinavian countries, has a large proportion of elderly people, an independent household structure for elderly people, and a universal service provision for the elderly. The second type, based on southern European countries, has a relatively small elderly population with a strong family structure and provides little institutional or home care services for the elderly. The third type, which includes all other countries, has a combination of various levels of aged populations, independent living arrangements for the elderly and service levels pitched somewhere between the first and second types.

One of the interesting points in the OECD data is that the proportion of institutionalised elderly in some countries dropped during the 1980s. In Australia, for example, the figure fell from 7 per cent in 1981 to 6.2 per cent in 1991. A similar trend can be seen in Canada, Denmark, the Netherlands, Norway and Sweden. In the United States, however, the figure went up from 3.7 per cent in 1980 to 5.1 per cent in 1990, and in Japan from 5.5 per cent to 6.4 per cent. These figures may indicate that in the last two decades many countries, particularly Scandinavian countries, placed much emphasis on community-care policy (such as home-help services) rather than institutional care. To what extent, and in what way, these policy shifts have been effective in each country is worth further investigation.

This chapter seeks to investigate the development of long-term care policy, with an emphasis on Japan and Australia, and to clarify the way in which their respective government policies have been changed. There are basically three policy areas in which the service provision and practice of long-term care have been developed and changed: medical care, residential care and community care.

DEVELOPMENT OF HEALTH-CARE SERVICES AND LONG-TERM CARE

The concept of long-term care can be defined first of all in comparison with that of acute health care. Table 7.5 shows the basic difference between the medical-care model and life-care model.* The

---

* The life model does not always apply to very elderly people, who frequently need medical care services as well as help with their daily life. In some countries it may be very difficult to get medical help after being discharged from hospital. For example, some medical care procedures, such as intravenous injections or the use of respirators, cannot be provided at home without medical supervision. In Sweden, small local hospitals, rather than large hospitals, provide medical home care for patients. However, this once more raises the problem of sharing care costs between hospital care and community care for the elderly with heavy care needs.

Table 7.5. **Models of care for the elderly**

	Medical model	Life (QOL) model
Purpose	Cure of illness	Enhancement of QOL
Outcome	Health	Independence
Target	Sickness	Handicap
Service setting	Hospital (institution)	Home/community
Staff team	Health centered	Inter-disciplinary

Source: Hiroi (1994).

implication underlying the two models is that high-level medical treatment may sometimes be inappropriate for elderly people who would be better treated with enhanced quality of life (QOL) in their daily activities by maintaining their physical and mental functions. In order to achieve this, long-term care for the aged must be provided. However, it is difficult to reorganise the existing service provision system and to change funding mechanisms because these changes are likely to clash with the service provision regime and its vested interests.

One of the basic policy strategies to cope with the increasing health care needs of the frail elderly is to introduce a distinction between acute care and long-term care, placing more emphasis on the latter and hence reducing the inappropriate use of resources. In some countries, including the United Kingdom, Ireland, New Zealand and Sweden, this distinction between general hospitals and long-term care hospitals was introduced some time ago.

In Australia, where the distinction is also clear, the States and Territories reduced acute hospital beds in the mid-1980s. From 1985/86 to 1991/92, the number of acute hospital beds in the public sector declined from 4.1 to 3.3 beds per 1 000 while the number in the private sector remained almost the same at 1.3 beds per 1 000. In 1991/92, the available acute hospital beds were 4.5 per 1 000, the numbers of acute hospital and aged nursing home beds per 1 000 were 4.2 and 4.6 respectively in metropolitan area, and 5.1 and 3.3 in non-metropolitan area (Australian Institute of Health and Welfare, 1994). This shows that the number of acute-care beds was controlled through the hospitals in the public sector, while in rural areas, acute hospital beds were being used for long-term care.

In Japan, the distinction was introduced fairly recently and is still in the process of development. In 1984, the numbers of general hospital beds and geriatric hospital beds per 1 000 were 8.7 and 0.6 respectively, compared to 10.1 and 1.5 in 1993. Also, the number of beds on other types of long-term care facility (see below) was 1.6 in 1984 and 3.6 in 1993. Though the number of geriatric hospital beds and other care facility beds increased during this period in Japan, the ratio of long-term care beds to acute care beds is low in comparison with that of Australia. Given the rapidly growing number of old-old in the elderly population in Japan, it is likely that a large number of frail elderly stay in general hospitals after medical care treatment in acute hospitals rather than being transferred to more suitable care facilities. The government is aware of the problem and has been trying to change the service structure by introducing various policy measures from the early 1980s.

The Japanese medical care system

Compared with western countries, the Japanese health service system has some distinctive features. First, primary health care and hospital care are not clearly divided. A distinction between clinics and hospitals is made only by numbers of beds; 20 or more beds constitutes a hospital, while less than 20 beds is defined as a clinic. People can freely visit either local physicians or highly specialised hospital doctors for medical examinations. It has been suggested that this free access system is ineffective in that patients tend to visit major hospitals to be examined and treated with minor sicknesses, thus creating long waiting hours for perhaps three minutes of consultation time. There is also criticism of the low quality of hospital services. However, the system as a whole has been deemed effective in encouraging people to have early medical examinations, enabling early treatment, and hence contributing to the reduction of national care costs.

Second, until fairly recently, there has been no differentiation between long-term care hospitals and general hospitals. Since the enactment of the National Health Insurance Plan in 1961, all Japanese citizens are covered under one of the social insurance plans. In many ways, this compulsory cover helped promote good health conditions amongst the Japanese. The introduction in 1973 of free medical and hospital care for the elderly has helped them obtain access to medical care services that had not been previously available.

However, the system experienced a number of problems during the decade following its introduction:

- free medical care for the aged invited a steady increase of medical expenditure in the health care budget;
- the system placed too much emphasis on medical treatment, whereas preventative measures, such as health promotion, were less effective; and
- there were imbalances in patient-payments between the various medical insurance programmes due to disparities in the ratio of the elderly in these programmes (Japanese Ministry of Health and Welfare, 1995c).

Introduction of long-term care hospitals in 1983

Various revisions have been introduced to the health service system and health insurance pro- gramme to cope with the increasing care needs of the elderly. Of great importance was the enactment of the Health and Medical Service Law for the Aged (HMSLA) in 1983, when the Specially Licensed Hospital for the Aged (Geriatric Hospital) was introduced. Hospitals which are deemed eligible for this category have wards in which some 60 per cent or more of the inpatients are elderly (around age 65+) with chronic disease, or have at least 70 per cent elderly patients with chronic disease and general patients with chronic disease (all ages). Medical fees are paid, according to a patient's monthly summarised fee points, through various social insurance schemes. These fees, along with the hospital- isation care-management fee, contribute to the improvement of nursing and personal-care facilities. This was a fundamental change of policy in the health care system (Japanese Ministry of Health and Welfare, 1996).

In 1986, the government revised the Medical Care Service Act with the enactment of the Medical Care Service Plan. The revision made it mandatory for prefectural authorities to set up health regions within their jurisdiction and to estimate the number of beds necessary in each region according to guidelines laid down by the Ministry of Health and Welfare. This revision was another measure intended to control the overall provision of hospital beds (Gang, 1987).

In 1992, the Medical Care Service Act was revised again and a new category of hospital was introduced for the first time. This category embraced the concept of long-term care beds. The basic ideas however are similar to those introduced in the Hospital for the Aged defined by the HMSLA of 1983.

The introduction of the concept of geriatric hospitals and long-term care beds, alteration of the payment system and the regional medical-care service plan illustrate a strong commitment by the government to control overall medical expenditure and to reorganise the medical service structure in response to the shift towards a more aged society.

Between 1985 and 1994, the number of geriatric hospitals increased from 710 (7.4 per cent of all hospitals) and from 85 503 beds (5.8 per cent of all beds) to 1 613 (16.4 per cent of all hospitals) and to 184 572 beds (11 per cent of all beds). This increase in the number of hospitals and hospital beds underlies a range of problem that have been facing hospital management.

In Australia, where the distinction between acute hospitals and long-term hospitals or nursing homes is clearer than in Japan, the issue of the over-use of acute hospitals, or inappropriate use of hospital beds (bed blocking) by older people has caused concern among policy makers and other interested persons. A detailed analysis of the issue revealed the complexity of the problem (Australian Department of Health, Housing and Community Services, 1991, pp 153-157). This report suggests that bed blocking by elderly persons is not as widespread as imagined. Rather, there is a small number of elderly people who tend to take up bed-days over a long period (Sax, 1993, pp. 70-71).

The issue of inappropriate use of acute hospital beds by elderly people should be investigated in relation to the provision and utilisation of other health and welfare facilities and services. Longer stay times are sometimes due to the inadequate provision of rehabilitation, long-term and residential care facilities and insufficient community care services. The interactions between health and long-term care facilities and community care are central issues which require careful examination.

RESIDENTIAL CARE

Health service facilities for the aged

Another step toward improved long-term care facilities in Japan was the establishment in 1986 of Health Service Facilities for the Aged (HSFA) by the amendment of the HMSLA. These facilities provide medical care and daily living support services to old people in need of care. The purpose of the facilities is to provide personal care, functional training and other necessary medical care for the elderly who are bedridden due to diseases, injuries, etc. They also offer help with daily living.

In 1988 there were 60 HSFA with 4 092 beds, increasing to 1 003 in 1994 with 85 547 beds. Given the short time since its inception, these figures show a steady and positive development. They also highlight the firm commitment by central government to changing the whole medical system. The HSFAs are intended to be the facilities that provide both health care and personal care, with special emphasis on rehabilitation services. They are also expected to improve the quality of care and reduce the cost to the government by levying a fixed-rate charge on users (Japan Ministry of Health and Welfare, 1987).

However, a study of the utilisation pattern of the HSFA in 1991 showed that 46.1 per cent of all patients stayed in the facilities more than 6 months and 25.4 per cent stayed more than 1 year. It also shows that 59.4 per cent of the referrals were made from the patients' home, 37.4 per cent from health facilities, and after a period of stay, 56.6 per cent returned home and 32.7 per cent were hospitalised. This means that quite a number of inpatients are being shuttled between hospitals and health service facilities (Koyama, 1993). The need for greater provision of long-term care facilities and further integration of service utilisation is apparent.

Long-term residential care

Apart from a small number of old people's homes run by private or charity organisations, almost all the old people's homes after the war were under the public control of central government, which provided capital and recurrent funding. Prefectural governments approved the establishment of the facilities and recurrent subsidies were based on the Daily Life Security Law which is equivalent to the Part III accommodations of the National Assistance Act in the United Kingdom. The result was that the old people's homes were restricted to low-income people without family support.

The history of old people's homes is similar across countries. The residential home was a last resort for those who could no longer live in the community without help from relations and neighbours. In the early history of these homes, physical, staffing and service conditions were poor and basic human needs for dignity, privacy and autonomy were often ignored.

The increase in the elderly population and the development of various social services after 1945 were to influence the future course of these old people's homes. Change can be seen in the integration of residential care homes with housing policy and in the development of a broader range of care facilities. The extent to which each country has achieved improvement of service standards and has integrated the residential care with other service areas needs to be examined (Brearly, 1977; Centre for Policy on Ageing, 1984; Judge and Sinclair, 1986).

In Japan, the Law for Welfare of the Aged (LWA) was enacted in 1963 and the provisions of the old people's homes were incorporated into the Law as the Care Homes for the Aged (CHA). Even in the days shortly after the war, appeals were made to the government at a national conference of the Old People's Homes Association that they needed additional subsidies to build and operate rooms for sick people in their facilities (Shimizu, 1994). A new category of old people's home was introduced as the Special Care Home for the Aged (SCHA). This is a facility for those who have severe physical and mental handicaps and can not seek care from other family members at home.

Unlike the CHA, the SCHA does not set any low income qualifications, but requires payment according to the income of residents and their family members under the schedules set by the government. The SCHAs are equivalent to nursing homes in the Western sense, administered however by the Health and Welfare Bureau for the Elderly, not by the Medical Care Bureau of the Ministry of Health and Welfare. This was a shift from the poor-relief related programmes for the aged to a more universal, tax-financed service provision.

Another category of home for the aged was incorporated into the Law in 1963. The Homes for the Aged with Moderate Fee (HAMF) are facilities for those elderly aged 60 and over who experience difficulties in staying at home in terms of family relations and housing conditions. Residents must meet certain income restriction criteria and pay "moderate fees" for running costs. HAMF constitutes a part of the public housing programme with basic care services.

The qualification for entering the SCHA does not require strict means-testing of applicants as is seen in the United States (Wiener, 1996). Rather, it requires payments, both from the applicants themselves and their main family income earners. This means that the fee policy differs from that of the Australian payment system for nursing homes, where residents are only required to pay 87.5 per cent of their pension (Australian Department of Health, Housing and Community Services, 1991). The pay policy in Japan has resulted in complaints and confusions amongst family members in relation to differing interpretations of what is meant by "Main Family Income Earners". Generally, however, such changes have been accepted as an unavoidable corollary to access to such facilities.

Ongoing issues

The number of beds in SCHA facilities increased rapidly from the introduction of the provision – from 41 606 in 1970 to 182 280 in 1992, an increase of some 440 per cent over 22 years. The number of beds of CHA increased from 47 924 in 1963 to 71 031 in 1970, decreasing slightly in 1992 to 67 678, while HAMF places increased from 7 527 to 19 416 during the same period. This suggests that the SCHA and the HSFA have been widely accepted as care facilities for those in need of care.

In contrast, the decrease in number of CHA beds and the small number of HAMF places suggest that the policy for residential care homes has not been in tune with comprehensive housing policies for elderly. In 1989 the government introduced the "Ten Year Plan", under which it promised to fund a housing programme of "Care Houses". A Care House is a residential facility for elderly people with moderate disabilities who are able to live an independent life with minor assistance, such as the provision of meals, cleaning, home maintenance, etc. The main characteristic which distinguishes the Care House from the HAMF is that placement is open to everybody, and no income restrictions are imposed. This is a small step towards a more universal housing programme which also provides some care services.

Private housing programmes for the elderly with moderate disabilities have been extensively developed in western countries. Different countries give different names to such programmes. In Sweden they are known as Service Houses, in the United Kingdom they are called Sheltered and Very Sheltered Housing, and in Australia they are called Hostels. Similar types of facilities can be seen in other western countries. All these programmes have proved to be effective in keeping elderly people out of institutional care and have widened the scope for aged care policy in the 1970s and 1980s (Tinker, 1994).

However, in recent years these housing programmes have raised a number of issues. First, people entering the facility are expected to pay entrance fees. Elderly who cannot afford to pay are not allowed to occupy a place in the facility and the government is required to make some financial arrangement and oversee the funding operation of proprietors investing in such facilities. Second, those who stay in the facility for a long period will deteriorate in their physical and mental capacities and hence need extensive care supports. Closer co-operation therefore between health and welfare services in each locality is necessary at the planning stage of these facilities.

The rapid increase of SCHA beds has also raised several issues to be addressed by the policy makers. First, the age distribution of residents in SCHA has shifted upwards. Residents aged 85 and over initially constituted 15.8 per cent of all residents, however by 1992 this figure was 35.3 per cent. Furthermore, the average age of residents in 1992 was 81.8 years. This inevitably has led to the facilities having to cope with many more severely handicapped elderly people with heavy and extensive care needs. It has also been maintained by those concerned with the operation of the facilities that closer co-operation with medical care services is necessary in dealing with some medical care demands. This relates to the issue of demarcation and interaction between acute health care and long-term care.

Issues have also been raised in relation to the respective boundaries of both community care and residential care. In 1982, the Inspection Bureau of the Administrative Management Agency published a report, "Present Issues in the Policy for Welfare of the Elderly", in which critical comments were made of the inadequate administration and inefficient use of resources in facilities. The report suggested:

- Some of the residents in the SCHA were not constantly bedridden and did not need any help with daily life, whereas some of the CHA residents would have been more appropriately accommodated in SCHA.

- Once a resident has been admitted, no further monitoring or review of the situation of family carers was undertaken. Therefore, despite receiving rehabilitation in the facility, many residents were unable to return home due to insufficient ongoing family support.

- Thus the Ministry of Health and Welfare was advised to take measures to improve admission procedures and make effective use of the facilities (Japan Administrative Management Agency, 1982).

There was criticism of the report for ignoring the heavy care burden on family carers as well as the housing conditions that militate against independent life of the elderly. Seen from the present stage of policy development, some crucial issues relating to long-term care were also apparent at that time, including:

- Inadequacies in rehabilitation services and medical examination before admission.

- Inadequacies in community-care service provision to support disabled elderly and their carers at home.

- A lack of a comprehensive assessment service and service co-ordination system to enable the elderly and carers to stay at home and make their own decision about if or when to enter an institution.

The Australian experience

In Australia, a comprehensive Aged Care Reform Strategy was introduced in the middle of the 1980s. It includes the setting of benchmarks for keeping the best balance of care between residential care and community care and the alteration of funding mechanisms. Individualised payment systems, based on the level of care received by each resident, have been introduced for both nursing homes and hostels. This has helped the institutions admit more handicapped people.

The expansion of the Aged Care Assessment Service across the country is another measure for achieving more integrated care services for the frail elderly in Australia. Although the service is mainly concerned with assessment of those who apply for admission to residential care, it has also undertaken the critical roles of consultation with clients, referral to, and sometimes co-ordination of, services in the community when needed. Thus the service occupies an important position in the integration of various kinds of services (Gibson, 1996; Australian Department of Health, Housing and Community Services, 1991; Australian Department of Health, Housing, Local Governments and Community Services, 1993).

The comparison between countries reveals the necessity for defined policy objectives with some kind of benchmarks or target figures for monitoring their implementation. It also shows that in order to achieve the objectives, financial arrangements must be secured that allow for shifts in service provision focus and change in operational mechanisms when required. Without these crucial foundations, intended reforms may not reach fruition.

COMMUNITY CARE

The concept of community care has been discussed in various ways, but there is a common understanding of the philosophy underlining the concept.

In Britain, the Report to the Secretary of State for Social Services, "Community Care: Agenda for Action" summarises the value and purpose of community care as:

- to enable an individual to remain in his own home wherever possible, rather than being cared for in a hospital or residential home;
- to give support and relief to informal carers (family, friends and neighbours) coping with the stress of caring for a dependent person;
- to deliver appropriate help, by the means which cause the least possible disruption to ordinary living;
- to relieve the stresses and strains contributing to or arising from physical or emotional disorder;
- to provide the most cost-effective package of services to meet the needs and wishes of those being helped; and
- to integrate all resources of a geographical area in order to support the individual within it. The resources might include informal carers, the National Health Service (NHS) and personal social services and organised voluntary efforts, but also sheltered housing, the local social security office, the church, local clubs, and so on (Griffith, 1988).

Expansion of service resources for community care

In order to increase service resources for community care, each country has introduced comprehensive strategies and has changed their financial allocation patterns. In Australia, Home and Community Care Services Programme was established in 1985-86. The aims of the programmes are:

- to provide a comprehensive and integrated range of basic support services for frail aged and other people with a disability and their carers;
- to help recipients to be more independent at home and in the community, thereby preventing their premature and inappropriate admission to long-term residential care and the enhancement of the quality of provision for those who remain at home; and,
- to provide a "greater range of services and more flexible provision to ensure the services respond to the needs of users" (Fine and Thomson, 1995).

In Japan, the government publicised "A Ten Year Strategy to Promote Health Care and Welfare for the Aged" (Golden Plan) in 1989 in order to increase service resources to cope with the rapidly increasing long-term care needs. The plan calls for an expansion of at-home welfare services to build a system in which "Whoever in need of long-term care will have easy access to the services necessary for his independence". The stated objectives of the plan are:

- urgent consolidation of domiciliary welfare measures provided by the local authorities;
- development of the "strategy for zero bedridden elderly";
- establishment of the "long life social welfare funds";
- urgent provision of institutional services;
- promotion of measures to ensure that the elderly live for some purpose;
- ten-year project for promoting scientific research on longevity;

– provision of comprehensive welfare facilities for the elderly.

The plan, broadly based on the philosophy of community care, demonstrates some distinctive features not seen in the previous health and welfare plans. First, specific target figures for basic community and institutional services are presented to secure the ongoing efforts, both of the central and local governments. Although the figures are rounded and not necessarily constructed on a solid basis, they have had a major impact on those concerned with health and welfare policies and service provision as well as on the whole nation because of the clearly stated objectives. Second, a rather specific policy objective is set out in terms of the strategy for "zero bedridden elderly", symbolised as evidence of the inadequacy or backwardness of the Japanese health and welfare services. This was also successful in raising wide concern among the people. Third, the government's assurance to invest some US$60 billion for the plan, based on the agreement between the Ministers of Finance, Local Government and Health and Welfare, was accepted as an indication of serious commitment by the government to community care.

Integrated community care services

In contrast to institutional care, community care has advantages in terms of giving more freedom and independence to people receiving care. However, if a client becomes frail and needs extensive care, he or she needs comprehensive support or "packaged services".

There are two fundamental issues in developing long-term community care services. First, who are service providers and second, who will take responsibility to co-ordinate services according to the needs of the client? We will take an example of home help service in order to see how far the services can respond to the long-term care needs.

Almost all the community care services for the aged in Japan have been provided by local authorities under the Law for Welfare for the Aged through cost sharing arrangements with the central government. As with the admission to residential care homes, home help services are provided to those who suffer from physical and mental handicaps and cannot be cared for by family members. The household must also be a recipient of public assistance or be of low income status.

In 1982, the restriction by income status was abolished and anyone who needed the service became eligible. However, the service standard was so low that two hours service, two days a week was the norm. In addition to this, home helpers mainly provided basic housekeeping assistance, such as sweeping, cleaning, shopping and cooking. They did not tend to provide personal care support such as toilet care, bathing, feeding and walking assistance. People who really wanted to stay at home but required a high degree of care had to buy services in the market place.

The reason for the poor standard of public home help services came partly from the common understanding that the services provided by local authorities were a part of the poor-relief programme and were thus of low quality. The poor standard however was recently brought into sharp relief decade with the announcement of a comprehensive and co-ordinated support system which includes day service, respite care, home nursing service and home care support centres.

Since the announcement of the Golden Plan, the government has rapidly increased the budget for home help services from 31 000 in 1989 to 92 000 helpers in 1995. The figure will increase to 170 000 by the year 2000. The increased provision of home helpers, the eligibility criteria and the standard of services have also been changed to such an extent that people have begun to express some trust in, and expectation of, the public support services in the community.

However, a number of issues remain unresolved before a fully-fledged home help service can be said to be in operation. These include:

– Expansion of service hours from a day-time basis to an around-the-clock basis.

– Provision of services of a personal care type, rather than of a house-keeping type.

– Integration of the service with visiting nurse and day centre or day care services.

– Inclusion of an emergency call system within the home help service.

- Appointment of home-help managers with greater expertise who can make assessments and referrals to service co-ordinators.

These arrangements have been highly developed in Scandinavian countries, where comprehensive and co-ordinated community care is provided. However, the extent to which such comprehensive and co-ordinated home help services are provided for those with heavy care needs may be scrutinised in terms of desirability, effectiveness and efficiency as part of community care as opposed to institutional care (Sundström, 1994).

Other community care services, such as respite care, day centre/day care, meals-on-wheels, home maintenance and home repairing service, have seen a steady development in Japan as in other countries. There are several issues to be discussed in relation to the provision of these services.

One of the issues is whether it is better to provide community-care services through a single service-providing body or by co-ordinating various service providers. In some areas, there is a tendency towards comprehensive service provision by a service agent who provides nursing care, respite care, day care/day service and home helpers, along with a home care support centre that will provide information, referral and advisory services. Another issue is whether or not to use a co-ordination model or a network model in which community service providers share all the responsibilities and mediate in service provision. In rural areas, comprehensive service provision may be prevalent, whereas in urban areas, the network model may predominate. Extensive care service may be better provided for by the co-ordination model, while community or social support may be better delivered by the network model.

Another issue that relates to community long-term care policy is the participation of the community in service provision. In Japan, numerous home help organisations, based on the objectives of mutual-aid arrangements, have been emerging in metropolitan areas in the last decade. This is partly because public home help service has been predominantly targeted at low-income people with some dependency, and has not sufficed for the service needs of people of middle income status.

Some local governments, particularly in metropolitan areas, have launched the establishment of semi-public home help services, aimed at encouraging community-based, mutual-aid activities. Local governments subsidise basic running costs, including the salaries of co-ordinators and clerical workers. With these arrangements, both helpers and clients can set up and run a mutual-assistance system. They receive some reward from the helped members, although the amount is far less than the market price. The payment can be understood as a token of gratitude from the helped members.

There were 452 such bodies in 1993 with 93 000 registered members. Of these, 27 000 persons were recorded as being active during that same year. Although the purpose of their activities is to complement the publicly provided services, they also often spontaneously take on critical roles ignored by inflexible public services.

These semi-public home help services organisations are situated between community-based volunteer activities and public and market services. How far and in what way such systems of semi-public home help service should be promoted and what their proper area of activities should be, may be an issue for further consideration.

Care management

In Australia and the United Kingdom, care management is a system by which macro policy can be mediated into field operation. Well developed needs assessment and care management can function as both a service co-ordinating system and resource allocation system. It is an indispensable part of mixed service provision in that clients are offered a service package according to his or her individual needs.

The roles of care management may be itemised as follows:

- providing information and advice to clients and making an assessment of their needs;
- tailoring services according to the needs of clients;

- purchasing services from public, non-profit and for-profit sectors; and
- monitoring and reviewing service provision.

However, the functions of care managers vary in each country. In Britain, care managers undertake all functions in the field of social services. In Australia, the Aged Care Assessment Team assumes the functions of advising, assessing and referring. However, service purchasing is carried out by the Community Options Projects, along with the mainstream home help services. In Japan, although the concept of care management has been introduced in the field operations, its major function is to give information and advice, and to make referrals. This means that functions of care management are closely related to the level of service provision in each locality. Differing functions of care managers in different countries may be related to the type of long-term care they provide.

FAMILY CARE

In western countries, over the past decade strong concern has been expressed about family care, given the tight financial positions of the governments. Various studies indicate that family members still play an important role for aged care both quantitatively and qualitatively, even in Scandinavian countries where generous home care service are provided.

In Japan, where more than half of the elderly people still live with their offspring, people's attitudes have nevertheless changed considerably regarding care services for elderly parents. First, the number of children per family has decreased to one or two, and many of these now leave home to seek employment in remote cities and stay there to marry. Second, a greater participation of women in the labour market after marriage makes it difficult for them to look after their old parents in need of extensive care – even when they live with them or near to them. Third, people's attitudes have been changed in favour of developing more generous social services. These changes are seen in various opinion surveys in relation to the proposed introduction of long-term care insurance schemes.

Policy measures in responding to the "caring for carers" consist of financial support such as tax relief and tax credits, care benefits and payment for care, and service support such as in-home assistance, respite services, and advice and support services. In principle, the financial support system offers a wide array of benefits to recipients, but just how effective such support will be is unclear. On the other hand, service supports may be of greater actual benefits to the recipients (Twigg, 1994). The issue was actively discussed in Japan in the process of working out the proposal of a long-term care insurance scheme as to whether and how much cash benefits should be given to the family carers (Japan Ministry of Health and Welfare, 1995a). It may be desirable for clients and their carers to be able to choose either or both of the services. However, it is also argued that this may require fairly extensive provision of services (Sundström, 1994; OECD, 1994).

Given the extensive range of home-care services currently available, particularly services such as round-the-clock home care, family carers have more scope for taking responsibility as "care-managers" in arranging various kinds of services. This provides another way of empowering family carers.

Nevertheless, all family carers may not be able or willing to take on this care management role, and so an initial assessment will often be necessary to establish who can best fill the role of care manager. Family carers will have to be provided with sufficient information, consulted and advised to enable them to decide whether they are willing to take on this role. Formal back-up services are vital. There have been reports of family carers who have cancelled applications for nursing home placement of their vulnerable parents after realising that they would receive adequate back-up whenever they required formal help in looking after them. If family carers cannot assume such care managing roles for whatever reason, professional care managers must take responsibility and intervene in the provision of home care and other services.

The policy of supporting carers should be examined in the wider context including labour, pension and incomes policy. For example, a report has been published which reveals the influence of improved care services on preventing the exclusion of women from the labour market (Research Institute of Medical Economics, 1996). Increasing taxes or social contributions in order to finance more services to support working carers may be an important way to widen labour market opportunities in economically-developed countries with less universal long-term care service provisions and rapidly ageing populations.

LOCAL HEALTH AND WELFARE PLANNING FOR THE AGED

Along with the implementation of the Golden Plan, in 1990, the Japanese government revised the related welfare services acts to delegate responsibility to local government, and to secure the steady implementation of the plan and the promotion of co-ordinated services at the local level. At the same time, the government made it mandatory for local governments to work out a Local Plan for Promoting the Health and Welfare for the Elderly, including local target figures for major care-related services based on needs research up to fiscal year 1992.

These strategies have also been seen in countries such as Australia and the United Kingdom. Making a local plan for long-term care and related services is one of the measures intended to promote the accountability of local authorities. Devolution of powers in the provision of services as well as modified financial arrangements between central government and local authorities has enabled local authorities to take initiatives for more effective social services.

The experience of local authorities in making health and welfare plans for their own populations certainly stimulates their sense of responsibility for long-term care for the aged. However, they often raise anxieties about the possible future heavy financial burden that may not be adequately covered by the government. Much depends on the financial position of local governments to implement the policies and on the will of the inhabitants. The issue of funding mechanisms, *i.e.* whether people opt for general taxation or social insurance for long-term care spending, is also central to the future course of long-term care.

In Japan, the Ministry of Health and Welfare has proposed a social insurance scheme for long-term care for the elderly similar to the German scheme. The proposal is scheduled for debate in the coming Diet session. The objectives of the scheme are:

– to increase the opportunities for user-choice of services;

– to provide more integrated long-term care services including both the health and welfare fields;

– to provide more flexible and efficient services; and

– to increase the efficiency of the expenditure for medical care and improve the situation of inappropriate bed use by elderly people.

The proposal intends to increase service provision of both institutional and community care in response to the rapidly increasing long-term care needs of the frail elderly, thus reducing the heavy care burden on family carers. Other policy objectives in introducing the new scheme are the separation of long-term care services from the acute medical care services, the effective use of medical resources and the containment of medical expenditure (Japan Ministry of Health and Welfare, 1996).

In order to achieve greater equity of services available for the elderly, a revision of the present relationship between pensions and the cost to the user of hospital, residential and community-based services will be needed (OECD, 1996; Hennessy and Wiener, 1996).

According to the Japanese Ministry of Health and Welfare, the cost of general hospital care, HMSLA, HSFA and SCHA are estimated to appoximate 500 000 ¥ (US$4 545), 400 000 ¥ (US$3 636), 330 000 ¥ (US$3 000) and 271 000 ¥ (US$2 464) per month, whereas, payments made by people using these facilities amount to approximately 39 000 ¥ (US$355), 39 000 ¥ (US$355), 60 000 ¥ (US$545), and 45 000 ¥ (US$409) respectively in 1996 and additional payments are also made by clients or their families for extra care attendance. The prices paid by clients are, therefore, if anything inversely related to the true cost of alternative provision schemes.

In Australia, the cost to the resident of nursing home care has been set at 87.5 per cent of the (flat rate) old-age pension (plus supplementary rent assistance) and a hostel resident also has to pay

85 per cent of the old-age pension plus rent assistance for his or her place. In Japan, however, there are no such links between residential-care charges and pensions.

This can also lead to other perverse incentives; for example, residents in nursing homes are only required to pay a relatively small proportion of their pension towards covering these costs, whereas remaining at home with a family carer and receiving some community care may result in much higher costs to the user than the residential-care option. The cost to the community in the coming years will be tremendous if such disincentives to opting for community care rather than residential care are allowed to burgeon.

However, it is reportedly very difficult to devise an adequate charging mechanism without compromising equitable service utilisation (Australian Department of Health, Housing and Community Services, 1991). Elderly people tend to under-utilise service resources when confronted by service fees, creating distress to themselves and their family carers. This is one reason why levying charges on a means-tested basis may be undesirable.

When reorganising financing, funding and charge mechanisms, it remains important to ensure equitable access to long-term care services as well as medical-care services, regardless of income. This calls for the introduction of some kind of assessment and/or care-management system, as described above. This could consist of a basic policy instrument for linking adequate financing and charging mechanisms with equitable service provision, including service targeting.

In terms of residential and amenity services, people may be encouraged to buy services on their own choice even if they are in care facilities. Basic attitudes towards care services may change in future generations of the elderly, who will be entitled to adequate pension benefits. They may take a consumerist attitude and prefer to buy better services. The whole service structure may have to adapt to these changes.

BIBLIOGRAPHY

AUSTRALIAN DEPARTMENT OF HEALTH, HOUSING AND COMMUNITY SERVICES (1991), *Aged Care Reform Strategy Mid-Term Review 1990-1991*, Australian Government Publishing Service, Canberra.

AUSTRALIAN DEPARTMENT OF HEALTH, HOUSING, LOCAL GOVERNMENTS AND COMMUNITY SERVICES (1993), *Aged Care Reform Strategy Mid-term Review: Stage 2*, Australian Government Publishing Service, Canberra.

AUSTRALIAN INSTITUTE OF HEALTH AND WELFARE (1994), *Australia's Health 1994*, Australian Government Publishing Service, Canberra.

AUSTRALIAN INSTITUTE OF HEALTH AND WELFARE (1995), *Australia's Welfare and Assistance 1995*, Australian Government Publishing Service, Canberra.

BREARLY, P. (1977), *Residential Work with the Elderly*, Routledge and Keagan Paul, London.

CENTRE FOR POLICY ON AGEING (1984), *Home Life: A Code of Practice for Residential Care*, Nuffield Lodge Studio, London.

FINE, M. and THOMSON, C. (1995), *Factors Affecting the Outcome of Community Care Service Intervention: A Literature Review*, Department of Human Services and Health Aged and Community Care Division, Canberra.

GANG, A. (1987), *Handbook of Health Care Planning*, Daiichi Houki, Tokyo.

GIBSON, D. (1996), "Reforming aged care in Australia: change and consequence", *Journal of Social Policy*, Vol. 25, No. 2, Cambridge University Press.

GRIFFITHS, R. (1988), *Community Care: Agenda for Action, A Report to the Secretary of State for Social Services*, HMSO, London.

HENNESSY, P. and WIENER, J. (1996), "Paying for care for the elderly", *The OECD Observer*, No. 201, August/September, Paris.

HIROI, Y. (1994), *Economics of Medical Care*, Nihonkeizai Shinbunsha, Tokyo.

JAPAN ADMINISTRATIVE MANAGEMENT AGENCY (1982), *Conditions and Issues of the Policies for the Aged: Results of Inspection*, Tokyo.

JAPAN MINISTRY OF HEALTH AND WELFARE (1987), *Health Service Facilities for the Aged and Related Materials*, Tokyo.

JAPAN MINISTRY OF HEALTH AND WELFARE (1995a), *Towards an Establishment of a New Aged Care system*, Gyosei, Tokyo.

JAPAN MINISTRY OF HEALTH AND WELFARE (1995b), *Demographic Data Book*, Tokyo.

JAPAN MINISTRY OF HEALTH AND WELFARE (1995c), *Annual Report*, Tokyo.

JAPAN MINISTRY OF HEALTH AND WELFARE (1996), *Health and Welfare for the Elderly, The Foundation of Social Development for Senior Citizens*, Tokyo.

JUDGE, K. and SINCLAIR, I. (1986), *Residential Care for Elderly People*, HMSO, London.

KOYAMA, H. (1993), "Development and issues of health care facilities", *The Quarterly of Social Security Research*, Vol. 28, No. 4, The Social Development Research Institute, Tokyo.

OECD (1994), *New Orientations for Social Policy*, Social Policy Studies No. 12, Paris.

OECD (1996), *Caring for Frail Elderly People: Policies in Evolution*, Social Policy Studies No. 19, Paris.

RESEARCH INSTITUTE OF MEDICAL ECONOMICS (1996), *Report on the Economic Effects by Improved Welfare Services*, Tokyo.

SAX, S. (1993), *Ageing and Public Policy in Australia*, Allen and Unwin, St. Leonards.

SHIMIZU, Y. (1994), *Social Welfare Services for the Elderly*, Kaiseisya, Tokyo.

SUNDSTRÖM, G. (1994), "Care by family: an overview", in OECD (1996), Paris.

TINKER, A. (1994), "The role of housing policies in the care of elderly people", in OECD (1996), Paris.

TWIGG, J. (1994), "Informal care for elderly people: policy issues and responses", Paper presented to the Conference of OECD on Long-term Care for the Elderly, in July 1994, OECD, Paris.

WIENER, J. (1996), "Long-term care reform: an international perspective", OECD, *Health Care Reform: The Will to Change*, Health Policy Studies No. 8, Paris.

COMMENTARY ON MR. KOBAYASHI'S PAPER

by

Claes Örtendahl
Director-General,
National Board of Health and Welfare, Stockholm, Sweden

Ladies and gentlemen,

I would like to use Professor Kobayashi's enlightening and stimulating paper as a starting point for a debate about whether the models presented in his paper will withstand the pressures of the 20 years following the year 2000.

My basic conclusion is that there is a risk that we may underestimate the dynamic forces of a changing environment for the over-eighty population.

Professor Kobayashi presented his paper by analysing the two possible models: a *life-care model* and a *medical model*.

There is one basic statement in Professor Kobayashi's paper to which I would like to refer to illustrate a possible problem of underestimating the impact of development in the field of medical technology:

"The implication underlying the two models is that high-tech medical treatment may sometimes be inappropriate for elderly people who would be better treated with enhanced quality of life in their daily activities through the maintenance of their physical and mental functions."

In one sense this statement is perfectly acceptable. The use of medical resources, such as acute hospital care for senior citizens, who have almost no justification for high-tech medical intervention, is not only a terrible misuse of resources, but also an utterly inhumane way of maintaining the life of the elderly, which deprives them of dignity and almost all quality of life.

But we should take care and watch our steps carefully. Let me try to spell this out by describing the Swedish experience in the area.

In 1991, a major change took place in Sweden from the point of view of old-age care. A clear distinction was made between the health-care system and the social-welfare system in caring for senior citizens. When they were in need of medical treatment, hospitals and doctors would be in charge, otherwise – if they still needed care – social workers were in charge. A patient in a hospital with no further need for high-tech diagnosis and treatment would from the economic point of view be regarded as a client of the social-welfare system of the local authorities and these had to pay for their clients stay in hospital.

Nursing homes – formerly a part of the health-care system – were taken over by the local authorities and their social-service departments.

The results were overwhelming. In almost no time, the number of hospital beds could be cut by 25 per cent. Length of stay in hospital was likewise dramatically shortened. Health-care costs shrank to a level which brought Sweden to the very bottom on the GNP share to health-list.

But this was not the whole story.

Age is not a disease. Nor is it a handicap. But the health dimension is a very important one for people over eighty. The evaluation of the reform gave a few clues about problems in a geriatric service based on a life-care model.

The handicaps that create loss of autonomy and dependence on children and society have more often than not, a medical name – a diagnosis. In some cases, medical intervention and rehabilitation can restore an independent life style. Not in all cases – but in many, and they are on the increase. To make this happen, you need medical skills within geriatric services.

The Swedish experience is that the causes of loss of autonomy and a dignified independent life style are not always well understood in the life-care model Swedish style. Disease and handicap in old age is not a steady state but fluctuates considerably. Treatment strategies in geriatric services are often provided by staff who have insufficient training to observe and understand changes in medical needs. Therefore, the strategies are maintained when they should be changed. And old people therefore sometimes suffer from both undertreatment and overtreatment in the new context.

High-tech medical procedures were previously often regarded as unsuitable for older patients. The reasoning behind this is still somewhat obscure. There were originally good reasons to be careful in not using heroic procedures on a frail patient. But there may have been also an underlying notion of disease and handicap as unavoidable and integral parts of ageing and dying, things that simply have to be accepted. Typically, many clients of the geriatric service system, are described as frail or demented, whereas in reality they are suffering from diseases that can be diagnosed and sometimes treated.

What is overlooked is not only possible curative medical procedures but sometimes also good palliative procedures. We found that terminally-ill cancer patients died in pain to an unacceptable extent, because the highly qualified resources and staff needed to provide palliative care were never actually available or even aware of these patients.

The fact that these patients were now in the social domain may even have made the medical establishment think that they were no longer their responsibility.

This could be an even greater problem, if it were to affect the strategies of medical development and research. There is one group of diseases, that more than anything else leads to a need for institutional geriatric care. These are neurological diseases of old age – dementia.

A breakthrough in the treatment of dementia, and there are research strategies that may in due time result in a breakthrough, would revolutionalise the whole concept of care of the elderly. I am sometimes a bit afraid that by defining the problems of old age as predominantly non-medical, we run the risk of concentrating less on the diseases of old age and putting less effort into research and development into how to cope with them.

The first conclusion is, then, that a risk that too little medical competence is available in the community setting. The Swedish experience indicates that we must find ways of stimulating the medical services to deal with health problems of old age within a life-care model. If this does happen, in turn, it could lead to increased the quality of life, less dependency on institutional solutions and – perhaps – thereby also lower total costs.

My second observation is a brief one, but one which may be very important.

The over-80s of 2020 in my country will not be like the over-80s of today.

They (we) will have much more money of their own, due to the long-term effects of pension schemes introduced as recently as in the 1960s and 1970s. They are well educated and will not readily relinquish control over their own lives. They will also know much more about the options for care and treatment than our parents' generation.

In the enlightening and stimulating presentation by Professor Kobayashi, not much reference was made to the possibilities of solving some of the problems of old age by empowering the over-80s.

On the other hand, I detect a lot of confidence in the effectiveness of good planning.

I would like to suggest that we should think a little less in terms of planning and monolithic models, and a little more in terms of citizens over 80 years of age making their own choices.

I still believe in community-style services for the elderly, but if we are to get credit for what we are discussing today in the year 2020, we may have to think of stimulating local authorities and others, to create a much broader spectrum of different forms of old age services for them to choose between.

I also use the buzz word "empowerment", because I think that in Sweden, we should try to concentrate on new ways of dealing with the two main problems of old age – passivity and loneliness. And these problems have not yet been successfully dealt with in our version of a life-care model.

To break the mould of top-down models could be one way of getting to grips with a cultural and social context of old age, which has taken away important functions of elderly people and made social contacts much more difficult for them.

Empowerment to let the over-80s find their own solutions may also require some rethinking in the way we construct pension systems. One problem we need to think about is the fact that today many citizens over 80 years of age use their pension system entitlements to accumulate money for their children, rather than to spend on themselves. Should we envisage creating more direct links between pension systems and old-age care?

In countries like Sweden, where unemployment and a very slow development of new businesses for employment is a dominant problem, we should not underestimate the economic possibilities and the employment possibilities that exist in the vast market for high quality services to the over 80s.

If the pension schemes and insurance schemes deal with the problem of an equitable distribution of wealth during old age, the model of the senior citizen as an informed and active client might be something to think of.

BALANCING SUSTAINABILITY AND SECURITY IN SOCIAL POLICY

by

Fritz W. Scharpf

Max-Planck Institute for Social Research, Germany

INTRODUCTION

Social policy in all advanced welfare states is confronted by two challenges, the requirements of maintaining, or achieving, international economic competitiveness, and the pressures of increasing financial burdens. At the same time, however, advanced welfare states differ significantly in their vulnerability to, and their capacity to cope with, these challenges.

The context: three types of globalisation

The most advanced welfare states all reached their present form during the first three decades after World War II, when international economic integration was only gradually recovering from the rampant protectionism that had followed the Great Depression. Significantly, this was also a period of rapid economic growth and of full employment during which the level of protection offered to those who were not, or no longer, able to find well-paid jobs could be quite generous. In comparison, the past two decades have been characterised by lower levels of economic growth and much higher levels of unemployment in most OECD countries. As a consequence, the sustainability of welfare state systems that reached their present form during the high-growth decades after World War II is generally in question.

At the same time, economic integration has progressed more rapidly than before, and the economic environment of advanced welfare states has changed fundamentally over the last two decades. These environmental changes have greatly reduced the capacity of policy makers at the national level to choose social policy goals, and to pursue these goals by the policy instruments traditionally favoured in their respective countries. Since these environmental changes have greatly contributed to the present difficulties of advanced welfare states, they need to be at least briefly considered here.

Capital markets

The first, and arguably most important, of these difficulties arises from the globalisation of capital markets which, on the one hand, have eliminated national boundary control over the outflow and inflow of financial assets and which, on the other hand, contributed to the increase of real interest rates from, on average, about 3 per cent in the 1960s to 6 per cent or more in the 1980s and 1990s.

As a consequence of increased capital mobility and tax competition, the power of all national governments to tax capital assets and capital incomes has been greatly reduced. By the same token, national monetary policy can no longer reduce interest rates below the international level in order to stimulate productive investment, and higher rates of interest mean that running fiscal deficits to expand aggregate demand has become more expensive. National governments have thus largely lost their ability to avert rising unemployment through strategies of macroeconomic management that were still effective in the 1960s and 1970s. Hence, the more social policy systems were implicitly premised on continuing full employment, the more they have come under stress.

Another implication of the rise in real interest rates is that productive, job-creating investments will only be undertaken in the private sector if their expected rate of return is correspondingly higher than it was two decades ago. As a consequence, wage earners and governments have had to reduce their own claims on the economic product in order to allow higher rates of return on capital. OECD countries differ in the extent to which they have accepted or tried to resist the shift in the terms of trade-off between capital and labour and/or between capital and the state. But the price of effective resistance was reduced private investment, a poor employment performance in the private sector, and greater burdens on the welfare state.

Competition from newly industrialising countries

In the present political discussion, more emphasis seems to be placed on the threat to employment and incomes in advanced OECD countries that is assumed to arise from the increasing competition from newly industrialising or ex-communist countries. These, it is claimed, have invested in the education of their labour force, and they are now able to combine skilled labour with Western capital and technology to produce advanced industrial goods and services under conditions in which not only wage costs, but also taxation and the costs of social and environmental regulation, are much lower than in the OECD countries.

But even if these generalised facts are, by and large, taken to represent real changes, it should be pointed out that the share of world exports captured by newly industrialising countries is still quite modest, even though there is reason to think that it will rise further. By the same token, however, the imports of industrialising countries are also rising, and OECD countries are particularly well placed to meet the need for the advanced capital goods that are associated with rapid industrialisation. By the same token, direct foreign investments by OECD firms in newly industrialising countries are mainly motivated by the hope of profiting from the rapid expansion of these markets. On the whole, therefore, it seems more realistic to consider the arrival of newly industrialising countries as a welcome enlargement of the world market for goods and services, rather than as a zero-sum conflict over market shares. It remains true, however, that competition from newly industrialising countries will induce structural changes within and among OECD countries. It is also true that these changes will be most painful among OECD countries with less productive economies, and that in the more productive economies, low-skilled workers are most likely to be hurt.

Competition among OECD countries

From a social-policy perspective, however, the competition which hurts most is taking place between the highly industrialised OECD countries themselves. They are generally competing with each other at roughly the same levels of productivity, labour costs, taxation, and regulation. Under GATT rules, they have largely eliminated trade barriers among themselves; and within the European Union, the completion of the internal market has gone a long way towards eliminating non-trade barriers as well. As a consequence, firms are now also free to move their production activities to the most attractive locations within the European Union, and for most practical purposes also within the OECD, without jeopardizing in any way their access to the home market. Thus, while nobody seriously believes that wages, taxes and social and environmental regulations could be brought down to the level of low-cost economies, investors, firms and the media are watching closely to see what competitive advantages might be created in other European Union member states, or in other OECD countries. For the same reason, changes in the flow of foreign direct investment among OECD countries are not generally interpreted as attempts to gain access to protected markets, but as responses to changes in international competitiveness. National governments find it hard to resist demands to eliminate these competitive disadvantages. Thus, if the internationalisation of the economy has intensified locational competition among nation states, that competition occurs mainly within the Triad and, above all, among members states of the European Union that have highly productive economies and highly developed, and hence costly, welfare states. It is here, if anywhere, that international competition is driving down wages and taxes on business and capital incomes, and that pressure is building up to reduce social regulations as well as social services and welfare expenditure.

Protection through international agreements?

As a response, it is often suggested that competitive deregulation and welfare cutbacks could be avoided, and should be controlled, through international agreements or through European regulations. In both cases, however, agreement would be extremely difficult to reach. When measures against "social dumping" or "ecological dumping" are sought to eliminate the advantages of low-cost competitors in newly industrialising countries, these are likely to refuse agreement for economic reasons. The same is true when Britain and some other member states of the European Union refuse to agree to economically burdensome harmonisation measures in the social-policy field. But even if uniform rules were sought among countries with similar levels of productivity and production costs and committed to high levels of social protection, the structural and institutional diversity of national welfare regimes would stand in the way of agreement.

First, there is the difference between countries that rely primarily on publicly-financed welfare services and transfers, and others that leave a much larger share to the market. Even though it is true, as Esping-Andersen points out in his contribution to this conference (see Chapter 2), that quantitative differences are much smaller if private expenditure for health and education are included in the comparison, it nevertheless is difficult to imagine a convention on levels of welfare provision that could include both the United States and Sweden. However, even among the public-sector oriented European welfare states, structural differences are enormous: France finances 82 per cent of its public welfare budget from payroll taxes, Denmark only 13 per cent. Italy spends 50 per cent of its welfare budget on pensions, Germany less than 30 per cent. And while in Germany health care absorbs 30 per cent of total welfare expenditure, the Danish health care systems gets by on 18 per cent of the welfare budget (Eurostat, 1995).

This list could easily be extended. If one adds to it the institutional differences between tax-financed, universalistic and service-intensive welfare systems of the Scandinavian variety on the one hand, and insurance based, corporatist, and transfer intensive systems on the European continent (Esping-Andersen, 1990), it should be clear that the harmonisation of welfare systems by international agreement, or even by European directives, could not easily eliminate the competitive pressures that are presently eroding the viability of all advanced welfare systems.

Thus, if competitive pressures arising from worldwide and European economic integration will continue, the sustainability of existing social-policy regimes must be discussed with regard to options that are available at the national level. But before we begin looking for solutions, it is also necessary to briefly consider those challenges to sustainability that have arisen, as it were, endogenously, and that would require painful adjustments and structural changes even if national governments were still able to exercise control over their own economic boundaries.

SUSTAINABILITY UNDER DIFFERENT PROBLEM LOADS

Challenges to national welfare systems may arise if either expenditure increase above expected levels or if revenues fall below expected levels. These pressures are felt most acutely in three areas of social policy: old-age pensions, health care and unemployment compensation.

Old-age pensions

In all OECD countries, average life expectancy has increased, and so have the expenditure of old-age pension systems. At the same time, birth rates are, and have been for some time, lower than they were in the past. As a consequence, the size of the economically active population is shrinking relative to the size of the population in retirement, but there are significant inter-country differences.

In some countries, the impact of cohort effects on the size of the active population is overcompensated by a rise in the activity rate of women with children. Significantly, these also tend to be the countries, in which birth rates have fallen less dramatically than in some other countries, where the labour market participation of women is lower. It seems therefore that birth rates, and thus the long-term problems of financing pension systems, as well as the present size of the active population, are positively related to conditions, such as child-care facilities and all-day schools, that allow mothers to seek employment in the labour market. As a consequence, countries with higher birth rates and higher participation rates will have less difficulty in the long run in financing their pension systems.

Beyond that, the viability of public pension systems is also affected by the mode of financing. There are four basic options: pay-as-you-go systems financed from general tax revenues; pay-as-you-go systems financed from payroll taxes; and funded systems financed either from payroll taxes or from mandated individual insurance contributions. While it is certainly true at the macroeconomic level that all outlays must be paid out of the current social product, funded systems nevertheless have an advantage over pay-as-you-go systems whenever the real rate of interest is higher than the real rate of growth (in the case of tax-financed systems) or than the growth of real wages (in the case of payroll-tax financed systems). Since that has been true ever since the late 1970s, pay-as-you-go systems are now generally facing greater difficulties than funded systems. In addition, payroll-tax based systems are also more squeezed by the relative decline of income from labour, either as a consequence of low employment or as a consequence of stagnating or falling real wages.

Health care

Like old-age pensions, the cost of health-care systems is affected by the longer life expectancy of the population, and by the fact that medical expenses tend to rise steeply toward the last years of a person's life if all technically available means for prolonging human life are utilised. But, again, there are significant national differences in service provision and financing which affect the impact of these changes on the viability of health-care systems.

With regard to service provision, the basic difference is between health care provided by doctors and nurses employed by a national health system, and health care provided by hospitals and private doctors on a fee-for-service basis. Regardless of whether they are tax financed or insurance financed, the former are likely to be under the control of an externally determined budget that can be, and is generally, used as a constraint on the expansion of health services and costs. By contrast, fee-for-service systems are more likely to expand services in response to new technical opportunities and to the ability of service providers to define new needs for medical treatment. As a consequence, the problems associated with national health systems are more likely to relate to the insufficient quantity, and perhaps quality, of the medical care available, while fee-for-service systems are generally able to provide quantitatively and qualitatively attractive levels of service, but tend to be more expensive and to generate endemic problems of cost containment.

The escalation of medical costs is most rapid under conditions where payment is private or through private insurance – with the consequence that insurance premiums may rise to levels that place adequate medical care beyond the reach of low-income groups. In compulsory insurance systems financed through payroll taxes, by contrast, there are usually collective-bargaining mechanisms or government regulations that attempt to contain the rise of non-wage labour costs. To the extent that these are effective, some of the qualitative and quantitative problems of public health systems are likely to appear here as well.

Employment and unemployment

Employment and unemployment, finally, constitute the problem area where conditions vary most among OECD countries. It is also central to any discussion of the sustainability of the welfare state.

Some countries are still able to leave much of the burden of income maintenance during unemployment to private firms, to the extended family or to private charity. For the highly-developed welfare states, however, there is no question that unemployment must be a core concern of the political system.

For welfare systems deriving large parts of their financial revenues from payroll taxes, moreover, the level of employment, as distinct from the level of registered unemployment, constitutes the most critical link between the labour market and social policy. This level is directly affected not only by changes in the economic environment, but also by specific characteristics of the welfare state itself. Thus, employment has been reduced in some countries by liberal rules regarding early retirement and disability pensions; at the same time, generous provisions for income maintenance during unemployment are not only likely to contribute to longer spells of unemployment, but also to impede the creation of private-sector jobs at the lower end of the labour market. On the other hand, the availability, or the lack, of certain social services has either contributed to or impeded the expansion of female employment. These are important connections to consider.

On the other hand, lower employment growth and/or rising unemployment will not only add to the burden, but also undercut the financial bases, of most other parts of national welfare systems. In this regard, however, the different modes of financing welfare state expenditure must be considered as a critical intervening variable that greatly affects the viability of the welfare state.

SUSTAINABILITY UNDER DIFFERENT MODES OF FINANCING

In principle, all countries have chosen combinations of three different approaches to financing their welfare expenditure: general tax revenues, payroll taxes, and mandatory (and subsidised) private insurance. Of these, systems that rely primarily on payroll taxes are presently most under siege.

Payroll taxes

Practically all OECD countries are financing some share of their welfare expenditure through payroll taxes, but they differ greatly in the extent to which this is true. France, for instance, is financing 82 per cent of its welfare budget from payroll taxes, Germany 74 per cent and the Netherlands 71 per cent. For Britain, the share is 53 per cent, while Ireland collects only 40 per cent, and Denmark as little as 13 per cent from wage-related contributions of employers and employees. In a closed economy, these differences are not of major importance. Payroll taxes, it is true, will increase the cost of labour and hence, if they are not compensated by reduced wage claims, will tend to make the use of capital relatively more attractive than the use of labour, and they will also increase the attraction of the black economy. Beyond that, however, the higher costs of labour may be passed on to consumers without further damage to employment levels.

In an open economy, however, and under conditions of intense internal competition, payroll taxes become more problematic. When exchange rates are fixed, increases of labour costs could no longer be passed onto consumers. Instead, they would reduce competitiveness and employment. With flexible exchange rates, the loss of international competitiveness might be avoided by devaluation (which would again shift the cost to consumers), provided that the central bank is willing to accommodate this inflationary solution. Thus, while the connection between payroll taxes and employment is generally negative, the strength of negative effects is contingent on several other conditions and hence somewhat uncertain.

There is nothing uncertain, however, about the reverse link. If employment shrinks, welfare systems financed from payroll taxes must either cut expenditure on transfers and services, or must raise the level of contributions – with the consequence that the increase in non-wage labour costs will contribute to the further decline of employment. At the same time, international economic competition will generate strong pressures to reduce the level of contributions in order to lower the production costs of firms. As a consequence, in the face of shrinking employment, payroll-tax based systems are likely to be squeezed by equally strong pressures to raise contributions in order to maintain levels of service, and to reduce contributions in order to avoid further losses of employment.

General tax revenues

To a somewhat lesser extent, welfare systems that are financed from general tax revenues are also vulnerable to the effects of globalisation and the increase in international economic competition. Since the exit options of capital and firms have expanded, countries must reduce, or at least avoid increasing, taxes on capital income and taxes that add to the production costs of firms. As a consequence, welfare spending must either be reduced or its costs must be shifted onto personal income taxes, property taxes and consumption taxes.

While the shift to these tax bases will not necessarily impede investment and employment (at least as long as value-added taxes are collected according to country-of-destination rules), they will again add to the attractiveness of the black economy. The main constraint is likely to be political, however. As the tax burden is shifted from capital income, and from the more mobile high-income groups, toward property, personal incomes and consumption, taxpayer resistance from the relatively immobile middle-income groups is likely to reduce the political feasibility of this solution.

Mandatory individual insurance

The third mode of financing is less generally practiced in highly developed welfare states, but it appears to be particularly robust under conditions of globalisation and international economic competition. The closest approximation is found in Switzerland, but elements of this mode of financing can also be found in other countries.

The basic principle is that every resident person is required to be individually insured against the typical social risks, and that the premium payments of persons with low incomes or without incomes should be subsidised from the state budget. In the Swiss case, this is essentially true of health insurance, where each individual is required to be insured, and where the premium payments to state-approved insurance corporations are subsidised by the state for low-income and high-risk groups.

The advantage of this source of financing is that it includes all residents, regardless of their status in the labour market, and draws upon all types of income. In this regard, this system is immune to changes in the functional division of income from work or from capital, or to changes between the status of being employed or self-employed. Moreover, while in Switzerland employee contributions to the pension system are collected at the work place, and are shared between workers and employers, this is not an inevitable feature of the model. They could well be financed, as is true in health insurance, through premium payments by the insured that will not appear as a form of non-wage labour cost, but as part of the individual consumption budget. In this case, they will not directly affect international competitiveness, and they will not be directly affected by changes in the level of employment. For that reason, a welfare state that is generally based on mandatory individual insurance contributions, subsidised for low-income groups, would be least vulnerable to the effects of globalised capital markets and international economic competition.

MOST VULNERABLE: PAYROLL TAXES AND GENEROUS RATES OF INCOME REPLACEMENT

After this overview, it is now possible to identify the highly developed welfare states on the European continent as "problem cases" where the sustainability of the present levels of social security is most in question. They are characterised by a combination of three features: a concentration on transfer payments, rather than social services; generous income replacement in case of unemployment; and payroll taxes as the major source of welfare finance.

Since they are largely financed through payroll taxes, continental welfare states are particularly dependent on high levels of employment. In the face of increasing international competition in the industrial sector, however, additional employment could only be achieved in service sectors catering for domestic demand. Such employment opportunities may exist in the public sector, as well as in the private sector. Continental welfare states, however, are structurally unable to exploit either of these opportunities. Instead, they even contribute to the further reduction of employment. This effect is best appreciated if the continental model of the welfare state is contrasted to the Scandinavian model on the one hand, and to the American model on the other hand.

The Scandinavian model

The Scandinavian model of the welfare state is characterised by an emphasis on social services, whereas continental welfare states place greater emphasis on cash payments. Thus, in 1990, public expenditure on "services for elderly and disabled people" plus public expenditure on "family services" amounted to 4.5 per cent of GDP in Sweden, 4 per cent in Norway, and 3.5 per cent in Denmark, but only to 1 per cent in France and 0.8 per cent in Germany (OECD, 1996a, Tables 2.5 and 2.8). This difference did not affect the viability of the welfare state during periods of high economic growth, but it becomes an important factor when full employment is no longer assured by growth in the industrial sector. Thus, in 1990, the public and social-service sectors (ISIC 9) did provide employment for 31 per cent of the working-age population in Sweden, but only for 16.5 per cent in Western Germany (OECD, 1994). This difference did account for the high overall employment/population ratio of over 80 per cent in Sweden, and the relatively low employment ratio of between 60 and 65 per cent in most continental welfare states.

However, since most of this service employment is financed from the state budget, the downside of the Scandinavian model is an extreme dependence on the conditions of public finance. If taxes cannot be raised because of taxpayer resistance, and if public sector deficits must be reduced, employment losses are likely to be immediate and large. Thus, the employment/population ratio in Sweden has fallen by ten percentage points within just three years, from 81 per cent in 1990 to 71 per cent 1993, and it has not recovered in the meantime (OECD, 1996b, p. 186). The fall has not been as pronounced in other Scandinavian countries, and in Norway employment continues to increase, but the Swedish example illustrates the specific vulnerability of service-intensive welfare states in which employment performance depends primarily on the public sector.

The American model

By contrast, there are countries with a small public sector, and a small volume of publicly financed welfare expenditure that also have very high employment ratios, and where these ratios have continued to increase during the 1990s. Among these countries are Switzerland, Japan and the United States. In the present political debate, it is in particular the employment success of the American model that is generally contrasted to the employment failures of continental welfare states. This success is primarily owed to an expanding market for privately financed and consumed services. To an extent, these are the same types of health care, family and education services which in the Scandinavian model are provided by the public sector, and which have to be purchased privately in countries with fewer welfare provisions.

At the same time, the private purchase of such services is facilitated by a relatively unequal income distribution in countries with a small welfare state (OECD, 1995). In the United States moreover (but not in Switzerland or Japan), an additional explanation is provided by dramatically increasing wage differentials since the 1980s (OECD, 1996b, pp 61-69) which permit a growing class of affluent consumers to buy more of the personal and household services provided by an increasingly impoverished lower class. The downside of the American model is the increasing share of households below the poverty line (OECD, 1995) and the problems of the "working poor".

The continental model

Since the continental welfare states are not service intensive, they do not benefit from the high levels of publicly-financed employment that is characteristic of the Scandinavian model. At the same time, however, relatively high levels of taxation and low degrees of income and wage differentiation have also constrained the evolution of a market for personal and household services in the private sector.

One contributing factor is the welfare state itself: since long-term income support for persons out of work and without alternative means of support is more generous than it is in the United States, this raises the reservation wage in the regular labour market. At the same time, high payroll taxes reduce the incentive to work. As a consequence, an American-type low-wage labour market could not develop in continental welfare states, and overall employment levels are generally quite low.

Thus the characteristic deficiency of continental welfare states is not the plight of the working poor – it is the plight of the long-term unemployed (who may also be tempted to combine income replacement with work in the black economy). Since these systems also rely on payroll taxes for a large part of their finance, they are also more likely to run into a fiscal crisis as employment recedes and as unemployment rises.

PERSPECTIVES

The implication seems clear enough: in order to increase their sustainability, each of these three types of welfare states must primarily attend to its specific problems. The Scandinavian model must reduce its dependence on very high levels of taxation; the American model must find ways of alleviating the distress of the working poor; and the continental model must find ways to increase levels of employment without running into the problems of the other two models. Since this is the most difficult challenge, I will focus primarily on potential solutions for the problems of continental welfare states.

Employment in internationally-exposed sectors

Under conditions of growing international economic interdependence and in the face of intense international competition, all OECD countries have difficulty in maintaining present levels of employment in the internationally-exposed sectors of their economies. In order to remain competitive, they must not only achieve continuous advances in labour-saving methods of production, but also more intensive co-operation with producers in low-cost countries.

Whether the resulting job losses can be compensated through larger volumes of production is at best uncertain. But it is certain that skill requirements in the exposed sector will continuously increase. Thus employment prospects for less skilled workers will continue to decline in the internationally exposed industrial and service sectors. If these groups are to find additional employment opportunities, they depend on an expansion of services in the domestic economy. In other words: in order to cope with their present problems, continental welfare states must find ways to translate a larger share of the incomes earned in the exposed sectors into additional demand for services that are locally provided and consumed, and hence not subject to international competition.

Employment in domestic sectors

To achieve higher levels of service employment, continental countries will not be able to move very far in the direction of the Scandinavian model. While it may be necessary and feasible to facilitate higher levels of female employment by providing more day-care facilities and all-day schools, continental welfare states are already operating at relatively high tax levels, and they would be bankrupted if they were to aim generally for Scandinavian levels of social services. A move in the American direction, by contrast, would be economically feasible, but institutionally and politically quite difficult.

The political difficulty is that voters in continental welfare states have come to expect minimal standards of social justice to be respected by public policy. In some countries, moreover, these standards are reinforced by constitutional law. There, service employment could not be expanded by simply reducing the level or duration of income replacement in order to create an American-type low-wage labour market at levels below the poverty line.

What could be politically more acceptable are schemes encouraging the creation of low-wage service jobs through programmes subsidising the incomes of persons working on these jobs. This is the logic of the "negative income tax" which, however, is presently considered financially unfeasible in light of the budgetary difficulties of all welfare states. On a more limited scale, the same logic is realised by the American "Earned Income Tax Credit" (EITC) that is discussed in some detail in Chapter 4. Similar "family credit" schemes exist presently in the United Kingdom, in Ireland and in Italy. They are generally aimed at working parents in low-wage jobs, and they use total family income as the criterion for subsidisation. If they are sufficiently generous, such schemes are highly effective in alleviating the poverty of families with small children and working parents.

Family credit schemes are less effective, however, in creating new employment opportunities in countries where a low-wage labour market does not already exist. It can only evolve if existing and start-up firms will invest in the marketing of new low-cost services and in creating new jobs. They are unlikely to do so, however, unless they are assured that workers will generally be available at wage costs below present levels – which also implies that unions must be willing to negotiate wage rates below the presently defined subsistence level. In either case, wages must be decided by the job, rather than by the greater or lesser poverty of the worker's family. By implication, that must then also be true of the income subsidy. Unions could not agree to wage rates below the present minimum unless they are assured that total income from full-time work at these rates will still be above the subsistence level, and employers would be less likely to invest in new jobs, unless they could freely select potential employees without regard to their family-income status.

For practical purposes, therefore, income subsidy is best defined as a supplement to the hourly wage. It could be paid by the employer, who would then be reimbursed by the tax office. On this basis, the scheme would require that an upper cutoff point be defined in terms of a "socially satisfactory hourly wage", and it would then provide partial compensation (say, at a rate of 50 per cent) of the gap between that wage and the wage that is actually paid by the employer (Chart 8.1). The effective lower cutoff point of that scheme would then be defined as the point at which wages plus supplement would be no higher than the replacement income provided for persons who do not work.

The advantage is that such a programme could encourage the development of a low-wage labour market without creating a population of the "working poor" below present levels of income replacement. Compared to the Scandinavian model, it also has the advantage of mobilising private resources, rather than having to finance additional employment exclusively from public funds. If successful, such a scheme would in fact largely pay for itself since each instance of additional employment will make a positive contribution (in terms of increased taxes and reduced outlays for unemployment support) to

◆   Chart 8.1.   *Income supplement for low-wage jobs*

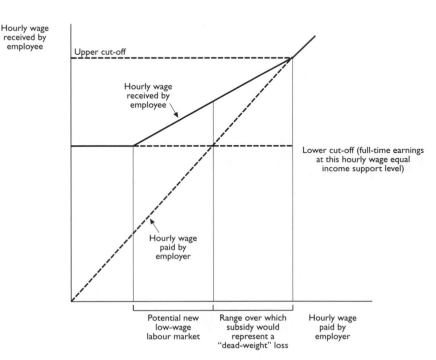

public-sector budgets as a whole. Net outlays would therefore be limited to those cases where persons who are presently working at wages below the upper cutoff would also benefit from the subsidy scheme (Scharpf, 1995).

In countries with minimum wage legislation, a necessary implication might be that the minimum wage paid by employers has to be reduced. Greater difficulties might be encountered in countries with strong union control over wages. Here, the success of the scheme would depend on the willingness of unions to conclude collective-bargaining agreements on wages below the present lower levels.

If that should present a difficulty, the continental welfare states which presently finance a large share of their welfare budget from payroll taxes involving contributions from both employers and workers, have an alternative option. By eliminating, or at least reducing, payroll taxes at the lower end of the wage scale, they would simultaneously reduce wage costs for employers and increase the take-home pay of workers. Depending on the size of the reduction, the effect on the labour market might be quite similar to that of the subsidy scheme described here.

BIBLIOGRAPHY

ESPING-ANDERSEN, G. (1990), *The Three Worlds of Welfare Capitalism*, Polity Press, Cambridge.

EUROSTAT (1995), *Statistische Grundzahlen der Europäischen Union*, No. 32, Statistisches Amt der Europäischen Gemeinschaften, Brüssel.

OECD (1994), *Labour Force Statistics 1972-1994*, Paris.

OECD (1995), *Income Distribution in OECD Countries*, Social Policy Studies No. 18, Paris.

OECD (1996*a*), "Social expenditure statistics of OECD Member countries", Labour Market and Social Policy Occasional Papers No. 17, Paris.

OECD (1996*b*), *Employment Outlook*, July, Paris.

SCHARPF, F.W. (1995), "Subventionierte Niedriglohn-Beschäftigung statt bezahlter Arbeitslosigkeit?", *Zeitschrift für Sozialreform*, Vol. 41, pp. 65-82.

SOCIAL PROTECTION AND THE LOW-SKILLED: THE DEBATE

Mr. PETER LILLEY, Secretary of State for Social Security, United Kingdom

A problem that all countries face as a result of global competition and the move from manufacturing to service industry is finding employment for all our people. The simple fact is that people will only be employed if the value of what they produce exceeds the cost of employing them.

The higher are the social costs we impose on employment and employers, either the lower is take-home pay to the employee or the fewer the jobs there will be. The latter result is more likely if pay is prevented from reflecting the productivity and value-added by employees either as a result of minimum wages, union resistance or other rigidities.

We all want people to have jobs. At the same time, we do not want to see the level of pay sink to such levels that people do not have reasonable living standards, particularly if the result is that they cannot meet their responsibilities to house and support their families. In the United Kingdom we have decided the best approach is to let wages reach the level set in the market place. The policy, which the United Kingdom has pioneered, is to impose the minimum of social and other costs on employers, but to top up the pay of those with low wages and high responsibilities.

We do not want to see anyone have low pay for the rest of their lives. We hope that, by getting into the labour market, they will gain the experience, the skills, the habit of work, the record of employment which will enable them to move to better paid jobs in due course. All the evidence is that people who spend a long time out of work have declining productivity, and therefore find it harder to get back into work. Our efforts are therefore geared to getting people into work as soon as possible, even into modestly paid jobs. There is evidence that over time, if you get a job you can improve your circumstances.

Ms. MADGA DE GALAN, Minister of Social Affairs, Brussels

Belgium is in the process of a major overhaul of its social security system, with the key issue being how the system is financed. The reform is still predicated on maintaining a combination of insurance and solidarity. This excludes the possibility of generalising the individualisation of entitlements, and of assuring an accessibility level to the low-income groups which would be reached only through state subsidies.

Even if Belgium intends to confirm that the financing base is still insurance, in other words employment-related social security contributions, the fact remains that the burden of such financing weighs too heavily on employees and employers, which prevents a balance between employment, competitiveness and the actual viability of our social security system.

There are two aspects to the financing issue. First, the need to compensate for the shortfall in social security receipts occasioned by the reduction in indirect labour costs: for example, when partial or full relief from social security contributions is granted. The other problem is the broadening of the revenue base to other types of income.

Since 1993, the volume of the alternative financing in our country has more than doubled. Even so, the figure is still low, with 75 per cent of Belgian social security receipts still coming from wage-related contributions in 1997 budget. One of the current challenges in broadening the financing base is that it needs to be geared to economic reality – which is characterised by a shift from labour to capital.

Under the Belgium system, accessibility for those on low incomes is guaranteed by law, for instance by reducing costs payable by the low-paid, by indexing automatically social security benefits, etc. Regarding health care, everybody's accessibility to treatment of the greatest quality is at the heart of the system's internal management practices. These are founded on greater empowerment of all actors. We anticipate an expenditure growth of 1.5 per cent each year, excluding inflation. The total budget is divided among the various care sectors upon the decision of the "financiers" and the actors of health care – social partners, mutual insurance companies and service providers. In the event of overruns, these are asked to propose adjustments within budgets, adjustments which must not affect the patient nor increase the state's transfers to the social security system as a whole.

Mrs. MEADOWS, Policy Studies Institute, United Kingdom

The discussion about low-skilled workers requires us to consider fundamental issues. What is the welfare state for? How can we promote social integration, the sharing of risks and the transfer of income across the life cycle? Doubts are increasingly being expressed about the best ways to achieving this objective, and in particular, whether state intervention is the best policy instrument.

There is a change in the perception of the state. If we look back in thirty years' time, we may find that there was a very brief period of history when the state was regarded as a sort of "benevolent parent" figure. In more and more countries, there is an increasing tendency to see the state as a sort of "policeman" figure. It is good at setting frameworks and rules. For that very reason, it is less good as a service provider, because rigid rules are not necessarily in the interests either of those who pay or of those who receive services. The flexibility in terms of delivering individual packages to meet individual needs and the real recognition of different family circumstances is difficult to achieve.

It may be that what is needed are a different set of institutions. Perhaps the principles of a social insurance model can be maintained without having to have these monolithic, bureaucratic state institutions, which dominate our public finances and national debates, and which often generate as much insecurity as they do security.

I would also like to suggest outright something which is often only implied. This is that our welfare states only worked as long as our labour markets were inefficient. In the past, companies sometimes employed people who were being paid more than their marginal contribution to production. Custom and practice led to the employment of people to open the gate, to operate the lift, to bring tea for workers during breaks in the working day. Furthermore, companies discriminated. They employed inferior men when superior women were available for employment.

Unskilled people tend to live in households with other unskilled people. In the past, the living standards of such households were underwritten by cross-subsidisation of the wages of low-skilled men. Pressures to be efficient and to end discrimination have together left unskilled households in a much more precarious situation than previously. In the absence of a reasonable level of income from work, taxpayers or social contributions are being used to subsidise living standards. It is, therefore, the very efficiency of our labour markets which is contributing to the increased stress being felt by our welfare states.

Mr. PULAY, Ministry of Labour, Hungary

One of the biggest tasks of continental European countries is creating additional jobs for the less-skilled part of the population. Subsidising the wages of the low-skilled workers in the domestic service sector could be part of the solution, but only part. There is a need for a range of policies to address the problem.

First, we must make clear that only services which are not traded internationally would qualify for any subsidy targeted at increasing low-skilled service employment. If the subsidy is general, the result is a distortion of international trade in services.

Secondly, we should consider whether the subsidy should go directly to employees or should be used to subsidise the demand for services. The latter should be preferred. To minimise costs, ideally governments should subsidise those on low wages or income only if they would not otherwise work. If subsidies are paid only to those employers who increase employment, the "dead-weight costs" of the subsidies can be minimised.

Furthermore, in many cases, there is a real need for domestic services, but at the prevailing market price the demand is not effective. For example, old people would like to get catering at home, but they cannot afford it. But at a subsidised price they could buy these services. By targeting the subsidies to certain services and to certain population groups by subsidising the demand side instead of the supply side, an approach half-way between the market solution of the United States and the public service solution of the Scandinavian countries can be achieved.

Mr. DAVIS, European Monetary Institute, Germany

The argument in favour of subsidising low-wage, low-income or low-skill workers implicitly assumes that further service jobs cannot be created at current wage levels. Hence it is argued that it is necessary, in order to generate employment in the service sector, to move down the labour demand curve, pay lower wages and cope with the social consequences through tax-financed top-ups of wages or incomes.

This is no doubt correct to a considerable extent. However, service jobs could be created even at current wages if further deregulation of the service sector were undertaken. In effect, this could move the whole labour demand curve upwards. An obvious example is that of the opening hours of shops, which have only been deregulated partially in Germany, but nevertheless there are hopes that considerable numbers of service jobs will be created. Further deregulation could help. Equally there could be further deregulation of hiring and firing so that employers are more ready to take on workers, given that the costs of dismissal would be less. A third area is to reconsider regulations which may hinder individuals wishing to set up businesses. In other words, subsidising employment may be one way forward, but there are other policies which are worth considering in addition.

Mr. LINDBECK, Institute for International Economic Studies, Sweden

Four issues must be considered when discussing the declining position of those with few labour market skills.

The first one is the controversy between those (including myself) who want to liberalise the labour market, deregulate it, and to allow more flexibility of relative wages, and on the other hand, those who do not believe in those solutions. The latter group will have to rely on public sector employment or similar policies.

A second observation is that various countries have moved towards contribution-based social insurance systems, with benefits dependent on how much has been contributed. The advantage of this approach is that the tax wedge becomes less of a labour supply problem, because if the capital value of expected benefits is equal to the value of fees, there is no tax wedge.

The third problem under discussion is the tax system, and in particular the effects of payroll taxes. It is often argued that a general payroll tax is particularly likely to reduce the demand for labour. Of course, if payroll taxes are increased by 5 or 10 per cent in a very short period of time, wage costs will increase and reduce the demand for labour. In practice, however, it has been raised by one or two per cent per year over a forty-year period. There has been plenty of time for firms to shift the payroll tax back to the household, either by a constraint on nominal wage increases, or by devaluations that have raised prices. Hence there is nothing especially bad about a payroll tax in general. In the long run, the payroll tax will be paid by wage earners, or more generally by all citizens.

But there is one exception – low-productivity workers. For low-productivity workers, wages are tied to minimum wage legislation or bargaining agreements. Thus wages cannot decline for these groups, and unemployment will result. Low-productivity workers are the victims of the payroll tax. The obvious solutions are to reduce the payroll tax for low-productivity workers, or to subsidise their earnings.

The theory of optimum taxation suggests that tax rates should be lower where the demand and supply elasticities are high. Interestingly, the elasticities of demand and supply of private household services are high because there is the possibility of substituting between home production and market production. It can be argued that it was a serious mistake to make indirect taxes as high on services as on goods, as has been done in many countries. These services are often both low skilled and labour-intensive. Cutting indirect taxes on purchases of household services, reducing the payroll tax for those providing household services, or giving a tax rebate for such expenditure may well promote employment for the low-skilled.

The final point which needs to be made is that it is not very helpful to discuss these other problems one at a time. Rather they should be discussed as a package – otherwise, we can do more damage than good when we reform one aspect of the system at a time. It is necessary to have system analysis rather than partial analysis of the issues.

Mr. ESPING-ANDERSEN, University of Trento, Italy

I do not believe that how the welfare state is financed is especially important. Take the extreme outlier, Denmark, where there is virtually no payroll tax. Danish workers cost the employer exactly the same as a German worker; they just want higher wages so that they can pay the higher income and consumption taxes. The total labour cost ends up about the same.

The two-earner family is a positive solution to the problem of creating a sustainable system of social protection. In both the United States and Scandinavia, the dual-earner family is now the norm. Dual-earner families create employment and social protection dynamics which interact with one another in a favourable way. First, the risk of poverty is low. The average poverty rate of two-earner families is a half or a third that of one-earner families. Secondly, their patterns of consumption are different. They consume services intensively because they lack time. Thus dual-earner families not only are more likely to have the resources to demand services, they also have greater needs for services, whether they are provided in the state or market sector. The result is a multiplier effect: dual-earner families require services; meeting the demand for those services creates more jobs and so increases again the demand for services.

The sustainability of the welfare state is therefore closely linked to this nexus of family responsibilities, the family's insertion in the labour market, and the orientation of social policy towards meeting the needs of such families.

Mr. SCHARPF, Max-Planck-Institut für Gesellschaftsforschung, Germany

In response to Messrs. Lindbeck and Esping-Andersen, I would agree that in closed economies, it makes little difference as to how the welfare state is financed. Any form of finance would be passed on to consumers. If you have open borders and relatively inflexible exchange rates, however, different systems of financing social expenditure may have different effects. Furthermore, payroll taxes on low-productivity jobs may be enough to price them out of the private labour market so they have a very direct impact on the viability of service employment.

Mr. HAVEMAN, University of Wisconsin-Madison, United States

In some sense, all of our efforts have been designed to find a way of having a welfare state that will simultaneously promote economic growth and employment with equity. And the reason why we want those objectives is that the current state is now perceived as giving us at least three important problems.

Problem number one is that the size of the income "pie" that each of our nations have is now perceived to be lower than it could otherwise be if we did business another way. Secondly, if we did business another way, we might reduce the number of "outsiders" relative to "insiders". The third thing that we gain by doing business in such a way as to promote growth and employment is a reduction in stress between different classes and, in particular, the resentment of taxpayers over the need to support large numbers of inactive people.

As the discussion at this meeting shows, there is no shortage of ideas as to how market-oriented societies can encourage the employment of low-skilled workers. For example:

- Lower the income available to low-skilled workers from sources that are an alternative to working. This may involve reducing benefit levels in certain social programmes, such as unemployment benefit levels or enforcing tighter controls on benefit recipients. Constraining access to unreported income may also be important.

- Deregulation of product markets (as discussed by Mr Davis).

- Subsidise low-skilled jobs, such as household service-related activities (as argued by Mr. Lindbeck).

- Subsidise the hours of work of low-skilled people (as I argued in my own paper).

- Reduce the taxation that is now applied to hours of work of low-skilled people through adjustments in the payroll tax (as suggested by Mr. Sharpf).

None of these options is cost-free. There is no free lunch. No matter what road nations choose, there are going to be disadvantages and side-effects and concerns and objections raised and political obstacles. But it is important to examine these costs closely in order to determine whether they are really so serious as to prevent reforms being attempted.

For example, Mr. Pulay raised the issue of the dead-weight loss associated with subsidising the hours of work of low-skilled workers. What does it mean to have a dead-weight loss associated with the subsidisation of the employment of low-skilled workers? The dead-weight loss will go into two pockets: the take-home pay of low-skilled workers that would have been employed anyway, and the reduction of the business costs of employers who hire low-skilled workers. The dead-weight loss turns into a subsidisation of low-skilled workers or those who hire them. What in economic theory is a dead-weight loss may turn out to be a social gain when such equity considerations are also taken into account.

CONCLUSION

Concluding address by Mr. A.P.W. Melkert,
Minister of Social Affairs and Employment, the Netherlands

This conference has debated the human dimension of socio-economic policy. The efficiency of the social contract is a key part of competitive policy, because success in this area translates into better economic performance. However, the nature of the social contract in our various countries does of course differ in response to the different attitudes in society towards the family, employment and retirement. The conference has therefore recognised that the relationship between children and parents through the life cycle is at the heart of the debate.

This conference has agreed that governments should not respond to the changing situation by simply providing more services and more protection. As there is a trade-off between wage developments and social standards with respect to the impact on employment, one effective approach might be for the social partners to pursue wage moderation. Another approach might be to strengthen the incentives for the provision of services in the private sector, which, through better job opportunities, could lead to a decrease in welfare transfers.

The changes that occur in our societies are not entirely predictable, but we can anticipate change and agree on the need to adapt to it. Thus, a central conclusion of the conference has been that social, education and employment programmes need to augment the capacity of the individual, the family and the labour market to adapt to change in ways that:

- sustain rising living standards for the whole population and encourage economic growth;
- address the existing practice in which the gender division of labour hampers the exploitation of the full potential of our economies;
- link inter-generational solidarity more consistently with labour-market strategy.

NEW PRIORITIES FOR SOCIAL POLICY

New challenges demand new answers. Innovative policies have to be developed in order to avoid sole reliance on either state-provision or self-provision, and these policies must enhance rather that hamper economic growth. A number of implications arise from this broad objective. They are not separate, but common elements of the same strategy.

If individuals are to be told to take risks and be flexible, there must be security

This calls for:

- a flexible social insurance system that supports mobility;
- some guarantee of minimum income when part-time or temporary work is undertaken as a way of retaining contact with the labour market;
- adaptation of the taxation system, for example, by broadening the tax base, both on the demand and supply side, to improve labour market prospects, particularly for those with low-earning capacity.

Adopting a social investment approach to social expenditure

This means taking a long-term view of costs and benefits. Short-term gains should be measured against the potential long-term cost of a single adult with few skills who has to be maintained largely on social benefits for 30 years, and who does not accumulate any pension rights during that time.

This points to:

– Preventing exclusion from the labour market:

  • those outside the labour market must be offered wider opportunities of employment, even if this requires unorthodox approaches.

– Greater investment in the young:

  • better child care and early education for young children;

  • support for parents who have to combine a job with raising children;

  • more focus on the transition to work by young people: this includes the provision of vocational training and "learner" jobs with lower wages.

– Maintaining human capital over the life-course, including:

  • lifelong learning as advocated by OECD Education Ministers in January 1996;

  • improving the capacities of older workers;

  • changing both individual and employer attitudes to older workers.

A new approach to ageing policies

The conference acknowledged the importance of moving away from a rigid three stage view of life as education-work-retirement, and towards an approach that is adapted to, and encourages, a more flexible approach to learning, working and leisure throughout the life cycle. Age should no longer be used as a criterion in labour-force adjustment.

This changed orientation involves:

– A pension guarantee more in accordance with basic economics:

  • the starting point, which seems to be economically affordable, must be that the promised pension will be delivered. It is important to maintain trust, particularly as younger workers are likely to be asked to take greater risks and be more mobile;

  • irrespective of the funding system (PAYG, capital funding, defined contributions) it seems to be realistic to allow for the notion that benefits have to be gradually geared to economic growth (with a minimum). This will apply whether the major pension provider is a public or private institution;

  • the pension guaranteed to the retired will give them a fair share of the economic growth to which they have contributed, whilst maintaining solidarity with those who have not been able to do so.

– Resisting the trend to ever-earlier withdrawal from work:

  • in order to preserve the retirement income system, a main pillar of security in our societies, the effective age of retirement must be raised. This calls for a wider range of policy responses than simply raising the age of entitlement to state pensions;

  • this will require major changes in labour-market institutions, wage-setting practices and attitudes on the part of employers to older workers.

– A more consistent response to rising care needs:

  • the promise to the very elderly is the right to health and social care on the same terms as anybody else. This will require a major increase in service jobs;

  • at the same time we can anticipate that in the future they (we) will be more active in organising and contributing towards the solutions, as committed, informed clients.

Taking a "zero tolerance" approach to long-term exclusion

We just have to say that long-term exclusion is not acceptable. Then other policy choices fall into place. If a minority are unable to take advantage of opportunities without greater help, some more direct intervention is required, including:

– offering education, training and work experience opportunities to adults, in return for a contract under which income support is received in return for active efforts to improve their own prospects;

– greater help to low-income families with children, to keep these children in education and training, rather than entering the labour market with no skills. The lesson we have learned is to provide better quality education from the outset, rather than patch on training for the unemployed at a later stage.

CONCLUSIONS

The conference has recognised the need for a social infrastructure in order to optimise economic growth. This implies re-shaping the welfare state into an economic performer.

The OECD will have to develop this analysis, in order to identify new strategies to supplement market mechanisms in raising the level of employment, and thereby help to make inter-generational transfers sustainable. This will also call for new policies designed to more closely align good family functioning with the labour market.

The building of the social infrastructure should be consistently integrated in the OECD's agenda generally, thus broadening the scope of its work. The Japanese Prime Minister has proposed a new "Initiative for a caring world" which the conference welcomed and supported, and which will form a central theme for the next meeting of OECD Social Policy Ministers in 1998.

Finally, an overall personal impression is that in spite of all problems the welfare state is facing or has to face, a certain optimism prevails. The discussions showed a wide variety of approaches and possible solutions. Not all of the suggestions were in unison, but the exchange of views was important in advancing mutual understanding.

MAIN SALES OUTLETS OF OECD PUBLICATIONS
PRINCIPAUX POINTS DE VENTE DES PUBLICATIONS DE L'OCDE

AUSTRALIA – AUSTRALIE
D.A. Information Services
648 Whitehorse Road, P.O.B 163
Mitcham, Victoria 3132   Tel. (03) 9210.7777
                           Fax: (03) 9210.7788

AUSTRIA – AUTRICHE
Gerold & Co.
Graben 31
Wien I   Tel. (0222) 533.50.14
                           Fax: (0222) 512.47.31.29

BELGIUM – BELGIQUE
Jean De Lannoy
Avenue du Roi, Koningslaan 202
B-1060 Bruxelles   Tel. (02) 538.51.69/538.08.41
                           Fax: (02) 538.08.41

CANADA
Renouf Publishing Company Ltd.
5369 Canotek Road
Unit 1
Ottawa, Ont. K1J 9J3   Tel. (613) 745.2665
                           Fax: (613) 745.7660

Stores:
71 1/2 Sparks Street
Ottawa, Ont. K1P 5R1   Tel. (613) 238.8985
                           Fax: (613) 238.6041

12 Adelaide Street West
Toronto, QN M5H 1L6   Tel. (416) 363.3171
                           Fax: (416) 363.5963

Les Éditions La Liberté Inc.
3020 Chemin Sainte-Foy
Sainte-Foy, PQ G1X 3V6   Tel. (418) 658.3763
                           Fax: (418) 658.3763

Federal Publications Inc.
165 University Avenue, Suite 701
Toronto, ON M5H 3B8   Tel. (416) 860.1611
                           Fax: (416) 860.1608

Les Publications Fédérales
1185 Université
Montréal, QC H3B 3A7   Tel. (514) 954.1633
                           Fax: (514) 954.1635

CHINA – CHINE
Book Dept., China National Publications
Import and Export Corporation (CNPIEC)
16 Gongti E. Road, Chaoyang District
Beijing 100020   Tel. (10) 6506-6688 Ext. 8402
                           (10) 6506-3101

CHINESE TAIPEI – TAIPEI CHINOIS
Good Faith Worldwide Int'l. Co. Ltd.
9th Floor, No. 118, Sec. 2
Chung Hsiao E. Road
Taipei   Tel. (02) 391.7396/391.7397
                           Fax: (02) 394.9176

**CZECH REPUBLIC –
RÉPUBLIQUE TCHÈQUE**
National Information Centre
NIS – prodejna
Konviktská 5
Praha 1 – 113 57   Tel. (02) 24.23.09.07
                           Fax: (02) 24.22.94.33
E-mail: nkposp@dec.niz.cz
Internet: http://www.nis.cz

DENMARK – DANEMARK
Munksgaard Book and Subscription Service
35, Nørre Søgade, P.O. Box 2148
DK-1016 København K   Tel. (33) 12.85.70
                           Fax: (33) 12.93.87

J. H. Schultz Information A/S,
Herstedvang 12,
DK – 2620 Albertslung   Tel. 43 63 23 00
                           Fax: 43 63 19 69
Internet: s-info@inet.uni-c.dk

EGYPT – ÉGYPTE
The Middle East Observer
41 Sherif Street
Cairo   Tel. (2) 392.6919
                           Fax: (2) 360.6804

FINLAND – FINLANDE
Akateeminen Kirjakauppa
Keskuskatu 1, P.O. Box 128
00100 Helsinki

Subscription Services/Agence d'abonnements :
P.O. Box 23
00100 Helsinki   Tel. (358) 9.121.4403
                           Fax: (358) 9.121.4450

*FRANCE
OECD/OCDE
Mail Orders/Commandes par correspondance :
2, rue André-Pascal
75775 Paris Cedex 16   Tel. 33 (0)1.45.24.82.00
                           Fax: 33 (0)1.49.10.42.76
                           Telex: 640048 OCDE
Internet: Compte.PUBSINQ@oecd.org

Orders via Minitel, France only/
Commandes par Minitel, France exclusivement :
36 15 OCDE

OECD Bookshop/Librairie de l'OCDE :
33, rue Octave-Feuillet
75016 Paris   Tel. 33 (0)1.45.24.81.81
                           33 (0)1.45.24.81.67

Dawson
B.P. 40
91121 Palaiseau Cedex   Tel. 01.89.10.47.00
                           Fax: 01.64.54.83.26

Documentation Française
29, quai Voltaire
75007 Paris   Tel. 01.40.15.70.00

Economica
49, rue Héricart
75015 Paris   Tel. 01.45.78.12.92
                           Fax: 01.45.75.05.67

Gibert Jeune (Droit-Économie)
6, place Saint-Michel
75006 Paris   Tel. 01.43.25.91.19

Librairie du Commerce International
10, avenue d'Iéna
75016 Paris   Tel. 01.40.73.34.60

Librairie Dunod
Université Paris-Dauphine
Place du Maréchal-de-Lattre-de-Tassigny
75016 Paris   Tel. 01.44.05.40.13

Librairie Lavoisier
11, rue Lavoisier
75008 Paris   Tel. 01.42.65.39.95

Librairie des Sciences Politiques
30, rue Saint-Guillaume
75007 Paris   Tel. 01.45.48.36.02

P.U.F.
49, boulevard Saint-Michel
75005 Paris   Tel. 01.43.25.83.40

Librairie de l'Université
12a, rue Nazareth
13100 Aix-en-Provence   Tel. 04.42.26.18.08

Documentation Française
165, rue Garibaldi
69003 Lyon   Tel. 04.78.63.32.23

Librairie Decitre
29, place Bellecour
69002 Lyon   Tel. 04.72.40.54.54

Librairie Sauramps
Le Triangle
34967 Montpellier Cedex 2 Tel. 04.67.58.85.15
                           Fax: 04.67.58.27.36

A la Sorbonne Actual
23, rue de l'Hôtel-des-Postes
06000 Nice   Tel. 04.93.13.77.75
                           Fax: 04.93.80.75.69

GERMANY – ALLEMAGNE
OECD Bonn Centre
August-Bebel-Allee 6
D-53175 Bonn   Tel. (0228) 959.120
                           Fax: (0228) 959.12.17

GREECE – GRÈCE
Librairie Kauffmann
Stadiou 28
10564 Athens   Tel. (01) 32.55.321
                           Fax: (01) 32.30.320

HONG-KONG
Swindon Book Co. Ltd.
Astoria Bldg. 3F
34 Ashley Road, Tsimshatsui
Kowloon, Hong Kong   Tel. 2376.2062
                           Fax: 2376.0685

HUNGARY – HONGRIE
Euro Info Service
Margitsziget, Európa Ház
1138 Budapest   Tel. (1) 111.60.61
                           Fax: (1) 302.50.35
E-mail: euroinfo@mail.matav.hu
Internet: http://www.euroinfo.hu//index.html

ICELAND – ISLANDE
Mál og Menning
Laugavegi 18, Pósthólf 392
121 Reykjavik   Tel. (1) 552.4240
                           Fax: (1) 562.3523

INDIA – INDE
Oxford Book and Stationery Co.
Scindia House
New Delhi 110001   Tel. (11) 331.5896/5308
                           Fax: (11) 332.2639
E-mail: oxford.publ@axcess.net.in

17 Park Street
Calcutta 700016   Tel. 240832

INDONESIA – INDONÉSIE
Pdii-Lipi
P.O. Box 4298
Jakarta 12042   Tel. (21) 573.34.67
                           Fax: (21) 573.34.67

IRELAND – IRLANDE
Government Supplies Agency
Publications Section
4/5 Harcourt Road
Dublin 2   Tel. 661.31.11
                           Fax: 475.27.60

ISRAEL – ISRAËL
Praedicta
5 Shatner Street
P.O. Box 34030
Jerusalem 91430   Tel. (2) 652.84.90/1/2
                           Fax: (2) 652.84.93

R.O.Y. International
P.O. Box 13056
Tel Aviv 61130   Tel. (3) 546 1423
                           Fax: (3) 546 1442
E-mail: royil@netvision.net.il

Palestinian Authority/Middle East:
INDEX Information Services
P.O.B. 19502
Jerusalem   Tel. (2) 627.16.34
                           Fax: (2) 627.12.19

ITALY – ITALIE
Libreria Commissionaria Sansoni
Via Duca di Calabria, 1/1
50125 Firenze   Tel. (055) 64.54.15
                           Fax: (055) 64.12.57
E-mail: licosa@ftbcc.it

Via Bartolini 29
20155 Milano   Tel. (02) 36.50.83

Editrice e Libreria Herder
Piazza Montecitorio 120
00186 Roma   Tel. 679.46.28
                           Fax: 678.47.51

Libreria Hoepli
Via Hoepli 5
20121 Milano   Tel. (02) 86.54.46
                           Fax: (02) 805.28.86

OECD PUBLICATIONS, 2, rue André-Pascal, 75775 PARIS CEDEX 16
PRINTED IN FRANCE
(81 97 04 1 P) ISBN 92-64-15557-0 – No. 49551 1997